THE ARISTOCRAT AS ART

We derive such dignity as we possess
from our status as art works.
Nietzsche, *The Birth of Tragedy*

THE ARISTOCRAT AS ART

A Study of the Honnête Homme *and the* Dandy *in Seventeenth- and Nineteenth-Century* French Literature

DOMNA C. STANTON

COLUMBIA UNIVERSITY PRESS
New York · 1980

The Andrew W. Mellon Foundation, through a special grant, has assisted the Press in publishing this volume.

Printed in the United States of America

Columbia University Press
New York   Guildford, Surrey

Library of Congress Cataloging in Publication Data

Stanton, Domna C
    The aristocrat as art.

    Bibliography: p.
    Includes index.
    1. French literature—17th century—History and
criticism. 2. Aristocracy in literature. 3. Conduct
of life in literature. 4. Dandies in literature.
5. French literature—19th century—History and criticism. I. Title.
PQ245.S7   840'.9'352   79–16657
ISBN 0–231–03903–4

For F. S. and A. S., and for my Sister who is not in this text.

For what *is* in this text, my thanks to Jules Brody who, as always, (re)read judiciously, Karen Mitchell and Bill Bernhardt who edited and advised, and Peggy Waller who helped turn the process into a product.

What this text should have been, only an other self can say: "All of our experiences with writing tell us that it is only after we have finished a text that we really know what it should have been." Butor, *Répertoire* III

CONTENTS

THE ARISTOCRAT AS ART

We derive such dignity as we possess
from our status as art works.
Nietzsche, *The Birth of Tragedy*

INTRODUCTION

"Interpretation," the introduction
of meaning—not "explanation." . . . There
are no facts . . . ; what is relatively
most enduring is—our opinions.
Nietzsche, *The Will to Power*

All men are created unequal: they are born with more or less talent in a superior or inferior milieu. That such inequalities exist and will not disappear through any natural evolutionary process is the fundamental notion underlying humanity's progressive attempts at egalitarianism. This conscious endeavor, however, is contradicted and undermined by the equally potent and perhaps more instinctive desire to assert the superiority of the self. Religion, as Nietzsche contemptuously noted, tries to thwart this basic will to power when it commands that we love our neighbor as ourselves (380:166 ff).[1] Available evidence suggests that we would prefer our neighbors to love us as we love ourselves—to acknowledge our superiority and their inferiority. Because our neighbors feel no differently about us, an unending contest is unleashed in which we often forgo our autonomy and join with others to increase our might. Enlarged in scope, the agon then assumes the configuration of "us against them." As with every individual life, society is crisscrossed with networks of "us and them" struggling for power and superiority. The tenor of entire societies is largely determined by the particular groups of individuals who manage to affix the banner of their superiority at the top of the pyramid.

The universal drive to manifest one's superiority is usually called "elitist," a less apt term perhaps than "aristocratic," which denotes, through its root, excellence or superiority elevated to a position of power. In this sense, all forms of government, democracy included, operate under aristocratic assumptions. As Thorstein Veblen observed, only the most primitive societies admit no hierarchical distinctions (512). This "savage" condition, according to Veblen, leads to barbarism, a predatory order of conquest in which the warrior-aristocrat tyrannizes a labor class consisting of all the women and foreigners (slaves). Under such a dispensation, might makes moral right and humanity is broadly divided into the worthy and the unworthy. In the final stage of "high barbarism," an aristocracy emerges whose tastes and privileges are specifically nonindustrious: war, rulership, sports, and priesthood. Now in Veblen's work, this physically and spiritually powerful male aristocracy is juxtaposed to a later one that arises when ownership of property and pecuniary strength replace the trophies of the predatory exploit as symbols of prepotence and prestige. This second type of aristocracy is dedicated to "conspicuous leisure," to the cultivation of nonutilitarian skills and the systematic refinement of a personal worldly manner, not only from a sense of the indignity of productive work, but also from a desire to display a capacity for idleness in such immaterial form as "manners and breeding, polite usage, decorum" (512:47). Broadly classified as branches of learning, these accomplishments, which cannot be attained by those who have to work, become "vouchers" of a life of leisure. The time, strenuous application, and discipline which they require constitute the only "labor" deemed worthy of an aristocrat.

Although Veblen did not analyze their substantive relation, the aristocracy of "conspicuous leisure" represents a less utilitarian, sublimated version of the nonindustrious aristocracy of "high barbarism." The leisured maintain a claim to spiritual superiority (priesthood) and insist on their dominion over others (rulership) without actually exercising either function. Their warring impulses are directed against those members of the community whom they label "outsiders," over whom they will prove or reconfirm their superiority in ways that are more obliquely violent. But it is the gaming impulse, originally channeled into sports, that seems most highly cultivated in the aristocracy of "conspicuous leisure."[2] In Johan Huizinga's formulations, play and

Introduction

aristocratic life, as voluntary activities, stand outside the realm of essential or traditionally "serious" needs, while at the same time they foster the illusion of their profound importance (265:39 ff; 264:7 ff). The participants in play constitute an exclusive team, who carve out a secluded playground, surround themselves with an air of secrecy, and are conscious of being apart-together in an exceptional situation. Within this precinct, the laws and customs of ordinary life yield to more obviously arbitrary conventions, designed to promote the mastery both of self and of others. In the most creative expression of play, according to Roger Caillois, *agon* is combined with *mimicry*, the transformation of self into another, more esthetic personage who enchants the spectator (107:158). Play stands as a metaphor for aristocratic life as a whole.

Beyond the factors of wealth and privilege that Veblen stressed, aristocracy, like play, contains an underlying esthetic impulse. It involves, it is *poiesis*. Unlike the artist who works with materials external to himself—and for this reason is potentially productive or utilitarian—the aristocrat uses the self as his raw material. Interested neither in what Huizinga calls the social vision of life (the amelioration of the world) nor in the religious (the forsaking of the world), the aristocrat *qua* artist aspires to dream-like or poetic activity, what Nietzsche calls the Apollonian (380:20 ff), and produces "by customs, by manners, by costume, by deportment the illusion of a heroic being" (265:37–39). Huizinga traces the elaboration of this ideal to a flight from unpleasant reality into illusion. He associates its content with a return to an imaginary, more perfect past, with an imitation of a preexistent hero or type that "ennobles life and its forms, fills them with beauty and fashions them anew as forms of art" (p. 39). It is in this sense that the Renaissance Humanist, for example, "imitates" the ancient sage. Huizinga fails to emphasize, however, that this imitation can only be a reformulation, a rewriting, an artistic idealization of the past through modern eyes. The Humanist may well admire the classical sage, but he is an expression of Humanism and not antiquity. Inevitably, the specifics of the "poetical vision of life" will tell us more about the esthetics of later periods than about the imagined and imaginary past.

3

Introduction

As Veblen makes clear, only those with sufficient economic freedom and prestige can easily express their artistic impulses. More specifically, however, the degree of proximity to the center of power will determine both the techniques needed to impress one's superiority on others and the nature of the image to be projected. When closer to the source of power, the aristocrat's tactics require no hostility or abrasiveness, since the basis of his prestige cannot be questioned. When this proximity decreases, as in societies which either admit to no aristocracies or valorize qualitatively different ones, the artist-aristocrat will be self-designated and will necessarily adopt far more aggressive tactics to impose his superiority. Whereas the image of the more powerful aristocrat will express society's cultural standards and tastes, that of the less powerful one will be jarring, even shocking. In either case, the artist-aristocrat's image is the means by which he manifests himself to others, emits signs which convey significant information, gives and gives off desired impressions. Because the elements of his projected image must justify his claims to superiority, they cannot be identifiable with the primary concerns of any other (competing) classes or groups. These elements, which have traditionally been branded as "superficial" or "insignificant," comprise aspects of self which the aristocrat imbues with new meaning and value. At the most elementary level, the signifying aspects of self are physical appearance and gestures; beyond these are the many forms of adornment, which help to mask natural deficiencies and display advantages. Adornment, the appropriation of objects to the self, extends, of course, beyond the body to all property—vehicles, houses, food—which exercises enhancing satellite functions around the central person. Finally, there are the multiple nuances of behavior—manner, manners, and language—which communicate complex meanings about the self and its attitude toward others.

Whereas we believe that words have significance, we do not generally attribute the same semiological status to nonverbal aspects of behavior. But language, according to Ferdinand de Saussure, is part of a much vaster science of semiology, which includes a variety of nonlinguistic systems: "Language is a system of signs that express ideas, and is, therefore, comparable to writ-

4

ing, the alphabet of deaf-mutes, symbolic rites, forms of etiquette, military signals, etc. It is, quite simply, the most important of these systems. It is thus possible to envision *a science which studies the life of signs within the life of society* . . . , we shall call it *semiology*. . . . Semiology would show us what constitutes signs, what laws govern them" (448:33).[3] More than any other "new" critic, Roland Barthes has used a linguistic model to address himself to the semiology of what he calls the rites, protocols, and spectacles of social life (41:79). In *Eléments de sémiologie*, he argues that gestures, clothing, food, and objects reveal the binary relation between social language and individual speech. If dress is language, then the specific way in which we dress is speech— *habillement* as opposed to *costume*. Analogous distinctions, applied to food or cars, for example, result in alimentary or vehicular speech. Paradigmatically, each of these "languages" comprises a system—small or large—with a number of categories among which individuals make significant choices. Within the language of dress and the category of head coverings, for instance, a top hat conveys different information about the wearer than a sailor cap. Syntagmatically, choices within each category—e.g., top hat, black tie, and patent leather shoes—tend toward consistency (the inconsistent would create the comic) and mutual reinforcement. Such choices, moreover, must be consistent intercategorically—e.g., black tie, champagne, Rolls Royce—to sustain the significance and the integrity of the system as a whole.

These semiological theories, which Barthes has tested in *Système de la mode*, have never been applied to individuals or specific human types. But they have particular relevance to the aristocratic desire to construct and deploy the self as a work of art. Every signifier which the aristocrat can control—looks, clothing, gesture, manners, speech—will be recruited into the expression of his superiority. Such an effort is more demanding of self-appointed aristocracies than of legitimized ones, whose members aspire to the established "sign equipment," what we call status symbols. Of course, individual signs or groups of signs will play larger roles in one aristocracy than another, and this creates different hierarchical structures which alter the overall effect of an aristocrat's image. There are, moreover, interaristocratic differences in the ways signifiers are made to signify "aristocratic" or "superior" which also determine the nature of the message. Hidden from view, the reasons underlying these variations must be sought in the codes and values of both the emitter and the receiver, the artist as well as the spectator. More than a simple emitter of signs to a destined person, however, the artist-aristocrat *is* a sign, a sign whose significance he understands better than his prospective audience. His entire person functions as an esthetic message, because his emitted signs are autoreflexive, designed to focus attention not on mere information, but on the *form* of the sign itself.[4]

Recurrent in human history, the phenomenon of the aristocrat-as-art is attested by such diverse types as the Chinese mandarin, the medieval knight, and the twentieth-century playboy. An unusual but compelling example is supplied by the Caduveo of Brazil, whom Lévi-Strauss describes in *Tristes Tropiques*. In their rigidly hierarchical society, which has both a hereditary aristocracy and ennobled individuals, the Mbaya lords relegate all work to inferior classes, from whom they distinguish themselves visually and verbally through a costume and jargon they alone may utilize. Surrounded by slaves who spare them physical effort, they devote their lives to leisurely pastimes, such as tourneys, that involve what Lévi-Strauss terms cruel games of prestige and domination. Fundamentally, however, they are obsessed with transforming their persons into art. This desire is based on a pervasive scorn for nature, "a sovereign contempt for the clay we are made of [which] . . . verges on sin," and which is expressed in a horror of the body and its functions (313:215). The Mbaya lord removes all facial hair, paints and tattoos his body, "the artist improvising on the living person," in intricate designs of incomparable beauty (p. 212). Consuming entire days, "the painting of the face confers on the individual his dignity as a human being; it effects the passage from nature to culture, from dumb animal to civilised man" (p. 220).[5] This attempt at self-transformation, part of a system which combines artifice, art, and game, exemplifies what Huizinga calls "the sublime vision of life."

The Mbaya model represents one fundamental system in the human repertory which varies little over the ages. This system,

Introduction

which I term the aristocrat-as-art, can be exemplified equally well by the *honnête homme* and the *dandy* in France, two types which may seem on the surface thoroughly dissimilar. The honnête homme, polite, modest, natural, reflects such expressed values of the age of Louis XIV as reasonableness, discretion, decorum. The dandy, on the contrary, condemned as a "fop infatuated with his appearance" (162 [1859]:s.v.), was dismissed as exhibitionistic, vain, affected, offensive. And whereas honnêteté was the principal secular ideal elaborated for an established nobility of the *ancien régime*, dandyism, formulated by a self-styled aristocracy, represents an ex-centric impulse, directed against the bourgeois-dominated postrevolutionary society. Now although such views are not inaccurate, the honnête homme and the dandy will be treated here as variant expressions of a single system. They will be interpreted as parallel incarnations of meritocratic minorities engaged in sublimated warfare against unworthy, vulgar, meritless majorities. In these sophisticated contests, the self, transformed into a system of signs that includes body, gesture, adornment, manners, and speech, gears its strategy to the captivation of others and to the imposition of its superiority. In the process of working out the connivance between the raw and the confected, the natural and the artistic, the means—stoic effort and rigorous discipline—became ends in themselves. Because success depended on factors which were indefinable, and to a large extent innate, honnêteté and dandyism ultimately delineate mysterious ideals which have all the markings of secular religions.

Although a comparative analysis of two types could proceed on the sole basis of the proposed internal connections, there is evidence that some nineteenth-century writers regarded the honnête homme as the dandy's ancestor and model. The author of *La Vie élégante à Paris*, for example, traces the lineage of *le fashionable*, a primary synonym for *le dandy*, from such honnêtes hommes as Bassompierre, Vardes, and the Chevalier de Gramont, through the dukes of Richelieu and Lauzun, to the Count d'Orsay, the renowned nineteenth-century French dandy (364:63, 68–69). And the *Larousse du XIXe siècle* associates both *le cocodès* and *le gandin*, two late synonyms for the dandy, with the *plumet* and the *marquis* of the seventeenth century (295:s.v.). Some dandy-writers

7

express a positive image of the honnête homme, among them Théophile Gautier in his remarks on Jean Chapelain: "[He] was, in fact, the consummate honnête homme, one who went out of his way to oblige, a sincere friend, a man of his word, charming, full of polish and moderation, perfectly suited to both the court and the town" (209:251).[6] But Gautier was far more interested in the so-called "preclassical" part of the century, which he idealized as encouraging the expression of personal rebelliousness and fostering enthralling adventures. Searching for seventeenth-century kindred spirits, Gautier glorified *Les Grotesques* and Paul de Musset *Les Originaux et extravagants du XVIIe siècle* (209; 369).[7] Stendhal, on the contrary, looked to the reign of Louis XIV for the passion and energy that his "pathetic century" lacked, and projected onto his dandy-hero, Lucien Leuwen, his own nostalgias: "We should have lived under Louis XIV; one spent one's time at court in the very best society, with Mme de Sévigné, the Duc de Villeroy, the Duc de Saint-Simon, and had nothing to do with soldiers except to lead them to battle and win glory if there was any" (487:I, 886).[8] For Stendhal and others, that aristocratic life did not have the cramped, stuffy profile which the first Romantics had created only to reject (412:320 ff). In 1858, Barante noted the revalorization of the seventeenth century's "noble aspect," born of disgust with postrevolutionary discord and chaos (30:I, 170).

As part of the distant past, seventeenth-century France became fertile ground for fictionalized history parading as historical fiction, a genre that frequently serves to express nostalgic visions of the better life. Gautier's *Mademoiselle de Maupin*, for example, demonstrates a (con)fusion of seventeenth- and nineteenth-century heroisms: side by side with his heroine, Madeleine d'Aubigny, who lived during the reign of Louis XIV, he places a fictional hero, D'Albert, who has the salient features of the dandy. In other texts, "reverse projection" makes dandies of "real" people from the *ancien régime*. The titular characters of Eugène Sue's *Latréaumont* and *Le Marquis de Létorière* are dandies by anticipation from the reigns of Louis XIV and XV, respectively. In *Un Dandy avant les dandys*, Barbey d'Aurevilly applied the term to Richelieu, Pascal and Rancé (38:IX, 218, 228). The title of this essay, however, as well as its contents, refers principally to the

Introduction

Duc de Lauzun (1632–1723), Mlle de Montpensier's betrothed, who was to become the archetype of the dandy in nineteenth-century French literature. This search for ancestors and models, this quest for a bygone aristocratic milieu, are but two indications that dandyism yearned to emulate an imaginary past—indeed, to recreate a prerevolutionary elite in a postrevolutionary world.

The tensions between modernism and nostalgia that are implicit in such a project were already patent in the case of Voltaire. In more than the chronological sense, the author of *Le Siècle de Louis XIV* stands midway between the honnête homme and the dandy. On the one hand, Voltaire articulated his nostalgia for the past in ways that announce Stendhal: "In the century of Louis XIV, I find consolation for all the stupidities of the present century" (520:577–78). His specific reference was to the poetic vision of luxury, esthetic and sensual pleasure he described in *Le Mondain*: "I love luxury and even indolence/All its pleasures, all the arts/Cleanliness, good taste and finery:/Every honnête homme is of such a mind" (vv. 9–12).[9] The *Lettres anglaises*, on the other hand, bespeak an admiration for a middle-class society free of aristocratic privilege and values. In urging the honnête homme to rectify injustice and ameliorate human ills, in advocating, like Montesquieu and Duclos, that he have a useful societal function, Voltaire transformed him into a virtuous citizen and thereby denied his aristocratic core. Voltaire's ambivalence between the esthetic and utilitarian or moral acceptances of honnêteté reflects a tendency that can be observed in successive editions of the *Dictionnaire de l'Académie Française*. In 1694, the following definition of *honnête* enjoyed prominence: "all the captivating qualities that a man can have in social life"; in 1718, these words were expunged.[10] The eighteenth-century honnête homme was on his way to being reduced to an honest man.

An identical reductionism underlay Rousseau's attack on *Le Misanthrope* where, as he saw it, Molière had shorn the honnête homme of his moral dimension: "[He] did not want to correct vices, but rather absurdities . . . he wanted to expose to public mockery all the faults that are contrary to the qualities of the *homme aimable* and the *homme de société*; after displaying so many other absurdities, the only thing left to depict was the

9

absurdity of virtue" (434:150).[11] And yet, Rousseau's moralism was counterbalanced by an equally powerful emphasis on feeling in the self-portrait of the *Rêveries* and the *Confessions*. As the model of the Romantic hero, even more than his surrogate, Saint-Preux, Rousseau announces the dandy's narcissism and rebelliousness. The rehabilitation of the passions, which led Saint-Preux to venerate spiritual love, was to lead by a parallel path to the sexual libertinism of the dandy-as-roué. The individualistic current, which equated the personal desire of the *homme sensible* with the good, ended logically in the dandy's justification of immorality.

The sequence—honnête homme, *philosophe*, *homme sensible*, Romantic hero, dandy—traces a diachronic line which literary history should consider. This study, however, will be only incidentally historical. It will center on comparisons between honnêteté and dandyism as independent, synchronic systems having discrete sets of constants and variables, i.e., as two elaborations of the same archetype, the aristocrat-as-art. As Lévi-Strauss has observed, such comparisons need not reduce one system to another; they may simply reveal the similarities, contradictions, dialectical relations and transformations that obtain between the two (310:98). Since the following pages deal primarily with a typology, they will attempt classifications of the elements in honnêteté and dandyism. A typology, of course, is an abstraction from a predetermined set of examples, none of which ever contains all the elements in the typology itself. The choice of examples in these instances is especially difficult, since we cannot say whether it was the social reality that generated the literary formulation or whether real people imitated or dramatized honnêtes hommes and dandies found in literary texts. Although the truth may lie in a mutually enriching but elusive combination of these two possibilities, I have chosen to focus on the literary pole in this dialectic, for it is in the formulation of an imaginary, fictive ideal, which could never be fully incarnated, that the typology achieves its completeness and greatest depth. When "real" individuals inhere in language as honnêtes hommes or dandies, they may be studied along with fictive examples as self-sufficient texts rather than the mimesis of reality. The critical question of influence, then, will not bear upon the relation between reality and literature; it will have relevance only within the literary corpus of honnêteté or dandyism where one text diachronically rewrites another in a process of continuation and discontinuation, imitation and novelty.

How does one determine the optimal size of the literary corpus for the analysis of honnêteté and dandyism? The question becomes urgent if we realize that even Barthes's concept of a "literature of worldliness" from Molière to Proust cannot fully span these two phenomena (42:227). Honnêteté must be traced to the Renaissance and ultimately to Greece and Rome, whereas dandyism, looking back to Regency and Romantic England, looks ahead to post-Victorian estheticism (Wilde and Beerbohm) and to the present-day snob. The problem of inclusiveness will seem less important if we note with Barthes that a phenomenon may be properly interpreted without observing all its instances, so long as the corpus used is sufficiently large and heterogeneous to permit a fairly complete system of similarities and differences to emerge, and to insure that recurrent elements are, in fact, constants. In order to maintain intensiveness and curtail the peripheral, the items in each corpus should be coeval and represent crucial moments in the elaboration of the system (41:171–72). In this light, the chronological limits adopted for this study—1630–1685 and 1830–1885—bear explanation. The year 1630 saw the publication of Nicolas Faret's *L'Honnête homme ou l'art de plaire à la cour*, the first important work on honnêteté; 1685, the date traditionally associated with the waning of French classicism, from which honnêteté is inseparable, also terminates the *oeuvre* of the Chevalier de Méré (d. 1684), its foremost exponent and most profound theoretician. This study will center on Méré's aristocratic or *mondain* vision of honnêteté, not only because it prevailed over the bourgeois (utilitarian or moralistic) conception of Faret and others,[12] but primarily because it provides a compelling seventeenth-century analogue to dandyism. As for the dandy, who arrived in France after the fall of Napoleon, he did not appear in important indigenous works until the establishment of the July monarchy in 1830. By 1885, however, the year after the publication of Huysmans's *A rebours*, the most extreme literary representation of dandyism in France, all the major dandy-writers had disappeared from the scene. Although there are dandyistic traces in Villiers de l'Isle-Adam, Bourget, Barrès, and Jean Lorrain, the 1880s and 1890s produced no figure comparable to Huysmans's Des Esseintes, who synthesizes the currents of dandyism, estheticism, and decadence. To find his equal, one must return to England, completing the cycle that began in 1830, and behold *The Picture of Dorian Gray*. In France, no imposing dandy-hero emerges after Des Esseintes until we meet Proust's Swann and Charlus.

Although the honnête homme appears more frequently in theoretical and essayistic writing and the dandy more often in fiction, both types underwent similar evolutions. Appearance and manners, which initially seemed the exclusive preoccupation of honnêtes hommes and dandies in 1630 and 1830, respectively, came later on to signify exalted visions of self and aristocratic philosophies of life. Only by treating honnêteté and dandyism synchronically, however, is it possible to analyze the elements in each typology and perceive their implications. This approach will also allow for emphasis on the recurrent images and words in each system. Although alternating shifts in focus from honnête homme to dandy within a single chapter present their problems, this procedure facilitates the description of thematic structures, and permits similarities and differences to emerge more clearly. Traditional literary historians may view the comparison of honnêteté to dandyism as bizarre; structuralist, post-structuralist, and semiotic critics may regard the project as traditional. I myself consider this study an introduction, or better yet, a continuation. I believe with Todorov that "scholarly research aims at approximate truth, not absolute truth. If descriptive science claimed to tell *the* truth, it would contradict its own raison d'être. . . . Imperfection is, paradoxically, a guarantee of survival" (500:27).[13]

CHAPTER ONE

PRE-TEXTS AND PROTOTYPES
The Parameters of Self-Definition

I have named those who were unknowingly
my workers and precursors.

Nietzsche, *The Will to Power*

What is an honnête homme? What is a dandy? Writers form these questions and arrive at their individual answers by decoding existing and antecedent texts, which they then go on to "rewrite." This process, which is basic to the phenomenology of any text, assumes added significance when the (writing) subject seeks to imitate or incarnate an imagined past or preestablished ideal. It could be argued that at an early stage the pre-texts and the prototypes to which seventeenth- and nineteenth-century French writers refer already contain the essential features of the honnête homme and the dandy, and the parameters of their eventual definition. Of course, even the identification and "recuperation" of such pre-texts entail interpretation, i.e., a translation that necessarily disjoins and distantiates the "imitated" from the "imitating" text. This first step generates the discontinuation which accrues in the rewriting process and which accounts for the ultimate individualization of its product. Viewed retrospectively, the sum total of these individualized, rewritten texts are the links of syntagmatic chains that comprise the literary corpora of honnêteté and dandyism, in which the honnête homme and the dandy may be said to exist in their own right, as autonomous, quintessential types.

The chosen past for both honnêteté and dandyism was not solely indigenous but foreign as well. Rejecting available domestic options, in a typically aristocratic search for the finer stuff, honnêteté looked to Renaissance Italy, and beyond to Greco-

13

Roman antiquity, while French dandyism turned to England, most immediately the Regency. But whereas the honnête homme defined himself as French, the French dandy remained an alien, less in the nationalistic than in the moral sense. The chief factor in the dandy's persistent, crucial foreignness was his desire to dissociate himself from bourgeois society. Unlike the dandy, the honnête homme did not equate foreign and superior, with the exception of the ultimate Greek and Roman models. Even where he copied foreign texts assiduously, the debt was concealed, as if its admission must indicate inferiority. Whether hidden, as in the case of the honnête homme, or displayed, as in the case of the dandy, the pre-texts of each type contain literary models and semantic kernels, broad thematic structures and minute details, which are subsumed with striking consistency in its own system.

The Honnête Homme

The quintessential prototype for the honnête homme was the Greek philosopher, the incarnation of virtue ($\kappa\alpha\lambda\acute{o}\varsigma$ $\kappa\alpha\gamma\alpha\theta\acute{o}\varsigma$), of the golden mean, and the source of such fundamental notions as human sociability. It was only as eminently social beings, devoid of pedantry, that Greek philosophers earned the label *honnête*: "People can only imagine Plato and Aristotle in the long robes of pedants," protested Pascal. "They were *honnêtes gens* and, like others of their kind, laughed with their friends" (393: 578, #533). Whereas Méré withheld such praise from Aristotle because of his "visibly contrived texts," he bestowed it generously on Plato and Socrates for speaking of the most speculative matters in a lucid, delicate, and captiving manner that was neither "artificial nor bookish" (340:I, 28–29). In the art of sociability, the ultimate Greek model for seventeenth-century writers was Alcibiades, Socrates' enormously seductive disciple, whose protean ability to "change without any effort both his appearance and his manner" (329:263) and be outstanding in all circumstances "always made him desirable among the most accomplished *honnêtes gens* and the most beautiful women of his time" (340:II, 42, III, 73).[1] In a global sense, however, it was Rome, not Athens, that provided the seventeenth century with its prime example of aristocratic society.

14

Pre-Texts and Prototypes

The age of Louis XIV looked to the age of Augustus for its model: "Everything was polished and refined during that reign," wrote Guez de Balzac, "everyone was learned and ingenious in the court, from Augustus to his valets" (29:I, 442). Among the familiars of Augustus, Balzac singled out Maecenas as "the perfect honnête homme of his time" (I, 446). In Saint-Evremond's eyes, this statesman, courtier, and patron of letters was an exemplar, "a winning man whom urbane and witty individuals tried to win over. . . . His tastes determined those of others; . . . they strove to adopt his manner and to imitate his personality as best they could" (438:IV, 111).[2]

For Roman stoics, principally Seneca, *honestus*, like the Greek καλόν, denoted the supreme good (i.e., virtue and honor), to the exclusion of such frivolous qualities as the sociability and worldliness for which Maecenas had been known. Balzac strongly objected to the charges that Seneca had leveled against Maecenas: "What he calls affectation, indolence, dissipation is gaiety, *galanterie*, delicacy" (24:I, 321).[3] Like other *mondains*, however, Balzac appreciated and appropriated into his concept of honnêteté the aristocratic elements inherent in the Senecan sage: born to command, he cannot be injured or controlled by anyone or anything because of an indomitable will and a capacity to master any interfering passion, but he prefers the quiet, exclusive companionship of his peers.[4] Rejecting the abstemiousness of Senecan retreat, the *mondains* insisted on the social connotations of *honestus* (honored, distinguished, respected), which pointed in a different and potentially divergent semantic direction from "virtue." The bivalent strain in *honestus*, its synonymity with *ingenuus* (freeborn, noble, or honorable), leads to *venustus* and *urbanus*, which denotes, in Quintilian, "the total absence of all that is incongruous, coarse, unpolished and exotic, whether in thought, language, voice or gesture" (413:II, 499). At the end of a tortuous, selective evolution, seventeenth-century writers referred casually to "that Roman urbanity" as if all Latin antiquity had prized this virtue uniformly. Attempts to articulate the exact components of the *vir urbanus*, however, were as numerous as they were unsatisfactory. Pellisson grappled with "this urbanity which the words *civilité*, *galanterie*, and *politesse* express only im-

15

perfectly, and for which our language has not yet found a suitable term" (445:120). Unable to offer their own analogue, the French simply naturalized *urbanité*, "the talent . . . which Cicero possessed, and which is all the more difficult to acquire since it is the most essential characteristic and the principal quality of the honnête homme" (120:I, 511–12).[5]

With the mention of Cicero we reach the crossroads where the most influential ancient texts have their intersection. The *De oratore* and *De officiis*, the "Bible of the *mondains*" (340:II, 141), provided a smooth reconciliation of stoic virtue with a latter-day worldliness. In *De officiis*, a treatise on statecraft, *honestum* is inseparable from the cardinal virtue of decorum or propriety (*quod decet*), a term which also embraces the components of gentlemanly deportment. With moderation as the key, Cicero's ideal man, like the honnête homme, will have neither an overmeticulous nor a slovenly appearance, and his manners, neither effeminate nor coarse, will be modest, affable, and courteous. Unremittingly self-critical, Cicero's paragon will do no less to perfect his craft than the actor or the artist (130:117, 151).

Rather than the statesman, however, it was the rhetor, as described by both Cicero and Quintilian, to which theorists of honnêteté consistently turned for a textual model. Although more technical and less philosophical, Quintilian's *Institutio oratoria* is itself a rewriting of *De oratore*; Cicero, cited repeatedly, is upheld as "supreme in all the qualities which are praised in each individual orator" (413:IV, 457). The eloquence to which the rhetor aspires in speaking or writing requires a "priestly" dedication, and involves a spiritual labor which is rewarded by supreme virtue and the highest art.[6] In the image of the ideal rhetor, theorists of honnêteté found a human work of art, able to captivate the will of his audience and cast a charm over the most resistant antagonist. He must display not his "nature," but that "which nature permits to be done to the greatest perfection" (413:III, 509); this appearance of naturalness conceals his effort and care, and accounts for his grace, ease, and elegance. Specifically, he must cultivate the urbanity of the Roman accent and articulate simply, distinctly, and smoothly, with a musicality that charms the ear and stirs the soul. This living work of art must exploit all aspects of delivery, including what Quintilian calls "physical eloquence"—the semiologically effective use of eyebrows, nostrils, neck, hands, or feet. A consummate actor, he must control his emotions the better to display his verbal art. Rejecting Ciceronian grandiloquence, Quintilian stresses a simpler idiom aimed at a "certain tasteful elegance that offends no one" (III: 299).[7] Wit, a particularly important weapon in the rhetor's arsenal, must therefore never be vicious, coarse, or buffoonish. Like all aspects of eloquence, wit can be enhanced through painstaking study and practice, but depends ultimately on an intuitive feeling, or what Cicero calls "a sort of subconscious instinct" (*tacito sensu*) of right and wrong (131:IV, 155); this artistic tact or taste, for which no rules exist, is inborn. According to the classical esthetics which underlie the ideal rhetor, Art veils over defects and perfects what is already there; Nature, inborn capacity, ranks first (131:III, 81).

The Ciceronian and Quintilian rhetor, along with the other aristocratic ideals of Rome and Greece, were obliterated—so went the seventeenth-century cliché—during those ignorant, uncouth centuries (72:159) labeled *le moyen âge*, the intermediate, indifferent gap between ancient and modern times (175a:58 ff). Even though knighthood represented the first aristocratic order on French soil, and the chivalric ideal had been inspired by such models as Alexander and Caesar (265:70–72), the seventeenth century, iterating the attitude of the sixteenth, viewed the Middle Ages as its antithesis and rejected its ties to any ancient culture but the classical past. "We have completely abandoned the Gothic order, which barbarism had introduced into palaces and churches," wrote La Bruyère; "we have recalled the doric, the ionic and the corinthian. . . . Analogously, we can achieve perfection in writing, and if possible, surpass the ancients only by imitating them. So many centuries had to pass before men could return to classical standards in the arts and sciences" (286:68, 15). This predominate stance did not prevent La Bruyère from occasionally praising the language and literature of the "dark ages" to criticize the modern idioms, or from extolling the virtuous knights of old to underscore the decadence of his contemporaries (pp. 431–34, 73; pp. 406 ff).[8] Nor did the widespread cliché affect the passion of the nobility and monarchy for reenacting medieval tourneys and pageants, as described in the romances and chronicles which the seventeenth century consumed for pleasure. But the imagined medieval praxis was transcoded from barbarous aggressiveness to aristocratic play, just as romanesque characters and adventures were rewritten—and the list ranges from D'Urfé's *Astrée* to La Fayette's *Zayde*—in accordance with standards of refinement that reflected and furthered the ideal of honnêteté. More specifically, the complex aristocratic system of duties and prohibitions known as courtly love—*honeste amandi* in Capellanus's twelfth-century rewriting of Ovid's *Ars amatoria*—constituted the literary prototype for relations between the sexes in honnêteté. Far from acknowledging the debt, however, the *mondains* looked with contempt upon the comportment of the courtly lover. Even Chapelain's *De la lecture des vieux romans*, the most notable seventeenth-century defense of the genuine amorous feelings and military virtues of the courtly lover, characterized the *chevaliers* as "honnête barbarians and respectable louts" who had no love for letters, no capacity for urbane conversation, no notion whatsoever of *l'art de galanterie* (119:20, 26, 28). In a barbaric, unartistic, imbecilic text like the prose Lancelot, therefore, no individual, concluded Chapelain, could hope to learn the incomparable art of honnêteté (pp. 14, 26).[9]

The honnête homme was undeniably indebted to the chivalrous and courtly ideal, at the very least for providing an indigenous antecedent text of the aristocratic self, which he went on to rewrite. Even more, as Huizinga has argued, the waning Middle Ages elaborated the socioliterary ideal of the courtier that served the next two centuries as basic (con)text (265). But the honnête homme chose to consider himself the direct descendant of the Renaissance. According to his mythical construct, when the luminous dawn of the Renaissance eliminated the shadowy swamps of Gothicism, the notion of the self-as-art was reborn. As Jacob Burckhardt put it, in his major work on the Renaissance, it was then that "the demeanor of individuals, and all higher forms of social intercourse, became ends pursued with a deliberate and artistic purpose"; these forms, he wrote, "meet us as a work of art" (97:223, 228). It is from this vantage point, which John White has called "aesthetic individualism" (523), that the Renaissance aristocrat rewrote the classical image of life as an object of emulation, replacing the Ciceronian notion of a useful citizen with the ideal of an established elite, consciously segregated from the vulgar herd, devoting its leisure to artistic perfection. No Renaissance text exemplifies that ideal more completely than Castiglione's *Il Cortegiano*, which purportedly transcribes the conversations of celebrated patricians in the most beautiful place in Italy. In this rarefied atmosphere of continuous pleasure, where nothing is more pleasurable than the leisurely discussion of a "fine question," the notion of the perfect courtier, "that never existed and perhaps never can exist," is conceived as a conscious analogue to the "Idea of the perfect Republic, the perfect King, and the perfect Orator" (113:196, 197). Devoid of any pragmatic intent, impervious to the problematics of realizing the ideal, the elaboration of the courtier partakes of a serene dream of human perfectibility.

Although one participant in Castiglione's text argues that the most gifted courtiers are often of humblest origin, noble birth is thought to represent a hidden seed or an inherent luster that enhances every quality and earns immediate esteem. Endowed further with beauty of face and body, the courtier dresses with a modest elegance that captivates even without speech or gesture. He displays his physical, military, and intellectual feats only for his peers, striving always to be "recognized as better than the rest," a sight "to feed the spectator's eyes" (113:38, 99). Unlike the French, whom Castiglione chastizes for abhorring letters, the courtier knows Greek and Latin, and is versed in the ancient poets, orators, and historians; he is also skilled in prose, verse, painting, and music. Above all, he must excel in the art of conversation, the principal occupation at court and the primary vehicle for displaying one's social being. Castiglione's specific precepts on conversation are a résumé of Cicero, but particular emphasis is placed on the courtier's nonchalance (*sprezzatura*), which will make his accomplishments seem effortless and all the more admirable: "Nonchalance ... often causes [an act] to be judged much greater than it actually is, since it impresses upon the minds of the onlookers the opinion that he who performs well with so much facility must possess greater skills than this, and that, if

19

he were to devote care and effort to what he does, he could do it far better" (p. 46); *sprezzatura*, then, marks the highest art, the one that "does not seem to be art" (p. 43). Like a consummate actor, the courtier will put artistry before all moral considerations: "If you have a beautiful jewel with no setting and it passes into the hands of a good goldsmith who with a skillful setting makes it appear far more beautiful, will you say that the goldsmith deceives the eyes of the one who looks at it? Surely he deserves praises for that deceit because with good judgment and art his masterful hand often adds grace and adornment to ivory or to silver or to a beautiful stone by setting it in fine gold" (p. 139). The courtier's relations to others are equally dominated by esthetic considerations: he has one perfect friend because "it is more difficult to attune three musical instruments than two" (p. 126); and he loves his perfect lady platonically, "beyond the manner of the vulgar herd," for "the sweetness of her voice, the modulation of her words, the harmony of her music" (pp. 346–47). Even the courtier's ascension to perfect virtue in Book IV, and his role, both *dulce et utile*, as the prince's guide in ethics and religion, do not diminish the accent on beauty and art. The courtier treats his life as a supreme canvas in which esthetic dignity remains the only lasting spiritual value. He is, first and always, an aristocrat who basks in his self-perfection, a work of art for the world to admire.

Whereas Castiglione had rewritten Cicero's *De oratore* and a nobiliary transcoded its substance into an aristocratic frame, French authors began by ignoring the *Cortegiano*'s esthetic vision in their quest for practical precepts to gain the princely favor.[10] Of the "bourgeois" treatises, as Magendie has called them (323), which stress a strategy of social *arrivisme* in the period 1600–1643, the most significant by far is Faret's *L'Honnête homme ou l'art de plaire à la cour* (1630). As its subtitle indicates, this text, which was reprinted eleven times before 1681, makes the semantic leap from the Italian *cortegiano* and the French *courtisan* to the *honnête homme*.[11] Summarizing the *Cortegiano* for pages at a time, without ever acknowledging his source, Faret outlines "the most necessary qualities . . . that the person who wants to succeed at court must possess" (188:9). While he recognizes the importance of noble birth, Faret insists that a person of lowly origins can become intimate with the great. The military remains the only valid profession, but only because it can lead to honor, renown, and nobiliary status. In the sartorial realm, however, Faret departs from Castiglione and foreshadows Molière's M. Jourdain: "The more you can put on without being encumbered the better; clothing is among the most useful expenditures made at court. . . . [It] opens doors . . . that are often closed to persons of the highest rank" (p. 91). He gives lip service to disinterested learning and reduces the courtier's knowledge to those modish subjects which can further his social ambitions—a "nodding familiarity with the most stimulating questions which are sometimes debated in high society" (p. 26).[12] Although faithful to Castiglione's precepts on politeness, consideration, modesty, and adaptability, Faret ignores the art of conversation. And rather than a "perfect friend," this honnête homme will have a henchman or public relations man to pave his way at court; his interest in women goes to those who have the power "to give men prestige" (p. 40). But when Faret, following Castiglione, insists that the honnête homme become the prince's virtuous mentor, his text reaches an impasse: an *arriviste* whose livelihood and success depend on currying the prince's favor is hardly in a position to reform him. And yet, it is not the unconvincing moral aims of the honnête homme as much as his fundamental indifference to esthetics that indelibly marks Faret's analysis of social climbing.

Faret's treatise, along with texts like Bardin's *Le Lycée* (1632), stimulated a corpus of reflection on the honnête homme, which not only obviated the need to return to foreign sources, like the *Cortegiano*, but also established a context and a code for the subsequent formulation of the aristocratic vision in France. This vision did not discard practical, utilitarian precepts; it merely reset them in a subtler, larger framework and ordered them according to the ideas of an indigenous Renaissance writer who was conceptually at loggerheads with the utilitarian Faret: Montaigne. In the seventeenth century, Montaigne's *Essais* were regarded as "the breviary of *honnêtes gens*," and their author as "the foremost master as well as the foremost example of nobility" (240:I, 231; II, 189).[13]

"The men whose company and intimacy I seek," Montaigne wrote, "are those who are called *honnêtes et habiles hommes*; the idea of these men makes the others distasteful to me. It is, rightly speaking, the rarest of human forms, and a form that is chiefly due to nature" (355:III.iii, 802).[14] In the *Essais*, the *honnête homme, habile homme*, and *galant homme* are the chief examples of the *nature bien née*, a term that refers to distinction of mind, *une tête bien faite*, rather than class origins or aristocratic appearance. The scholar Adrien Turnèbe is a case in point: "The cut of his gown and a certain manner that might not be considered civilized by courtly standards . . . are things of no value. . . . Inwardly, he was the most polished soul in the world" (I.xxv, 139). Montaigne may occasionally cite Castiglione, but his vision of the true aristocrat departs radically from the courtier model. Although he sometimes saw himself as the king's virtuous counselor, in keeping with the ideal of the *Cortegiano*, he recognized that the pursuit of this ambition would have meant betraying his nature and sacrificing his passion for freedom (I.xxvi, 123; II.xvii, 626; III.ix, 947, 976). Courtiers become so bound to court life that they are out of their element anywhere else; the honnête homme, on the contrary, is "an all-around man" (III.ix, 964), a supple nature who abhors "fastidiousness and confinement to certain particular ways" (III.xiii, 1061), a citizen of the world, a member of a universal elite, whose personification is Socrates: soldier, philosopher, friend, musician, dancer, "a personage with all the models and forms of perfection," the living contradiction of those who are "hardly good in a single vein" (p. 1090).[15]

"To compose our character is our duty, not to compose books, and to win, not battles and provinces, but order and tranquillity in our conduct. Our great and glorious masterpiece is to live appropriately" (p. 1088). For Montaigne, the art of life constitutes the only meaningful and honnête occupation: "My trade and my art is living" (II.vi, 359).[16] In the pursuit of this art, Montaigne follows, at the outset, the Senecan model of retreat as the precondition for the *otium* or *oisiveté* that is basic to all modes of elite existence. In *De l'oisiveté*, however, Montaigne confronts the difficulties involved in endowing his "full idleness" with a form and purpose that will save it from degenerating into a disordered "shapeless" mass (I.viii, 33–34). Because this self-created form and order, which require "husbanding one's will" (III.x, 980) and bridling one's passions, comprise an independent code of ethics and internal court of law, management of the private life is more demanding and profound an art than management of the public life (III.iii, 787). Devoted to self-knowledge and self-realization, this self-sufficient life includes, contrary to Seneca, the enjoyment of all reasonable appetites in the name of a virtue which is finally, as for Epicurus, inseparable from the pleasure principle (I.xx, 80). Montaigne considered himself "born for company and friendship" (III.iii, 801), and prized, even more than the solitary pleasures of reading and meditation, opportunities for conversation. Social intercourse in its original sense, conversation is "the most fruitful and natural exercise of our mind," he wrote in *De l'art de conférer*, "sweeter than any other action of our life" (III.viii, 900). Refusing to converse with "ill-born and vulgar types," especially the monomaniacal pedants who would contaminate and bastardize his judgment (p. 904), he seeks the kind of vigorous and invigorating confrontation of minds that overlays a secret but essential order: "I receive and acknowledge any sort of blows that are straightforward . . . but I am only too intolerant of those that lack form. . . . I will argue peaceably a whole day if the debate is conducted with order. It is not so much strength and subtlety that I ask for as order. . . . So in a concert of instruments we do not hear a lute, a spinet, and the flute; we hear a rounded harmony, the gathering of these disparate elements into a fruitful whole" (pp. 903, 909). Like the private, exclusive life, conversation with *honnêtes gens* has nothing to do with pedantic weightiness of substance and everything to do with beauty of form: "graciousness and beauty satisfy and occupy me as much as weight and depth, or more" (III.iii, 797).[17]

The art of conversation that Montaigne delineates ultimately stands as a metaphor for the *écriture* of the *Essais*, as Regosin has observed (422:115). Just as freedom, idleness, and social intercourse require order to have meaning, so too must the self be circumscribed and enclosed within a form if it is to be apprehended and understood in a world ruled by uncertainty and instability, where "all things are in constant motion" (III.ii, 782): "In modeling this figure upon myself, I have had to fashion and compose myself so often to bring myself out, that the original model has grown firm and somewhat formed itself" (II.xviii, 647–48).[18] Montaigne revealed in the very fabric of his text—and he was, as he knew, the first to do so (II.vi, 357)—how the self becomes art as it transforms itself into a (verbal) artifact. The narcissism inherent in taking the self as the subject and substance of art—"I am myself the matter of my book" (preface, I, 10)—must be attenuated to ward off charges of presumption. Thus Montaigne initially dismisses his enterprise as folly and madness, his subject as frivolous and vain, and like Socrates, from whom he learned the delicate art of self-depreciation (II.vi, 358–60), he presents an excessively modest and mocking self-image to disarm his readers—a most effective strategy of persuasion, as McGowan has shown (321). An integral part of this tactic is the antiwriter pose—"I am less a maker of books than any other thing" (II.xxxvii, 764)—and his insistence that the *Essais* are the artless meanderings of an unfettered mind recorded for the amusement of some friend or relative "who may take pleasure in conversing with me again in this image" (II.xviii, 647). Behind this *sprezzatura*, however, is the wish to appeal (*plaire*) to the happy few, the unidentified members of his spiritual circle: "Besides this profit that I derive from writing about myself, I hope for this other benefit, that if my humors happen to suit and appeal to some honnête homme before I die, he will try to meet me" (III.ix, 959).[19] Although he may claim to portray his nature fully and uninhibitedly—"I expose myself entirely" (II.vi, 359)—the decorous naturalness to which Montaigne aspires is modeled after Seneca's *Epistles*, with their captivating "undulating and diverse" style (II.x, 392), and particularly Plato's dialogues, where Socrates "makes his soul move with a natural and common motion" (III.xii, 1013).[20] Such texts have a "poetic gait, by leaps and gambols" (III.ix, 971), for which no rules exist (III.i, 773), but which produce the most irresistible kind of beauty: "Charms . . . which glide beneath naturalness and simplicity easily escape a sight as gross as ours. They have a delicate and hidden beauty; we need a clear and well-purged sight to discover their secret light" (III.xii, 1013).[21] By forging an *écriture* which is equivalent to aristocratic *parole*, Montaigne inscribed an image of self which seemed to capture being in the process of becoming, of testing itself out (*s'essayer*). At bottom, however, it was the writing that made the man, the art and act of writing which endowed Montaigne with his form and essence: "Painting myself for others, I have painted my inward self with colors sharper than my original ones. I have no more made my book than my book has made me" (II.xvii, 648). His offspring, as he implied in *De la ressemblance des pères aux enfants*, was a self created through and in a text, a form to behold and to become: "It serves me as a rule. . . . This public declaration obliges me to keep on my path, and not to give the lie to the picture of my qualities" (III.ix, 958).[22]

It was a rich convergence of elements that made Montaigne a model for the seventeenth-century honnête homme: his views on professionalism, pedantry, education, and conversation, his brand of stoicism and epicureanism, his comfortable distance from religion and independent attitude toward other established codes. Even more, however, it was his vision of a select society devoted to the beautification of life and, above all, his representation of self as art that determined the substance of seventeenth-century honnêteté. Through his views, and especially his example, Montaigne injected a new intellectuality into the aristocratic typology, and a new worldliness into the typology of the intellectual. Without the coalescence of these two strains, honnêteté would never have evolved in the form in which we know it.

The exclusive ambiance that Montaigne idealized, like the palace in which the Cortegiano is devised, already prefigures the life of the salon, that center of aristocratic sociability first established through the conscious efforts of the Marquise de Rambouillet. Her revulsion at the crudity of court manners[23] impelled her to create *la chambre bleue*, an oasis of refinement that was probably a reproduction of her native Italian environment. By numerous accounts, hers was a more selective milieu than any other aristocratic stronghold: in l'Hôtel de Rambouillet gathered "the most urbane members of the court and the most polished among the fine minds of the century" (497:I, 443). It attracted notable persons who wished to partake of its prestige, bathe in its exclusivity; by their admission, they further enhanced its powerful aura in the eyes of the nonadmitted. Although a matter of faith and illusion, social being or nonbeing seemed to depend on her recognition: "You cannot claim to belong to high society unless you are known to her;" wrote Madeleine de Scudéry, one of the salon's habitués (453:I, 262).[24] In her thirty-year reign (c. 1615–1648), the Marquise defined a new elite, above society's pyramid and outside courtly protocol, based on the principle of exclusivity. This conscious effort of a group to assert itself against others constitutes the new dimension that Rambouillet's salon grafted onto earlier models of honnêteté.

The guiding spirit of this salon, the chief source of its amusements, was Vincent Voiture. The butt of verses that rhymed *Voiture* with *roture*, this wine merchant's son countered that true nobility came from action, not station: "He who is born a commoner can be reborn a nobleman and fill his life with splendor despite the obscurity of his origins" (518:II, 150). And yet, the very fact that Voiture, Isaac Benserade, and Jean Ogier Gombauld, for example, ennobled themselves or were ennobled by the group would seem to contradict the claimed indifference to rank. If writers were not admitted on an equal basis, their inclusion nonetheless attests to their social promotion, as well as to the nobles' concerted effort to conjoin intellectuality and aristocracy. The mutual benefit derived by the nobles who frequented the salons and the authors who glorified them in their work did not go undetected: "Writers . . . serve to extend the dominion of noblewomen and to maintain their reputation and their power: reciprocally, the women do the same for writers" (467:I, 23).[25]

Life in *la chambre bleue* aspired to all the embellishments and subtleties of art. Utilitarianism and specialization were banished: "The conversation there is not learned, but it *is* reasonable," wrote Chapelain; "nowhere on earth is there more good sense and less pedantry" (120:I, 215). The acclaimed unpretentious worldliness of Rambouillet's own brand of learning was the test for all aspirants: "[She] knows almost everything worth knowing; but she knows it without appearing to know it; to hear her speak one would say . . . that she speaks only out of simple good sense and experience of the world" (453:I, 261).[26] The primary virtue was sociability, a willingness to transcend individual differences for the common pursuit of esthetic pleasure. In a collective poetic undertaking like *La Guirlande de Julie*, sociability was raised to the level of art; inversely, the love poetry promoted in this salon sublimated passion into a refined game. Nowhere is this more apparent than in Voiture, the poet who delights as much in hiding as the (female) reader delights in discovering the secret meaning. As his titles alone suggest—*Verse written with the left hand on a page facing a mirror placed inside the cover of a notebook*—he wants to dazzle with the virtuosity of his linguistic acrobatics. Self-discipline for pleasure and for applause was the underlying principle of the poetry and the various intellectual parlor games played by artists and aristocrats alike. Along with these pastimes, Rambouillet's world included ballets and plays in which members themselves became part of the processes of art. Even her renowned tricks involved an esthetic component. During an outing, Voiture writes, the habitués of l'Hôtel were suddenly greeted by twenty-four violinists hidden near a fountain, two girls dressed as Diana and a nymph, and a youth who represented Paris: "No one uttered a word, dazzled by so many things that stunned their eyes and ears" (293:67).[27]

The esthetic vision of life which literature has ascribed to Mme de Rambouillet and her group became the model for the form and substance of the honnête life. That many theorists, including Méré, had been received at l'Hôtel corroborates the interpretation of this salon as the birthplace of honnêteté.[28] Chapelain and Balzac, who moved in Rambouillet's orbit, helped integrate early bourgeois theorizing into an esthetic framework that recalls the *Cortegiano*, just as Méré was later to retheorize a vision abstracted from her example. However, her salon has also been described by literary historians as the birthplace of *préciosité*, although no such concept or school of thought existed in the seventeenth century, any more than French classicism did, from which it has traditionally been substantively differentiated. And the term *précieuse*, which was in circulation since the fourteenth century, is hardly used as a noun until 1650–1660, and then only pejoratively.[29] No individual claimed that label, nor did any contemporary apply it to Madeleine de Scudéry, that alleged exemplar of *préciosité ridicule* (201:16–42). Scudéry's ideal, as every page of *Le Grand Cyrus* confirms, was honnêteté, effectively transformed into a kind of romantic heroism, a latter-day drawing room version of courtly love. Her extensive and intensive analyses of love, a rewriting of the texture of *L'Astrée*, prefigure the predilection for psychological dissection in "classical" literature as well as in later theorizing on honnêteté, of which her own texts constitute an elaborate feminist version. In fact, the outpouring of satirical literature against the so-called pedantic and prudish, unnatural and unaristocratic *précieuses* (and not the *précieux*) may well represent a threatened and threatening male response to feministic assertions of power over sex and logos in seventeenth-century society.

Whatever its motive and intent, this satirical corpus on *préciosité* revels the logical, if extreme, consequences of the aims of Rambouillet and aristocratic honnêteté. Thus the urge of the honnête homme to exclusiveness, the desire to be superior, inherent in Rambouillet's efforts, become explicit in definitions of *les précieuses*: "Certain members of the fair sex, who managed to set themselves apart from the crowd, and to constitute a unique breed and caste" (410:I, 12). This group is so elitist as to form an independent country with its own history and laws, or even a secret sect demanding solemn life-long vows (467:I, xl; I, 71). Although membership may be hereditary, as in traditional aristocracies, it is granted primarily for social and intellectual merit, irrespective of class origins: "There are no commoners in their domain, since learning and *galanterie*, by definition, are illustrious and noble" (467:I, 173). Equality within the sect goes hand in hand with extreme contempt for outsiders: "When there is only one *précieuse* in a gathering, she is exhausted with boredom and annoyance; she yawns, doesn't answer when spoken to, and if she does answer, it is off the point to show that she isn't thinking about what she's saying. . . . If another *précieuse* arrives, they join forces . . . their carrying on, as they laugh in people's faces, is the most insufferable thing in the world" (357:517).[30] This lack of civility surfaces at the slightest sign of an outsider's presence; because La Grange and Du Croisy do not dress like members of *le beau monde*, they are immediately dismissed by Molière's *précieuses ridicules*. Their more significant concern, however, is to be courted in strict conformity to the rules of *la galanterie*, which has nothing to do with passion. For their express desire is to live life itself as art: "Let us weave at our leisure the fabric of our novel," Magdelon asks Gorgibus, in opposition to his vulgar obsession with the bourgeois institution of marriage (sc. iv). Of a piece with their views on the art of love is the *précieuses*' linguistic puritanism, the heroic lengths purportedly taken to refine language, banish the crude word, not as signifier but as signified. By substituting abstract periphrases for the concrete and the material, language itself is to be transformed from a mere system of communication to an artistic guessing game, as befits aristocrats: "Of necessity, a *précieuse* must speak differently from the masses," insists l'Abbé de Pure, "so that her thoughts may be understood only by people whose lights surpass those of the vulgar herd" (410:I, 58).[31]

These attitudes toward language and love already suggest that the *précieuses* strove to transform the self into art. Submitting to self-imposed disciplines, they developed a semiotics of physical language and assumed collectively a set of signifying stances: "They lean their head on their shoulder, grimace with their eyes and mouth, and have a contemptuous air and a certain affectation in their whole demeanor" (357:517). Even a reflex response like a smile could be controlled to convey precise psychological nuances, and thus could be classified in a repertory that included, by Pure's account, "the white tooth," "the gracious eye," and especially the *faux semblant*: "It's a natural artifice, by which the mechanism of the face radically changes its configuration, just as the scene changes in the theater to depict different subjects or to enthrall the audience. Thus although the spirit is unchanged and has the same haughtiness, the *faux semblant* brings a soft expression to the face" (410:II, 162).[32] The metaphor of the stage and of the face as a machine obeying the will reveal a seriousness of purpose which transcends the banal charge of affectation, the criterion by which *précieuses* were judged *ridicules*.

In their satirical representation, the *précieuses* of 1650–1660 exemplify the inauthentic version of the aristocratic ideal of honnêteté. *Préciosité ridicule* served as the necessary partner in the binary *paraître/être*, the sign of the exaggerated, inartistic expression of the elitist impulse, which had to be exorcized precisely because it was a most tempting possibility. The "vices" of this *préciosité* are the caricature of native tendencies of honnêteté itself, not a separate, isolated phenomenon. Méré, in fact, found such "vices" in Voiture, and refused him the title of honnête homme. He chastized Voiture's obsessive need to advertise his superiority and display his agile mind, to the point of using tasteless stylistic tricks, intellectual obfuscation, and hyperbolic emotionalism; these were the marks of vanity and vulgarity, the failure to create the illusion of naturalness. For Méré, inauthenticity characterized Voiture's entire being: "He often said fine things, but I felt that he was more an actor than an honnête homme; to me, that made him insufferable" (339:484–85).[33]

The differences between Méré's view of Voiture or Molière's view of the *précieuses ridicules* on the one hand, and the honnête homme on the other, are only of degree, not kind. The similarities have more to tell us than the differences: *préciosité* (−) and honnêteté (+) share the same elitist impulse, the same desire to create a consummately artistic—and of necessity artificial—secondary self designed to exact recognition of superiority through an elaborate strategy of seduction. To the realization of this goal the honnête homme and the "affected" *précieuse* devoted their exclusive energies, as did the dandy two centuries later. In at least three important areas, dandyism was, in fact, more akin to negative *préciosité* than to honnêteté. Both favored more obvious and extreme means of self-assertion, had a greater contempt for nature and a more visible respect for artifice, and both were the objects of satire and ridicule. Although dandyism and honnêteté transcend the notion of a closed côterie, to which *préciosité ridicule* was relegated, all three postulate a philosophy of life for the superior being who is as much artist as aristocrat.

Dandyism

If honnêteté evolved gradually and gracefully, dandyism, true to its nature, arose meteorically and explosively. No sooner had dandyism been born in England, during the Regency (1811–1820), than it invaded France along with the conquering English army.[34] But it was not the English dandy in the flesh as much as his literary representation that fired the French imagination and stimulated imitation of a type depicted in texts both foreign and domestic. On French soil, this corpus of material generated not a duplication but an interpretation, a rewriting that led to the literary phenomenon of the French dandy.

Just as the *Cortegiano* epitomizes Renaissance Italianization, the dandy stands as a synecdoche for the image and impact of England in nineteenth-century France. In both the Renaissance and the nineteenth century, the foreign model imposed itself in the aftermath of heavier intellectual currents—Humanism in the first case, and in the other, the Enlightenment and Romanticism. It was the *philosophes*, notably Voltaire in his *Lettres anglaises* (1732), who first looked to England for political, philosophical, and literary inspiration. Extended by d'Holbach and Diderot, along with numerous translators, uninterrupted by the Revolution or Napoleon's rise, England's influence on France found its strongest endorsement in de Staël's *De la littérature* (1800). Her belief that the Republic will necessarily bring French culture closer to the English overlays a desire for intellectual "progress" and an avowed preference for the "Literature of the North." Like Voltaire, de Staël sees in Shakespeare's work an esthetic, unknown to prerevolutionary France, that symbolizes the essential English character. Voltaire had described the Bard's plays as "brilliant monsters," full of energy and sublime passion, but still bizarre and savage (522:81–84); analogously, he saw the archetypical Englishman in terms of an old cliché as barbarous, somber, and eccentric.[35] Rationalizing and synthesizing the disparate elements contained in that cliché, de Staël derives from the English philosophical spirit a natural penchant for melancholy and ennui ("melancholy poetry is the poetry best suited to philosophy" [473:I.xii, 180]). Ennui, linked to a somber imagination, determines the uncontrolled eruptions of energy, the violent and bizarre passions both of the individual Englishman and of English literature; even their humor, by French standards of civility, is morose and misanthropic. At the same time, de Staël's hope for a synthesis between "French urbanity" and "Shakespearean energy" goes beyond Voltaire's criticisms to provide a valorization of a basically non-French—even anti-French—psychoesthetic outlook.

31

With Chateaubriand we find a further shift toward positive representation of Englishness and its literary manifestations. Whereas in 1800 he had denounced the primitiveness of Shakespeare's style and dramaturgy, by 1822 he was ready to dismiss the Bard's "defects" as useless defenses against his overpowering genius and to admit that "England *is* Shakespeare" (126:I, 409). Three years later, Stendhal was to make Shakespeare the symbol of the Romantic battle against the classicism of Racine (486).

Those who looked to Shakespeare in their ardor to bury the *ancien régime* and renew French art were precisely those who also fought the importation of English aristocraticism. When Stendhal speaks of "the dreadful misfortune of our anglicization" (482:233), he is not referring to romanticization, but to the obsessive imitation of the material signs of English upper-class life. "Everybody has a passion for horses, dogs, fabrics and carriages from England," writes an observer as early as 1802; "a person of elegance would be ashamed to outfit himself anywhere else" (3:399). One might have expected the defeat of France in 1815 to check this anglomania, but by a process that Freud calls identification with the aggressor, it grew in intensity: English perfumes, china, pastries, restaurants, and clothes became the rage. Even the English passion for sports found French imitators who proliferated boxing matches, pigeon shoots, and equestrian societies with appropriate texts on the rules of racing. Cock fighting, however, was the last straw: "That is the state of urbanity, good taste, and elegance of manners in the land of Francis I, Lauzun and Richelieu!" (347:114).[36] Reaffirming France's preeminence in prerevolutionary Europe, Balzac urged his country to recapture the scepter with which she had for so long ruled art and literature, elegance, civility, and taste (21:I, 350). Such resentment and indignation betray a fear of destruction by an alien force. Primitives will deal with this fear by classifying the foreign as evil; the civilized are more likely to devalue and dismiss it through contempt and/or ridicule. Accordingly, the upper-class Englishman in the 1820s became the object of satire. In a wide variety of texts, ranging from travel accounts, like Jouy's *L'Hermite de Londres* and Pichot's *Le Voyage en Angleterre*, to the reflections of Chateaubriand and Stendhal, the French evolved what Reboul has called "the English myth" (420). It was this corpus that contained the first literary representation of the English dandy in French literature.

Although at first glance they may seem diametrically opposed, the dandy reproduces the major traits of the Englishman as seen through the prism of Shakespearean drama.[37] The most notable ingredient added to the older typology is affectation—the conscious manifestation of archetypal traits, which are now constituted into a "system" of distinctiveness (277:I, 96). Thus, the English penchant for melancholy is transmuted into the dandies' purposeful cultivation of an "unhappy air" (485:1441). The lack of civility was calculated as well: "Nothing succeeded in London like insolence" (126:II, 78). As Pichot saw it, the dandy had simply made virtues of the most obvious English vices, many of which had been imitated from the French. English upper-class life of the 1820s was losing "its solemn ways, its natural originality, independence, and dignity and assuming those frivolous charms which until now had belonged exclusively to the French character. England does not hide its admiration for Parisian pleasures; it considers them indispensable to the enjoyment of life. Undoubtedly, the two sexes fashion themselves tolerably well after the model they constantly have before their eyes; but they remain imitators and lose their national physiognomy" (397:285). When Pichot suggests that nineteenth-century English aristocraticism was itself a rewriting of the French, it is for the sole purpose of stressing his own country's superiority. France, he argues, no longer considers the power to dictate the whims of fashions a valid claim to eminence. Chateaubriand was to put it succinctly: "The new breed of Englishman is infinitely more frivolous than we are" (126:II, 79).[38]

Among the newer "vices" cultivated by "frivolous" English dandies was the emphasis on external adornment: "We are judged more by our clothes than our qualities," complained Jouy; "if a man isn't dressed in the latest fashion, he must settle for last place in the esteem of high society" (277:II, 71-72). One must spend endless hours "getting laced up and squeezed into a corset, arranging the folds of a cravat that strangles you as if you were in the pillory, having your hair greased, your face painted, and all that in order *not* to look *comme il faut*" (277:I, 338). In Jouy's and other early texts, sideburns and mustache, boots, whip, and horse converge to produce a military look (I:341). It is, however, as an uncouth and blustering soldier that the English dandy first appears in French texts: racing through the London streets in his tilbury, knocking people over, vaunting the price of his horse and the skill of his jockey, or simply assuming ridiculous military poses: "They often have a toothpick in their mouth, a piece of straw picked up in their stable, or, to give themselves a military air, a lighted cigar, whose smoke suggests that inside their head there is only a vacuum, vapor, and fog. Sometimes you see these heroes of tavern and stable nonchalantly seated on a horse, closing one eye, bringing a lorgnette up to the other, and on their arm, a crooked stick, the perfect emblem of their mind" (I:341–42).[39]

Until the publication of Bayard and Wailly's revisionist *Anglais et français* (1827), the fashionable Englishman remained a vapid and ludicrous type. However, in this play, which seeks to dispel the prejudices of the French, the central character, Sir Richard, exemplifies what he preaches: "the young gentlemen are in no way ridiculous. . . ." (52:282–83). The marriage between a Frenchman and an Englishwoman that he helps engineer at the play's close suggests a significant shift in attitude. By 1830, in fact, the most negative elements in the image of the dandy had become signs of superiority. This countervalorization of a set of negative signs must ultimately be ascribed to a new corpus, which brought together the two typologies that French writers had first classified as mutually exclusive: the Romantic hero and the dandy. The author of this corpus, of course, was Lord Byron, whom the French discovered only to claim, with Chateaubriand, that they alone could understand and revere him as he deserved. To the extent that the poet's favor in England was at an ebb at the moment of this discovery, Chateaubriand was right. Although he also sensed the difference between the "real" Byron and the mythic creation that Byron himself did much to fashion and promote, Chateaubriand recognized that the myth remained the only reality (126:I, 419). In French eyes, Byron became "Shakespeare's brother," the living model of the Romantic hero and uncontested leader of French Romanticism.[40] As a rewriting of antecedent texts, Byron's work contains traces of Rousseau's lyricism and

Voltaire's irony, Chateaubriand's ennui, Young's melancholy, and Goethe's philosophical anxiety (185). His hero unites a number of prototypal traits—the child of nature, the man of feeling, the gloomy egoist, the Gothic villain, the noble outlaw, and the rebel (498)—into a single image of which Byron was personally the most striking incarnation.

Whatever else Byronism may contain or imply, it is primarily an aristocratic system which exalts the self as it condemns established social, moral, and religious codes, humanity, and the universe at large. Because of his refusal to be content with what others consider absolutes, because of his mysterious, "satanic" crimes, the Byronic hero is doomed to lose or be denied sublime love, but his lack of fulfillment is a sign in and of itself of superiority. Whether a languid and decadent aristocrat (Harold), an aggressive chieftain (the Giaour, Conrad, Lara), or a metaphysical hero conversant with the spirits of the universe (Manfred), he affirms his difference and wards off contact with "breathing flesh" (*Manfred:*II.ii, 57), by a haughty exterior which, like "some mysterious circle thrown/Repell'd approach" (*Lara:*I.vii). Beneath the proud isolation and superior contempt of this riveting figure, however, there exists a suffering hypersensitivity that must be protected from public exposure. The mask that the hero dons, the outer covering over the precious inner core, would become for French writers the point of intersection between dandyism and Byronism, or more accurately, between two different visions of Byronism itself.[41]

"I had a tinge of dandyism in my minority," wrote Byron in 1825, "and probably retained enough of it to conciliate the great ones at five-and-twenty. I had gamed, and drank, and taken my degrees in most dissipations, and having no pedantry and not being overbearing, we ran quietly together. I knew them all more or less, and they made me a member of Watier's [the Dandy Club]" (101:I, 447). The French seized upon this revelation: "From his admirers' hands, the great poet . . . accepted initiation into the secrets of their Dandyism," wrote Chasles; "from them, he receives . . . baptism into that fatuousness which will leave its mark on his entire life" (123:3). Byron's allegiance to what Chasles saw as a secret, quasi-religious order was already manifest in *Beppo*, and especially in *Don Juan*, a work ignored by the French in 1820 but rediscovered in 1830 and acclaimed the greatest of Byron's poems.

At first glance, *Don Juan*'s positive impact on French dandyism is hard to reconcile with the narrator's presentation of an amiable, well-mannered hero or his expressed opposition to the dandy:

> Nothing affected, studied, or constructive
> Of coxcombry or conquest; no abuse
> Of his attractions marr'd the fair perspective,
> To indicate a Cupidon broke loose,
> And seem to say, "Resist us if you can"—
> Which makes a dandy while it spoils a man (XV, 12).

And yet, Don Juan's naturalness and sincerity are part of a strategy of self-representation—"Be hypocritical, be cautious, be not what you *seem*, but always what you *see*" (XI, 86)—a dictum realized through his protean capacity to become all things to all people. More than Don Juan's masks, however, it is the narrator's persona which incarnated to the French the spirit of dandyism. Toward any universal problem or principle, this narrator, inclined "more to laugh than scold" (*Beppo*:lxxix), displays the bemused skepticism, the casual cynicism of the urbane man—and his irony does not spare the values affirmed in the earlier works or even the seriousness of writing. That Byron "manages his pen with the careless and negligent ease of a man of quality," as Sir Walter Scott had noted (452:186), is fully confirmed by the tone of *Don Juan*:

> I don't know that there may be much ability
> Shown in this sort of desultory rhyme;
> But there's a conversational facility,
> Which may round off an hour upon a time.
> Of this I'm sure at least, there's no servility
> In mine irregularity of chime,
> Which rings what's uppermost of new or hoary,
> Just as I feel the *Improvvisatore* (XV, 20).

The rejection of the professional's servile bonds, the aristocratic contempt for artistic order—as narrative linearity disappears under the sheer weight of digressions in *Don Juan*—are underscored by the narrator's express desire to play the improvisor.

Echoing the stance of a Montaigne or a Voiture, this narrator is Byron's self-representation as a work of art.

Confronted with the task of amalgamating what they regarded as two Byronic models of aristocracy, French writers for the most part encoded the taxonomy of a Harold, Lara, Conrad, and Manfred as the dandy's hidden essence, while the apparent self was to exhibit the elegance, seductiveness, and nonchalance of the central character or the narrator of *Don Juan*. Within a single text, then, the dandy could be *X* and not-*X* at the same time—suffering and blasé, alienated and captivating, morose and witty, a rebel and a social arbiter. Alfred de Musset, who was baptized "Byron's brother," at times dissociated the two models, or at others, as in *Les Caprices de Marianne*, projected them simultaneously onto two different characters. The callous and debauched seducer of *Les Marrons du feu* and the determined pursuer of an unattainable ideal in *Namouna* are Musset's versions of the Don Juan figure, enriched by the forms of Byronic anguish. In yet another amalgam, the bohemian Jeunes-France of the 1830s championed the satanic and the debauched, and imitated to the letter the orgies described in *Childe Harold*, which they read as autobiographical: "We greatly admired the exploits of the young lord and his nocturnal bacchanalia in Newstead Abbey with his young friends covered in monk's robes," wrote Gautier, " . . . those banquets . . . seemed to us the supreme expression of dandyism because of the absolute indifference toward things that terrify the human race" (207:50).[42] Going beyond the "facts" of the legend, the Jeunes-France and their militantly republican cohorts, the *bouzingots*, banded together to display an aggressive iconoclasm in replication of the Byronic outlaws—a community of chosen outcasts at once aristocratic and primitive. Rejecting Don Juan's elegance, they continued to imitate what Gautier called "the complete physical picture of the young Byronian"—long dark hair with mustache or full beard, expansive forehead, striking pallor, melancholy eyes and lowered lashes (p. 97). For Gautier, the incarnation of this literary portrait was Pétrus Borel, who "could have posed for the Byronic hero" (p. 22).

Consciously anachronistic in their revolt against bourgeois life, the Jeunes-France clung to the early Byronic model after other dandies had discarded it. As Chateaubriand noted in 1839, the somber and suffering melancholy of the 1820s had been replaced by the insolent, conquering demeanor of the well-groomed dandy (126:II, 72). Reduced to clichés in the 1830s, the traits of the early Byronic hero became food for satire. Thus Balzac dismisses as an uncombed Byron a dandy who aspires to literary genius, and mocks Charles Grandet, who apes before his mirror a famous portrait of Byron (19:II, 87; III, 515). So familiar had the elements of the Byronic stance become, so extensive their imitation, that the Nancy provincials decode Lucien Leuwen's genuine melancholy as a dandyistic technique of self-promotion: "His horses, his tilbury, and his liveried servants made him the object of the young people's envy in Nancy and its environs. His dark melancholy when he was alone in the street, his distractedness, his impatient and seemingly hostile gestures, were considered fatuousness of the highest and most noble kind. The most enlightened saw it as a skillful imitation of Lord Byron, who was still much discussed at the time" (487:I, 953–54).[43] Stendhal and Balzac were suggesting what Barbey d'Aurevilly explicitly stated: by the late 1830s, Byron had become "horribly cliché" (34:80–81). Barbey, perhaps his last disciple, continued to fuse the early and the late Byron. In *Les Diaboliques* (1874), Mesnilgrand still combines the sartorial elegance of a Don Juan with the ennui, despair, frightening mien, and satanic passions of Lara and the Giaour; even silent and contained, "there [is] . . . something in him of the Byronic hero" (38:I, 266). But in retrospect, this phrase applies globally to the dandy in French literature. For Byron had added to the form of the Regency dandy a content and a context without which the rich development of French dandyism would never have taken place.

Coming in the wake of Byronism, a number of "fashionable" English novels, translated from 1825 to 1830, furthered the acceptance of dandyism as a model for self-assertion. Texts like Hook's *Merton*, Lister's *Granby*, or Ward's *Tremaine* proposed a more detailed and penetrating image of the Regency dandy than had either French satirists or Byron himself. The most influential by far, however, was Bulwer-Lytton's *Pelham or the Adventures of a Gentleman* (reprinted in France eight times between 1828 and 1840). Although it was hailed by French critics as the complete

manual of dandyism (400:551), its author's expressed aim was
rather to show "a man of sense . . . gradually grow wise by the
very foibles of his youth" (95:I, x). But the "unfashionable"
dénouement—Pelham's marriage for love, quiet life, and devotion
to profession—was ignored in favor of the hero's "foibles," that is,
his dandyism. This reading of the novel was tantamount to rewriting.

Pelham's dandyism, like the literary representation of *préciosité*, defines itself by an opposition to vulgarity in all forms,
which subsume traditional aristocratic pastimes as well. With a
characteristic *précieux* penchant for hyperbole and periphrasis, he
defines sportsmen as "a species of bipeds" foreign to the human
race (95:II, 33–34); marriage is a calamity, passionate love absurd,
and bourgeois morality thoroughly contemptible. Pelham praises
what the mob condemns: "Why stigmatize vanity as a vice," he
asks, "when it creates, or at least participates in so many virtues?
I wonder why the ancients did not erect the choicest of their
temples to its worship" (II, 127–28). In his code, the pleasure principle alone deserves devotion: "There is no content like that of the
epicure—no active code of morals so difficult to conquer as the
inertness of his indolence" (II, 105). French cuisine sends him into
fits of ecstasy: "Exquisite *foie gras*!—Have I forgotten thee? Do I
not, on the contrary, see thee—smell thee—and almost die with
rapture of thy possession?" (I, 138–39). This sexualization of the
oral and divinization of the trivial is the sign of passion for the
subtle and the delicate, which Pelham commends as supremely
philosophical: "Nothing is superficial to a deep observer! It is in
trifles that the mind betrays itself. . . . He who esteems trifles for
themselves, is a trifler—he who esteems them for the conclusions
to be drawn from them, or the advantage to which they can be put,
is a philosopher" (I, 280). The antithesis of the "barbarous"
Englishman, Pelham is an esthete, as his views on the "divine" art
of dress confirm. His sartorial theory is built on the maxim,
"Nature is not to be copied, but to be exalted by art" (I, 277). The
subtle, innovative refinements of his quiet black costume betoken
an artistic concern for the "gently pleasing," not the "sublimely
astonishing" (I, 274). His manners observe the same mysterious
esthetic of understatement: "While you are enchanted with the

effect, it should possess so little prominency and peculiarity, that you should never be able to guess the cause" (I, 40). Although he prefers the polite and unpretentious ease of what he terms "French manners," he discovers that a cold, aloof or insolent "English air" furthers notoriety and prestige. Depending on the milieu and his specific aims, he will alter his manner at will. A philosophy of self-control, rather than of pleasure, Pelham's dandyism predicates a "most daring resolution" in what is ultimately a quest for power: "Manage *yourself* well and you may manage all the world" (II, 39).

The power that Pelham achieves through the esthetic strategies of dandyism is modeled after the career of Beau Brummell, the paradigmatic dandy. Bulwer-Lytton's novel, in fact, contains in the person of Lord Russelton a fictional refraction of Brummell; along with Felton in Hook's *Merton*, Beaumont in Ward's *Tremaine*, and Trebeck in Lister's *Granby*, these characters served to enhance the myth that the Beau himself was the first to create and promulgate. The fascination of this myth lies in the meteoric rise, power, and fall of one who had neither extraordinary station, wealth, nor what we conventionally call talent. The son of a wealthy and powerful civil servant, Brummell exploited the vogue of the self-made man and described himself as the son of a "very superior valet," thus stressing the feat of his eminence as "the supreme dictator, laying down the law in dress, in manners," "the mighty genius . . . at whose nod the haughtiest nobles of Europe . . . quailed" (95:I, 480, 204). Byron, in a sentence, depicted the thrust of this fantastic career: "I . . . was in favor with Brummell (and that was alone enough to make a man of fashion at that time)" (337:261). Captain William Jesse, Brummell's first biographer, puts him on a par with Napoleon: between them they "divided the attention of the world" and they died in the same country, less than a year apart (274:I, 308). In this hyperbolic climate, Brummell's ascension to power, however much facilitated by the patronage of the Prince of Wales, was credited as his own remarkable achievement. The prince, often described as the butt of Brummell's wit, as the man-in-waiting at the Beau's sartorial rituals, served as foil to the dandy's enormous though fragile prestige. Their mysterious break was to be Brummell's undoing.

Pre-Texts and Prototypes

The notoriety that came from waging "open war against his royal enemy, assailing him with ridicule in all quarters" (I, 27), could not counterbalance the lost commercial credit that the regent's patronage had assured him. Bereft of this resource, Brummell had to flee the society that he had dominated for twenty years.

In Bulwer-Lytton's fictionalized account of Brummell's story, dandyism represented "the only course which could place him in a prominent light, and enable him to separate himself from the society of the herd of ordinary men whom he held in considerable contempt" (95:I, 135). This contempt covers all forms of vulgarity, including, as with Pelham, the conventional components of English nobiliary life. Thus Brummell (Lord Russelton) disdains equestrian sports because "he [can]not bear to have his tops and leathers splashed by the greasy galloping farmers" (I, 81). His disdain for the herd extended to sexuality as well: besieged by female admirers, he seems never to have had an affair. The mystery of his abstinence sparked many speculations that became part of the legend—that he had been spurned in his youth and was taking revenge on the entire female sex, that women distrusted and feared him, and more frequently, that he suffered from an excess of self-love. Lister's Trebeck, for example, can "keep up a silly *persiflage* with a thousand pretty nonentities . . .; but it is mere habit or mere idleness; they excite no interest, and they seem to know it" (347:36–37). With never an intimation of homosexuality, Trebeck's contemptuous indifference enhances his appeal to women and underscores his superiority to other men's vulgar desires.

Brummell's dandyism laid special stress on physical appearance. The illustration of his name, the Beau was reputed to be of Apollonian beauty. And for one whose origins could not explain it, his aristocratic air was all the more extraordinary. But it was principally his sartorial elegance that won him his celebrity and the title "Father of Modern Costume." "His chief aim was to avoid anything marked," writes William Jesse, "one of his aphorisms being that the severest mortification a gentleman could incur was to attract observation in the street by his outward appearance" (274:I, 55). Shunning all extravagance as a despicable attempt to attract the vulgar, Brummell was "visible" only to the eye of the connoisseur. The creation of his public self, a ritual that took at least two hours to achieve, centered on the perfection of his cravat: "It appears that if the cravat was not properly tied at the first effort or inspiring impulse, it was always rejected. His valet was coming downstairs one day with a quantity of tumbled neckclothes under his arm, and being interrogated on the subject, solemnly replied, 'Oh, they are our failures.' Practice like this of course made him perfect, and his tie soon became a model that was imitated but never equalled" (I, 56). This perfectionism marked every "mytheme," or element of the legend: his coiffure required three hairdressers, his gloves were made by two craftsmen—one for the thumb, the other for the fingers and hand (a number Bulwer-Lytton increased to three in *Pelham*)—his boots were polished in champagne, and his furniture and bibelots brought from the continent by a special courier. Known as "Prince of Gourmets," he was credited with legendary gastronomic exigencies. When asked about his distaste for vegetables, he reportedly replied: "I once ate a pea" (I, 109).

Brummell's superior manners ran the gamut from amiability to hostility. No one, according to Jesse, "possessed the art of pleasing to a greater degree," but neither did anyone surpass Brummell in the English art of "cutting" with an indefinable look that repelled familiarity or a raised eyebrow that quashed pretension (274:I, 109). His insolence was diversely interpreted as a defense, a "stepping stone to notoriety," or in Bulwer-Lytton's characterization of Russelton, sadistic revenge against a hostile nobility: "It was because *I trampled on them* that, like crushed herbs, they sent up a grateful incense in return. Oh! it was balm to my bitter and loathing temper, to see those who would have spurned *me* from them if they dared, writhe beneath my lash, as I withheld or inflicted it at will. I was the magician who held the great spirits that longed to tear me to pieces, by one simple spell which a superior hardihood had won me" (95:I, 214–15). Such hyperbolic bitterness and rage coexisted in the Brummellian legend with a plethora of delicate and elegant *bons mots*. More than his society verse, or even the treatise on *Male and Female Costume* that he apparently wrote (135:145–46), Brummell's witticisms were considered the verbal illustration of his dandyism. As Hazlitt observed, Brummell's sayings were predicated on devaluating the important through "utmost nonchalance and indifference" on the one hand, and on the other, on "exaggerating the merest trifles into matters of importance." Hovering "on the very brink of vacancy," they are paradoxically, for Hazlitt, proof of Brummell's genius: "He has touched the *ne plus ultra* that divides the dandy from the dunce. But what a fine eye to discriminate: what a sure hand to hit this last and thinnest of intellectual partitions! . . . it is truly the art of making something out of nothing" (253:152–53). Beyond Brummellian wit, Hazlitt had aptly described the dandy himself: an artifact created *ex nihilo*.

"He crossed the Channel with a caustic line from Lord Byron's Don Juan," Arnould Frémy wrote in "Le Roi de la mode" (1836), the first French article devoted to Brummell (198:256).[44] Although the man had been living modestly in Calais since 1816, French writers showed no interest in the legendary Brummell before 1830, when Byron valorized in their eyes the dandyistic posture. Even then, no writer of any nationality articulated the spiritual implications of the Beau's achievement until Barbey d'Aurevilly's *Du Dandysme et de George Brummell* (1845). Neither a biography of the man nor a history of the phenomenon, Barbey's analysis seeks in Brummell the key to the concept of dandyism: "He was dandyism itself" (38:IX, 228). Bent on discrediting the charge of superficiality, Barbey argues that Brummell was an intellectual "even in the kind of beauty he possessed," who managed to dominate an entire society by his evanescent airs (p. 257). His clothes and manners, like his temperament and wit, were means toward profoundly artistic ends: "He was a great artist in his way; but his art was not special, not limited to a particular time. It was his life itself. . . . He enthralled with his person, as others do with their works" (p. 254).[45] The last step in a development begun by Byron and amplified by Bulwer-Lytton and the Brummellian legend, Barbey defined the dandy as both artist and work of art, a synthesis of intellectuality and aristocracy. A pivotal point in the trajectory of French dandyism, Barbey's work became the model for Baudelaire and Huysmans. Reading/rewriting that text, Baudelaire disregarded the emphasis on a peculiarly English phenomenon and defined dandyism as a symbol of modernity and a sublime quest for moral and artistic perfection. Where affectation seemed to Barbey the only appropriate response to the dandy's social context, Baudelaire declared artificiality to be essential to art and Huysmans, in *A rebours*, proclaimed it the ultimate value.

The contrast between Huysmans' apotheosis of artificiality and Jouy's satire of affectation dramatizes the distance that the dandy in France traversed from the 1820s to the 1880s. If the change from a negative to a positive valuation confirms the dandy's integration in France, the redundant seme of artificiality reaffirms the consistency of the system. That artificiality was the specific element that distinguished the *précieux* from the honnête points to a notable disjunction between honnêteté and dandyism. And yet, the pre-texts and the prototypes of these two systems reveal a more fundamental comparable pattern. Thus, in classical texts on the one hand, and Shakespearean texts on the other, seventeenth- and nineteenth-century France saw substantive models to be emulated. What these models lacked in aristocratic worldliness was appropriated from a later era—Renaissance Italy and Regency England—in which French writers found a nonindustrious, conspicuously leisured type, preoccupied with the art of appearance and manners, dedicated to displaying and receiving recognition of superiority. This model, which had predominantly esthetic connotations in the formulations of Castiglione and Bulwer-Lytton, was reduced to a strategy of social *arrivisme* in the texts of Faret and Jouy, the first indigenous rewriting of the honnête homme and the dandy, respectively. The eventual enrichment and valorization of that model as a philosophy of life for the superior man—artist and aristocrat—can be ascribed to Montaigne and Byron. The emphasis which seventeenth- and nineteenth-century writers placed on the honnêteté and dandyism of Montaigne's and Byron's texts served to (con)fuse the typologies of the aristocrat, the intellectual, and the artist. That the esthetic was the linking value among these three typologies may explain why the extreme expressions of honnêteté and dandyism were *préciosité* on the one hand and decadence on the other. These extremes, however, also confirm that honnêteté or dandyism as a system was more than a sum of its antecedent, pre-textual parts; it was a higher synthesis which seventeenth- and nineteenth-century French texts alone inscribed.

The Semantic Field of Honnêteté and Dandyism

Exogenous in origin, the Greek philosopher, the Roman *honestus*, and the Renaissance courtier or Humanist for the earlier century, and the Shakespearean Englishman, the Byronic hero, or the Regency dandy for the later, have what could be called an essential etymological function. They do not reveal the endogenous linguistic dynamics by which *honnête homme* and *dandy* became the signifiers of the system of the artist-aristocrat in seventeenth- and nineteenth-century France. For in addition to antecedent types, there were numerous coincident ones which bore basic similarities to the honnête homme and the dandy, and could, therefore, be used to define them. These types and the terms that serve as their signifiers do not properly constitute a paradigm for honnête homme or dandy, because they cannot be scaled according to any fixed set of traits. Rather, they form a semantic field, a constellation of signs that revolve around the central concepts of honnêteté and dandyism, with *honnête homme* and *dandy* as their key terms.[46]

That *honnête homme* and *dandy* can be proposed as the key terms of two semantic fields is a function of our temporal vantage point. We can regard the literature of a past period as closed text and determine which are the dominant terms by such criteria as quantitative repetition and qualitative richness. Of course, we cannot explain why *honnête homme* and *dandy* prevailed over other terms. To argue that they contained certain nuances lacking in others is, at best, simplistic: other signifiers could have been given, and were often given similar semantic components. And aside from *why*, it is *how* a group puts a term into circulation, and how a society receives it—in other words, how speech (*parole*) specifically makes language evolve—that remains mysterious. This complex process of exchange from sender to receiver, and receiver back to sender, with its attendant incomplete or distorted communication, even its short circuits, lies outside the parameters of this study. My specific subject of concern is the seventeenth- and nineteenth-century effort to delimitate the semantic field of honnêteté and dandyism, to articulate the semantic components of the constituent terms in relation to one another. This conscious metalinguistic undertaking revealed the inadequacies of language as a precise tool, and confirmed the need for speech, for individual formulations. However, this effort not only reflected but also increased the instability of the semantic field—especially the key terms *honnête homme* and *dandy*.[47] An examination of the ways in which the signified of each signifier in the field was enriched or impoverished and the signs waxed or waned in their relationship to the key terms illuminates the evolution of the honnête homme and the dandy themselves.

Although the semantic field of honnêteté is smaller than that of dandyism, the term *honnête homme* in its period was not any easier to define. In a letter to Bussy-Rabutin, Corbinelli formulates a frustrating problem in semantics: "When someone is called an *honnête homme*, it irritates me that one person should understand one thing by this term, and another person another. I want people to have a clear idea of what they call *le galant homme*, *l'homme de bien*, *l'homme d'honneur*, *l'honnête homme*. Don't waste your time basing definitions on usage, because that way, most of these terms become synonymous . . . my definitions . . . may be good or they may be bad; but finally, I am determined to have definite ideas" (100:I, 338–39).[48] Corbinelli's irritation at the freedom of speech, his annoyance at language's lack of clarity and stasis, underlie his need to formulate his own definitions. The situation is more complex, however, than Corbinelli intimates. In addition to the four terms that he includes in the semantic field of honnêteté, one also has to contend with *l'homme habile*, *l'homme de qualité*, *le bel esprit*, and *le courtisan*. By and large, the terms in this field are formed on the model *homme*, preceded or followed by adjective (*habile*, *galant*) or followed by adjective phrase (*de* + noun [*qualité*/*honneur*/*bien*]). This basic structure was taken from the Latin either as a literal translation (i.e., *vir bonus*) or as an analytical version of an earlier synthetic form (i.e., *honestus*); even *bel esprit* reveals traces of it, since the mind (*esprit*) stands as a metonymy for man (*homme*). And since analogy is the basis for all lexical enrichment, it is perhaps not mere accident that *le courtisan*, which did not conform to this structure, had one of the briefest conjunctions with *honnête homme*.

The title of Faret's *L'Honnête homme ou l'art de plaire à la cour* dates the inclusion of *le courtisan* in the semantic field of honnête homme as 1630 at the latest. Earlier texts on the *courtisan*—Nervèze's *Le Guide des courtisans* (1606) and *Le Courtisan français* (1616), de Refuge's *Traité de la cour ou instruction des courtisans* (1616)—do not even use the term *honnête homme*. And yet, Faret's equation of honnêteté with success at court was not long lived. The advent of a more exclusive salon society posed new goals for the aristocrat, and in the process, *courtisan* was devalued as materialistic, grasping, self-seeking. For Méré, *les courtisans* are "irritating negotiators rather than people of good company," whereas *les honnêtes hommes* "who are neither miserly nor ambitious . . . have no goal other than to spread joy everywhere" (340:II, 122, 70). Although Molière might well extol *l'honnête homme de cour* and even *le courtisan* in his *Critique de l'Ecole des femmes*, that type could not survive the explicit charge of turpitude leveled in the moralist tradition that culminates with La Bruyère,[49] or of bourgeois occupationalism that is repeatedly made in the *mondains'* texts.

The strong antiprofessional bias inherent in honnêteté also explains why *le bel esprit* ceased to be used as a positive term after 1630. Promoted at first by the salons to describe a quick and scintillating mind adept at conversation and poetic improvisation, the term became synonymous with "pedant" (296:573–75) and was in disfavor by mid-century. Bouhours's essay on *Le Bel esprit* (1671), which (re)valorizes the concept by distinguishing the creative mind from the imitative and the professional, seems to have had little effect (79:148–93). Similarly, in his posthumous *Réflexions diverses*, La Rochefoucauld fashioned an entirely favorable definition of the term: "A *bel esprit* always thinks nobly; he brings forth ideas that are clear, attractive and natural; he presents them in their best light, and he embellishes them with all the appropriate adornments; he embraces the tastes of others and banishes from his thoughts what is useless or might offend"

(294:527). This emphasis on ease and sociability, coupled with an intuitive capacity to make artifice more natural, delineate an amalgam of artistry and aristocracy which is synonymous with honnêteté itself. By La Rochefoucauld's own admission, however, the pejorative overtones of *bel esprit* were too widely accepted to be ignored: "Since the epithet has been applied to an infinite number of bad poets and boring authors, it is more often used to ridicule people than to praise them" (p. 529).[50] By that token, however, the downward trajectory of the term may also indicate his society's continued resistance to the upward mobility of the artist/intellectual.

Rather than ennoble the bourgeois intellectual, the seventeenth century was bent on intellectualizing or civilizing the noble. Continuing the trend away from Faret, Jacques de Caillières's *Fortune des gens de qualité* (1661) uses *homme de qualité*, as well as *gentilhomme*, interchangeably with *honnête homme* (106:312–13), while relegating the art of the courtier to the domain of strategic goals: "I don't claim here to fashion an honnête homme, I presume that he is one already," declares the author, "and that he only needs guidance to arrive at his goal" (p. 24). The cleavage between "inner" qualities and their successful social application also appears in Chalesme's *L'Homme de qualité* (1671). And yet, since *homme de qualité* was so clearly an index of caste, abstract nouns were often added to justify the identification with *honnête homme*. Thus Molière's Alceste commends a "man of quality, merit, and courage" (*Misanthrope* IV.i, 147); and in a chapter entitled, "De la nécessité de fréquenter d'honnêtes gens," Marmet speaks of "persons of quality, merit, and virtue" (329:234). This phrasing confirms that rank did not suffice for inclusion among the *honnêtes gens*. Méré spelled out the indispensable distinction between quality as birth or rank and the inner quality designated by honnêteté: "We can certainly say that a man is of high quality or of high birth; usage allows it. But within the word *quality*, to lump together the advantages of royal birth with those that come from being physically attractive, valiant, or honnête is something that a person who knows what he is talking about certainly avoids" (340:I, 99).[51]

Pre-Texts and Prototypes

Méré's concept of merit had little to do with orthodox notions of moral virtue. But insofar as honor has traditionally been the touchstone of the aristocratic code, the dictionaries of Furetière, Richelet, and the Académie Française cite *homme d'honneur* (*homme de probité*) as a synonym of *honnête homme*. Accordingly, Scudéry described Conrart as an honnête homme "worthy of being held up as a model when defining the true *homme d'honneur*," and spoke of his justice, constancy, loyalty, and magnanimity (141:II, 107). But most writers who treated the two terms synonymously limited the moral connotations of honor to frankness and sincerity. "You need only show yourself as you are to be recognized as a superior honnête homme," wrote Choisy to Huet; "you are frank and sincere; you have the frankness of a true *homme d'honneur* who has nothing in his heart that he feels the need to hide" (357:521). More often, however, the *mondains* contrasted the flexibility and delicacy of the honnête homme to the ponderous rigidity of the *homme d'honneur*. "Most of these *gens d'honneur*," observes Saint-Evremond, echoing Montaigne, "have a certain rigidity which makes their strict conformity to the code even less appealing than the insinuations of a scoundrel. I find in these 'honorable' men . . . an irritating soberness or a deadly dullness" (438:III, 262).[52]

As with *l'homme d'honneur*, the semantic development of *l'homme de bien* signaled the break with traditional moral codes. In 1630, Faret, following the *Cortegiano*, had expressly equated the two terms (188:39).[53] By 1650, however, Bussy-Rabutin eliminated *homme de bien* from the semantic field of honnêteté because of the term's marked religious connotations (100:I, 342). And by the century's end, it was principally religious writers who tried to reconcile the two concepts. But even these efforts were questioned by those, like Bourdaloue, who insisted on the incompatibility between Christian and mundane values: "There are two moralities which formally contradict each other, that of Jesus Christ and that of the world. If we examine the maxims of both we will find none that are not in absolute opposition" (323:627). In the same period, La Bruyère pointedly chose *l'homme de bien* to express his moral ideal (286:360, #55), whereas Méré, ignoring the religious connotations of that term, praised *l'honnête homme* as the subtler and more demanding notion: "One could be a true *homme de bien* and a truly *malhonnête homme*. You need only be just to be an *homme de bien*, but to be an honnête homme you must be versed in all sorts of proprieties and be able to put them into practice. It also seems to me that one could be the most honnête of all men without being the most just" (339:429).[54]

In the semantic field of honnêteté, terms with moral connotations, like the *homme de bien* and the *homme d'honneur*, evince marked shifts of meaning and value less often than those with predominantly social implications, like the *habile homme*. Whereas Montaigne had used *habile homme* interchangeably with *honnête homme*, by the mid-seventeenth century, when it took on the modern meaning of adroit, *habile* assumed negative connotations. Saint-Evremond, for example, identified the *habile homme* with the practical, shrewd bourgeois mentality, as opposed to the sensitivity the honnête homme displayed in his leisurely pastimes: "We see fewer *honnêtes* than *habiles gens*: more good sense in commerce than delicacy in conversation" (439:III, 27). In La Bruyère's ironic view, however, *habile homme* and *honnête homme* were becoming synonymous, a sign of the moral decadence of *les grands*: "The distance between the *honnête homme* and the *habile homme* is becoming less pronounced each day, and is on the verge of disappearing. The *habile homme* is one who hides his passions, knows his own interests and sacrifices many things to them, and who has managed to acquire wealth or to preserve it. The *honnête homme* is one who does not commit highway robbery, does not kill anyone, whose vices, in short, are not scandalous" (286:360, #55). Pejorative shades vanish, however, when the adjective *habile* follows the noun: "It is the fool's part to be a nuisance; an *homme habile* can sense whether his presence is fitting or annoying" (p. 148, #2). While the synonymity to "adroit" is sustained, La Bruyère's *homme habile* has the sensitivity that Saint-Evremond had attributed to the honnête homme alone. This valorized notion came full circle back to Montaigne when Méré used *habile homme* (and not *homme habile*) interchangeably with *honnête homme*: "Gambling produces good results when you conduct yourself as an *habile homme*," he writes; by the same token, "if you always gamble like an honnête homme, you sometimes gain more by losing than you actually lose" (340:III, 164, 166). More important, Méré imbues *habile homme* with the philosophical substance of honnêteté, in contradistinction to what he recognizes as its more limited acceptation: "To judge from the way people view what we call an *habile homme*, you would think that this quality only involves gaining a position of power; but it consists much more in finding happiness in life" (III, 141). With Montaigne, Méré reaffirms for *l'habile homme*, as he does for *l'honnête homme*, a philosophy of happiness and self-sufficiency: "[To be *habile*] is to make good use of things in our control in order to live more happily" (II, 84).[55]

A similar ambivalence is found in the terms *galant homme*/ *homme galant*. In Monet's dictionary (1636), the adjective signifies both the admirable, the socially appealing (which is equated to *honnête*) and their antithesis: "1. seemly in whatever he does; remarkable, distinguished, outstanding; 2. honnête, of good humor and good manners; 3. rogue, wicked, worthless, good-for-nothing; 4. arrogant; haughty, domineering" (349:s.v.). While none of these meanings disappeared before the end of the century, as the dictionaries of Richelet and Furetière attest, others accrued which delineated the notion of a ladies' man. *Galant* suggested an elegant, well-dressed man, and particularly in the salons, *un amant*. The ambiguous sociosexual components of *galant*, however, led to numerous attempts to clarify the signified by creating a number of signifiers. Motteville, for example, distinguished *la galanterie*, a negative term that implied promiscuous sexual relations, and *le galant*, a negative type known for his lack of civility toward women, from *l'esprit galant* or *l'esprit de galanterie*, an ideal social stance indistinguishable from honnêteté: "I would like men to show the deference toward women that *honnêtes gens* must show, and in their company, to act always in a spirit of honnêteté and *galanterie*" (308:33-34, 50-52). If, for Motteville, the positive or the negative value of the sign depended on the presence or absence of that valorized term, *esprit*, for others meaning hinged on a grammatical rule. The position of the adjective determined two different but equally positive meanings, according to one observer: "The expression 'he's an *homme galant*' means that he is gracious and that he tries to appeal to women by a manner both deferent and honnête. The expression 'he's a *galant homme*' means that he behaves nobly and handles all sorts of situations with ease" (488:208–11). The latter may recall *l'homme habile* and the former *un amant*, but they are both aspects of honnêteté. Indeed, Vaugelas confirmed by his analysis that *galant* (as opposed to *galand*) was as polysemic as *honnête*: "Others said that . . . it was, in a word, a synthesis of *le je ne sais quoi* or a gracious manner, a courtly air, intelligence, good judgment, politeness, urbanity, and joyfulness—and all this without constraint, affectation, or defect of any kind. Here, you have all the makings of an honnête homme in the style of the court. This view was accepted as closest to the truth, and yet it was felt that this definition was still incomplete and that there was something more in the meaning of the word that could not be expressed" (510:477). Notwithstanding the frustrating elusiveness of the notion and the incapacity of language to express it, Vaugelas's analysis was hailed by the Académie Française in its *Observations . . . sur les remarques de M. de Vaugelas* (1704). And in the Academy's own dictionary, *honnête homme* stands as one of the definitions of *galant homme*. Even the perfectionistic Méré could not fundamentally disagree, although he made a slight distinction between the two styles of sociability: "a *galant homme* is simply an honnête homme who is more scintillating or lively than his usual self" (340:I, 20); thus "the difference between them is so slight that there is a considerable margin for error" (III, 139–40).[56]

Méré's remarks on *galant* could apply to the semantic field of honnêteté as a whole: because the differences were minute, the terms tended to be fused and confused. And yet, if Méré's own views are an accurate index, we can discern a development in the concept of the honnête homme during the fifty-five-year period under consideration: *le courtisan*, *l'homme de qualité*, and *l'homme de bien* were devalued and disjoined from *l'honnête homme*, whereas *l'homme habile* and *l'homme galant* were conjoined to the key term.[57] These semantic developments point to the discarding of traditional notions of aristocratic merit—rank, fortune, or virtue—in favor of an ideal of worldliness and sociability. And it is this ideal which underlies Bussy-Rabutin's pithy and symptomatic definition of *l'honnête homme* as "a man of refinement who knows how to live" (100:I, 342). Seventeenth-century dictionaries, although conservative and reductionist like all dictionaries, are unanimous in attesting the growing importance of the *mondain* definition. Furetière (1690) and the Académie Française (1694) list the moral definition of *honnête* as primary ("consonant with honor and virtue") but give the *mondain* ideal considerable weight: "*Honnête homme* . . . also includes all the appealing qualities that a man can have in society. . . . Sometimes, too, one calls *honnête homme* a man whom one considers only for his appealing qualities and worldly manners. In this sense, *honnête homme* means nothing more than *galant homme*, a man of good conversation and of good company" (162:s.v.). As early as 1680, however, Richelet's dictionary had stressed the sociability of the honnête homme, ignored the element of virtue, and played down the notion of honor: "honnête (courteous, urbane), who has honnêteté, civility, and honor (the honnête homme is the man who prides himself on nothing)" (426:s.v.).[58] However summary, Richelet's definition bespeaks a generalized acceptance of the *mondain* ideal of honnêteté.

Where the definitions of honnêteté left off is where discussion of dandyism must begin. For on the level of the signified, its terms do not refer to those notions of rank, fortune, or virtue which ostensibly were discarded from the ideal of honnêteté. As a result, the semantic field of dandyism seems to include fewer variables, but they appear in a more striking array of signifiers. Although the explanation for this may be partly sociological, since a heterogeneous society puts more terms into circulation than a homogeneous one (334:44), such a view overlooks the nineteenth-century passion for enlarging the dimensions of "literary language." It also overlooks the fact that French dandyism, a synthesis of Byronic Romanticism, English and indigenous aristocraticism, filled its semantic field with terms appropriated in the process of emulating and rewriting earlier texts. Not only were English terms introduced into French and new meanings given to the signified of existing French signifiers, but in a final stage, new indigenous terms proliferated that signaled the establishment of the French dandy as a type.

A look at some indigenous seventeenth-century terms that were appropriated into the semantic field of dandyism dramatizes its conceptual differences from honnêteté. If the true honnête homme is, as La Rochefoucauld and others after him insisted, "the man who prides himself on nothing" (294:349, #203), his opposite is *le fat*, the pretentious, arrogant fool. Other kinds of *fats* were the author "who prides himself on being *bel esprit*" (286:349, #20), the social butterfly who draws attention to himself by his servants, clothes, and carriages (286:98–99, #27), and the nobleman who flaunts "the false luster of his noble birth" (72:30, v.22). By a process of countervalorization, in the nineteenth century *le fat* came to incarnate an ideal of sociability with explicit connotations of power and eminence. "There are, strictly speaking, no more *fats*," wrote Raisson in 1829, "those transcendent *fats* who sparkled in society, dictated the laws of finery and fashion, conquered women, dominated men and whose manners the young hastened to copy and whose style they imitated" (415:191). Raisson regards the dandy, by comparison, as a degenerate form of the species; most commentators, however, saw no break between them. Julien Sorel, for example, must learn the ways of "higher fatuousness" in London before he can be called a dandy (487:I, 484). But Lucien Leuwen's *fatuité*, displayed to exact respect from a hostile provincial society, also implies that he is an insensitive seducer of women, a Don Juan. It is this component, absent from earlier usage, that frightens Mme de Chasteller, Lucien's love, as she wonders whether the label *fat* does in fact fit the man. In general, however, "fatuous" Don Juanism has positive connotations in the dandy's eyes. *La fatuité*, argues Balzac's Henri de Marsay, "[is] the sign of an incontestable power wielded over the female populace. A man loved by several women is credited with having superior qualities" (19:V, 287). This superiority was often expressed as scorn: "Intrigued by the contempt of *le fat*, stimulated by his affected claim that it was impossible to draw him out of his utter stagnation, and spurred by the aura of a blasé sultan, women pursued him even more eagerly than at first" (19:IV, 532). Negative behavior which seeks a positive response (e.g., intrigued, stimulated, spurred, pursued) lies at the heart of the dandy's strategy. The hero dandies of Barbey d'Aurevilly's *La Bague d'Annibal* (1840), *Un Amour impossible* (1841), and *Les Diaboliques* (1874) are all called *des fats*. His treatise, *Du Dandysme et de George Brummell*, bears the inscription, "Of a *fat*, by a *fat*, for the *fats*" (38:IX, 216).[59]

Semantically enriched and positively defined, *le fat* is the most important of the older French terms to be appropriated by dandyism. In addition, there was *le petit maître*, originally used of the Frondeurs in the 1640s, and later as a synonym for *courtisan* (286:205, #7). In the eighteenth century, Diderot, like Marivaux in *Le Petit Maître corrigé* (1734), saw the type as "drunk with self-love," "affected," "pretentiously dressed" (165:XVI, 271). By 1821, Jouy could define the dandy simply as "[a] name given to excessively fatuous *petits maîtres*" (276:I, 338). Similar equations occur in the case of three other eighteenth-century types: *le muscadin*, *le merveilleux*, and *l'incroyable*. These peculiar substantives (*l'incroyable* reportedly used the adjective obsessively; *le muscadin* favored musk lozenges) referred to notable sartorial and political eccentrics. The converse of *le petit maître*, they espoused royalism in a democratic era; Lucien Leuwen, for example, is labeled *muscadin* for his presumably anachronistic, aristocratic attitudes (487:I, 780). In its extended sense, the *muscadin* denoted "[a] more or less authentic dandy" (154:s.v.), the *merveilleux* signalized the Parisian dandy of the 1830s (363:I, 234), and the *incroyables* were equated with "dandies, lions, the fashionable" (295:s.v.). Of all eighteenth-century terms, however, it was *le roué* (literally one who deserves the rack) which enjoyed the widest circulation. First associated with debauchery in the circle of the Duc d'Orléans, the *roué* designated "a man of the world who has neither virtues nor principles, but who gives his vices a seductive facade and who ennobles them only by dint of grace and wit" (388:VI, 34).[60] Thus the dandies of *La Comédie humaine* compose, in Balzac's view, "the world of the Parisian rakes" (19:IV, 377). Both Musset in *Namouna* and Baudelaire in his *Notes sur Les Liaisons dangereuses* saw the archetypal *roués*, Lovelace and Valmont, as the dandy incarnate.

Where the *roué* and the *fat* were countervalorized, positive prerevolutionary terms often were given negative connotations in the corpus of dandyism. *L'homme du monde* is a case in point.

Ronteix grants the type all the social graces, but dismisses him as a parrot (432:20); Paul de Musset characterizes him as a calculator beneath his sociability (391:407–9); and Ancelot's *L'Homme du monde* (1827), outwardly an elegant style setter and a gifted diplomat is, like the *roué*, inwardly an amoral seducer. And yet, there was no more unanimity of opinion regarding nineteenth-century terms than there had been for seventeenth-century ones. Baudelaire, for example, embraced the *homme du monde* as "a spiritual citizen of the universe"—a literalization of the term that harks back to Montaigne (51:II, 689). Semantic contradictions are equally apparent in the relation of *dandy* with the *homme élégant* and the *homme comme il faut*, two prerevolutionary signifiers modeled on *honnête homme*. Thus, because of Balzac's expressed dislike of affectation and rudeness, the dandy is chastized in *Traité de la vie élégante*, and the *homme élégant* is valorized with Brummell as his prototype. But in his *Théorie de l'élégance* (1844), retitled *Manuel de l'homme et de la femme comme il faut* in 1862, Chapus refused to accord Brummell the title *homme comme il faut* or its synonym, *élégant*: "He dressed well . . . but he had many pretensions, which are never compatible with an elegant appearance" (122:107–8).[61] From the 1820s to the 1880s, however, most writers on dandyism, from Jouy to Barbey (277:I, 338; 38:I, 336), equated *élégant* and *dandy*.

With the exception of *le fat*, the native French terms in the semantic field of dandyism pale in importance alongside the lexicon from across the channel. Some of the English terms, like the French, evoked mid-seventeenth-century types, notably the Restoration beau, immortalized in Farquhar's *The Beaux' Stratagem* (1707). As the term suggests, *les beaux* had a French manner about them, and differed from the contemporaneous *petits maîtres* only by their "more urbane and splendid appearance" (397:286). This appealing exterior led Barbey to insist that *les beaux* were more French than English: "As we see, then, the very name they bore points to the French influence. Their grace was like their name. It wasn't indigenous enough, nor tinged enough with the uniqueness of the English people, with that inner power that it would one day contain" (38:IX, 238). Although he regarded the death of Richard ("Beau") Nash in 1764 as the end of one era and Brummell's advent in 1794 as the beginning of dandyism, Barbey used *beau* and *dandy* interchangeably with reference both to Brummell and to his own fictional heroes. "Under the term 'beau' . . . do not include anything frivolous, slight, or narrow," says the narrator of *Le Rideau cramoisi*, " . . . because you would not have the right idea of my Vicomte de Brassard, in whom intelligence, manners, physiognomy, everything was expansive, substantial, opulent, full of patrician stateliness, as befit the most magnificent dandy I have known, I who have seen Brummel [*sic*] go mad and d'Orsay die" (38:I, 17).[62] Like the Vicomte de Brassard, Balzac's Baron Hulot was a well known member of "the batallion of the Empire *beaux*" (19:III, 155). In the corpus of dandyism, *le beau* is identified with the brilliant officers of the Empire and often denotes an older dandy.

The *beau* and other "despots of elegance" (e.g., the *buck* and the *macaroni*) who preceded the dandy in England play a minimal role in France when compared to *le fashionable* and *le lion*.[63] Imported (c. 1817) and used concurrently with the term *dandy*, *le fashionable* was first associated with sartorial obsessions; but with the publication of Ronteix's *Manuel du fashionable* (1829), it was made to include "every action at every time of life: it is the art of dressing, eating, walking, speaking, loving, sleeping. . . . In a word, it is the art of living" (432:10–11). Nonetheless, in Ronteix's argument, the artistic and elegant French *fashionable* is the antithesis of the fatuous, stupid English dandy: "An enormous cravat, an inane air, an immense monocle stupidly aimed at some bloated face, and you have a dandy, god damn!" (pp. 18–19). In the same vein, Balzac ranks *le fashionable* with *l'élégant*, his own preferred term, far above the mere dandy, "a piece of boudoir furniture, an extremely ingenious mannequin . . . but a thinking creature . . . never!" (22:97). A comparison between the 1835 and the 1830 versions of the same text, however, reveals that Balzac substituted *dandy* for *fashionable*, and gave the term the connotations of power that Maxime de Trailles deserves (408:122). Mortemart-Boisse sustained the conjunction of the two terms, even though his was a wholly negative description: "*Le fashionable*, note it well, is not a courteous man; he represents the triumph of the bizarre and the singular over the natural. The thoroughbred English *fashion-*

able must have a facile contempt for people and things. . . . He must never feel emotion, smile affectionately, be happy or unhappy . . . [his reserve] toward everyone must be taciturn, haughty, insolent" (364:66–67). This archetypical Englishness, however, accounts for the consistent equation of the *fashionable* and the dandy in the works of Gautier and Barbey.[64]

The 1840s witnessed the decline of *le fashionable* and, with a proliferation of articles, novels, plays, and treatises, the ascendancy of *le lion*.[65] The etymology of this term prompted debate. It was traced alternately both to *lionne*, Voiture's name for a celebrated redhead, and to the lions which drew spectators to the Tower of London in the seventeenth century. Some grouped *lion* with the *incroyable*, *merveilleux*, and *beau* (19:I, 755; 51:II, 712), and considered Richelieu an exemplar of the type (158:11). Others stressed the term's exotic resonances: "M. de Cernay," wrote Sue in *Arthur*, "was very curious about all kinds of *lions* and as soon as an Arab, a Persian, an Indian, a foreigner of any distinction arrived in Paris, M. de Cernay had him introduced to him. Was it in order to attract even greater attention with these conspicuous and strange acolytes?" (489:I, 177–78). *Lion* also generated analogies to the king of beasts that served to underscore the dandy's aura. "Women love prodigiously those who proclaim themselves pashas, who seem to be accompanied by lions and executioners, and walk in an array of terror," declared Balzac. "There is in these men an assurance in their actions, a certainty in their power, an arrogance in their look, a leonine consciousness, which exemplifies for women the kind of strength they all dream about" (19:V, 299–300). These connotations of terrifying power were extended by metaphorical allusions to jaguars and tigers in the representation of the dandy. In other contexts, however, the meaning of *lion* did not go beyond "celebrity" (e.g., *un lion politique, un lion littéraire*). Lucien de Rubempré, for example, refers to Marsay, Vandenesse, and Manerville, "the dandies who had previously mystified him," as "the *lions* of this age" (19:IV, 786). Barbey saw here a distinction of degree rather than kind. In 1840, he called *les lions* "the princes of dandyism": "they are the elite of the elite, the cream of the elegant and fashionable world" (36:1).[66]

After the vogue of the *lion* and the *fashionable*, no single term enjoyed wide currency. *Gentleman* did not undergo the semantic enrichment of other English terms, perhaps because the term primarily suggested "incomparable correctness of speech and manners" (154:s.v.). By that token, *gentleman* was often opposed to *dandy*. The insolence of M. de Marigny "was not gentleman-like," wrote Barbey, "[it] smacked of the feather-brained dandies" (38:V, 94). The gentleman also disdained all forms of exhibitionism: if the predilection for sartorial eccentricity is not checked, Barbey argued, "*le gentleman* will no longer exist" (37:[9/1/1856]5). Conservatism of this type reflects the view of Vigny, who used *gentleman* as analogue for his own stoical ideal, one which bore considerable likeness to the honnête homme: "[it is] *l'homme d'honneur* himself who is held by convention to a standard of good conduct and propriety which even religion could not attain; for there are a good many things that a priest would do which a *galant homme* could never do" (515:II, 1011). Sue's definition, written at about the same time, is no less reminiscent of the honnête homme: "This English word *gentleman* does not mean *gentilhomme* in the aristocratic sense, but a perfectly well-bred man of very good company, no matter what his origins" (489:I, 88–89). Because of its association with English aristocraticism, however, the term generated such variants as *gentlemen riders* or *sporting gentlemen*, which also served to describe the dandy (53:252; 364:70). In Baudelaire's description of Delacroix's dandyism, the imperturbable English gentleman plays an important role (51:II, 757). And for Gautier, Baudelaire himself "belonged to that sober dandyism which rubs its clothes with sandpaper to take away their Sunday-best and brand-new look so dear to the philistines and so undesirable for the true gentleman" (212:2). Writing in this tradition, Hippolyte Taine in 1864 simply equated the two terms: "We have gentlemen, dandies, lords who preach the gospel of savoir-vivre" (495:173).[67]

The ambiguous semantic relationship between *gentleman* and *dandy*—term A = term B, and term $A \neq$ term B—reflects a pattern that characterizes the entire semantic field of dandyism. But whereas the *gentleman* exemplified socially acceptable norms, and the term remained semantically stable, the dandy whose behavior was purposefully problematical never ceased to generate pejorative neologisms. "There is an abyss between the *lion* and the *gandin*," wrote Barbey, "but what about the abyss between the *gandin* and the *petit crevé*! at least dandyism, with its haughty stiffness, had a certain grandeur" (38:I, 23). Rather than a degeneration, however, the neologisms suggest, on both the level of the signifier and the signified, a return to the prerevolutionary *muscadin* and *incroyable*. Thus *le gandin* (a young sheep) denoted a vain, bored, impertinent, and eccentrically dressed type of the 1850s, as did his successor in the 1860s, *le petit crevé* (whose name evoked the slashed sleeves in fashion during the seventeenth century). In the 1870s, *le gommeux* and *le poisseux*, appellations derived from resinous or slimy substances, were but two more signs for "a young man who becomes ridiculous by his excessive elegance and pretentious air" (430:s.v.). In the same vein, *le pommadin* (one who uses pomade) was defined as "*gandin*, imbecilic, affected," and *le boudiné* (who resembled "a sausage standing on two feet") represented "one of the last incarnations of the *gommeux*" (154:s.v.). Terms of the late 1870s and the 1880s, *sgoff, zing, tchink, pschutt, vlan,* while they may suggest dash, impact, surprise, or shock, were bizarre to the point of lacking a recognizable semantic base, or semblance to French morphology.[68]

The offensiveness ascribed to the dandyistic types that came and went after 1850 perpetuated the pejorative nuances that have always been implicit in the term *dandy* itself. Although its etymology is uncertain, all speculations have included the element of disparagement. *Dandy* has been traced, for example, to the sixteenth-century *dandiprat*, a coin of little value and, by extension, an insignificant, contemptible fellow. Or, as Barbey argued (38:IX, 239), its origins may reflect the Old French *dandin*, an apparent analogue for dandiprat, a small bell, and by extension, a stupid, dawdling fellow; this noun gives the verb *se dandiner*, "to sway back and forth nonchalantly, either on purpose or for lack of control" (162 [1835]:s.v.). In literary texts, the term takes on positive connotations with Rabelais's Perrin Dandin—an honorable, successful arbiter of lawsuits—only to lose them with the ludicrously maniacal judge of Racine's *Les Plaideurs*, the rapacious arbitrator of La Fontaine's *L'Huître et les plaideurs* and the self-defeating nobiliary pretensions of Molière's *George Dandin*. The same intimation of stupidity and affectation reappear in *Yankee Doodle Dandy*, a satire of the provincial and vulgar appearance of American troops, and especially, the allegedly pretentious costumes and manners of George Washington. Stupid and crafty, inept or successful, comic or threatening, these hesitations and ambiguities anticipate the polysemous nineteenth-century dandy.

Like the key term itself, the entire semantic field of dandyism, with the exception of the English *gentleman* and the French *élégant, homme comme il faut,* and *homme du monde,* contained at the outset a large negative component. Whether devalorized, like *homme du monde,* or countervalorized, like *fat* and *roué,* virtually all the terms in this field sustained a fundamental ambivalence that commingled the offensive with the appealing. Although each of the primary terms in the field of honnêteté also had some pejorative resonance (*habile, galant,* the amoral nuances of *honnête* in religious usage) the ideal of the honnête homme, unlike that of the dandy, was predicated on eliminating the offensive and on incarnating the appealing exclusively. From yet another perspective, the nature and dynamics of the seventeenth- and nineteenth-century semantic fields themselves illustrate the same distinction between the appealing and the offensive. The subtle manipulation of a small (and neat) set of existing terms in the earlier century contrasts with the continuing (and bewildering) onslaught of new bizarre or foreign terms in the later period. If both fields are characterized by contradictory tendencies to assimilate and disassimilate any single term and the key term, the size of the nineteenth-century field creates an added confusion that seems to parallel the dandyistic penchant for mystification. Indeed, unlike the seventeenth century, the nineteenth-century metalinguistic commentary does not allow for a conceptual pattern to emerge in the definition of the aristocrat. Although the very same signified—eccentric dress and offensive manners—keep reappearing throughout the field, this redundancy defies attempts to schematize—another linguistic parallel to the mysteriousness of dandyism.

In the last analysis, however, the exploration of the semantic fields of honnêteté and dandyism allows perhaps only one firm conclusion: the semantic confusion observed within each of these fields testifies to the evasiveness and vitality of the concepts at the center. The essayists, moralists, novelists, lexicographers who grappled with the problematics of honnêteté and dandyism do not, predictably, pinpoint their "essence." On the contrary, their semantic speculations point rather to the indefinability of that essence. The answers to the questions "what is an honnête homme?" "what is a dandy?" therefore must be sought, not in linear comparisons with their prototypes, not even in those contemporary texts which speculated on relations between name and thing. The only meaningful definitions will be found, if anywhere, in the structures and signposts of the honnête homme's and the dandy's own quintessential text.

CHAPTER TWO

SELF-ASSERTION AND
THE METAPHORS OF WAR

Every specific body strives to become
master over all space and to extend its force
(its will to power). . . . But it continually
encounters similar efforts on the part of
other bodies and ends by coming to an
arrangement ("union") with those of them
that are sufficiently related to it:
thus they then conspire together for power.
The Will to Power

Nietzsche, *The Will to Power*

The assertion of superiority always entails a component of aggression. For assertiveness (from the Latin *ad serere*) literally defines the other as slave, as a devaluable "servile" object whose essential function is to underscore, by contrast, the superiority of the master. If slaves, originally the booty of war, have largely disappeared as a class—an institutionalized sign of power and eminence—the desire to enslave others has persisted, concealing its original violence beneath more "civilized" expressive modes. We now recoil at the thought of a body branded with the master's name, but not at the idea of the liveried servant wearing his master's insignia, or of the woman bearing her husband's name. The power seeker can always find ways of using his dependents as sign-producing objects to affirm his proprietary status. "Free" beings, however, will resist a subjection that offends their sense of personal worth and denies their own desires to dominate others. It is, therefore, only by veiling the drive for conquest, by sublimating "assertion" into agon, or even into leisurely, playful contest, that the power-seeking subject can hope to captivate the autonomous object. A necessary partner, this object is the adversary, whose specific identity determines the coordinates of the struggle at any given moment. The contest will be more overt or covert depending on the perceived status of the contestants, the obstacles confronting them, the contest in which they vie for superiority, and the code which they embrace.

Conquest and Context

The quest for supremacy of the honnête homme and the dandy is inscribed in a language of military conquest, an extended vocabulary of domination and subjection, that transforms society into a metaphorical battleground. Contrary to what conventional ideas of "progress" might lead us to expect, however, it is the writers on honnêteté who stress the need for concealing aggressiveness. Even the relatively unsophisticated Faret recognizes that a head-on attack will jeopardize the entire campaign (188:96); and at the end of the century, La Bruyère delineates a circuitous strategy which leaves the victim oblivious to "the power and control that we want to exercise over his mind"; for if he knew, "he would throw off the yoke out of shame or impatience" (286:144, #71).[1] A prudent, patient approach, understated to the point of imperceptibility, is the optimal means of "subduing" the intended victims (294:441, #254). In particular, accommodation and self-effacement—the antitheses of one's hidden, fundamental goals—will serve to captivate the other, bind him with handcuffs (421:20), carry off infallible victory (188:44). The honnête homme will play the part of the conquered the better to conquer.

The acid test of honnêteté was the mode, not the fact, of conquest. "We should not want to vanquish, like barbarian rulers, at any price," Méré insists repeatedly, "but rather like heroes, in a way that gives pleasure even to the vanquished" (340:I, 52). They must enjoy their defeat and collaborate in a civilizing process that affects the form and, ultimately, the substance of aggression. "Barbarian" brute force and gross physical prowess are transmuted into spiritual goals, as concrete verbs seek new objects in the abstract, mental realm: "to besiege minds" (188:93), "to subjugate the minds of others" (141:II, 276), and even further along the axis from war to play, "to win people over at will" (340:III, 152). Méré's consistent preference for the term *win* over *vanquish* reveals a subtle but essential shift from the meanings of "capture" to those of "captivation." The more noble conquest will win over—not overrun—the object of its aggression: in François de Caillières's words, "this great art of manipulating the feelings of others and winning their affection [is] the *chef d'oeuvre* of the human spirit" (103:9).[2]

When viewed through the lens of honnêteté, Alexander and Caesar stood forth as models antithetical to the "barbarian princes" of old. Among honnêtes gens, these fascinating figures became "the subject of all our conversations," writes Saint-Evremond; "every one of us has become the champion of one or the other" (438:I, 201).[3] His own *Jugement sur César et sur Alexandre* (1663), a case in point, is a distillation of a rich tradition in which Plutarch's *Lives* in Amyot's translation and Montaigne's *Essais* had been the major sources; further interest in these exemplary warriors was generated by Vaugelas's translation of Quintus Curtius' *Life of Alexander* (1646) and Ablancourt's version of Caesar's *Commentaries* (165). From Grenailles's *L'Honnête garçon* (1642) to La Bruyère's *Caractères* (1688), every text in the seventeenth-century corpus measures Alexander and Caesar critically against the standards of honnêteté. For Méré, who ranks the conqueror and the hero low on his scale of values, *l'honnête conquérant* in the middle, and of course, the honnête homme at the top (340:I, 5; III, 90), Alexander's merit lay in his primary concern for intellectual, not physical superiority: "He must have had—don't you agree?—true greatness of heart and breadth of spirit to think upon matters which ordinary conquerors never seriously entertain" (I, 31). And yet, as Méré often argued, especially in his late essays, Alexander was unduly attached to conquering as a profession, and frequently neglectful of such qualities as civility and grace (II, 44; III, 81). Like most of his contemporaries, Méré saw in Caesar a closer approximation of the ideal of honnêteté. Beyond mere valor, Caesar had showed rare social and intellectual attributes. In planning his campaigns, he had occasionally revealed an unattractive technicity and meticulousness, but his style had an eloquence which Méré prized even over Cicero's—a noble simplicity worthy of the consummate honnête homme. And despite his inordinate ambition, Caesar had demonstrated a remarkable ability to captivate the minds of all who knew him (I, 6; II, 30). For this preeminent reason, Méré concluded: "I consider him the greatest man in the world, and what pleases me even more, I find it hard to imagine a more perfect honnête homme" (339: 26).[4]

The paradigmatic role played by these ancient conquerors in the system of honnêteté fell, in the first decades of the nineteenth century, to a latter-day warrior who achieved mythopoeic eminence during his own lifetime. Napoleon Bonaparte ranked above all his predecessors, wrote Stendhal, even Alexander and Caesar (484:XVII, 180, 195–96). As the incarnation of the ideal of will and power that lies at the core of Balzacian thought, Napoleon's exploits seemed nothing short of epic: "[He] is as great a poet as Homer; he wrote poetry just as Homer waged wars" (21:I, 354).[5] With the disillusionment that followed Napoleon's final defeat and exile, however, aggressiveness had to be displaced from the real battlefield to compensatory, functionally equivalent, socioesthetic spheres. The only alternatives left to the frustrated Vicomte de Brassard, insisted Barbey d'Aurevilly, were contemplation and dandyism, now that there were no longer "daily opportunities for heroic acts as there had been during the Empire" (38:I, 20). The explicit connection made here between Napoleonic self-assertion and dandyism is confirmed by descriptions of those, like Julien Sorel, who model their strategy for conquest on the ideals contained in the *Mémoriale de Sainte-Hélène*, the text that Stendhal's hero is, in fact, reading when we first meet him. It is the image of Napoleon that motivates his departure from Verrières to the seminary and finally to the Hôtel de la Môle, where he becomes a full-fledged dandy. In a similar spirit, Balzac's Lucien de Rubempré, rather than use the favor of women, prefers to drive triumphantly through "the thick ranks of the aristocratic or bourgeois mob. . . . The example of Napoleon . . . suddenly loomed before Lucien who, in self-reproach, cast his calculations to the wind" (19:IV, 517). According to Vautrin, mentor both of Lucien de Rubempré and Eugène de Rastignac, the superior man must ultimately throw down his own glove to society, ever ready and able, "like Napoleon, to wage battle, knowing that a single defeat would spell the ruin of his fortunes" (III, 44).[6]

In the wake of the Napoleonic epic, the dandy exhibited an intense urge for conquest, which Baudelaire described as an exclusive passion for domination (51:II, 82, 709). This open assumption of aggressiveness, a trait that the honnête homme had done his best to conceal, suggests that for the dandy militancy was more than a metaphor. The rise and fall of Napoleon, the ultimate self-made hero, inspired in his admirers the desire to emulate and even to outdo the naked, brutal aggression on which he had founded his unparalleled career. As Chateaubriand observed, Napoleon's example had set off a collective regression marked by a thirst for savage warfare: "His miraculous military feats bewitched the young, and taught us to worship brute force. His unprecedented good fortune encouraged the most wildly ambitious to dream of reaching the heights that he had attained" (126:I, 1005). In post-Napoleonic society, this desire was all the more imperative in the absence of meaningful military life. Thus, whereas honnêteté had affirmed its superiority over and against established nobiliary values, according to which the military remained the only acceptable profession, dandyism, similarly opposed to the context in which it was elaborated, reaffirmed the conquering impulse as truly *noble*, but in the extended rather than the literal sense of that word.[7]

Whether aggressiveness was consciously manifested or conscientiously concealed, whether invoked in its raw or sublimated forms, it had to overlay by its very content a fund of arrogance, self-love, and vanity. These traits, which Augustinian Christianity labels moral faults, become virtues in the Nietzschean code for the *Übermensch*. To call them otherwise, Nietzsche argues in *The Genealogy of Morals*, is to speak the language of slaves, who seek to restrain the power of the strong for their own survival, and so affirm the spiritual supremacy of altruism and charity over egotism and self-assertion. In diachronic terms, he explains, "it is only after aristocratic values have begun to decline that the egotism-altruism dichotomy takes possession of the human conscience . . . it is the herd instinct that asserts itself" (380:160). In a far-reaching Augustinian critique of the noble ethic, La Rochefoucauld, as Nietzsche perceived (385:197), had made this dichotomy the essential structure of human behavior: egotism, self-interest, self-love, pride, and vanity comprise the essence of a power-seeking humanity, altruism only the mask. "Magnanimity scorns everything in order to have everything," wrote La Rochefoucauld (294:437, #248), recognizing that when egotism is forced underground, altruism emerges as the most effective technique for dominating others. In this sinuous battle for supremacy between equally voracious egos, the neo-Augustinian Jansenists emphasized the particular adroitness of the honnête homme. "This honnêteté, which was idolized by the pagan sages," notes Nicole, "is really nothing but a more intelligent and more clever form of vanity than is found among ordinary people" (375:III, 136). Because honnêtes hommes understand that overt vanity, like overt aggression, provokes reaction and resistance, they captivate the other's ego by feeding it: "seeing that open violence is precluded in their case, they must seek other means, and substitute artifice for force; and the only other means they do find is to satisfy the vanity of those whom they need, rather than try to tyrannize it" (III, 127). This strategy is so artfully executed, claims Nicole, that vanity even assumes the appearance of Christian charity. But as Pascal reminded the honnête homme: "the self is hateful: you may hide it, Miton [*sic*], but you can't get rid of it" (393: 584, 597, #455).[8] For Damien Mitton had based his entire theory of honnêteté on "self-love under control" (244:55), a notion that La Rochefoucauld only extended when he defined the honnête homme precisely as "a man who prides himself on nothing" (294:430, #203).[9]

With the surge of Romantic individualism, when overt narcissism became a sign of superiority, Barbey d'Aurevilly could define dandyism itself as the "product of a vanity that has been too much maligned" (38:IX, 222). Looking back to Bulwer-Lytton and forward to Nietzsche, Barbey's treatise aims to revalorize the quality that has been crushed by Christianity's contempt for the world and despised as the lowest of human sentiments (pp. 222, 226). To the contrary, no feeling is more useful than the thirst for applause, he argues, nor does any impulse spring from a wider variety of sources and encompass more domains than the vanity which the dandy or *le fat* exemplifies.[10] From a more poeticized, nostalgic perspective, Baudelaire regarded dandies as "representations of what is best in human pride," in fact, as "the last representations of human pride," soon to be engulfed, along with other relics of old-style aristocracy, in the rising tide of democracy (51:II, 711–12).

As Baudelaire's statement implies, the aggressive expression of pride will necessarily vary with the perception of one's relative power and prestige in the social hierarchy. When part of the recognized ruling class, the power seeker may well present "the man . . . accustomed early in life to the obedience of other men" (51:709).[11] That Baudelaire, however, considers the dandy as the (re)incarnation of this prototype reveals a large dose of personal wishfulness. It also suggests a dreamlike return to an imaginary past, when a prepotent noble class held unquestioned sway over the other estates. Such immanent "aristocratic" power was, in fact, illusory even in the seventeenth century. We know that after the wars of the Fronde the power of the French nobility became largely symbolic, that distinction and rank were henceforth identified with sign, not referent: the privilege of holding the king's candle at the *coucher*, or his shirt at the *lever*. He was the master, the nobles were the slaves: "They had become, as the King wished, so many mendicants, capable only of obedience" (409:134).[12] And yet, the distinguishing signs of the noble—he alone could carry a sword, hoist a weather vane over his manor, occupy certain pews in church, and display a coat of arms—coupled with his hereditary rights at court, had a persuasive reality when viewed from below; they betokened a prestige to which the bourgeois ceaselessly aspired. In the look of the other, if not of the king, the nobility found the subserviency that reaffirmed a bygone glory. The peasants and tradespeople whose livelihood depended on the nobleman's wants, the artists to whom he could take a stick, these were slaves who still confirmed his mastery.

Already in the seventeenth century, the noble who enjoyed "the obedience of others" did so only through the symbols of his lost power. And gradually, even the power of those symbols was lost. During the nineteenth century, the numerous official deaths and resurrections of the nobility expressed the now hopeless marginality of the class on which the existence of the *ancien régime* had been based. The reinstitution under the Restoration of hereditary titles, which had been abolished by the Revolution, stimulated ambitions that were to be dashed under Louis Philippe, who enthroned, through policy as much as personal style, the bourgeoisie as society's new ruling class. For the nobles, as Balzac remarked, 1830 consummated the work of 1790 (19:VI, 229). Abolished once again in 1848, restored in 1852, the nobility was nonetheless undermined by Napoleon III, a monarch who refused to ennoble any of his subjects. The hope of regaining nobiliary power in the 1870s vanished with the Third Republic's denial of any inherent differences of birth among its citizens.

The decline of the nobility did not put an end to aristocratic aspirations in the nineteenth century. On the contrary, distinctiveness and prestige were pursued with an aggressiveness that the absolutism of the *ancien régime* had precluded. As Balzac emphasized in *La Duchesse de Langeais*, however, it was not the old, legitimate nobility which manifested this will to power (19:V, 147–52). For instead of being stirred into action, instead of forging new arms suitable to the struggle of the times, the old nobility retrenched into enclaves, practicing the kind of debilitating seclusion that Lucien Leuwen sees in Nancy as a sterile fear of the present. The vacuum created by this situation could henceforth be filled by anyone who demonstrated his worth in competition against the unleashed aggressions of all others. In this context, the dandy's nostalgia over the demise of nobiliary power was conjoined with his optimistic belief, voiced by Balzac's Raoul Nathan, that the "reign of true superiorities" was near (19:II, 137).

When Barbey judged that Stendhal was a *"déclassé* by the accidents of birth and life, but naturally aristocratic" (34:117), he was commenting on a new class of men, both real and fictional, that included dandy-writers like Balzac's Raoul Nathan and Emile Blondet, or Baudelaire's Samuel Cramer, as well as Stendhal himself. Emancipated by the Revolution from his role as the noble's servant, the nineteenth-century artist found himself autonomous but "classless," incapable, because of his "aristocratic" values, of returning to the class whence he came. In its larger acceptation, however, the notion of *déclassement* transcends all questions of class origins in the literature of French dandyism. As Stendhal's texts are the first to reveal, the dandy may be born a peasant (Julien Sorel), a wealthy bourgeois (Lucien Leuwen) or even a blue-blood (Octave de Malivert), but he always perceives himself as *déclassé* because he is convinced that he belongs rightfully to a class for which there no longer exists a model. This is, perhaps, what Baudelaire had in mind when he wrote: "Dandyism makes its appearance primarily during periods of transition, when democracy has not yet become all-powerful and when the aristocracy has not been completely shaken and debased. In the turmoil of such times, a handful of men who are *déclassés*, disgusted, devoid of occupation but rich with native powers, may conceive the idea of founding a new kind of aristocracy" (51:II, 711).[13] Creatures of talent, dandies are a self-selected *happy few*, who claim membership in a *classe à part*. The dandy's *déclassement* thus constitutes the basis for his *reclassement*.

In a broad sense, the transitional sociopolitical (pre)condition which Baudelaire stipulates for the rise of the "new" aristocrat had been operative for honnêteté as well. Both the seventeenth and the nineteenth centuries witnessed the consolidation in the state's hands of a power destined to undermine the influence and the prestige of a nobility that had incarnated aristocratic values—to render it, in Baudelaire's words, "shaken and debased." It was this development that catalyzed the particular type of struggle which the honnête homme and the dandy waged in the assertion of their superiority. There are, of course, obvious differences between the societal contexts in which honnêteté and dandyism arose and the perceived status of these self-appointed "new" aristocrats. With a legally constituted and universally accepted nobility at its core, honnêteté stood in a palpably more direct and intimate relation to power. It is, in fact, because of this relational disparity that the honnête homme seems as far from the dandy as does the conformist from the revolutionary.

"Always conform . . . to the customs of the country in which you live, because otherwise you will be considered a fool or a wretch," Marmet warned the honnête homme (329:262). This had been the wisdom of Montaigne, who hated civil strife perhaps even more than injustice; this was also the lesson of the Fronde, whose only visible fruit was the self-defensive, repressive intensification of absolutism. In this climate, criticism of the king was unheard, if not unheard of. "The safest practice is to honor and fear him, and to speak of him only with admiration," wrote Sévigné (461:I, 573), intimating that fear of the master could be concealed by feeding his vanity, the sign of acceptance of his eminence.[14] By the same token, acceptance of the parity of egos within the nobiliary circle, which included bourgeois intellectuals, had to be conveyed through conformity to the social code; nonconformity was defined as an offensive attempt to set the self above the other. As Molière revealed in *Dom Juan* and *Le Misanthrope*, the central characters' refusal to play the game by the accepted rules hides a desire to gain superiority by improper means: "I want to be distinguished," declares Alceste (*Mis*.I.i, 63). Nonconformity, whether laughable, as in the case of Alceste, or initially successful, as in Dom Juan's, provokes wrath and eventual punishment. The honnête stance, however, is not represented by the rigidly conventional Don Carlos, but by Philinte, who argues only for superficial conformity, the display of surface signs: ". . . in polite society, custom decrees / That we show certain outward courtesies" (I.i, 65–66). With Orante, Philinte exhibits the behavior that is expected of him, but the hyperbolic register of his compliments tell us that he is, in fact, playing a conscious, obvious game that does not reflect or affect his elusive inner being. His behavior signals a strategy designed to conceal from others a negative opinion of humanity which he admits only to Alceste:

> Why, no, these faults of which you so complain
> Are part of human nature, I maintain,
> And it's no more a matter for disgust
> That men are knavish, selfish and unjust,
> Than that the vulture dines upon the dead,
> And wolves are furious, and apes ill-bred.   (I.i, 173–78)[15]

The conjunction of external conformity with inner, critical independence that Philinte exemplifies is but a particular instance of the general position laid down by Méré: "We owe something to the customs of the land where we live, so as not to offend the public's respect for them, even though these customs may be bad. We owe them only outward respect, however: we must pay them their due, but refrain from condoning them in our hearts for fear of offending universal reason, which condemns them" (339:88). Whereas he associates inner conformity with the common, unenlightened mind (340:III, 94–95), Méré ultimately ascribes the independence of the honnête homme not to some transcendental concept of universal reason, but to a private, intuitive sense of discrimination: "The mark of a solid mind is to be taken in neither by fads nor by customs, to make no judgment unless we see clearly what we are judging, and to disregard any authority whatsoever when we see . . . that it shocks good sense" (II, 71).[16]

The honnête homme was no more a conformist than the dandy was a revolutionary. Both, however, were discriminating strategists. In prerevolutionary absolutist France, the appearance of conformity was a ludic necessity; in postrevolutionary bourgeois France, on the contrary, outer nonconformity was considered requisite for distinction. But the need for distinction and domination dictated their own limits: they preempted the possibility of overthrowing or forsaking society. The dandy's separatist strategy could have no meaning if separation actually occurred.[17] Although this incapacity to break formally with society substantially reduced his status as a revolutionary, the dandy nonetheless had to *appear* to be, as Camus notes, "always on the verge of revolt, on the fringe" (108:72), posing the threat of a break, which he never would or, like Alceste, never could realize. The dandy needed the conventions and laws of society as the backdrop to his posture, the cliché against which to dramatize his originality. Thus, while Baudelaire emphasized the dandy's penchant for opposition and revolt, he also acknowledged his confinement to "the outside limits of social convention" (51:II, 710). And Barbey, conceding that dandyism was not a revolution against the established order, explained that the dandy "plays with the law and still manages to respect it. He suffers from it and takes revenge on it while submitting to it; he appeals to the law at the same time that he evades it; he governs it and, alternately, is governed by it" (38:IX, 230). This elusive and reversible master-slave relationship with respect to law has an agonistic, even a game-like quality that Barbey captured when he defined the dandy as the unclassifiable "caprice in a symmetrically structured class society" (p. 311, #25).[18] The word *caprice* itself reveals the limits of the dandy's revolt and its fundamental inoffensiveness (447:168). An *agent provocateur* who tested to see how far he could go, the dandy did not fundamentally threaten the social order. In Camus's formulation, the dandy was to the revolutionary as *le paraître* is to *l'être* (108:151).

In politics, as in other expressed attitudes, signs of opposition mattered far more than the specific stance. At one end of the spectrum, bohemian dandies, like the Dadaists a century later, launched systematic attacks against the law in the name of anarchy: "What was most characteristic of our Bohemia was our open rebellion against all prejudices, I would almost say against all laws," wrote Arsène Houssaye. "Sheltered there as in a citadel from which we made belligerent sallies, we derided everything. We had placed ourselves outside the law" (260:I, 310).[19] Recognizing the futility of what was ultimately more a ludic than a revolutionary activity, Petrus Borel abandoned the tomahawks and poisoned daggers that lined the walls of his quarters, the *Tartar War Camp*, and became a Republican instead. Until 1848, other writer-dandies, notably Stendhal, Balzac, and Baudelaire, occasionally championed the Republican cause against the bourgeoisie. Looking back to the Revolution of 1848, however, Baudelaire interpreted his own involvement as the product of a thirst for vengeance and the pleasure of destruction—aggressive impulses which the superior man must sublimate, he argued, if he is to rise above the mob (51:I, 678–79; II, 106–7).

Baudelaire, like Balzac, Barbey, and a majority of the fictional dandies, chiefly exhibited a political conservatism vis-à-vis the democratic trends of the times. They idealized the prerevolutionary sociopolitical structure in which, they claimed, the aristocrat had reigned supreme.[20] In *Lucien Leuwen*, the central character and the authorial persona express their preference for the elegantly corrupt courtly pleasures of the *ancien régime* to democratic life among the boorish American puritans (487:I, 761–62; 822–23). This "snobbery of the anachronistic," to quote Jean-Pierre Richard (425:69), was marked by a return to the textual politics of the honnête homme. The Balzacian dandy, for example, who aspires to actual political power in addition to the substitutive power of dandyism, outwardly embraces the existing political order while inwardly he despises it. Eugène de Rastignac by his public statements admits belonging to the July Monarchy, but identifies with the aristocracy by personal conviction; thanks to this strategy, he becomes a count and peer of France. Still other dandies, especially in the works of Gautier, manifest their superiority through political disengagement. "To act in opposition," Baudelaire wrote in his essay on Gautier, "means becoming somewhat philistine oneself, doesn't it? We constantly forget that to insult the rabble is to become part of the rabble" (51:II, 106–7). The dandy, then, might transform his private rather than his public life into a statement of political opposition, a possibility most fully realized by Des Esseintes. The impulse underlying an existence wholly fabricated "against the grain" is revealed at the novel's close when Huysmans' hero shouts in impotent rage, "So crumble, society!" (266:268).[21]

Where the true scope of his opposition is a secret hidden from public scrutiny but revealed to the reader, the dandy appears outwardly to be less revolutionary than he is inwardly. At the same time, his private rebellion has no effect on the social order or the status quo. Ultimately, this is true even of the dandy's attraction to criminality, a mode of revolt valorized by Byron's texts. For the dandy, the underworld represents a primitive and savage subculture where he can flex his muscles and achieve, by personal might and cunning, victories that society denies him. Eugène Sue's Rodolphe finds in *les bas-fonds* stimulating, agonistic situations that allow him to "play the role of Providence" (492:283). Because he is a force of Good and not Evil, however, Prince Rodolphe's "beneficent machinations," his "charitable treacheries," are anything but incendiary (p. 283); they simply represent the nineteenth-century rendition of the (good) prince's love for the incognito. The proverbial princely desire to behave like "normal" beings is the underlying cliché of Baudelaire's *Perte d'Auréole*: "Now I can wander about incognito, commit base acts and indulge in the grossest debauchery, like ordinary mortals" (51:I, 352).[22] Despite his wholly pejorative view of the simple and the lowly, Baudelaire's artist-dandy has no politically subversive intent or impact.

Other versions of the attraction to criminality involve a second character, a type of double with which the dandy forms a couple. Des Esseintes, for example, tries to transform a street urchin into an assassin, but does not engage personally in any criminal acts. This kind of secret pact between thinkers and doers is best illustrated by the relations between Balzac's Vautrin and protégés like Rastignac or Rubempré: the rebel/criminal proposes a Faustian pact with an aspiring dandy, who recoils before its criminal implications. Or as Richard has put it, the association between Vautrin, as the tyrannical father, and the protégé, as the initiated son, overlays a series of antinomies—cause/effect, determinant/determined, actual/potential (424:107). Vautrin represents will, thought, and action outside the law, whereas the protégé is to reap results within its confines: "If you were willing to become my student," promises the "Tempter" to the power-hungry Eugène, "I would put everything within your grasp. Your every desire would be instantly fulfilled. . . . For you, all civilization would become ambrosia" (19:II, 980–81). But the dandy achieves no power in criminality: Vautrin's pact with Lucien ends in the dandy's suicide, and his association with Eugène, which lasts but one day, results in his own imprisonment.[23]

Rather than actually engage in criminality, the dandy prefers to stay within the precincts of the law, exploit it to his own advantage, and at the same time, stand secretly above it. With the notable exceptions of Julien Sorel and Lucien de Rubempré, the Stendhalian and Balzacian neophyte loses his scruples, but maintains a histrionic appearance of conformity that allows him to operate unhindered.[24] A celebrated dandy, like Maxime de Trailles, is capable of anything and everything, according to Balzac, but masks his unscrupulousness beneath a brilliant veneer that remains impenetrable to the enforcers of society's codes (19:VI, 61). More importantly, however, Maxime de Trailles, Henri de Marsay, and other eminent dandies in *La Comédie humaine* place themselves "above all laws" (V, 11). This is the mark of the truly superior man, as Paul de Manerville realizes in his confession to Marsay: "You can . . . put yourself above society's laws, . . . accepted conventions. . . . As for me, I belong to the masses. I must play the game according to the rules of the society I am forced to live in" (III, 88–89). What Manerville must have in mind is the self-made aristocrat's capacity to superimpose his own law where it does not conflict visibly with legal strictures—an impulse confirmed by the secret association that Marsay and Trailles form with other dandies for the explicit purpose of conquering society (V, 14–15). Unbeknownst to the world, the thirteen *Compagnons de l'ordre des dévorants* become "kings . . . and more than kings, judges and executioners who had forged wings for themselves with which they could sweep through society from top to bottom; they refused to lower themselves and play a role in it because their power was unlimited" (V, 16).[25]

The Secret Society: Within and Without the Citadel
Balzac's conspirators consciously fashion their association on the model of the criminal gang because of the immense power that accrues to each member of such a collective unit. The access to the militant energies of peers, which the individual gains, buttresses his personal campaign for power, although, of course, it requires him to give up, in return, some of his autonomy and uniqueness. From this perspective, the Balzacian *confrérie* represents a particular instance of the economy that regulates those exclusive and exclusionary associations which have been formed throughout history in the pursuit of power and prestige. Like the metonymic *ordre des dévorants*, dandyism and honnêteté, as collective phenomena, share striking features with what Georg Simmel has called "the secret society." Exclusive, clandestine groups flourish, he argues in *The Secret and the Secret Society*, during periods "in which new contents of life develop against the resistance of existing powers," and they involve an assertion of power over and against a much larger "potentially and ideally subordinate group of human beings" (465:347, 357). Such groups may be organized along several possible lines: they may, for example, include all who are not explicitly excluded, or else exclude those who are not explicitly included. Secrecy itself may vary in degree and kind: the

individuals may be known, but not the group to which they belong; conversely, the existence of the group may be known, but not the membership, its purpose or rules. In any of these structures, secrecy may be total or consist merely in withholding some privileged knowledge. The degree of secrecy will usually depend on the relative advantages of enclosure and exposure. Whereas enclosure assures the totality of the secret and augments the power derived from its exclusive possession, exposure confronts the excluded with their unworthiness and sharpens their desire for inclusion. But exposure, however slight, always involves the risk of betraying, and perhaps of losing, to the excluded both the secret and the prestige it confers. Thus the more enclosed may represent the stronger secret society, which has the power to cut itself off from others, whereas the more exposed may signify an inability to maintain a place apart, a citadel, that will be both visible and impregnable.

Openness and enclosure, in Simmel's analysis, emerge as the respective structural principles of democracies and aristocracies. In the case of purposefully created aristocracies like honnêteté and dandyism, this antithesis becomes axiomatic. Both the honnête homme and the dandy belong to the kind of secret society that excludes everyone who is not explicitly included, whose existence is known but whose purpose and rules are largely hidden. Formed by a superior minority in reaction against an unworthy majority, these societies are rooted in a hostile act of separation aimed at the same adversary: the bourgeois. The object of the noble's satire as far back as the thirteenth century, the inept, uncivilized, pro-fane bourgeois remained a visible target of contempt in the *Siècle de Louis XIV*, all the more so since it was in this period that the middle classes secured a powerful foothold—social, political, and economic—that would grow increasingly firm throughout the *ancien régime*. It was, in fact, the wealthy bourgeoisie, not the impoverished nobility, who could afford the luxurious pastimes required of an aristocratic posture; whence the contempt (and resentment) of a fictional but typical nobleman: "I have often been amazed to see how pleasures are handed over to the bourgeoisie which should be reserved exclusively for persons of our quality" (104:9–10). In Molière's plays, it is M. Dimanche who has the money and Dom Juan who cannot pay his bills; it is the penniless Sotenvilles who marry their daughter to a rich George Dandin; and it is the bourgeois gentilhomme who would buy the company of a noble woman at any price, as indeed he does. What money cannot buy, however, is a spiritual dimension that spells out the aristocrat's essential difference: "The humors of a Gentleman," proclaims J. de Caillières, "are totally different from those of a merchant" (106:213–14). Méré lumped together such defects as "an uncouth, common air, one that smacks of the courts, the bourgeoisie, the provinces, and commerce" (339:57–58), in keeping with a basic principle of his aristocratic ideal: "Everything connected with a profession offends" (340:III, 142). Like the merchant and the lawyer, the bourgeois scholar with his imitative mind and unsociable personality was barred from the *mondain* in-group: "I cannot understand," writes de Pure, "why a scholar . . . always has such tasteless attitudes, so alien to the public's, so contrary to those of an honnête homme" (410:I, 173). The differences between the private society of honnêtes gens and the bourgeois at large often lay in subtle but radical nuances: "Their civilities, their compliments, and their ways of writing are totally different" (106:213–14).[26]

The attenuated terms in which the honnête homme justified his contempt for the archetypal bourgeois reflected his belief, which satires of *préciosité* had stressed, that more extreme modes of expression were in and of themselves vulgar. Moreover, although Saint-Simon was to describe the era of Louis XIV as "the long reign of the vile bourgeoisie" (440:IV, 802), the honnête homme could afford the luxury of moderation because the middle class was still legally and socially inferior. In the nineteenth century, however, when the bourgeoisie became, in the words of Vigny, "the mistress of France" (515:II, 1163) and imposed its ideals of utility and profit, the dandy could no longer merely emphasize his difference and spiritual superiority: he expressed a primitive aggressiveness that is more characteristic of the excluded than the exclusive. The Jeunes-France, for example, ventured forth from their Bohemian enclave with a savage urge to scalp grocers, philistines, and bourgeois alike, and to display their trophies on their belts (207:97). And Baudelaire, who regarded the supremacy of the bourgeois as the reign of mediocrity, ascribed to the dandy the specific goal of combatting its triviality (51:II, 711). Preferring retreat to confrontation with an enthroned bourgeoisie that crushes all intelligence, virtue, and art (266:267), Des Esseintes in 1885 is the only dandy who seals himself off in his own private domain.

The steady encroachments of the bourgeois mentality made it all the more imperative to establish aristocratic enclosures. On the simplest level, both dandyism and honnêteté utilize spatial constructs to distinguish the vital center from the vast, dismal periphery, localizing aristocratic "urbanity" in the city, bourgeois "provinciality" on its outskirts and beyond. In what constitutes a topos common to both corpora, the superior being in the provinces feels exiled, imprisoned.[27] Conversely, the literary voyage from the provinces to Paris is repeatedly used to underscore a radical difference of standards. By Parisian norms, Molière's *précieuses ridicules* are nothing but piteous and pretentious provincial imitations of the genuine article. In the Balzacian scheme, a dandy potentate in the provinces, like Victurnien d'Esgrignon, must build his power base from zero once he arrives in Paris. And Rastignac, who suffers for his own provincialism under the contemptuous gaze of Trailles in *Le Père Goriot*, displays an equal scorn, upon becoming an eminent dandy in *Illusions perdues*, for the newly arrived Rubempré.

Although a haven by comparison with the rest of France, Paris did not necessarily provide the ideal aristocratic milieu. Seventeenth-century writers often maintained that Parisians were more concerned with professional productivity than with polish (244:36). From a broader perspective, Méré argued that no city could claim to be the locus of honnêteté: "the mores and manners of the city are not noble; *le grand monde* cannot bear them" (340:I, 87). His recurrent referent, *le grand monde*, is an abstraction for a universal aristocratic society transcending the prejudices and the limitations of any specific place. Alongside *le grand monde*, the court leaves much to be desired, even as the proverbial proving ground in the qualities of honnêteté. If Méré concedes that those who have not trained at court often lack certain essential nuances, he also questions the benefits to be reaped there,

80

among men who are neither prone to self-improvement (II, 123; III, 142) nor worthy of imitation (II, 110). Thus, "we must consider the court and *le grand monde* separately, and remember that the court, whether out of habit or whim, sometimes approves of things that *le grand monde* would not tolerate. In order to judge and evaluate correctly the ways of *le grand monde* and even those of the court, we have to imagine the collective opinion of the most outstanding honnêtes gens of all the courts in the world if they could be assembled in one place" (II, 111). However impracticable such a world-wide synod might be, this vision of *le grand monde* translates opposition to a court that, in Méré's view, had no real comprehension of authentic worth: "Even at court, where everything seems so refined and polished, most people have only a limited understanding of excellence: anything beyond that limit, passes them by or bowls them over" (III, 155).[28] Explicitly ranked above *les grands seigneurs* and the princes who constitute the court (II, 74; III, 76), Méré's society of honnêtes gens is superior to all (except, one might assume, the king himself).

Neither *la cour* nor *la ville* was spiritually large enough to contain the ideal of honnêteté.[29] Paradoxically, the actual locus of *le grand monde* was the small, exclusive space that we know as the *salon* and that the *mondains* called *le cabinet, le réduit, la ruelle,* or *l'alcôve.* Signifiers for the most exiguous and intimate of seventeenth-century rooms, these signs served as metaphors for the sanctuary in which a choice group or *cercle* could retire to the pleasure of their own company.[30] Such enclosures owed their existence to the same motives that underlay *la chambre bleue* and consciously strove to duplicate its brilliant and powerful model. After the decline of Rambouillet's circle in the 1640s and its virtual demise during the Fronde, habitués like Scudéry and Sablé were among the notable women—some fifteen, by Somaize's account (467:I, 205–06)—who created the enclosures wherein honnêteté developed and thrived. As in *la chambre bleue,* the members of Scudéry's côterie shed their personal and professional problems to bask in a poetic atmosphere which Pellisson, "the Apollo of the Saturday session," described: "In this ambience, their minds were indeed well disposed to receive inspiration from Apollo. . . . The whole group felt it: it filled the whole palace and, if what they say is true, poetry, passing through the antechamber, the chambers, and even the wardrobes, filtered as far as the servants' quarters . . . a tall lackey composed at least six dozen burlesque verses. But our heroes and heroines concentrated on madrigals; never have so many been composed nor so quickly. Hardly had one person finished declaiming a madrigal than her neighbor felt another teeming in his head. In one place, someone recited four verses; in another someone else wrote twelve. Everything was done gaily and without effort" (138:17–18). Aside from purportedly improvised poetry, Scudéry's circle, following Rambouillet's example, valued spirited banter—"challenges, replies, retorts, attacks, rejoinders" (p. 18)—which rivaled, in Pellisson's eyes, the heroic narratives of *Le Grand Cyrus* and the diversions of Boccaccio's *Decameron* (p. 38).[31]

In the côterie of Mlle de Montpensier, where Segrais officiated, literary portraits became the rage. This ritualistic activity, which La Grande Mademoiselle brought to life from the pages of *Le Grand Cyrus*, was given permanent form in her *Galerie des portraits*, a not too distant model for Molière's "scène des portraits" in *Le Misanthrope*.[32] The purposely elitist nature of this and other pastimes had been underscored in Sorel's *Maison des jeux* (1642), where card games or *le jeu de paume* and *boules* are rejected precisely because they are enjoyed by "all sorts of people, lackeys and lords alike, and are equally accessible to the ignorant and uncouth as to the educated and refined"; those games are allowed which "can appeal only to persons of quality who have been reared on *civilité* and *galanterie*, have judgment and knowledge, and are adept at all kinds of discussions and repartees [which] others could never master" (323:403–4).[33] Hermogène, who is to Sorel's fictional company what Voiture was to *la chambre bleue*, proposes as appropriate verbal games *le coeur volé*, *la chasse à l'amour*, and *le jeu du mariage*, as well as the fashioning of proverbs and riddles. The challenge provided by such hermeneutic games, in which combatants matched wits much as knights clash swords (138:29), found its culminating expression in the maxims perfected by Sablé's côterie. Abandoning her influential Parisian salon, which had formed and launched many an aspiring honnête homme (268:28), Sablé built an elegant retreat at Port Royal, where one could converse on everything from gourmet cooking to metaphysics with the likes of Jacques Esprit, Nicole, and Pascal, Mesdames de Montausier, Maure, and Longueville, and of course, La Rochefoucauld and La Fayette. It was this milieu, as Ivanoff has shown, that generated the texts of the major aristocratic and Jansenist *moralistes* (268).

The notion of secret, ritual activities carried on within a secluded space underlies not only the spirit of specific seventeenth-century circles, but the corpus of honnêteté itself. The numerous treatises framed as conversations imply a specially reserved, self-contained locus endowed with such reality that its shape requires no concrete description. The tacit assumption that the reader knows that space and place is combined with the recurrent caveat against disclosing in-group preoccupations to inferior outsiders: "They would make bad jokes about it," explained Méré, "although there is nothing in the world as excellent or as true" (339:625). Because of the essential differences between the included and the excluded, the source of joy for one is misery for the other (p. 522). Thus, only the initiates are worthy of concern: "One must appeal . . . above all to *les honnêtes gens*," declared Marmet; "as for the others, you needn't bother about them" (329:149). This radical exclusivity constitutes, for La Rochefoucauld, proof of aristocracy itself: "The mark of a true honnête homme is the desire always to be in the company of *honnêtes gens*" (294: 430, #206).[34]

Any compromise with the principle and the praxis of exclusivity threatened the very nature and the goals of the secret society. The splintering of *la chambre bleue* into factions unleashed rivalries that La Bruyère likened to wars among nations (286:203, #4), and resulted in a relaxation of standards and consequent openness that spelled decline. Like La Bruyère, who looked nostalgically back to the Hôtel de Rambouillet as a golden age lost forever (p. 394, #10), Molière's characterizations of Célimène in *Le Misanthrope*, or of Uranie in *Critique de l'Ecole des femmes*, who welcomes "all sorts of people indiscriminately" (I.i), are symptomatic of what occurs when vanity usurps the place of aristocratic discrimination. Conversely, to venture beyond one's circle is to risk contact with those whom the creation of the circle was specifically designed to exclude. Attending a concert at the home of a noblewoman, Sapho in *Le Grand Cyrus* finds "one of those random gatherings where the door is open to everyone, where you sometimes see a hundred people you never saw before and would never want to see, and where you also see every irritating and trying person that you know" (141:II, 155). No wonder, then, that Saint-Evremond yearned for societies "where *honnêtes gens* could conveniently withdraw" (438:IV, 295).³⁵

Although he expressed a need for greater enclosure, the honnête homme, like all prerevolutionary nobles, in Balzac's terms, was "always someone apart" (22:50). Baudelaire, in turn, extolled the idea of an aristocracy "which surrounds itself in solitude" (51:II, 107), but bourgeois society had little room for such citadels of meaningful prestige. Except in the minds of provincial dreamers, like Victurnien d'Esgrignon, the court, over and against which the society of *honnêtes gens* had proclaimed its superiority, no longer even existed as a viable alternative (19:IV, 369 ff). In the Paris of *La Comédie humaine*, however, the Faubourg Saint-Germain is the Balzacian counterpart to the Hôtel de Rambouillet—the site of the aristocracy's separation from the rest of society: "This space between a class and a whole capital, is it not a material consecration of the spiritual distances that should separate them? In all creations, the head has its assigned place" (V, 145–46). And yet, Balzac also recognizes that this symbolic place has lost its magic: it holds only by tradition what it once possessed in reality (V, 151). Nonetheless, the various salons of the Faubourg Saint-Germain, and those of the slightly more bourgeois Chaussée d'Antin, precisely because they are *considered* impregnable, must therefore become targets in the struggle for social eminence.³⁶ In fact, once family ties gain him an initial admission to Mme de Beauséant's salon, Rastignac "conquers the right to go everywhere" (II, 874), is launched into *le beau monde*, and shortly becomes the peer of Trailles and Marsay. But whereas the neophyte views the salons as his "battlefield" (V, 731), the scene of his "glory or his downfall" (417:13), prominent dandies dismiss them as insufficiently exclusive, and attribute their decline to their domination by bourgeois women (19:III, 205, 223–24; V, 228). The superior man, according to Balzac, is repelled by "the sterility of salons, their emptiness, their shallowness" (V, 230).

Self-Assertion and Metaphors of War

The decline of the salon is one of the chief reasons why English-style clubs proliferated in nineteenth-century France. The Jockey, the most celebrated by far, achieved such stature that no aspiring *lion* could afford not to belong; among its members we find the foremost dandies in *La Comédie humaine* (II, 579).[37] When Baudelaire, however, criticized the members of Le Jockey in 1861 (51:II, 812), he was not only erecting new barriers between insider and outsider—a constant aristocratic concern—he was also pointing to the shaky foundations of all nineteenth-century enclosures. But exclusiveness was so imperious a need that the dandy recreated in public places symbolic modes of distancing. At the theater and the opera, for example, the *loge* became the visible but inaccessible precinct from which one could view and be viewed by fellow dandies in their circular enclosures, oblivious to *hoi polloi* below. It is in the *loges* that the Stendhalian and Balzacian dandy-neophyte perfects his worldly education by observing the masters, who in turn scrutinize him. In addition, certain cafés like Tortoni's are reserved for members of the in-group; they enter such places through the back door, a practice common to secret societies, because as Musset writes, "the front steps have been invaded by barbarians, that is, by stock-exchange types" (367:III, 1105–6). Novelists ranging from Stendhal to Barbey depict the dandy having lunch or an after-theater ice at Tortoni's, or merely leaning against a balustrade, a toothpick in his mouth.[38] The stylized poses, the appearances at specific times in carefully designated places, share a similar motivation with the ritual observances that members of secret societies impose upon themselves. "Know then ... that there are certain times and certain places where *les fashionables* must be seen," declares Mortemart-Boisse (364:317–18). Even certain public thoroughfares are consecrated to the dandies' use—the Bois de Boulogne, the Jardin des Plantes, the Champs Elysées. By Musset's account, the Boulevard des Italiens (ironically labeled, after 1816, the Boulevard de Gand) is left to the masses in the morning and from three to five in the afternoon, but at other times becomes the exclusive preserve of the initiated (367:III, 1104–9). The focus of all Parisian pleasures, this circumscribed territory marks off the length and breadth of the dandy's world: "*There* is the universe. On the other side of the street lie the Indies"

(p. 1105). In a similarly hyperbolic vein, another writer calls the Boulevard de Gand "the center of the world, the end of everything, the supreme goal of so many efforts, the last word of so many ambitions" (391:184), in short the crowning arena of the agon of dandyism.[39]

In the absence of permanent citadels, the opera, the café, and the boulevard are transformed into the private, ritual locales where the dandy comes to see, but essentially to be seen: "*Le fashionable* . . . counts only so long as he is seen," insists Ronteix; "he must not worry about seeing or admiring, but being seen, being admired" (432:58,65). Accordingly, Barbey proposed *nil mirari* as the motto of dandyism (38:IX, 239–40). Whether he aimed to shock by blatant tactics (perhaps best illustrated by the leashed lobster Gautier promenaded through town) or to impress by his quiet refinement, the dandy was to be self-possessed in total indifference to the mass of humanity in his path. In truth, however, he wished to humiliate the foolish arrogance of the bourgeois who ruled the world (51:I, 291), and dominate them by the sheer superiority of his presence. This hidden need to impress an inferior other conflicted with the more aristocratic desire to act for one's own exclusive pleasure. Baudelaire, chastizing those who performed for others (II, 719), imagined a completely autonomous dandy type, who resolves this potentially humiliating contradiction. The outwardly indistinguishable, "invisible" *flâneur*, whom he depicted in *Les Foules*, enters at will the bodies and minds of the unsuspecting masses, dominating them silently for his solitary enjoyment (I, 291). With this complete self-sufficiency, he creates a secret society of one, an isolated tower of refinement. For Baudelaire, such unitary solitude is one of the manifestations of genius (I, 700); it is also one of the conditions of heroism: "the true hero entertains *himself*" (I, 682).[40]

Although these exclusionary tactics may recall the *confréries* of old, the society of dandies remains essentially what Sartre calls "a participation of solitaries" (447:168). Each dandy's enterprise may be supported and furthered by the existence of the secret society, but he is first and always aggressively independent, removed from all others, other dandies included. "I haven't a single friend!" one of Barbey's spokesmen declares proudly

(38:IX, 308), uttering one of the topoi of the fictional dandy from Julien Sorel to Des Esseintes. It is only in the most desperate straits, at the end of *A rebours*, that Des Esseintes finally expresses the wish to find a kindred spirit (226:211). Earlier dandies, like Stendhal's Octave de Malivert or Gautier's D'Albert, endure their painful solitude, determined to be under obligation to no one who could compromise their autonomy. The sullying effect of "friendships" was vividly summarized by Baudelaire: "Many friends, many gloves" (51:I, 654). Such determined insulation from peers was a function not only of the dandy's desire for autonomy, but of his quest for supremacy as well. The battle, carried from the outland to the inland, had to be waged against the only worthy opponents: his equals. Although in theory aggressive impulses were to yield ground to respect for one's peers (22:92–93), the inner circle depicted in Balzac's novels, for example, is a stage for savage power struggles waged by the law of the jungle. As Mme de Beauséant instructs the neophyte Rastignac in *Le Père Goriot*: "Strike pitilessly, you will be feared" (19:II, 912). Victurnien d'Esgrignon's successes breed plans for destruction that come to fruition; in the end, society's lions observe his demise with sadistic pleasure. As "king of the dandies" with unrivaled power, Marsay does extend a magnanimous hand to his emulators, Manerville and Rubempré, but in the universe of the dandy, the mentor almost always emerges as his disciples' archrival. Ancelot's Count de Senanges is "perpetually armed against the success of others": "He had already feared more than once that the scepter of fashion might be wrested from him; and he felt a violent resentment whenever he saw some young man appear on the social scene who was endowed with all the qualities that age would soon take away from him" (8:611).[41]

Although the circle of the honnête homme seemed built on a horizontal, egalitarian model, conceived in opposition to the hierarchical structure of seventeenth-century society, rivalry remained a powerful motivating force in this as in every aristocratic society, according to Nietzsche (385:493). Explicit in the *Cortegiano* and its early rewritings, this "antagonistic drive" (p. 493) surfaces only occasionally in the later *mondain* texts. "Excellence does not always impress the most eminent *honnêtes gens*," admits Saint-Evremond; "each individual is so jealous of his own merit that he is almost incapable of tolerating anyone else's" (438:III, 249–50). Beneath the beguiling, polished surface, the self views others as the enemy it yearns to enslave (393:584, 597). And yet this agonistic tension does not undermine the surface stability of the circle; there exists a latent "agitation without disorder," to use the phrase that defines the closed world of *La Princesse de Clèves* (290:24). But La Fayette's novel also suggests that close friendship, even unguarded communication, is virtually unachievable among *honnêtes gens*. Only *in extremis* do the Duc de Nemours and the Vidame de Chartres ever exchange the secrets of their private life. Because intimacy disarms and makes for vulnerability, the honnête homme must distrust his closest friends: "this precept may seem shocking," confesses Marmet, "but it is often indispensable" (329:224–25). Méré concurred: "I observe that excessive trust in what are called *friends* usually does not have a happy outcome" (340:III, 150–51)—and his italics, along with the cynical "what are called," bear witness to a subjacent hostility. Autonomy is a primary consideration which precludes receiving sustained help from peers: "an honnête homme hates nothing more than dependency on others, even on his best friends" (III, 151). Thus, while magnanimity remains a basic aristocratic virtue, it is tempered by the recognition that generosity invariably breeds resentment; in the words of La Rochefoucauld, "there is hardly anyone who is not ungrateful at receiving great favors" (294:444, #299).[42] In this moral climate, the structures of exchange vital to friendship are replaced by superficial contacts according to the implicit principle: "separate, thus equal." Within the enclosure, the essence of human relations was distance, as each honnête homme, to paraphrase Nietzsche, wrapped himself "in the cloak of external, spatial solitude" (385:515).

If the honnête homme shunned friendship with peers, he strove to emulate those rare masters who alone possessed and exemplified the secret knowledge on which all claims to superiority are ultimately based. The choice of such a model, however, was no easy task: "One finds very few of these excellent teachers on honnêteté," observed Méré, ". . . one must therefore try to find them on one's own or through the recommendation of people who have sound judgment, and pattern oneself on the most accomplished" (340:III, 71). Although this process of formation by another involves a temporary compromise to one's autonomy, it is amply rewarded when the honnête homme appropriates the knowledge of the master, and even more, when he surpasses him (III, 71). From a collective perspective, moreover, the presence of expert masters within the closed society renders it self-sufficient and reconfirms its superiority to all rival institutions. Méré pointedly argued that a novice could learn far more from him in a month than in a lifetime at court (78:XXX[1923], 520–21), let alone from the *collèges* far beneath the court (340:I, 30). *La science du collège*, useless, even detrimental (I, 173), is rejected in favor of *la science du monde*, as F. de Caillières entitled one of his treatises on honnêteté (103), which the in-group alone possessed and dispensed. "Nothing is more effective than *l'école du monde*," agreed Morvan de Bellegarde, "in training the mind and bestowing that aura of *politesse* which can be acquired only by frequenting people who are *polis*" (61:preface).[43]

The dandy resisted the notion of a secret "science" of dandyism as a compromise to his superior individuality. An all-encompassing code of dandyism would contradict his very essence, argued Barbey: "It cannot be repeated often enough: what makes a dandy is his independence. If this were not so, there would be a fixed code (or legislation) for dandyism, but no such thing exists" (38:IX, 250); if it did, "anyone at all could be a dandy; there would be a prescription to follow and nothing more" (p. 310). There are, to be sure, dandyistic principles and traditions, "but all that is governed by whim" (p. 311). Put another way, as a collective group, "dandies, by their personal authority, establish a law above the one that governs even the most aristocratic circles . . . and they succeed in winning acceptance for this mobile law which is, at bottom, nothing more than the daring of their own personality" (p. 240). Baudelaire, to the contrary, did not subscribe to the idea of a "mobile law" but to a "doctrine" that delineates a "haughty" and "belligerent caste," an unchartered institution "outside the law, but having its own rigorous laws, by which all its subjects are strictly bound, no matter how fiery and independent their natures may be" (51:II, 710–11).[44] Rigid or mobile, the rules of the secret society constituted the epistemological weapon that legitimized both the dandy's and the honnête homme's assertion of superiority. Contained within that code were not only the numerous precepts that specified the qualities requisite to becoming a dandy or an honnête homme, but on a larger scale, the criteria that defined dandyism and honnêteté as meritocratic societies.

The Secret Society and the Meaning of Merit

"Today, thanks to God and to the Revolution, it is merit alone that determines one's position in society," declared Raisson in 1828 (415:195–96). Some nineteenth-century writers believed that the Revolution, by eliminating distinctions of birth, had made intrinsic worth the only valid means of self-assertion. Paradoxically, perhaps, the honnête homme in the absolutist *ancien régime* subscribed to the very same belief. Whether it was the nobility's diminished power that made rank a secondary consideration, or the need to distinguish true aristocracy from mere hereditary privilege, honnêteté was equated with merit alone. "Because you are a duke, I do not have to respect you, but I do have to bow to you," wrote Pascal. "If you are a duke and an honnête homme, I will give its due to each of these qualities. I will certainly not deny you the courtesies that you merit as a duke or the esteem that you merit as an honnête homme. But if you are a duke and not an honnête homme . . . you can be sure that I will feel for you the inner contempt that the baseness of your spirit deserves" (393:367). *Contempt* and *baseness* are powerful signs, which spell out the agonistic impulses that motivated their use. In more restrained language, Méré advanced the same principle: "The heart and mind are the only real sources of true superiority . . . all the rest is mere show" (340:I, 39–40). To La Rochefoucauld, already *duc et pair*, the attainment of honnêteté could not even be matched by the possession of a kingdom: "I know of nothing finer than nobility of heart and loftiness of mind; these are the mainsprings of that perfect honnêteté which I value above all else and which I deem preferable, for human happiness, to the possession of a kingdom" (294:728–29).[45]

Self-Assertion and Metaphors of War

Such manifest indifference to the traditional marks of distinction—rank, fortune, professional status—covers over a barely disguised contempt for the gross values of those outside the precinct of honnêteté. Inside the circle, the principle of meritorious equality was embedded in a verbal sign: the honnête homme, relieved of his class-revealing name, was reclassified and reclassed under an equalizing anthroponym, conferred as part of the rite of acceptance in the secret order. This widespread practice in the seventeenth-century salon began with Rambouillet (*Arthénice*, a virtual homonym for Artemis) and Voiture (*Callicrate*, the arbiter of beauty; *El Re Chiquito*, the mini-king, because of his physical size) and was continued in Scudéry's circle. But whereas in *la chambre bleue* the key to an anthroponym lay in the individual's perceived traits or function in the group, in Scudéry's côterie, to judge from Pellisson's *Journée des madrigaux*, names had their roots in *Le Grand Cyrus*, the *roman à clef* where Conrart appears as Théodomas, Raincy as Agathyrse, and the author herself as Sapho. Not only do these single-term names preclude the presence or absence of the nobiliary "de," but their crypto-classical morphology suggests the emulation of an idealized past, a mythical place distant from the everyday, contingent world. In the same way, the anthroponyms that dot the conversations and dialogues of the corpus of honnêteté, in works like Bouhours's *La Manière de bien penser* or Vaumorières's *L'Art de plaire dans la conversation*, require classical keys for their deciphering and fill out the image of private, spiritual territories of elite populations consciously, perhaps even arrogantly, turned in upon themselves.[46]

By comparison, the largely fictional corpus of dandyism includes a panorama of social classes in which the superior man can and must be set off from the mass. In this narrative space, the dandy's name signals his preeminence immediately both to the reader and to his fictional audience, insiders and outsiders alike. Just as the code name of the honnête homme evoked exalted classical models, the dandy's harks back primarily to the "ancient" prerevolutionary nobiliary world as a sign of difference from the crowd and kinship with the elite. Thus Balzac's Lucien adopts his mother's name, de Rubempré, because of his "mortification at hearing himself called Chardon [thistle] in salons where

91

all others bear sonorous names encased in titles" (19:IV, 819). With the possible exception of Julien Sorel, who becomes M. le Chevalier de la Vernaye with M. de la Môle's help, the dandy is not reclassified by his peers, but renames himself in a basic gesture of militancy. If Balzac, who added the nobiliary "de" in 1831, Gérard Labrunie, who became Gérard de Nerval, and Barbey, who exhumed the long-discarded patronym d'Aurevilly, are typical, the passion for noble names was equally pervasive in dandyistic life as in literature. Nestor Roqueplan even coined a label for the person whose alias represented an appropriation of the noble's identity: "The modern Mascarille . . . calls this resurrecting the *ancien régime*. . . . These Mascarilles date from the Restoration; but they have proliferated at an alarming rate. France is becoming a country of Mascarilles, and with *all* of us equal, we will *all* be nobles" (433:139–40).[47]

Roqueplan's hyperbolism notwithstanding, other, equally significant morphological means were used to express disdainful distance. Nobiliary anthroponyms from foreign countries served just as well to underscore the complementary notions of difference and superiority; whence the dandies who are English lords (Walmore in Ancelot's *Le Dandy*; Falmouth in Sue's *Arthur*; Sir Williams in du Terrail's *Rocambole*) or noblemen of Russian (Korasoff in *Le Rouge et le noir*), German (Rodolphe in Sue's *Les Mystères de Paris*), and Spanish origin (Pinta in *La Comédie humaine* and Ravila de Ravillès in *Les Diaboliques*). Even non-nobiliary foreign names, like Samuel Cramer, set the dandy apart from common French stock. Gautier's Daniel Jovard, who cannot tolerate the six "ridiculous" letters of his "dreadful" name, finally chooses a pseudonym so full of k's and w's and other "romantic consonants" that, as the author comments satirically, "a postman would need six days and six nights to spell it" (210:91–92). Gothic and medieval-sounding anthroponyms, like Elias Wildmanstadius, which Roger (alias "de Beauvoir") interpreted as compensation for the lack of nobiliary titles (53:123, 125)—even classical ones, like Anarchasis and Albertus, eponymous heroes of works by Beauvoir and Gautier—were designed to convey exclusionary and aristocratic hostility to contemporary society.

In the case of the honnête homme, the adoption of classical anthroponyms, and more broadly, the denial of mere rank as a sign of merit, served as a means of asserting superiority over a hereditary aristocracy. This strategy, which was functional in an age when everyone who mattered bore a title, was useless in the nineteenth century, when the nobility had become irrelevant in the bourgeois power structure. The dandy's concern with his name, an obsession which finds hyperbolic expression in Henri Beyle's 171 pseudonyms (477:191–244), overlay an effort to posit a symbolic accord between "nobility of character" and "nobility of rank" (122:40), on the understanding that the latter could be signified by various morphological means, and that the former constituted the preeminent consideration. This is why Barbey discounts Mesnil-grand's high nobiliary rank in favor of his natural, spiritual qualities: "He was profoundly aristocratic—not merely by birth, caste, or social rank, but by his nature; because he was *himself* and no one else, and would have been what he was, even as the lowliest cobbler in town. He was an aristocrat, in short, as Heinrich Heine said, 'by his magnificent sensibility' and not in the bourgeois manner, like those social climbers who love external signs of distinction" (38:I, 264).[48] Although in most fictional instances the name and the thing were made to coincide, the dandy is dubbed *un patricien de nature* from Balzac to Barbey, the natural aristocrat of his society (22:93; 38:I, 280). Whatever his origins, argues Baudelaire, the dandy possesses extraordinary natural distinction which has nothing whatever to do with rank (51:II, 309–10).

In another area of human activity, wealth and fortune play a role that is functionally equivalent to the noble name. As an aristocracy of merit, honnêteté rejects the archetypically bourgeois equation of money with inherent value. Philinte, like Cléante, Monsieur Jourdain's future son-in-law, gives no information about his financial standing. This deliberate silence confirms Méré's contention that wealth is not a sign of merit, not even a vehicle for displaying honnête qualities; "Socrates' poverty," he observes, "did not prevent him from being as generous as Alexander, who possessed so many treasures and kingdoms" (340:III, 160). In fact, wealth may be detrimental to the realization of the ideal because of a human tendency to think its acquisition meritorious; but honnêteté "is far above that sort of thing" (I, 38).[49] In the nineteenth-century world dominated by rich bourgeois, however, such compensatory maneuvers were no longer possible; wealth became the source and symbol of the dandy's power. Dériège, for example, specified that the *lion* required an income of at least 40,000 francs (158:12); and Barbey went so far as to declare Brummell's wealth the necessary foundation of his elegance (38:IX, 262). In these and other instances, the dandy rejects the bourgeois connection between wealth and hard work; he will inherit money, acquire it somehow, sometimes from those whom he deems fit only to serve him, but without professional exertion of any kind. When Rastignac, for instance, realizes that money is the "tool" with which one "digs the vineyards" of Paris (19:II, 917), he extracts various sums from his self-sacrificing family, from his association with Vautrin, and finally from gambling—that aristocratic pastime which has always held the promise of immediate acquisition without demeaning effort. In undisguised contempt for the sacrosanct notions of solvency and thrift, Baudelaire speculated that for the dandy "unlimited credit might suffice" (51:II, 710). Like the aristocrat who puts no stock in his noble name, his dandyistic prototype is a rich man, "reared in luxury" who "does not desire money as something essential . . . he relegates that crude passion to vulgar mortals" (p. 710). That Baudelaire's Don Juan despises money, and even more his servant's passion for it, underscores the essential difference between the aristocrat and the petty bourgeois (I, 627). His dandy values money only because it relieves him of the common man's concerns, and allows him to translate his fantasies into realities, to feel and to think in absolute freedom and independence (II, 709). In this sense, argues Baudelaire, the ultimate basis of the new aristocracy is founded on "the most precious, the most indestructible faculties and the divine gifts that work and money can never bestow" (II, 711).[50]

Whereas their expressed attitudes toward rank and wealth as criteria of merit contained subtle dissimilarities, the honnête homme and the dandy alike had no use for productive activity of any kind. Signs of productive, professional activity were anti-thetical to Pascal's vision of the honnête homme: "We should not be able to say of a man, 'he is a mathematician,' or 'a preacher,' or 'eloquent'; but that he is an honnête homme! that universal quality alone appeals to me" (393:588, #647). These *gens universels* "are not called poets or mathematicians, etc., but they are all these things and judges of them all" (p. 583, #587). Going beyond Montaigne, Pascal's honnête homme is both nothing in particular and everything in general; he embraces the most intui-tive and intellectual forms of knowledge, he is even capable of judging practitioners of all professions, without exercising any himself. In Nicole's terms, he strives for no "insignia" other than honnêteté (375:III, 141). This posture was a weapon to be used against the courtier and the conqueror as well as the bourgeois, since the antiprofessionalism of the honnête homme extended even to that traditionally aristocratic vocation of statesmanship. In a jab at Castiglione and his French imitators, Méré criticized the desire to become confidant to a king: "The most outstanding honnête homme would be the last person to get involved in such a thing" (340:III, 76). Far from opposing the monarchy's efforts to render the nobility ineffectual, the honnête homme, in a display of reaction formation, valorized nonproductiveness and uselessness as a sign of aristocracy.[51]

In a society which enthroned bourgeois practicality, the dandy's praise of uselessness represented a conscious rewriting of a bygone aristocratic ideal that was deliberately hostile. "At a time . . . when people's minds are being deadened by the single ideal of utility," observed Baudelaire, "I don't think there is great harm in exaggerating a bit in the opposite direction" (49:II, 344). Because a useful man is fundamentally "hideous" and all productive func-tions are "vile" (51:I, 679, 684), according to Baudelaire, his dandy, going beyond the honnête homme, incarnates the antithesis of utility. Openly evoking the economic system and social roles of the *ancien régime*, Baudelaire chastized those who are "subject to the *taille* and the *corvée*" as fit for "the stable, that is, for the practice of what are called *professions*"; "a dandy," by com-parison, "does nothing" (p. 684). Such vehement statements reca-pitulate pronouncements on nonproductiveness that pervade the corpus of dandyism from the 1830s onward. It is "the essence of *le fashionable* never to work," declares Ronteix (432:123); or, as Balzac writes more discreetly, "a man accustomed to working cannot comprehend the elegant life" (22:41). At the same time, to insure that idleness is correctly deciphered as superior disdain and not ineptitude, the dandy must combine professional apraxis with evidence of boundless potential. Henri de Marsay "will be whatever he wants to be," insists Paul de Manerville: "I would not be surprised to learn one day that he is the minister of foreign affairs. Nothing ever stands in his way" (19:V, 277). Maxime de Trailles, in Balzac's view, could have been Richelieu, Mazarin, or Potemkin (VII, 729). Here, as often, Baudelaire had the ultimate word: the dandy is "a rumbling unemployed force," and in an even more striking oxymoron, "an unemployed Hercules" (51:I, 657, II, 712).[52]

In its extreme form, the commitment to uselessness went so far as to preclude the production of a literary text. A typical fictional situation depicts the dandy as *un artiste manqué* who possesses the necessary talent but refuses to labor like a bourgeois craftsman. As Gautier's D'Albert explains: "To take a thought from the imagination's mine . . . set it down in front of me, and from dawn to dusk, a chisel in one hand, a hammer in the other, strike, carve, scrape, just to take at the end of the day a pinch of dust to sprinkle over my writing—that is something I will never be able to do" (211:249). This refusal to produce a tangible work of art, an object of consumption to be sold in the marketplace to vulgarians, becomes proof of uncompromising artistry. Baudelaire's Cramer, "a man known for his brilliant, artistic failures," represents, even more than an "unemployed Hercules," "the God of impotence," a phrase which ironically underscores his greatness (51:I, 553).[53] The moment he begins to produce—a work on the gospels and a treatise for industrial use—Cramer ceases to be a dandy.

It was, however, also an age-old aristocratic axiom that a man could write if he appeared not to take his writing seriously. In a society of peers who shared the antiutilitarian, antibourgeois assumption, this fiction could easily be maintained by rejecting professionalism and financial gain, and by treating art as a gratuitous game. On this basis, Scudéry distinguishes between the man of letters and the honnête homme who writes as a "charming diversion" for himself and his friends, but never for the masses (454:III, pt.2, 1083, 1087). Accordingly, Saint-Evremond characterized his works as *bagatelles* which helped him while away the time (439:III, 62). Since Plato and Aristotle were *honnêtes gens*, in Pascal's eyes, it followed that "they amused themselves in creating their *Laws* and their *Politics*; they wrote them for fun" (393:578, #533). As aristocratic play, honnête art emulated the example set by Montaigne's *Essais* and avoided the meticulous constructions for which bourgeois pedants were noted. "I am not interested in putting the contents of this work into a set order," writes Méré at the beginning of a late essay, "or in making careful distinctions between the subjects that come to my mind; ... such obvious procedures are suitable only to professional pedagogues and I am not one of those; my only method is to follow a natural order, sometimes even according to my personal whims and tastes" (340:III, 103). Refusing pedantic distinctions and constructions to follow his superior, whimsical taste, Méré was exemplifying the ideal that Saint-Simon laid down for himself and for elite society: "no trace of the poet ... every mark of the honnête homme" (440:I, 623).[54]

Under the influence of Byron, dandy-writers assumed in their own works a stance that was even more exclusive and nonchalant than that of the honnête homme. Typical is Stendhal's expressed annoyance that his "reveries" would be read by all that "human rabble" (484:XXIV, 216); his proclaimed desire for no more than one hundred readers (482:328), or his famous dedication "To the Happy Few." Similarly, Barbey addressed his treatise on dandyism to a handful of unknown appreciators, as if for the members of Montaigne's elite: "He wrote this little bit of a book without authorial pretensions ... solely for his own pleasure and that of the thirty people, those unknown friends which one can never be sure of and never boast of having in Paris without enormous conceit" (38:IX, 216). Barbey's refusal to call himself an author, his modest characterization of his lengthily researched treatise as a tiny and pleasurable book, reenacts the standard pose of the honnête homme, but with the added hostile implications that such anachronistic attitudes carried in the nineteenth-century context. More than the substance of such statements, however, it is the tone of dandyistic texts, after Byron's *Don Juan*, that communicated aristocratic disdain. Casual or loose structure, coupled with narrational impertinence, irony, and cynicism are, as Prévost and Carassus have shown, the principal elements of an authorial dandyism that refuses to take one's own work seriously (408; 109). And yet, this stance was not uniformly maintained: at other times, the very same writers underscored their profound seriousness. Whereas in *Namouna*, Musset treats art as an amusing pastime, in *Les Nuits* he idealizes it as the most sublime and painful endeavor. And if Baudelaire declared that he had poured into *Les Fleurs du mal* all of his passion and loathing, he also dismissed it as an "essentially useless and absolutely harmless [book] which was written," he said, "solely for my own amusement and to exercise my passion for obstacles" (51:I, 181).[55] Whether the dandy-writer dismisses his writing as diversion and love for obstacles, or whether he exalts it as a serious agon, he is laying down a double challenge—to the bourgeois perception of the literary work as a commodity for consumption, but primarily to the archbourgeois notion of "work" itself.

Leisure and War: The Problematic "Repos du Guerrier"
The aristocracies of dandyism and honnêteté were determined to exemplify what Veblen calls "conspicuous leisure," the deliberate abstention from all recognized forms of labor as an essential sign of superiority (512). That writers on honnêteté and dandyism did their utmost to present their literary productions as aristocratic leisure and not bourgeois labor did not, however, prove to be sufficient or satisfactory. Balzac, for example, tried to reconcile through paradox the potential contradiction between art and leisure by classifying the artist as "an exception: his idleness is work and his work leisure" (22:42). The author of *Traité de la vie élégante* looks forward to the day when "the idle," in his extended meaning of that term, "will no longer be fetishes but veritable gods" (p. 56). In this arrogant perspective, the dandy, *l'oisif* (p. 57;

21:II, 28), is even more exalted than a god; he enjoys his *repos* "without ever having labored" (22:41).[56]

Extolling the glories of *l'oisiveté*, Scudéry delineates her own fantasy of omnipotence that challenges the prerogatives of divinity: "If indolence could provide this blessed *repos*, which is so great a pleasure, why then would it be such a bad thing for me to enjoy it in peace?" asks Amilcar in *Clélie*. "Why, I ask, would you criticize me for praising and loving idleness, and for preferring it to work? After all, is there anything more pleasurable than having nothing to do and doing everything one wants?" (454:IV, pt.i, 55). Such idleness and indolence, argues Amilcar, is the only condition befitting an honnête homme: "A *galant homme* of leisure is a philosopher who does nothing because there is nothing in the world worthy of his attention; he is a man who, seeking wisdom in different ways from ordinary men, seeks only pleasure, without concern either for the public good or for the hundreds of things that cause all life's turmoil. He is happier . . . than those ambitious and ever-diligent people with all the honors that they acquire through ceaseless efforts" (IV, pt.1, 56). Whereas Amilcar, in a peculiar amalgam of worldly and stoic views, distinguishes between the *oisif* and the *fainéant*, an odious type who lacks both heart and mind, Méré proposed the archetypal *fainéant* as the model of the honnête homme: "There have always been certain *fainéants* without an occupation, who were not, however, without merit; they thought only of living well and looking debonair. It may well be from such people that we have inherited this essential word. They usually have gentle dispositions and tender hearts; they are proud and courteous, daring and modest, neither miserly nor ambitious . . . ; their only aim is to spread joy everywhere and their greatest concern is to merit esteem and win affection" (340:III, 70).[57] Although a dandy-writer might have transcoded Méré's benevolent honnête homme into a figure of malevolence, he would nevertheless have agreed fundamentally that leisure was the prime condition for the exaltation and preeminence of the self.

Leisure is not, however, an unproblematic mode of life, as Montaigne had discovered. To reject the activities that define traditional notions of human esteem is to invite confrontation with the existential nothingness of the self. Under such a dispensation, pleasant leisure may well degenerate into that painful state called *ennui*. Whether it refers to the *taedium vitae* or the Horatian *cura*, that "agitated indolence which torments us" (*Epistles*:I, xi, 29), whether it signifies superficial boredom or profound metaphysical *Angst*, ennui is the inner psychological equivalent of the aggressiveness which the aristocrat has always turned against the society without. It involves a microcosmic psychomachia of which aristocratic behavior, in its varying degrees of hostility, is the macrocosmic projection. The intrusion of ennui sets the stage for that "other scene," the inner space of the self as the ground of tension and strife.

"At the same time on the same day one can be amused and bored by the same thing. Extended pleasures cease being pleasurable" (455:57–58). The life of pleasurable leisure cannot evade the cruel dialectic which Scudéry underscored in her significantly entitled essay, *De l'ennui sans sujet*. Nor could the vast array of splendid pastimes in La Bruyère's description of the Sun King's court forestall the destructive presence of ennui: "Men are bored in the end by the very things that enchanted them in the beginning: they would forsake *the table of the Gods*, and with time, lose their taste for *divine nectar*" (286:339, #145). Even among the king's favorites, as Mme de Maintenon observed, "there is nothing quite like the ennui that consumes them" (317:170–71). In Pascal's grim, relentless perspective, all forms of worldliness owe their existence to the chronic need for dealing with the terror and pain of human emptiness. Honnêteté, falling into the global category of Pascalian *divertissement*, becomes an "activity," which, like all secular (pre)occupations, unconsciously aims at distracting humanity from the spectacle of its fundamental, universal misery. Without such diversion, leisure would open into the paradigmatic abyss of Pascalian *repos*, not that suprahuman serenity to which all beings aspire in emulation of the divine, but an intolerable state of suspended animation, of total inactivity: "Nothing is so unbearable to man as complete *repos*, without passions, without preoccupations, without diversions, without work" (393:586–87, #622). This *repos* makes man experience "his nothingness, his desolation, his inadequacy, his dependency, his powerlessness, his emptiness. Forthwith, there will rise up from the depths of his soul ennui, melancholy, sadness, grief, vexation, despair" (#622).[58] And thus does this *repos* lead inevitably to ennui and, in desperation, to a resumption of *divertissement*. Although Pascal never labeled honnêteté a *divertissement*, he did insist that this secular ideal could never make man fully happy because it veils over the truth of human nature and the human condition (pp. 552, #426; 584, #597). Not surprisingly, then, the unfinished apologia of Jansenist belief that he addressed to an anonymous individual, who may have been Mitton, Méré, or some hypothetical, imaginary prototype of honnêteté, sets forth a purposefully terrifying picture of the human condition caught up in the vicious cycle of *repos* > *ennui* > *divertissement*.[59]

The *mondain* treatise, by comparison, does not deal with ennui as a problem inherent in the ideal of honnêteté. The term, where it appears, refers to various destructive behavioral signs. Aside from boredom, which satires on *préciosité* had branded as *malhonnête*, depression, melancholia, or grief are, for Méré as for Faret, negative signs to be repressed or eliminated at all costs from the manifest self: "above all, he must take care never to display unhappiness" (188:51; 340:II, 49–50).[60] But the internal, and more global connection between ennui and honnêteté suggested by the *moralistes* can be deduced from the re-presentation of the Pascalian cycle in the texts of *mondain* writers like Méré and Saint-Evremond, and particularly from their defense and valorization of the *divertissement* that Pascal had condemned. Because he believes that God alone can be his own source of felicity, Saint-Evremond welcomes *divertissement* to avoid ennui: "If we are to live happily, we should not think too much about life; but rather get out of ourselves often and . . . avoid confronting our own misfortunes. *Diversions* are so called for the *diversion* they create from trying and painful subjects . . . : which is proof enough that it is difficult to overcome the hardships of our condition by strength of will but that, if we are clever, we can ingeniously get around them" (438:IV, 12–13). And Méré, who compared "a profound *repos*" to a death-like torpor and apathy, argued that "if we seek diversion with a little care and a lot of casualness we can find the cure without even knowing it" (339:561, 418).[61] Although Méré would never have reduced the subject of his life's work to a "diversion," his and other *mondains'* conscious avoidance of ennui through diversionary activities may be considered a fundamental element in the impetus toward honnêteté.

On an axis that differentiates the repressed from the acknowledged, theorists of dandyism, unlike the *mondains*, explicitly traced the psychic impulse underlying their ideal to a demoralizing leisure. "Dandyism," proclaimed Barbey, "is the product of a bored society" (38:IX, 255). In its most salient literary manifestations, this ennui was a form of *Weltschmerz*, which Musset, speaking for his entire generation, had called *le mal du siècle*: "Condemned to *repos* by the rulers of the world, delivered over to vulgarians of all kinds, to idleness and ennui, the young saw those foaming waves ebb away for which they had readied their arms. All these anointed gladiators felt deep within their soul an unbearable misery" (367:III, 71–72). In fictional texts, as in Musset's *Confession*, the causal relation between ennui and dandyism becomes a topos. Eugène Sue's Arthur, for example, attributes his dandyism to "an indefinable . . . imperious need to occupy my restless, chronically discontented spirit, to search for . . . some unforeseen accident that could free me from the bleak and painful apathy that crushed me" (489:II, 11–12). For Fromentin's Olivier d'Orsel, dandyism would seem to be a militant response to ennui and that related ubiquitous monster, vulgarity: "Do you know my greatest concern? To kill ennui. Whosoever renders this service to humanity would be the true slayer of monsters. Vulgarity and boredom. In their entire mythology those uncouth pagans imagined nothing as insidious or terrifying. They are very much alike: both are ugly, flat, and pale, although multiform, and both give an image of life that is enough to disgust you from the day you are born. Vulgarity and boredom are inseparable, moreover, a hideous couple that not everyone can see. Pity those who catch sight of them too early! *I* have known them always" (200:241–42). Although the disgust, the crushing apathy, and the unbearable misery that these dandies describe fall within the semantic range of Pascalian ennui (284:662), the term also refers to those complementary, intensely personal longings for the infinite and for nothingness specific to the Romantic sensi-

102

bility. Thus dandyistic ennui included what Musset described as "a rejection of everything on heaven and earth, which you might call disenchantment or, if you like, *desperation*" (367:III, 74). Gautier's Albertus, however, points to another component of ennui, an overwhelming feeling of staleness, unrelieved even by the gamut of human experience, which the common man can never hope to experience, much less have the discrimination to reject (205). The ugliest monster in Baudelaire's "infamous menagerie of our vices," ennui "would gladly make a wreckage of the earth/ and swallow the universe in a yawn" (51:I, 6).[62]

With a distinctly Romantic penchant for *delectatio morosa*, the dandy valorizes, seeks, articulates and displays the ennui that the honnête homme had devalorized and repressed. Because this tendency was so widespread, Barbey could comment sarcastically that "the *gens d'esprit*" of his own "fascinating times had stolen the capacity for boredom from the fools who were once its exclusive possessors" (38:XI, 13). Whether out of boredom or melancholia or some anxiety-ridden combination of the two, the dandy exhibits ennui as a sign of exquisite sensibility, and ultimately uses it as an instrument of conquest. Such is the lesson Julien Sorel derives from Prince Korasoff's remarks on the art of manifest boredom: "You have the look of a Trappist . . . you are overdoing the principle of graveness. . . . A melancholy air can never be good form; what you need is a bored air. If you are melancholy, it means that you lack something, that something has gone wrong. *That's a sign of inferiority.* If you are bored, on the other hand, it means that the person who has failed to please you is inferior" (487:I, 590).[63]

The dandy is not troubled by the ostensible contradiction between the reality of ennui and its affectation, between a painful inner state and a deliberate pose. As Baudelaire reminds us: "the dandy is blasé or pretends to be, for reasons of strategy and caste" (51:II, 691). Artifice or sincerity, the source is irrelevant; what matters is the effective production and emission of the sign in the pursuit of superiority. For ennui, as sign and/or catalyst, triggers a determined and sometimes desperate quest for new sensations with heroic overtones. Some dandies seek escape from ennui in the underworld, while others pursue the sensations of sadism; as

103

Balzac's Count de La Palférine explains: "You feel a perpetual afternoon ennui. You are idle, you do harm rather than do nothing" (19:VI, 829).[64] Still others turn to alcohol and drugs. Brummell, according to Barbey, often experienced "the thrill of that other life which lies at the bottom of potions, which beats faster, resonates, and dazzles" (38:IX, 251). Although Baudelaire in *Les Paradis artificiels* extolled the vitalizing pleasures of alcohol and warned against the destructiveness of hashish, the attraction to drugs, which culminates in Gautier's exclusive Club des Haschichiens, underscores the dimensions of a quest most richly expressed in the odyssey of Des Esseintes.[65] He creates sensations never before experienced, and yet, not even his most imaginative experiments, whether with perfumes, foods, jewels, flowers, lights, furniture, or sex, can remedy his incurable ennui.

The dandy's quest for freedom from the curse of ennui assumes Sisyphean dimensions, which, by definition, obviate any lasting solution. As Barbey put it, dandyism "only half escapes . . . the ennui of this idle existence" (38:IX, 251). The dandy can never completely escape from ennui, nor does he really try, since to admit satisfaction and accept gratification is to valorize forces both outside and within the self which essential dandyistic narcissism must militantly deny. Ennui may be a monster, but for the dandy, heroism lies in living with it rather than in slaying it. Ennui, declares Barbey, "is the basis of everything and for everyone, all the more so for the soul of a dandy. As someone said very cleverly but very sadly: Dandies surround themselves with all of life's pleasures, but like a stone that gathers moss, without being affected by the coolness that covers it" (IX, 312, #27). In Barbey's metaphoric stone, we may see the obstacle which the dandy deliberately interposes between his perfect self and an imperfect world. Writers like Barbey saw in this defiant stance the substance of a new kind of heroism: "the hero of idle elegance—the dandy hero" (p. 308). In a profoundly unheroic world, this form of heroism was the only one left.[66]

The heroic lesson that dandyism drew from the problem of ennui was derived by honnêteté from repressing and sublimating the problem itself. The ability to conceal all traces of melancholy, grief, or boredom was considered a victory over the self. And as

Self-Assertion and Metaphors of War

Scudéry pointed out, "[it is] perhaps more glorious to conquer oneself than to conquer others" (454:II, pt. 1, 471).[67] Because the one was so clearly predicated on the other, Méré could dub the honnête homme as superior to any hero esteemed by the world (340:III, 90). That the seventeenth-century aristocrat ostensibly overcame the ennui of a life of leisure, and that his nineteenth-century counterpart refused to, should not obscure the more essential secrecy with which both revealed to the world only those traits required to captivate and dominate. Uselessness, whatever its problematic consequences, was a sign enlisted in a strategy to confound and exclude the profane and the productive.

In its most meaningful implication, the systematic uselessness of the honnête homme and the dandy afforded the necessary privacy and retreat for cultivating those rarefied forms of appearance and manners which were the vouchers and the trophies of "conspicuous leisure." The privileged enclosures in which the honnête homme and the dandy grew and triumphed contained the secrets that had to be grafted onto the self—in the last analysis, the superior man's only decisive weapon. Rejecting the extrinsic tokens invoked by traditional aristocracies to justify their claims to eminence—rank, wealth, professional praxis and prestige—the honnête homme and the dandy mobilized all the physical and mental resources of the self into sign-producing strategies geared to mastery over the adversary. Combining an agonistic stance with what Caillois calls *simulacre* (107), this heroic self-mobilization would emerge as nothing less than self-creation. Leisure, the condition *sine qua non* of merit and beauty, was to be put to the service of a noble and ennobling *poiesis* in which self-selected and select human beings were to figure both as the principle of form and the stuff of content.

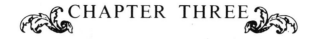

CHAPTER THREE

THE SELF-AS-ART
A Poetic Text and Its System

> No longer the *artist*, he has himself
> become *a work of art*.
>
> Nietzsche, *The Birth of Tragedy*

"**W**e know of certain people," wrote Morvan de Bellegarde, "who are consummate works of art" (63:176). La Rochefoucauld before him had marvelled at the rare combination of nature, chance, and method that seemed to underlie particularly seductive individuals: "it is as if they followed the rules of the great masters and produced perfect pictures" (294:522). This kind of person attunes "his air and manners to his facial expressions . . . his tone of voice and words with his thoughts and feelings" to create an imcomparable "harmony," a perfect "cadence" (pp. 508–9). Méré, who compared the ideal symmetries and proportions of words and deeds to "a kind of architecture," perceived that the captivating person of the honnête homme was "like a comprehensive painting" (340:II, 37, 35).[1] Two centuries later, the dandy was hailed as "a walking portrait" (38:I, 267). That he fashions a cravat as Phidias sculpted a block of marble (21:II, 49), that he infuses a mere glove with beauty proves incontrovertibly, insists Barbey, that the dandy is "an artist in all things" (38:XVI, 77), and even more, that "he creates the same effects with his person as others do with their works of art" (IX, 254). For Baudelaire, even the most admirably "productive" artists—Edgar Allan Poe, Eugène Delacroix, and Constantin Guys (51:II, 309–26, 691, 759)—were prime examples of dandies, who "have no function other than to cultivate the idea of beauty in their person" (II, 709).[2]

The Self-as-Art

This series of perceptions and appreciations, although they span two centuries and cover a variety of references, share the striking characteristic of describing human beings as if they *were* artifacts, not mere resemblances. When that passage from simile to metaphor is effected, when the honnête homme or the dandy is depicted as a painting, an architectural monument, a verbal or musical composition, he is being viewed as a specific kind of thing—a collection of signs situated at the crossroads where esthetics and semiotics intersect. Now although Saussure included "social phenomena"—military signals, symbolic rites, and the forms of etiquette—in the semiological enterprise, he specifically excluded art and all forms of individual and creative speech (*parole*) (448:33, 42).[3] Subsequent semioticians, however, have concentrated their efforts on the verbal, pictorial, musical, and kinetic arts, and their various permutations in the theater and cinema. Continuing in the tradition of the Russian formalists and the Prague Circle,[4] Juri Lotman in *La Structure du texte artistique*, to cite a recent example, conceives of art, in addition to folklore, mythology, and other manifestations of culture, as a "secondary modeling system"—a derivative and partial translation of some of the factors, structures, and devices of language (316:36–37). In so doing, Lotman applies to art the notion, most notably represented by Barthes, that all semiotic systems of any magnitude presuppose language in their formation and require it for their analysis (46:79–80; 46:8–9). Lotman would argue, along with Benveniste, that in comparison to the primacy of language, *the* model for all human semiotic activity, art represents an interpreted rather than interpreting, a derived rather than engendering, system (68:II, 50, 61–63). Works of art, and by extension, artistic genres, whether synchronically or diachronically perceived, even the artistic products of an entire epoch, constitute in Lotman's analysis texts of secondary language(s) (316:95–97, 390, 392). As the sum of all available data for the construction of a system, "the text," in Lotman's terminology, is the macrounit of all artistic semiotic systems.

The linguistic model underlying Lotman's theory of the secondary semiotic system lends itself particularly well to the analysis of honnêteté and dandyism, versions of an artistically modeled "artistocratic self" which exist for us through the medium of language. These are both systems of self-representation in which physical, visual, and kinetic substances play a major role; nonverbal elements, however, can be apprehended chiefly through linguistic representation and metalinguistic analysis which, to use Barthes's term, are nonisologous with substances inherent in the system itself (41:117). Enclosed in the *écriture* of the past, the representational system of the artistocratic self falls within the realm of what Barthes, after Hjelmslev, calls "connotative semiotics"—the study of secondary "languages" whose plane of expression is language itself (256:161; 41:163 ff.). Although the application of the linguistic model to nonlinguistic phenomena has caused considerable uneasiness (and for some, an impasse) in semiological research,[5] this methodological procedure must be used, even if it necessarily affects the perception and content of the message, in the absence of any other, more viable means of semiological investigation.[6] As Barthes repeatedly cautions, however, the linguistic model is only a propaedeutic or heuristic tool (41:82).[7]

In comparison with the primary semiotic system, the artistocratic self necessarily comprises a very narrow "language." The pertinent object of investigation, delimited through the medium of the self, inheres in three "natural substances" that are common to all (normal) human beings: a body, behavior—which includes physical (movement, gesture) as well as psychosocial manifestations (manner, manners)—and speech. Each of these "natural substances," however, can be divided into a number of categories and subcategories (i.e., body > face > eye) each of which in turn involves a number of paradigms (eye: shapes/colors/sizes). An individual may be conceived as a compendium of "choices" made from within each of these paradigms, choices which particularize the traits of his body, the way he acts and speaks. In this sense, an individual's self-representation may be defined as an act of personal "expression," or *parole* in contrast to the all-inclusive *langue*, the repertory of all possible traits that may be called upon or combined from among the three primary substances. The term "choice" thus extends beyond behavior and speech to those elements of the "natural" body that may be altered or transformed (e.g., weight, color of skin, hair, etc.). The ultimate choices that make up the self-as-art are determined largely by a society's values, its codes, and the arbitrary meanings it ascribes to various physical, behavioral, and verbal signs. These meanings, of course, have been rationalized and legitimized diachronically, and sometimes cross-culturally, in the bodies of knowledge and lore that we call, for example, physiognomy, etiquette, and verbal style. Thus, haircut, handshake, humor, or grammar are some of the signifiers that convey extensive information about individuals and help classify them within the spectrum of recognized social types. In addition to various behavioral codes and systems, there are available in every culture numerous objects among which an individual makes choices that also determine perceptions of the self. Dress and other forms of bodily ornamentation, for instance, which serve, as Flugel observed, both to hide the body and display it in altered form and extended size, increase the signifying capacity of the self (193:20–21, 34).[8] Virtually all societies possess languages of dress and decoration, small or larger sets of discrete signs that emit differing, even contradictory meanings. The relation between the signifiers (*beads, gray flannel suit*) and their signified (*hippy, businessman*), although ostensibly arbitrary when viewed from an aprioristic perspective, will appear less so a posteriori once it has been successfully rationalized and legitimized by the contextual culture. The choice of signs in each category of dress or ornamentation (i.e., necklace, suit of clothing) and their intercategoric combination constitute *sartorial speech.* As Barthes has shown in his *Eléments de sémiologie*, equivalent languages are also inherent in furnishings, foods, and other objects; these can be connected to the self and made to convey a range of meanings which varies with the richness of the semiological language.[9] Even the people with whom a man surrounds himself, or if he is powerful, those whom he appropriates, become self-reflexive sign conveyors; a king, as Pascal perceived, needs individuals who are recognized as his objects in order to convey the message of his royalty (393:504–5, #44). Although in themselves and on their surface extrinsic and intrinsic "properties" may appear limited in scope, they can, when selected and consciously organized in certain patterns, contribute to the development of an elaborately expressive "language," that is, *poetic speech.*

When Baudelaire speaks of the dandy as an artist "whose person radiates far more poetry than his works" (51:I, 553)[10] or when Balzac observes that his treatise on elegance contains the principles that render life poetic (22:63), they are not referring to a lyrical or ideological mode of feeling. Rather, they are underscoring the notion that the self-as-art is, by its very nature and definition, poetic as an operational mode, as a linguistic function. In Jakobson's classic definition, "the set (*Einstellung*) toward the message as such, focus on the message for its own sake, is the POETIC function of language" (272:356).[11] Just as with language in its poetic function, the physical appearance, dress, manners, and speech of the dandy and the honnête homme are not means conducive to pragmatic ends; they are autotelic, autonomous objects of contemplation (129:17). We may view this kind of message, with Riffaterre, as a self-contained, self-reflexive monument which imposes its mass, or more precisely its form, on the receiver's attention (429:30–31). The intentionality of this self-referring message, which is revealed in the metalinguistic analysis of qualities requisite to honnêteté and dandyism, promotes and provokes yet another level of response: it leads back systematically to the sender or producer, and foregrounds the power of his artistry.[12]

As the receiver focuses on this provocative message and the processes that account for its impact, multiple meanings accrue. On one level, there is the experience of what Jakobson terms "frustrated expectation," i.e., the message runs contrary to (or beyond) expectations, which are based on the codes (norms or contexts) to which it seemed likely to conform (272:363). Such deviations, perceived successively at various stages or in various parts of the message, create tensions and ambiguity, produce the unexpected and surprising, which are the very signs and preconditions of poeticity (272:370–71; 270:363–66; 316:120). Or, as the Russian formalists say, there occurs a defamiliarization or singularization, which inhibits automatic, habitual, and mundane responses and forces the receiver to new, unaccustomed, and heightened perceptions (318:176, 178). In trying to interpret poetic

111

messages, the receiver as decoder discovers unexpected possibilities and gains added, highly condensed information that
generates a "total reevaluation" of the significance of the whole
(272:377). Such "surplus" information, although keenly perceived,
often proves to be untranslatable or irreducible to discursive
terms; with Moles one might call this kind of message *esthetic*
information (348:124–69). On a more verbalizable level, "surplus"
information also derives from the addition of a connotational
stratum to the whole message and its marked units. The denota-
tional, the meaning normally ascribed to a sign, which in
Jakobson's schema constitutes the referential function (272:353), is
virtually eliminated; or as Eco observes in his analysis of the
poetic message, denotations are continually transformed into connotations (173:139; 174:274). The accumulation of new connections between a signifier and a connotational signified results in
what Lotman terms a new semantic (316:129–31).

In the elaboration of the self-as-art, units are selected from
heterogeneous physical, behavioral, and verbal areas—and for
Lotman heterogeneity itself is an aspect of artistic effect (pp.
383–84, 389)—and combined syntagmatically to create a new
structure. Because the units are selected only insofar as they are
conducive to poeticization, in combination their formal characteristics will necessarily reveal to the beholding eye the parallel-
isms, symmetries, and equivalences which are inherent in the
poetic function. In Jakobson's famous formulation: "The poetic
function projects the principle of equivalence from the axis of
selection into the axis of combination. Equivalence is promoted to
the constitutive device of the sequence" (272:358). Such equivalences have an intentional mnemonic function which prolongs the
effect of the message, a phenomenon that is both a sign and result
of poeticity (318:176). Repetition, convergence, and overdetermination are among the techniques that must be used to reinforce
and extend the impact of the poetic message of the honnête
homme and the dandy, since the aristocratic self *is* human, and in
contrast to what we usually call art, does not possess a durable or
immutable form.[13] On the other hand, the human, perishable
artifact does have at its disposal a variety of linguistic and nonlinguistic elements—intonation and gestures, for example—to insure

that it will be decoded in accord with the emitter's precise intent. For similar reasons, the phatic function, which prolongs or accentuates contact and communication (272:355), although not indispensable to art in the traditional sense, is essential to the self-as-art in the same way that it is essential to conversation among speaking subjects.

The notion of the poetic function, with its deviations, new connections, surplus expression, and connotational and nondiscursive content, illustrates how a relatively small number of signifiers in one language can produce a veritable battery of signs. From this perspective, the system of the artistocratic self, which represents a selection of signifiers in a set of languages—physical, behavioral, and verbal—may be viewed as a vast, polysemic text for semiological analysis. The specificity of this system, however, is not fully conveyed either by the concept of the poetic function[14] or even by Lotman's inclusion of collective bodies of work under the rubric "the artistic text." Since there exists a poetic speech common to all honnêtes hommes and to all dandies, which forms the abstract prototypes delineated in the métalinguistic part of the corpora, it would be more meaningful to speak here of an *idiolect*, and by extension an *écriture* in Barthes's sense: "the language of a linguistic community, that is, of a group of people interpreting all linguistic statements (*énoncés*) in the same manner" (41:93). This idiolect does not evolve haphazardly, like "natural languages," from mass usage, but emanates from a particular group, in this case the writers on honnêteté and dandyism, who consciously elaborate a code and frame the rules for its articulation. Just as the metalinguistic texts spell out the code to which any single artistocrat must be referred, so too does each individual, like any other esthetic message, give insight into its own generating code (316:97). In keeping with the notion of an idiolect, the artistocratic self must display a sufficient number of elements in the code in order to be properly deciphered and identified as one of the idiolectic community, but at the same time, may emphasize certain features or introduce certain permissible variants. Each honnête homme or dandy must demonstrate his competence through mastery of the entire code, but must also create a personal performance. It is, in fact, that performance which will reveal his faults—and not merely his errors, as in language (46:220)—and will determine his merit in the eyes of others.

The intention to communicate a message is consistently emphasized in seventeenth-century metalinguistic texts, which analyze the optimal type of emission for insuring proper decoding and for eliciting the desired response(s). Considerable attention is devoted to the faculties necessary for deciphering signs, distinguishing the right from the wrong, the superior from the inferior, since members of the idiolectic community are always cast in the dual role of emitter and receiver. They are involved in the kind of two-way, reversible process which Mounin regards as a constitutive criterion of communication, but which art forms or secondary sign systems, by comparison, usually do not exemplify (365:89).[15] The picture changes, however, when the receiver stands outside the idiolectic community: as a human body which acts and speaks, s/he shares a common "language" with the emitter, but not a common code (the artistocratic idiolect). Although such a receiver is more germane to dandyism than to honnêteté, in neither system is the stranger to the semiotic enclave ever regarded as a crypto-analyst capable of reconstructing from the message the (secret) code that underlies and informs it. Nor is s/he granted the full prerogatives of a speaking subject, but merely the function of responding to the stimulus of the poetic message. That response, which the emitter can manipulate—modify or prolong—by a variety of strategies, may be instinctive and unknowing, but bears witness to the esthetic impact that the artistocratic self achieves both as message and as medium.

In comparison to language, the artistocratic idiolect, like most secondary semiological systems, is not characterized by what Martinet has called the phenomenon of double articulation (332).[16] Whereas language consists of a finite number of units of minimal significance (monemes), each of which can be subdivided into non-signifying, distinctive formal units (phonemes) that can be recombined to create millions of messages, art and other secondary systems are concerned only with signifying units; the non- or subsignifying, because they are not perceived, are not pertinent.[17] Unlike many other systems in which the identification of significant units poses major difficulties,[18] the metalinguistic texts of honnêteté and dandyism are specifically designed and even structured to define the principal signs. Although each semiological unit may require for its articulation one or several linguistic units, it can be classified according to the "substance of its expression"—the body, behavior, speech, dress, and other sign-conveying objects.

In this system, however, the relationship between signifier and signified implements a poetic rather than a merely linguistic mode. A signifier like a look or a slow gait is stripped of its referential or utilitarian meaning, and is contextually marked in such a way as to operate exclusively on a level where it transmits connotational and esthetic information. Function is consistently disjoined from sign as a precondition of poeticity. But unlike the prototypical poetic text, all signifiers in the system of the self-as-art are the "form of expression" for the "substance of the content" *honnête* or *dandyistic*, a signified for the idea of superiority. Each signifier, then, functions within the limits of a single binary opposition: it is $(+)$ or is not $(-)$ honnête or dandyistic; one assertion excludes the other. The metalinguistic corpus defines the signifiers than can or should emit the signified honnête or dandyistic—a taxonomic enterprise—and explores the degree to which any one signifier can be modified on the plane of expression without altering the substance of the content; the permissible morphological variants that still maintain the signified intact; the freedom of execution and performance that will produce no change in ultimate meaning.[19] The signifiers in the system, be they concrete (wig or hand) or abstract (grace or eloquence), thus fill an essential synecdochic function. They do not only convey connotational and esthetic information; they reveal the nature of the emitter. To the informed receiver, the part announces the whole.

The sign in this system goes beyond the tautological equation between signifier honnête/dandy = signified honnête/dandy to the proposition that signifier A or B or C^n = signified honnête/dandy = superior. A connection between a form and a content is established that is both arbitrary and nonarbitrary. Seen from an objective aprioristic perspective, the relation between the signifiers *vest*, *air*, or *irony* and the ultimate signified *honnête* or *dandyistic* is as arbitrary as the relation between the signifier m-a-n and the idea *man*. But whereas in language, as Benveniste among others has argued, no individual is free to alter the necessary connections between signifier and signified (8:I, 49–55), in the system of the self-as-art those connections are unnecessary and alterable. Old signifiers are modified or eliminated and new ones are added with a deliberateness uncharacteristic of any but the most linguistically minded idiolectic communities. Seen from the a posteriori perspective already sketched out in "Pre-texts and Prototypes," these very same signs, like those of language, seem less arbitrary or even partially motivated because the link between a signifier and a signified has been rationalized and legitimized through time.[20] Tradition has, in fact, wholly dispelled the arbitrariness of such "universal" prepoetic signs of superiority as a beautiful face, grace, eloquence, and so on. The specific connections between a signifier and a signified which honnêteté and dandyism valorize constitute the particularly creative elements in these systems. Although such connections are rationalized in the metalinguistic texts, their unexpectedness contributes to their poeticity; were they perceived as wholly natural or conventional, they would have virtually no semiological or esthetic impact. As they are organized and emitted in the system of the self-as-art, the arbitrary complementarity of every signifier and signifed assumes a solidity and a solidarity that makes us perceive it as valid, necessary, poetic.

In combination, these relatively motivated signs are not necessarily emitted in a linear sequence. Whereas in ordinary language no two linguistic signs can be articulated simultaneously by one individual, the entire sign system of the artistocratic self could conceivably function at a single instant and be perceived in its entirety through visual, auditory, and subliminal senses. In this respect, the system bears a closer resemblance to painting and the other pictorial arts, which are spatialized, than to musical or verbal texts.[21] And yet, poetry, among all the verbal arts, "imposes a global perception" by virtue of its iconic and spatial components (150:175).[22] The system of the self-as-art, however, differs from even the most revolutionary of poems in that its signs are not emitted according to (or even in stylistic deviation from) a predetermined order or a preexisting grammar. A graceful walk, for example, need not be perceived before a particular sign of politeness in order for meaningful communication to occur. As Saussure reminds us, however, linguistic syntax provides only one of many syntagmatic models (448:188). With reference to the three types of relations between signs that Hjelmslev outlined—solidarity (two units necessarily imply one another); simple implication (only one necessitates the other); and combination (neither necessitates the other) (256:53–61)—the signs in the system of the artistocratic self could be said to function for the uninformed receiver by combination, and for one who possesses the code by a type of solidarity. In the latter instance, perception of one sign begins a generative contextual process which creates the expectation that other signs in the system will emerge, a justified expectation since the presence of an emitter involves at the very least signs of physical appearance. Unlike some semiological systems (i.e., the code of traffic signals) this one emits a continual chain of signs with no nonsignifying space in between (41:137). Of course, the contextual pressure of one sign on all others to signify honnêteté or dandyism may not be realized. Although neither the seventeenth- nor the nineteenth-century metalinguistic corpus specifies the required number of signs to identify the emitter as an honnête homme or a dandy—and that omission may be consciously related to the lifelong extension and comparative "unboundedness" of this poetic text[23]—the greater their number, the more overdetermined and incontrovertible the message. The syntagmatic model that operates here is, therefore, not simply paratactic. Like a poetic message, which forms a whole that is more than the sum of its parts, the syntagm is cumulative, incremental, and in that sense, architectural, monumental.[24]

At the juncture of its syntagmatic and paradigmatic planes, the system of the self-as-art reveals the relative value of its constituent signs. Each of the primary categories—body, dress and ornamentation, behavior, speech—and their various subcategories (paradigms) contains varying significant units, which may be equal in value or hierarchically scaled. In some paradigms or categories, the number of units may simply reflect the adequacy or inadequacy of language to accommodate the semiological specificity of the signs and the esthetic information that they carry. Concrete objects, like an eye or a cravat, require only one linguistic sign as their signifier, whereas signs of a more abstract or spiritual nature, which are more likely to defy linguistic adequation, tend to generate multiple signifiers—*négligence, grâce, air aisé; civilité, politesse, urbanité; impertinence, insolence.* Whether the number of signs depends on a generative, analogical process, or on the neutralization of differential variants, there exist in the system semiological isomorphs and semantic isotopes whose very redundancy operates with an emphatic effect to enrich a particular paradigm or category. Within each system, some paradigms or categories will prove to have greater value and will be regarded as more significant than others. These differential valuations, which accrue along the length of the syntagm, converge to fashion the "texture" of the aristocratic self and to reveal significant variations between honnêteté and dandyism. Since the categories and the aims of each are substantially the same, the more important of these variations will take place not on the level of the signifier or the ultimate signified (aristocratic, superior), but rather in those subtle intermediary planes where the emitter determines the precise form of the signifier's expression and injects particular connotational and esthetic nuances into the sign.

In the last analysis, however, the variations between the honnête homme and the dandy cannot simply be ascribed to causes intrinsic to the systems themselves. No semiological system, after all, evolves independently of the values or the ideology of the culture which produces it. As Barthes observed in *Le Degré zéro de l'écriture*, no poetic text, even the most deliberately iconoclastic, can ever escape the contemporaneous parameters of the theory, conception, rules, or modes of *écriture* (41). The conception of the esthetically appealing and the beautiful, as well as the prevailing artistic principles and rules in seventeenth- and nineteenth-century France, necessarily determine, both paradigmatically and syntagmatically, the signs and the system of the self as poetic text in each period. This does not reduce the honnête homme and the dandy to mere locus of representation and re-production. As with the interrelation between *langue* and *parole*, the seventeenth- and nineteenth-century codes contain a finite number of possibilities out of which the systems of honnêteté and dandyism were constructed, and these systems in turn affect the shape, scope, and hierarchical structure of the contemporaneous esthetic codes. Although every culture harbors a diverse number of such codes at any one time, developed and dominant codes will be found side by side with peripheral and developing ones. For purposes of simplication, we can speak, with Lotman, of an artistic text as the manifestation of an *esthetic of identity*, which supports and reconfirms the dominant artistic values in the culture, in comparison to an artistic text as the manifestation of an *esthetic of opposition*, aimed at supplanting and/or destroying the prevailing cultural hegemony (316:392–406). From this perspective, the honnête homme may be said to exemplify an *esthetic of identity*, the dandy an *esthetic of opposition*. In the metalanguages of each period, we can call the esthetics of honnêteté, *l'art de plaire;* that of dandyism, *l'art de plaire en déplaisant*.

L'ART DE PLAIRE

"In order to become and be known as an honnête homme, the most important factor, in my view," writes Méré, "is to discern in all things the best means of captivating others (*plaire*), and to be able to put them into practice" (339:55). The comprehensive art of honnêteté predicates knowledge and praxis of a single element, the sign *plaire*. Inversely, the same sign comprises the chief means for perceiving the many manifestations of honnêteté: "In whatever form it appears it is always captivating (*plaît*), and that is essentially how we can recognize its presence" (340:I, 75). This capacity, whose pertinence transcends the domain of sociability, surpasses all conventional notions of merit and virtue. The cleavage may be gauged by the strikingly disparate messages that signs emitted by two individuals (probably the Count de Grammont and the Maréchal de Créquy) conveyed to Saint-Evremond: "One of them had all sorts of appealing qualities. . . . He seemed to have the innate ability to captivate everyone. The other had so many fine qualities that he could be sure of winning approval wherever people take any account of virtue. The first never failed to draw people to him. The second was a little on the proud side, but it was impossible to refuse him one's esteem. In a word: people took pleasure in succumbing to the first one's *insinuations*, but they were sometimes annoyed that they could not avoid being impressed by the other's merit" (438:IV, 128–29). Even where merit (or virtue) does not have to overcome such resistance, its impact is of a different order from the pleasurable seduction wrought by the signs of the aristocratic self. "Those who know of nothing more appealing than virtue," Méré writes to one of his disciples, "have not felt those piquant charms that are apparent in your person and your slightest gesture. They have a secret power that would confound the highest wisdom" (339:350).[25] In this kind of superiority, visible signs (*are apparent*) overlay a rich connotational stratum (*those piquant charms*) but they generate an even deeper process whose workings remain ambiguous, mysterious, untranslatable in discursive terms.

The *secret power*, which Méré evokes to describe the effects of the self-as-art, replicates the fundamental notion of seventeenth-century esthetics. The capacity, hidden behind the surface signs, to penetrate the receiver imperceptibly to the very core is the functional analog of a paradigmatic ability to emit a poetic message powerful enough to "stun, enrapture the beholder" (72:127), enmesh him in invisible bonds (p. 169), "grab him by the guts" (348:I, 883). Synonymous with *enchanter* (<*incantare*) and *charmer* (<*carmen*) in their etymological sense, the connotational semes of *plaire* suggest ideas of magical control over the other. Alongside this bewitching power, the rules of esthetic codes become irrelevant. This is the essential argument that Guez de Balzac used to defend Corneille's ability to *plaire* against the mechanistic strictures of Georges de Scudéry:

> Since the French poet's *Cid* has had such an appeal . . . wouldn't it be true to say . . . that he has achieved his aims even though he didn't take the Aristotelian route or use the clever methods outlined in the *Poetics*? But you say, Sir, that he has dazzled people's eyes and accuse him of spells and magic. . . . You yourself will admit that if magic were allowed it would be an excellent thing. It would really be wonderful to be able to perform miracles in all innocence, make the sun come out at night, prepare banquets without victuals or servants, change oak leaves into money, and glass into

diamonds. This is what you are criticizing in the author of *Le Cid*, who admits having violated the rules of art, and thus forces you to admit that he possesses a secret more effective than art itself; and since he does not deny having taken in the entire court and nation, the only conclusion that you can draw from all this is that he is cleverer than the entire court and nation, and that a deception which takes in so great a number of people is not a fraud but a conquest (204:454).[26]

Fraud or deception is a charge to be leveled, not against one who casts poetic spells, but rather, against the producer of obvious, showy signs which can only bewitch vulgarians. Anything but magical, "ostentatious ornaments . . . are only good for flim-flam" (340:II, 72); their emitter is automatically "suspected of a certain falseness" (339:296–97). The ultimate model for esthetic conquest, however, is to be found beyond magic in the domain of sexuality. The sustained vocabulary of entrancement and bewitchment which defines Corneille's poetic strategy builds on the same erotic paradigm that informs Méré's vision of Cleopatra's "conquest" of Caesar: "That alluring Queen of Egypt had little *éclat*. . . . . She wasn't so beautiful that one was instantly taken aback; but when one looked closely, there was a magic about her: it was by her subtle and exquisite manner that she held Caesar for three or four years as if he were under her spell" (340:II, 46). More than a metaphor, *plaire* involved a simultaneous erotization of the poetic process and poeticization of the erotic process through which the honnête homme, like Corneille, like Cleopatra, captivated their respective victims in the manner of a latter-day Circe, "the way a beautiful enchantress beguiles her lovers" (339:80).[27]

In the aristocratic system of seduction, aggression, usually associated with masculinity, yields to the proverbial, circuitous, serpentine *insinuation* of the female. Working subtly beneath the surface of the other, the emitter "winds his way in and makes his presence felt imperceptibly" (441:98–99), achieving the powerful and lasting effect of "a lingering poison or a magic spell" (340:III, 136). In this type of ("feminine") communication, the superior man shows pliancy and accommodation, writes La Rochefoucauld, as he develops the strategic implications contained in *insinuation:* "he knows how to find out and follow the mood and disposition of those he deals with, and by attending to their interests, he advances and establishes his own" (294:527). F. de Caillières advocates a similar strategy composed of "certain detours, seasoned with certain accommodations, designed to control without their knowing it the minds of those to whom he seems to defer" (103:20–21). Consumed by the receiver, this ambiguous message, which contains surface and subsurface signs, manifest as well as connotational and nondiscursive "esthetic" information, furthered the artistocrat's self-reflexive goal "to be first . . . in the hearts and minds of those around us" (340:I, 72). This ultimate of artistocratic intentions required the continual emission of "almost imperceptible things" (pp. 14–15), an infinite number of nuances (78:XXXII[1925], 452) injected into signs of physical appearance, manner, manners, and speech, which Méré described as "hidden qualities whose source cannot be discovered. They are also the most dangerous. It is the people who have them that win our hearts over. We never forget them because they never lose their appeal" (340:II, 17).[28]

The Body as Signifying Surface

"It is the face that dominates our outward appearance," Faret notes; "that is the part of us which pleads, threatens, flatters, and expresses our joys or sorrows, and in which others read our thoughts before our tongue has had time to express them. The eyes perform that speech function particularly well, and it is through them that our soul flows very often out of us and bares itself to those who are there just waiting to steal its secret" (188:94). Even the unsophisticated Faret conceives of the face, but especially the eyes, as a signifying system that functions more rapidly than human speech. Faret still operates, however, on the age-old view of physical signs as the visible counterpart to inner spiritual qualities—the eyes, for example, as mirrors of the soul. More subtle analysts are aware that the decoder may easily unearth secrets that should remain concealed, and urge the honnête homme to manipulate his facial expressions so that only the desired messages are conveyed: "Try to compose your face in such a way that at all times, in all places, and all kinds of encounters only those inner feelings will be visible which are the most favorable and advantageous to you" (329:166). Far from being a mere datum of nature, a predetermined or immutable set of physiognomic signs, the face is asked to operate like the very stuff of art, malleable matter than can be molded to perfection.[29]

Although Méré ascribed specific and arbitrary meanings to individual physical features, he was primarily concerned with the generalized *Gestalt* designated by the comprehensive term, *la mine*. Only two among the possible *mines* were adequate to the strategy of the honnête homme—*la grande mine* and *la bonne mine*. The first of these, as the adjective *grand* suggests, was appropriate only to the very "great"—emperors, kings, princes, and lords—whose rank and life style could sustain physiognomic signifiers that connoted preeminence. Those, however, who on the referential plane lacked the correlative station and wealth would necessarily be compromised by a *mine* "that gives a hint of greatness ... someone who is not a great lord but is unfortunate enough to have the look of one must try to get rid of it; at first it may fool people, but in the end they will despise him" (340:II, 21). Writing to an aspiring honnête homme with *une grande mine*, Méré thus emphasized the need for mutation and muting: "You are more resplendent ... than I would like; you should try to correct that" (p. 21).[30] His expressed preference for *la bonne mine* is rooted in the notion that the less imposing is the more alluring, as the case of Cleopatra demonstrated: she had little *éclat*, but enormous *charme* (p. 46). Accordingly, Méré ranked signifiers of physical substance below those of spiritual source. The beauty of women and the *bonne mine* of men, he warned, will always run a poor second to a certain "cleverness and turn of mind that can take care of everything as long as there is nothing offensive about the person" (p. 46). Although extraordinary physical beauty might have seemed a necessary feature of the self-as-art, it was in fact considered a negative sign in honnêteté. "Beauty—at any rate, great or extreme beauty—might be useless and even harmful," writes Méré, "because it stifles and overwhelms. ... Besides, we are easily bored looking at only one thing; this kind of beauty always looks the same: after we have seen it once, we no longer find anything exciting about it" (p. 38). In this discriminating view, the uniformity of overwhelming beauty renders the initial excitement of its perception short lived, and eventually, shallow in its effect; superior by far is the understated kind of beauty "that one can scarcely see . . . that is hidden as if behind a veil" or "a cloud" (339:528–29).[31]

The system of honnêteté, like French classical esthetics, valorized those hidden and ambiguous forms of beauty, known as *les agréments*, for their extended and profound effect: "a great wealth of *agréments* cannot be exhausted; new ones are always emerging that we had not noticed. This is what revives our interest and keeps us from ever being bored" (340:II, 38). Referring to the precise qualitative difference between beauty (−) and *agrément* (+), La Fayette leans on the paradox that Nemours was "the most attractive and handsome man in the world" and that this was "the least admirable thing about him. What did set him above all others was his incomparable merit and an *agrément* in his mind, on his face, and in his movement which no one else had ever possessed" (290:10). It was *agrément*, not *beauté*, that accounted for the seductions of Helen of Troy; inversely, the *agréments* displayed by Aesop, compensating for his irregular features and proportions, made him far more attractive than the merely handsome Nero (340:II, 37, 46–47). In honnêteté, the physical signifier stands in permanent need of a spiritual, that is, a connotational dimension; when that is added, even ugliness and deformity lose their conventional meanings and become positive, indeed, poetic signs: "often, in fact, a deformed man proves to be more appealing than another who seems picture-perfect" (I, 19).[32]

The infusion of the spiritual into the physical as the principal support of significance is especially apparent in the generalized category which seventeenth-century writers, after Cicero, called "the eloquence of the body," a language so powerful and persuasive as to penetrate far beneath the resistant surface of the receiver. Balzac wrote of Maecenas that his physical eloquence "swept past the external senses in an instant and made its way to the soul, whose defenses had immediately crumbled" (28:452). Even in repose, the stance of the body could convey through semiological signs the subtle messages of delicacy, gaiety or seriousness (340:II, 14). But the essential sign emitted by the body, whether in action or in repose, was *grâce:* "It is a seasoning which lends appeal to a person's slightest gesture. . . . It is the beauty of action and repose which reveals itself in the perfect balance that the body observes, whether in motion or at rest; in the last analysis, it is a *certain air*, full of natural allurements and free of artifice, which accompanies the body's every stance, active or inactive, with the result that as our eye dwells on it, our mind simultaneously gives its tacit approval" (323:710). More than perfect bodily proportions, the multifaceted quality of *grâce* partakes of that indefinable "attic salt" (340:II, 39; 117:181) which makes any trait or gesture enticing; it sparkles like a "ray of Divinity" and "enraptures the eyes and hearts of all" (188:18, 20). Conversely, where *grâce* is lacking, all other signs of honnêteté lose their value. The Maréchal Saint-Luc "had in him the makings of six *honnêtes gens*," according to Tallemant des Réaux, "and yet one couldn't say that he was an honnête homme. . . . He did nothing with grace" (497:II, 113). In honnêteté, as in seventeenth-century esthetics, *la grâce*—"even more beautiful than Beauty itself" (291:II, 6)—ranks as a primary synecdoche for *ce qui plaît.*[33]

Closely related to *grâce* and *insinuation* in substance and importance, *l'air*, with its further connotations of lightness and immateriality, suggested the fluidity of a body that has no contours, of flesh made spirit. The soul of *la bonne mine*, as Méré dubbed it (340:II, 6), this *air* took numerous and redundant linguistic forms. As the antithesis of rigidity, angularity, and abruptness, *l'air aisé*, *libre*, or *dégagé* provided an autotelic sign for effortless, free-floating mastery. "People who attempt difficult things," writes Méré, "should go about it in such an easy manner that we are left with the feeling that it doesn't cost them any effort" (p. 32). Whereas constraint attests the novice's ignorance, ease, nonchalance, or *négligence* identifies a master of honnêteté (p. 121); thus no effort must be spared to acquire it and perfect it (pp. 20, 22). Even if the receiver should surmise the underlying effort, in other words, intuit the antithesis of the sign itself, the positive value of the message need not be lost. "Although we may sense the effort, as long as it is not visible it can do no harm," declares Méré, "for it is excessive zeal which is unappealing" (p.

125

34). Excessive zeal, like excessive visibility, is enough to negate the stature of self as poetic text.

When La Fayette wrote that the Duc de Nemours was always the exclusive center of attention because of an *air* that pervaded his person (290:11), she pointed to the impact of this single sign on all others. By the same token, shadings between this global *air* and other signifying units tended to blur. The difficulties encountered by those who tried to translate its multiple semiological properties into discursive terms produced, moreover, a number of linguistic variants homologous with *aisé, libre,* or *dégagé.* Although Vaumorières claimed that the meaning of *air* changed with each adjective or adjectival phrase appended to it (511:II, 2), in practice, the differences between *l'air noble, les airs des cours et du grand monde, l'air honnête, le bon air,* or *l'air* in general were so minimal that these discrete linguistic signs were semiologically isomorphic. In an effort to circumscribe the specific connotations of the neologism *le bon air* (340:I, 42), writers called upon *la bonne grâce* and *l'agrément.* For Bussy-Rabutin, *le bon air* was to *la bonne grâce* as the acquired to the natural, the beautiful to the pretty, and esteem to friendship (100:I, 333). But these distinctions parallel those that Méré established between *le bon air* and *l'agrément:* "*Le bon air* is immediately visible, it is more regular, more conventional. *L'agrément* is more ingratiating and sinuous, it goes right to the heart by more covert ways. *Le bon air* inspires more admiration, *l'agrément* more love" (340:I, 42–43). In a later essay, Méré describes two kinds of *bon air:* while one echoes his earlier definition, the other merges semantically with the qualitatively superior *agrément:* "The first and most common [kind of *bon air*] favors pomp and splash: the other is more modest and discreet. The first is closely allied with beauty, and I find that it soon becomes boring; but as for the other, which is less conspicuous, the more you contemplate it, the more you cherish it. In the first there is always something essentially false and illusory; the second is more real although more difficult to perceive and I feel that it approximates the power of *agrément* . . . it appeals most to people of sophisticated taste" (II, 23). In this accumulation of binary oppositions—pomp, splash/discreet, less conspicuous, difficult to perceive; illusory, false/real; becomes boring/cherish, appeals—Méré has encapsulated the paradox of the poetic function: the hidden is more real (and more captivating) than the visible. Emanating from the textual or physical body, this secret "esthetic" information is the highest form of eloquence.[34]

The Language and Speech of Adornment

Throughout the corpus of honnêteté, the proper sartorial signs, more than specific physiognomic or corporal ones, are said to "open doors" (188:91; 117:307). In 1688, La Bruyère still rehearses this cliché, but with considerable bitterness: "a piece of gold braid more or less will get you in or keep you out" (286:314, #71). Such signs may be especially arbitrary, and yet they provide the in-group with criteria for determining who has the necessary competence for admission. Now, at the height of the seventeenth century, the upper-class sartorial lexicon to which La Bruyère refers was, by any standard, extravagant, dazzling, at times fantastic. The military look of the 1630s—boots, sword, mustache—with its emphasis on the practical and the functional, had given way by 1665 to a highly ornamental, "feminized" style, marked by a blatant superfluity which was all the more significant. The doublet had been reduced to a minuscule vest that almost reached the armpits; but through it and over it billowed a bouffante shirt and a *rabat* that fell halfway down the back. The *rhingrave* looked like a full petticoat or apron (only a recent discovery has proved that it was a pair of breeches after all). Dazzling *aiguilletes* and gold and silver threads dotted this costume, while *canons* and *rubans* fell from shoulder to sleeve and from knee to shoe. Some nobles wore five or six hundred ribbons at one time, enough, as one commentator put it, for children to hide in (323:490). In this perspective, Pierrot's description of nobiliary attire in Molière's *Dom Juan* is probably free of exaggeration:

> What a lot of contraptions an' doohickeys those courtier fellows do put on themselves! I'd get lost in all o' that, I would, an' I had my jaw hangin' down watchin' it. . . . They got shirts that got sleeves that we could get inside of, you an' me, just the way we are. 'Stead o' breeches they got 'em a great big apron as wide as from here to Easter; 'stead of a doublet, a little old waistcoat that don't even

127

come down to their sole aplexus; 'stead o' neckbands, a great big lace neckerchief with four big linen tassels that hangs down over their stomach. Then they got other little neckbands at the end o' their arms, like, an' then great funnels o' lace on their legs, an' then on top o' all that such a lot o' ribbons, *such* a lot o' ribbons, it really makes you sorry for 'em. Why, they ain't even the shoes that ain't all loaded with 'em, right from one end to the other; an' the way they're fixed up, I'd sure as heck break my neck. (II.i)

With the exception of the small doublet, the elements of this costume were indeed expansive, as Pierrot's repeated use of *great big* suggests. Layer upon layer of clothing and ribbons enlarged the natural dimensions of the body; without the *canons, manchettes,* and *galands,* wrote Conrart, the Duc de Candale would be nothing more than an atom (323:491). Moreover, the ornate *talons rouges* with their high, block-like heels and squared-off toes gave the wearer a broad, strutting, even arrogant gait. But by far the most significantly expansive element of this attire was the wig. What had begun as mere compensation for natural defects with the addition of a few postiches became a consciously artificial sign that reached its most sumptuous and fantastic form in the *allongé* or full-bottomed *perruque* of the 1660s. Not only did it hide the face, it transformed it. "Courtiers," as La Bruyère critically remarked, ". . . have a countenance which is not clearly recognizable, but obscured and encumbered by a mass of hair that does not belong to them but which they prefer to their own, and weave into a covering for their head: it hangs halfway down their body, alters their features and prevents us from knowing a man by his face" (286:239, #74). A logical complement to the dimensions of the costumed body, the wig enlarged the powdered and perfumed face to leonine proportions. Capped off with a plumed hat, the seventeenth-century noble was larger than life itself.[35]

Implicit in the discourses and treatises on honnêteté, this sartorial code assumes particular significance within an absolutist monarchy, which from 1633 on tried to legislate the apparel of bourgeoisie and nobility alike. In 1660, for example, Louis XIV forbade the bourgeois gold and silver fabrics, embroideries, passementerie, and clasps (353:67). Within the nobility itself, the king made finer distinctions by granting his favorites permission, formally signed by the royal hand, to wear articles like the *justaucorps à brevet*. Such a sign flaunted the artificial connection between signifier and signified (46:270); radically but deliberately arbitrary, it highlighted the power of the ultimate sign maker, the Sun King. The arbitrariness and the dominance of these unnecessary and alterable signs did not escape La Bruyère's detection: "Ultimately we criticize this or that fashion which, however bizarre it may be, adorns and embellishes us while it lasts and from which we derive all the advantage we can hope for, namely to be attractive (*plaire*). It seems to me we should even admire the inconstancy and fickleness of men who successively attach the labels of *agréments* and *bienséance* to completely opposite things; who use in comedies and masquerades the same finery and ornaments that had once conveyed soberness and utter seriousness, and that so little time makes so much difference" (286:395, #12).[36] Nonetheless, because the right sartorial signs do provide essential embellishments, the part of wisdom is to conform to "the fashion which has been sanctioned by the most admired of the great and *honnêtes gens*, and which lays down the law for everyone else" (188:92). Nonconformity made no sense to Molière's Ariste in *L'Ecole des maris*:

> In clothes as well as speech, a man of sense
> Will shun all these extremes that give offense,
> Dress unaffectedly, and, without haste,
> Follow the changes in the current taste (I.i, 43–46).

Anything but a sign of heroism or artistry, sartorial originality was a contemptible attempt "to be noticed at all costs" (61:428). Or, as J. de Caillières put it some years earlier, emphasizing the connection between material signifier and spiritual signified, "The strangeness of a person's dress makes us rightly suspicious of his character" (106:204).[37]

Conformity did not reduce the significance of sartorial signs to zero, since the nobiliary code was in and of itself an idiolect that partook of *parole*, not *langue*. Conformity did not render one invisible; on the contrary it betokened membership in a caste which displayed signs qualitatively and quantitatively different from those of hoi polloi. There was no need to advertise superiority through originality when the costume of one's caste did so automatically. Within this idiolectic context, however, the honnête homme still had to distinguish himself from his peers. He could do so not through striking sartorial signifiers, but rather by the way in which he emitted them and the connotational semes that he injected. It was the poeticity of his own sartorial speech that determined his special worth. In the case of the Duc de Nemours, it was a style so personal that it could never be properly replicated: "he had . . . a way of dressing which was always copied by everyone but which remained inimitable" (290:10–11). This capacity to fashion and display signs of ornamentation with an indefinable *agrément particulier* constitutes what Méré claimed to be the first to call "elegance" (78:XXXI[1924], 494)—a quality which he attributed to an equally indefinable *négligence*: "It is almost like a woman who wears beautiful clothes and expensive finery which she does not bother to assemble meticulously. This lack of concern which smacks of greatness is proof enough that she attaches no importance to such things. I also think that the handsomest and whitest shirt is more becoming when slightly rumpled than if it hasn't a crease in it" (339:156). Artistic "negligence," as opposed to vulgar "neglect" (63:28), is, like *agrément* itself, more enticing because of its ambiguity and imperfection. It further connotes the artistocrat's superiority to the petty minds obsessed with their own splendiferous adornment.[38] Visible concern expressed through overly visible dress was counterproductive: "I have yet to meet a man on whom dazzling brilliance and magnificence looked good" (339:669). Like a painter who wants to portray his subject to greatest advantage, argues Méré, the honnête homme must not affix to his person "anything too dazzling that might cause our gaze or thoughts to dwell on it too long" (340:II, 41). Within the prescribed limits of the code, the honnête homme must aim, rather, for an understated simplicity, concretizing the dictum that less is more.[39] Blatant and understated, essential and trivial, normative and individualized—these were the mixed messages that the sartorial system of honnêteté conveyed.

The Self-as-Art

The Meaning of Manners

"Manners, which we dismiss as trivia, are often what determines whether men form a good or bad opinion of us: taking a little care to have pleasant and polished manners forestalls their negative judgments. It takes almost nothing to be thought proud, impolite, contemptuous, uncooperative: it takes even less to be regarded as the very opposite" (286:160, #31).[40] That the success of the system of self-representation depended on the most minute of signs, on virtual "nothings," was, for the honnête homme, an incontrovertible fact. These "nothings," however, were thought to partake of a finer substance than either the body or its adornments. In this system, manners, rather than concrete or physical signs, contained the spiritual qualities that served as an index of the artistocrat's heart and mind.

The global unit of significance in the discourse of sociability—what we traditionally call courtly behavior—was *civilité*, an unmotivated sign which drew its meaning from conventions rationalized through time. In Nicole's view, *civilité* is one of those "simple laws of decorum, whose authority originates in a consensus among people who have agreed to condemn those who do not obey them. . . . This is why we owe to those around us the civilities laid down by the *honnêtes gens*, even though they may not be governed by clearly stated laws" (375:I, 237–38). Despite this lack, *civilité* comprised both elementary and sophisticated rules designed to convey esteem and consideration. That message had to be successfully imprinted on the receiver's senses before it could reach the necessary core. "When we are not convinced by our senses that people like us and have regard for us," observed Nicole, "it is difficult for our heart to believe it or to believe it deeply. Now civility is a quality that does produce this effect on our senses and through the senses on our minds; if we do not show civility, this neglectfulness will produce a chilling effect in others which often goes from the senses right to the heart" (I, 241).

Although some writers treated *civilité* as synonymous with *politesse*, others, as the century wore on, tended to differentiate between the two by classifying the first as surface and the second as substance. For Bussy-Rabutin, *la politesse* "has greater solidity and range than *civilité*, which has only the outer trappings" (100:I,

334). Eventually, *politesse* became a generalized sign of spiritual and moral worth, *impolitesse* the unmitigated sign of worthlessness (60:9, 374). In Jacques Esprit's analysis, true *politesse* dwells in the soul and makes our "thoughts, predilections, and feelings *honnêtes* and *délicats*"; it is from the soul that *politesse* draws the honnêteté and *délicatesse* with which it infuses men's "actions, their conduct and their entire person" (184:I, 438–39). So powerful was the term—its modern, more superficial meaning appears only at the end of the century—that the honnête homme himself could be defined as "a man who is *poli* and who knows how to live" (439:III, 172), one who possesses "this extraordinary knowledge . . . the essential element of which is *la politesse*" (79:181). With the connotations of polish, refinement and elegance that it still contained from the Latin *politus*, *politesse*, like *civilité* and *urbanité*, with their synonymous etymons, represented the ultimate sign of civilization, the essence of culture. In the esthetic strategy of the honnête homme, it constituted the key to triumph over others: "One can't be sure of captivating others with a keen mind, remarkable talents, and magnificent manners," wrote Bellegarde, "but no one can resist the charm of true *politesse*" (60:II, 381).[41]

The specific manifestations of *politesse*, *civilité*, or *urbanité* varied with the receiver and the context. The choice as to which precise behavioral signs should be emitted depended on a prior reading of the hidden message that lay beneath the surface of the other—a form of semiological incursion that could be carried out only by "a most penetrating mind" (340:III, 160). This process of "getting inside" the other struck Méré as magical, but once again, contains a sexual note implicit in his metaphor of "penetration": "There seems to be a measure of sorcery in this art, for it instructs us in divination, which is how we discover a great number of things that otherwise we would never know. . . . It requires that we penetrate people's unspoken thoughts and, very often, their most closely guarded secrets" (II, 107–08). In a more strictly semiological perspective, the other can be "read" like a layered text in which manifest signs, when properly decoded, give a clear rendering of latent, hidden, even unformed messages: "nothing goes on in people's hearts or minds without leaving some trace on their face, in their tone of voice or in their actions, and when we become familiar with this language, there is nothing so hidden or so complex that we cannot uncover and unravel it" (p. 76). This capacity to decipher "almost imperceptible signs" is a competence, "a mode of knowledge that can be learned like a foreign language in which, at first, we understand next to nothing" (p. 107). Once the receiver's secret code has been deciphered and his language read, the emitter can select from the vast repertory of possible behavioral signs those that will best convey the intended message. From Faret to Méré, theoreticians agree that, at this performative stage, *souplesse*, a form of *insinuation*, becomes the dominant factor, the "sovereign precept" (188:70). "Through an innate suppleness, the persona . . . of an honnête homme . . . must transform itself, as the occasion warrants" (340:III, 157), writes Méré; "certain people are so naturally supple that they can turn themselves any which way . . . ; this kind of person succeeds in everything; but it takes a miracle to find one" (II, 19).[42] Interchanging the semes of flexibility, talent, and magic, Méré spells out the strategic feat of *l'art de plaire*.

Accommodation to the needs and wishes of others was the precondition for their seduction. "Whosoever is accommodating can confidently hope to be captivating," dictated Faret (188:70). Anything but facile or perfunctory, *complaisance*, in its rich seventeenth-century sense, predicated, once again, the decoding of hidden messages and undeclared desires: "We are delighted with people who do what we want without being told" (340:II, 107). Beyond the mere production of ingratiating signs, *complaisance*, buttressed by *souplesse* and *insinuation*, was to suggest a free, intentional, creative activity. Chalesme advocated *complaisance* "both refined and delicate . . . [which] must seem free and grounded in reason if we want it to have the anticipated effects" (117:167). These and other concerns and motifs converge on Madeleine de Scudéry's analysis of that fine point of *complaisance* which allows neither adulation nor harshness, self-abasement nor contrariness: "The *complaisance* we want . . . yields without weakness, praises without flattery, and adjusts judiciously and ingenuously to various times, places and people: without affectation or vulgarity it makes social life delightful and our existence

more comfortable and enjoyable. . . . If possible, we must acquire
. . . that *honnête complaisance* which gives pleasure, harms no
one, adorns the mind, makes for a congenial temperament . . .
and, in keeping with principles of justice and nobility, constitutes
the secret charm of human society" (454:III, pt.2, 742–44).[43] As
the redundant *with* and *without* suggest, even at the level of
syntax, *honnête complaisance* demands deft, unceasing negotiation
between ever changing alternatives that manages life as if it were
the stuff of art.

The supreme test of the honnête homme's manners was the
ability to handle the whims and outbursts of others, to manipulate
the violent and distasteful messages emitted by bilious, sanguine,
melancholic, or catarrhous types, which could disturb the polished
surface of life in the salon. As Bellegarde explained, *complaisance*
"teaches us to sympathize with the weaknesses of some people, to
endure the whims and eccentricities of others, to espouse their feelings and bring them back to their senses in a gentle and sinuous
manner out of a genuine desire to win their affection (*plaire*)"
(60:II, 374). Although this manipulative capacity underscored the
honnête homme's superiority over others, the primary controls
were directed, of necessity, toward the self. It was axiomatic that
the honnête homme should not emit any disruptive sign, or express
any emotion detrimental to the harmonious, suave discourse of
sociability which he orchestrated. Specifically excluded were all
traces of gloom or unhappiness that might threaten or repel others
(188:51); bitterness and cantankerousness would surely arouse
enmity, so would excessive seriousness that might be decoded as
judgmental (340:II, 49–50; 339:574). In the eyes of Philinte,
Molière's exemplary honnête homme, this was the "sickness" of
Alceste which earned his ridicule:

> You overdo your philosophic bile;
> I see your gloomy fits and have to smile . . .
> I'll tell you frankly that this malady
> Is treated everywhere as comedy.
> (*Mis.* I.i, 97–98, 105–6)

Even excessive reserve and withdrawal conveys the negative
message of disdain for the other: "in society there is nothing so

malhonnête as to be withdrawn and wrapped up in oneself" (340:II, 121).[44]

These extensive prescriptions did not imply the desired absence of all signs of emotion. If that zero degree were in fact achieved, the honnête homme "would be offensive to everyone, even to himself" (II, 49). For Faret, the safest and most effective sign was "an appealing coolness" (188:101), a posture which, with added psychological and philosophical significance, Philinte was to call *le flegme* (*Mis.* I.i.166). The more confident Méré went farther: "to the extent that decorum allows, we must give to others, even in the slightest matter, some sign of thought or feeling" (340:III, 79). As the terms "some," "slightest," and "to the extent" suggest, Méré was drawing a fine line, striking a delicate balance that was based on semiological and esthetic principles of measurement and dosage. For so long as signs of anger or sadness were *bienséant*, appropriate to the context, so long as they were managed adroitly, they could effectively produce *le bon air* (II, 49). At the top of Méré's list, however, we find under various synonymous and isomorphic guises, "honnête and scintillating gaiety" (p. 49), "a gentle, playful and even amusing humor" (339:56), "easy and lively approachability" (511:I, 38). This group of expressions suggests a mode of affability antithetical to excessive gaiety and hilarity and, at the same time, compatible with a kind of seriousness that could inspire respect (III, 145). With skill and effort, insisted Méré, the consummate honnête homme could acquire the right mixture of affective signs, and display that "perfect temperament" which has "powerful charms for winning affection" (II, 113: I, 10).[45]

The tendency to substitute for the more primitive, energetic emotions a small set of consummately civilized signs finds its clearest demonstration in discussions of love. Passionate love had no place in a system predicated on total control over internal feelings; Faret states in no uncertain terms that the smitten can have no use for his precepts (188:98). Moreover, because it subjugates and enslaves, passionate love, Saint-Evremond noted, had been wisely avoided by the honnêtes hommes of old: "The *galants* of antiquity had a deep aversion to servitude. . . . They reserved for themselves the freedom to go from one sex to the other at will.

Love for women would have sapped the inner strength of those great men . . . and might have diminished the greatness of their lofty spirits" (438:III, 278–79). This image of woman as Circe, a role which the honnête homme essentially assigned to himself, overlay an avowed fear of becoming object rather than subject, slave rather than master. As Marmet warned: "You must not . . . become too attached to a lady, or for too long a time, because you might become an object of amusement; this kind of activity, on the contrary, should *be* an object of amusement for an honnête homme" (329:71–72).[46]

Prescriptions against passionate love did not, of course, preclude the manifest signs of love. Just as repression is the necessary partner of sublimation, the rejection of passionate love in the system of honnêteté went hand in hand with the valorization of the nonmarital or extramarital varieties which have always been the aristocrat's diversion and a mark of his superiority over both the bourgeois and the mere warrior. So integral was love to the aristocrat's sign equipment that it was feigned where it was not felt. "Love is not just the simple passion it is everywhere else," observed Madeleine de Scudéry, "but a necessary and seemly passion; all men must be lovers, all ladies must be loved. Indifference is not allowed; those who are capable of such hardheartedness are condemned as criminal; that kind of freedom is so shameful that those who are not in love at least pretend to be" (141:II, 5–6). Although she did not advocate such role playing, it was not pretense itself so much as its obviousness that aroused her displeasure. Her critique of Aristhée (Chapelain) makes this clear: ". . . I believe that his *galanterie* is all in his mind: he hides and displays it at will, and controls it so completely that I can't believe there is any other explanation. Not that he doesn't do and say all the things that love makes people say and do; but, in my view, he says and does them all too well" (II, 16–17).[47] What Scudéry rejects is a perfect, mechanical production of signs, a conformity to the code so total as to be incredible. Her objection is grounded not in ethics but esthetics; her dissatisfaction is less with the presence of artifice than with the absence of artistry.

In a treatise entitled *S'il faut qu'un jeune homme soit amoureux*, Sarasin distinguishes between the vulgar amorous behavior of the many and the rarefied performance of the few:

136

"the common folk cover love over with fake diamonds that they idolize because they do not know their true value and follow them blindly over the precipice; the *honnêtes gens*, on the contrary, replace these spurious stones with the genuine adornments that love deserves, thus raising it to that level of perfection where those who know how to love find true happiness" (445:200). The oxymoronic *genuine adornments* and *know how to love* suggest the distance that separates passion from poiesis, raw nature and its stylized, estheticized version. ". . . Without all the motions we go through," explains Amilcar in *Clélie*, "love would not be what it is. Many things," religion and love among them, he adds, "owe their beauty to ritual" (454:V, pt.2, 561). This kind of ritual was the backbone of the code of *galanterie*, a system comprised of discontinuous units of significance combined according to a set of rules, a grammar of amatory behavior which, in texts like Scudéry's *La Carte de Tendre*, found expression in a sustained topographical metaphor. Like any language, the system of *la galanterie* required competence; Scudéry chastized the "large number of people who get involved in something they don't understand" (453:X, pt.2, 473). The rules governing the so-called *précieux* code of behavior were, of course, appropriated from the medieval art of courtly love, in which the male role required faithful submission to a dominant, demanding female who looked down upon her slave from an inaccessible pedestal. Women, wrote Scudéry, "make glorious conquests and lose none of the lovers they have subjugated. . . . The honor of our ladies depends chiefly on keeping the slaves they have acquired in obedience"; for the men "it is equally essential that they be in love and in misery" (141:II, 60).[48] The honnête homme as lover was cast in the part of Céladon and not Hylas, Werther and not Don Juan. It is with reference to this polar antithesis that the performance of the Duc de Nemours is tested. A consummate Don Juan, he is metamorphosed into a consummate courtly lover only for a short time before signs of temerity, indiscretion, and calculation, indicative of libertinism, reveal the transformation to be illusory, and ultimately, the very notion of courtly love to be mere myth (290).

Conversely, the mythic nature of the code of *galanterie* explains why the required submissive posture carried no real threat of subjugation and castration. Participation in the art of courtly love was viewed, rather, as an integral aspect of the self-reflexive strategy of seductiveness. In context, submission to women was but the sexualized analog to the *complaisance* that the honnête homme artfully displayed to his peers. Since in the *art d'aimer*, as in the *art de plaire*, it was the criteria of art which determined the precise components of signs, the honnête homme rejected those archetypal courtly signs which were unappealing by seventeenth-century standards. Lancelot, for example, running wildly across fields at the thought of displeasing Guinevere, seemed ludicrous to Chapelain's contemporaries, "the most un-*galant* man who ever lived" (119:30–31). Complaints and tears, the literary staples of the courtly lover, were considered annoying and unattractive (454:III, pt.2, 1353 ff.). "There is nothing so improper," we read in *Clélie*, "as to carry the art of love to the point of misery, and to love so intensely that we cease being lovable and capable of being loved" (p. 1367). The ironic sequence (*the art of love, to love, lovable, being loved*) dramatizes at the level of lexicon and syntax the witty and ludic parodies of courtly metaphors in Voiture's poetry. Only in this climate can one understand the meaning of this admission by Méré: "wanting entertainment, [a lady] commanded me to amuse her by pretending that I was madly in love with her, and by playing the role of the desperate lover" (339:707).[49]

Ludic or serious in tone, the amatory message that the honnête homme addressed to his lady was not private or secretive communication, but rather a means for displaying his artistry to all the members of his circle. Perfect lovers, in Scudéry's opinion, were those who knew how to be "as appealing to others as to their beloved; the rarest thing in the world," she added, "is to find a man who can love you with style" (453:X, pt.2, 470). Where form claims priority over substance, even *galanterie* matters less than *l'air galant*, a style which "gives an inexplicable charm to everything we do, to everything we say" (p. 466). In the last analysis, this was the essential competence to be acquired at the school of love: "I maintain that no man who ever possessed the *air galant* ever shunned the company of my sex; to be perfectly candid I would add that a man must even have had, at least once in his life, some slight amorous inclination . . . some small sentimental involvement if he were truly to acquire the *air galant* . . . in order to accomplish this, he would have had either to be in love or to have wanted to captivate someone (*plaire*)" (pp. 467–68). It is symptomatic of honnêteté that the seme *love* is systematically desexualized here, whereas the seme *plaire* takes on an opposite sexual charge. In this highly eclectic version of the courtly code, love represents an indispensable stage in the construction of the self-as-art, and woman an instrumentality of competence in the *art de plaire*. As Chalesme explains: "Since women are naturally averse to all kinds of coarseness, a man who frequents them can hardly wish to go on offending their sense of delicacy. On the contrary, without even knowing it, he develops the desire to please them, with the result that he adjusts whatever is offensive in his language or demeanor to the gentleness of their company and behavior" (117:197–98). In this perspective, women, more than men by far, become "essential to achieve perfection in honnêteté" (340:III, 75).[50] By that very token, they are not inaccessible subjects to which the honnête homme slavishly submits, but to the contrary, objects used in the elaboration of his own poetic text. On this level, the artistocrat's relationship to women is substantially the same as his strategic rapport with men. But at the deeper level, the predominant role of women in fashioning the signifying surface underscores the "female" principle at work in this system of esthetic seductiveness.

The Art of Conversation

"There are . . . various airs, tones, and manners," La Rochefoucauld observed, "which often determine what is pleasing or displeasing, delicate or shocking in conversation; few people possess the secret of using them well" (294:510). This reflection builds on the premise that underlies the extensive commentary on the language of social intercourse in the system of honnêteté. Conversation, the activity which enlists all the multifarious signs of the self-as-art—what La Rochefoucauld refers to summarily here as *airs*, *tones*, *manners*—is concerned primarily with the form of the message as its content. The rules that govern this kind of discourse are geared not merely to impart information but to promote certain attitudes and arouse certain value judgments about the emitter. This performance, going far beyond linguistic competence, pursues at every point a poetic rather than a utilitarian function. Thus, the statements made by a plaintiff in the law court, a merchant in negotiations, or a king in political council—"none of these deserves to be called 'conversation,'" stipulates Scudéry. "Such people may, of course, speak ably of their professional interests and affairs, and yet, not have that delightful talent for conversation which is life's sweetest charm" (455:2–3). This use and kind of language—unproductive, gratuitous, esthetic—are intended to constitute and to procure "the greatest pleasure of *honnêtes gens*" (pp. 2–3), "the most exquisite pleasure that persons of refinement can experience" (60:II, 392).[51]

Such a mode of discourse predicates the existence of an idiolect, which is the particular achievement and property of an elite caste. "We must speak the language of the *honnêtes gens* of whatever country we are in," insists Scudéry, "and avoid just as carefully both the language of the vulgar masses and of the pseudointellectuals, as well as the language spoken by certain people which takes a little from the court, a little from the masses, and a lot from the town, and is the most bizarre of all" (454:IV, pt.2, 415). This "language of the *honnêtes gens*," which reflected the values that forged the idiom of French classical texts, was abstract, periphrastic, euphemistic—"pure," in Méré's term, an esthetic denomination derived from a sociopolitical model. In what Méré repeatedly calls *la langue pure*, cleanliness is identified with class, purity with nobility, impurity with the *profanum vulgus* (340:III, 132). And yet, since Méré understood vulgarity to be primarily a function of mind, not of rank, this idiolect excluded "lower-class words and expressions" and "bourgeois speech" which were used even among royalty (p. 131). Inexact and inappropriate usages were also signs of linguistic impurity; so were the neologisms and phonological eccentricities that cropped up at court (454:IV, pt.2, 407). In language, as in dress, innovations were ruled out as vulgar means of self-distinction (104:74), among these, improper *liaisons*—"you zopen, you zapprehend, you zaspire"—in which Méré claimed once again the court indulged

(340:III, 114). The diction of the *honnêtes gens* was to be marked by "a soft and pure accent . . . [an] inexpressible air of nobility" (454:IV, pt.2, 418), that was essentially Parisian but slightly modified by "the turn of phrase and the accent of *le grand monde*" (340:III, 114).[52] As with the signifier and its mode of articulation, the purity of the signified was to distinguish the honnête homme from the best of courtiers. "We should carefully avoid talking about things that are disgusting or that evoke unpleasant thoughts," Méré insisted in *De la délicatesse dans les choses et dans l'expression*, "let us remember that when we discuss unpleasant subjects we become almost as unappealing as the subject itself. Even the finest people at court can use this advice" (p. 125). To speak of the disgusting is to be disgusting: logo is ego. Conversely, when semantics, diction, and usage are purged of all possible contaminants, when they are free of all intrusive peculiarities that would hamper their effect, then language can operate with the special efficacy of art. As La Rochefoucauld recognized: "There is just as much eloquence in our tone of voice as in our choice of words" (294:309, #44).[53]

The goal of the idiolect, a metonym for the fundamental intent of the system of the self-as-art, was elegant and eloquent communication. An object of beauty, this mode of expression was frequently compared to what Pascal termed "a speaking portrait" (393:582, #578), the kind "which persuades by its gentleness, not by its power" (p. 582, #584). As with every other element in the system, the keynote remained understatement, ambiguity, a subtlety that verged on invisibility. "When speech is too blatantly beautiful, that beauty is usually false and . . . it immediately offends people of good taste," Méré wrote to a friend. "I advise you . . . to favor only the most discreet form of beauty in language, the kind that seems to be hidden behind a veil. Because it *is* hidden, we seek it out when we know it is there, and the more we look at it the more we love it. . . . By scrutinizing them, we discover in these forms of beauty subtle qualities that reveal themselves slowly . . . we find them even more beautiful in their substance than in their appearance" (339:3–4). This refusal of ornamentation and obviousness reflects a generalized contempt for grandiloquence. Brilliant arabesques, luxuriant turns of phrase were decoded, in linguistic as in sartorial speech, as signs of vulgarity. "Although this sort of language may dazzle the ignorant and the foolish, I can assure you," says Méré, "that it is just as indecorous as the speech of the masses and that neither royalty nor *honnêtes gens* have ever used it" (340:III, 116). Similarly with elaborate images and even classical *sententiae*: "the masses and common people love them, but the *honnêtes gens* cannot stand them" (II, 120; III, 126). The more sophisticated theorists were no more receptive to Ciceronian *bona dicta* than they were to his rhetorical stance in general. While Faret and Chalesme considered them powerful indices of a keen mind (188:83; 117:182), Méré and Pascal devalued them in no uncertain terms: "a maker of *bons mots*, a bad sort" (393:589, #670).[54]

When Méré advocated a *langage propre*, he was not suggesting mere simplicity but a pure, terse, dense mode of expression whose model he found in the dialogues of Plato and the parables of Jesus. This is what he understood, in contradistinction to *la grande éloquence*, by *la haute éloquence*, and perhaps more accurately, *la subtile éloquence* (340:I, 59–62; III, 108–9), a mode of discourse which contains "an indescribably natural turn of phrase" (III, 129), all the more effective for not being conveyed by external rhetorical apparatus: "to be eloquent without appearing to be" (p. 125). The same subtlety characterized the narrative structure of the discourse. While it gave the appearance of spontaneous and unstructured speech, it contained on a deeper level, like Plato's dialogues, like Montaigne's *Essais*, "a secret and natural order," "[a] well-hidden order" (339:23; 340:III, 108), which satisfied the need for structuration, the foundation of beauty (339:22). Gratuitous complexity or obscurity, on the other hand, gained through *galimatias* or *équivoques*, was quite simply "a false *agrément*," "a shoddy trick . . . which is ill-suited to *honnêtes gens*" (340:I, 63; II, 116). That such techniques connoted vulgar affectation rather than eloquence confirms Pascal's celebrated maxim: "True eloquence has no use for eloquence" (393:576, #513).[55]

In truly eloquent discourse, where form is content, subject matter is but a raw material put to the service of an ultimate, autotelic intent. From this perspective, writers on honnêteté could justifiably argue that the most inconsequential of subjects, and not the most ponderous, provided the best opportunity for demonstrating superior artistic ability. "A man must have great manners, a great deal of *politesse*, and even a great deal of inventiveness to make felicitous remarks about the most trifling subjects," observed La Bruyère; "to jest in this manner is to create, to make something out of nothing" (286:148, #4). Whatever difficulties insignificant subjects posed, they could not compare with those attendant upon the expression of a compliment. Inevitably self-interested, such communication had to appear natural and disinterested to the addressee; trite and overworked, the topoi of the encomiastic genre had to be imbued with freshness and originality. These were some of the rhetorical problems explored by Vaumorières in his essays on *The Art of Praising Properly*, a detailed analysis of the negative effects of untimely, excessive, or even straightforward compliments, and the positive value of those that are laced with "a delicate seasoning" (511:I, 226). Méré used the same alimentary metaphor to underscore the subtlety of this art: "To avoid looking like an ordinary flatterer and to give some flavor to compliments which almost always have a certain distasteful 'something' about them, we would do well to use subtlety and wit and to make them more spicy than sugary. The seasoning, however, must not be in any way excessive; on the contrary, we must find other, more flattering kinds of praise by dressing up a compliment to look like an insult, and by criticizing in the people whom we want to please qualities that they are really glad to possess" (340:II, 124–25).[56] In this rhetorical strategy, piquancy is injected to transmit an ostensibly negative message, which on a deeper level communicates a positive one about the receiver, and ultimately, the emitter as well.

If praise required piquancy, wit, which always contains an element of aggression, had to be modulated in the direction of gentleness. Any trace of hostility, anger, contempt, bitterness, or resentment would immediately alienate the other and undermine the seductive strategy, whence the need for "a playful wit which is in no way malicious, unjust, or shocking to anyone" (340:II, 83). For identical reasons, La Rochefoucauld endorses a delicate, even flattering way of poking fun, which touches only upon faults that the emitter perceives the receiver is willing to acknowledge (294:528). At the same time, wit should not be so mild as to become insipid, saccharine. The most artful blend is a rare kind of "gentle . . . piquant . . . and soothing wit" (340:III, 172), which produces "the same effect as salt in a stew" (117:181), charms as it attacks, seduces as it stings (340:III, 172). To this deft management of nuances, writers on honnêteté opposed "lower-middle-class pedants" and "common buffoons," whose tasteless, mannered jesting, with its *brocards*, *quolibets*, and *turlupinades*, knows no bounds (511:I, 76; 340:II, 120). Qualitative as much as quantitative, these limits made all the difference between the vulgar and the aristocratic, the offensive and the appealing. "We laugh at many things that we do not love," wrote Méré, "but we love everything that gives us pleasure (*ce qui plaît*)" (III. 171).[57]

At every juncture in the art of conversation, the emitter had to maintain the closest correspondence between his verbal signs and the nature and disposition of the receiver(s) (393:582, #584). To orchestrate his performance in perfect synchronization with the other's *amour propre* is to insure, in Pascal's words, "that the listener will be, as it were, forced to surrender" (393a:326, #15). This synchronization is predicated on the all too easily forgotten fact that conversation is dialogue and that, as La Rochefoucauld reminds us, the consummate speaker must also be a consummate listener: "One of the reasons why we find so few people who seem reasonable and appealing in conversation is that almost everyone is more concerned with what *he* wants to say than with giving straight answers to what is said *to* him. Even the cleverest and most accommodating people do no more than merely look attentive, but their eyes and their thoughts wander, they are in a rush to get back to what *they* want to say. They don't realize that by trying so hard to please themselves they will never please or persuade others, that attentiveness and responsiveness in conversation are among the highest attainments we can achieve" (294:333, #178). La Rochefoucauld confirms that listening has a semiology of its own and represents a vital form of activity: "There exists an eloquent silence which is sometimes used to approve or to criticize; there is a mocking silence, there is a respectful silence" (p. 510, #4). This is precisely what Nicole conveyed in the oxymoron, "the language of silence" (375:III, 115). And yet, the most strategically effective silence by far acts as a blank page on which the other may inscribe his discourse. The chief conductor of the *musica mundana*, the honnête homme produced through nonverbal and verbal stimuli opportunities for others to put on their conversational performance. "A person who wants to charm people," explained F. de Caillières, "should expend much less effort in showing off his own intellectual qualities than in helping others exhibit theirs; he should try to single out, discreetly and delicately, those things that they have done or expressed well. The ostensible sacrifice of his own interests is an ingenious subterfuge which will advance him further in people's esteem and affection than all the marvelous things that he could have said" (103:19). Somewhat more cynically, but with full awareness of the constructive uses of duplicity, La Bruyère noted that "a person who leaves your company satisfied with himself and with what *he* has said is thoroughly satisfied with *you*" (286:155, #16).[58]

The inscription of this mode of conversation extended beyond the parameters of the system of the self-as-art. In an ultimate fusion of that self with art, the honnête homme's *parole* became, not merely the substance of the corpus of honnêteté, as the large body of *dialogues*, *entretiens*, and *conversations* attests, but in fact the most valorized mode of seventeenth-century *écriture*. According to the views of an entire generation, a written text could fashion the mind, even increase linguistic competence, but only speech could achieve what Scudéry called "the *agrément* of language" (454:IV, pt.2, 419). Thus an artistic speaker was *ipso facto* an excellent writer, but not necessarily the reverse: "A person who is good at speaking is also good at writing," insisted Méré; ". . . a person cannot write well without being able to speak well. It turns out, however, that those who care only about writing well often have a listless, almost lifeless way of speaking. By favoring this kind of soft-talk, they gradually lose all sense of natural usage" (340:I, 71). This *natural usage*, the mark of artistocratic speech, was precisely the type of *écriture* that Pascal and his contemporaries extolled in exploring the hidden sources of *l'art de plaire*: "When we see the natural style we are wholly astonished and

thrilled, because we expected to see an author and find a man."
"Honnêteté is the rule" (393:595, #675; 585, #610).[59]

L'ART DE PLAIRE EN DÉPLAISANT

"*Everyone* loved d'Orsay so naturally and so passionately that he even got men to carry his picture in their lockets! Whereas the only thing that dandies get men to wear is you-know-what, and they *give pleasure to women by offending them*" ("*plaisent aux femmes en leur déplaisant*") (38:IX, 312, #29). In Barbey's statement, we find the peculiar juncture of contraries that characterizes the system of dandyism: a perverse interplay of attraction and repulsion that fulfills a need to captivate people who are deemed inferior, and who will lionize the very individual who showers them with contempt. "He offended too many people *not to be sought after*," Bulwer-Lytton had written in *Pelham*, an observation quoted in Barbey's treatise with this comment: "Doesn't this remind you of those powerful and debauched women who sometimes have a desire to be beaten?" (pp. 275–76).[60] Nineteenth-century society, Barbey argued, was like a debauched woman; what he termed "naive and spontaneous seduction" could not serve the dandy's strategic goals (p. 276). Nor could the subtle, imperceptible enthrallment which the honnête homme produced with pleasure for emitter and receiver alike. A stronger "stimulant" had to be added (p. 276), a new strategic component had to come into play in which the preeminence of one partner required the humiliation of the other.

The collocation of antithetical signs in the expression *plaire en déplaisant* reflects the synthesis that marks the shift from classical to Romantic esthetics. Art, hereafter, would blend the grotesque with the sublime, the bad with the good, the ugly with the beautiful (262:191). "A certain blemish," Hugo writes in the *Préface de Cromwell*, "may be inseparably linked to a certain type of Beauty. . . . Remove one and you remove the other" (p. 70). Just as the ugly achieved its own independent value in Romantic esthetics, *déplaire*, in an analogous development, became an autonomous poetic principle. "Even where [Baudelaire] offends," Gautier noted, "he does so intentionally, in accordance with an esthetic all his own, and after lengthy reflection" (212:40). Baudelaire subscribed to this esthetic not only as a Romantic, but as a theorist and practitioner of a dandyism which afforded him "the aristocratic pleasure of displeasing" (51:I, 661).[61] Conjoined through the preposition *en*, however, the expression and the notion of *plaire en déplaisant* contains a paradox that allowed for a fusion and confusion of cause and effect. This fundamental ambiguity in the system of dandyism provided the space for diversity, a notion which Baudelaire considered integral to all artistic expression (II, 578). From the repertory of possible signs, the dandy could select those which he as emitter and/or others as receivers regarded as *plaisant* or *déplaisant*, combine them in various dosages and create his own variant system to communicate his particular brand of dandyism.

As individual as his modes of expression might be, the dandy shared the preeminent goal of the honnête homme to captivate others (*plaire*). Under the impact of the antonym *déplaire*, however, *l'art de plaire* underwent subtle but significant modifications that delineated an esthetics of power rather than of persuasion. When Barbey stated that it was Brummell's vocation to *plaire*, he hastened to add that his sway over others was owed not to amiability but to inordinate power: "the coquettishness of powerful men can be very slight and yet seem irresistible" (38:IX, 274, 311, #23). The art of seduction, which is defined as the vocation of a large group of fictional dandies (8:628, 487:I, 594), is associated not only with magic, as in the seventeenth century, but with demonic, satanic strength. Ponson du Terrail describes the dandy-criminal Sir Williams as "the most seductive of demons" (403:IV, 294); Eugène Sue's Marquis de Létorière, who possesses "the art of captivation and seduction to the highest degree" (491:36), can cast spells on man or beast, and is called the devil incarnate (pp. 6, 25, 120, 174–77). If the dandy is "[the] modern-day Satan" (21:III, 648), Satan, following the example set by Nerval's adaptation of *Faust*, often assumes the dandiacal guise. In Balzac's *La Peau de chagrin*, Satan has "the style of an old *fat* who still keeps up with fashion" (19:IX, 176); in Gautier's

Albertus, Belzébuth resembles "a *merveilleux* from the Boulevard de Gand" (205:49); and in Soulié's *Mémoires du diable*, the devil is likened to a *fashionable* (469:14).[62] The honnête homme, we recall, founded his prowess on a serpentine capacity; in the nineteenth-century version of the *art de plaire*, the dandy has become the serpent.

Already implicit in the vision of dandy-as-demon is the mysterious connivance of attraction and terror which emerges as a further variant of the seme *plaire en déplaisant*. Baudelaire's definition is prototypical: dandies are "privileged beings in whom prettiness and awesomeness are so mysteriously blended together" (51:II, 712). Whereas the strategy of the honnête homme partook of a "secret enchantment," the dandy, the incarnation of Romantic predilection for mystery (I, 657; II, 131–32), presented an impenetrable surface which was designed to "attract like an enigma," as Barbey put it (34:I, 114), to produce the impression of "a palace within a labyrinth" (38:IX, 311), or even "those boxes filled with Asiatic poison" (I, 218). The ultimate dandy, Brummell was particularly adept at pouring out "perfectly equal doses of terror and affability, out of which he concocted the magic potion of his influence" (IX, 256). The recurrent use of *terreur*, *crainte*, *peur*, and *effroi* were so many signs for the kind of esthetic impact that dandies, like Romantics after Chateaubriand, strove to make. If nineteenth-century writers on art and aristocracy, like those of the seventeenth century, valorized the signifier *étonnement* (51:II, 616), it was, however, with increased emphasis on its more primitive, etymological sense—a stunning, unsettling, fearful effect: "the most beautiful form of amazement," Barbey specified, "is terror" (38:IX, 256). By that token, the verb *étonner* absorbed the hostile semes contained in *plaire en déplaisant* (p. 256). As Mesnilgrand, a character in Barbey's *Les Diaboliques*, explains to an inferior: "My dear fellow . . . men . . . like me have always existed for the sole purpose of astounding men . . . like you" (I, 258). In Baudelaire's definition, dandyism brings together "the pleasure of astounding" with "the haughty satisfaction of never being astounded" (51:II, 710).[63]

The cultivation of astonishment, like the need to *plaire en déplaisant*, is rooted in a programmatic perversity that was inherent in the Romantic notion of merit. "You have not understood this century," Prince Korasoff says to Julien Sorel, *"always do the opposite of what people expect of you.* That, upon my honor, is the only religion of our time. Be neither foolish nor affected for then people would expect of you foolishness and affectation, and you would not be observing the rule" (487:I, 480). "One of the marks of dandies," generalized Barbey in his treatise, "is never to do what is expected of them"; their systematic contrariness impels them "always to come up with what is unexpected," "always what is singular" (38:IX, 282, 230, 302). This persistent emphasis on the rare reflects the valorization of originality—a term which in the seventeenth century had predominantly negative connotations—as the condition sine qua non of superiority: the dandy, like the nineteenth-century artist, cannot exist "if he doesn't have a certain exquisite originality" (p. 249). No one knew this better than Baudelaire, the most vocal among nineteenth-century writers to identify the dandy with the poet as parallel deviations from bourgeois-philistine codes; whence his definition of dandyism as "the ardent desire to become one of a kind" (51:II, 710).[64] With the cultivation of deviance as a principle, *bizarrerie* emerges logically in Baudelairean esthetics as a positive sign: "The beautiful is always bizarre. I do not mean that it is willfully and consciously bizarre for in that case it would be a monster run right off the track of life. I say that it always contains a slight bizarreness, naive, involuntary, and unconscious, and that it is precisely this bizarreness which makes it Beautiful. . . . The measure of bizarreness that constitutes and defines individuality, . . . plays in art (—the aptness of this comparison will, I hope, make up for its triviality—) the same role as flavor or seasoning in food; foods do not differ from one another, leaving aside their usefulness or nutritional value, except for the *idea* they reveal to the tongue" (II, 578–79). Although this countervalorization of a negative linguistic sign represents an important, and consistent, difference with seventeenth-century esthetic strategy, Baudelaire's analysis also points to the substantial similarities between dandyism and honnêteté. *Bizarrerie*, injected here in carefully measured quantities (*slight*, *measure*) has essentially the same function as the "salt" which spiced the seventeenth-century system. Moreover, although the bizarre, individual touch may seem spontaneous, there is, to use another cliché, a cook behind the stew, a controlling consciousness which imparts an order to the product of art that is no less rigorous than the structure of a complex machine: "There are no accidents in art, any more than there are in mechanics. A felicitous discovery is the simple result of good thinking. . . . A painting is a machine all of whose systems are intelligible to the trained eye" (II, 432). This conception of intentionality has global implications for the system of the artistocratic self. "A man's idea of the beautiful," writes Baudelaire, "is imprinted in the way he dresses, it rumples or stiffens his suit, softens or sharpens his gestures, and in the long run, even subtly marks his facial features. He ultimately resembles the person that he would like to be" (II, 684). It is in this context that the equation of poet with dandy takes on its particular relevance—the individual who illustrates by his textual *corp(u)s* the significance of modernity as a system: ". . . a person's dress, coiffure and even his movements, his look and his smile (each period has its own walk, look and smile) form a whole that has a vitality all its own" (II, 695).[65]

The Body as Signifying Surface

"To be beautiful is to possess a magic quality that makes the world smile on you and welcome you with open arms: before you have even spoken, everyone is already predisposed in your favor, ready to agree with you; you walk down a street, you appear on a balcony and in a flash you have friends and mistresses in the crowd. You don't have to be lovable to be loved, you are spared all the mental effort, all the polite concern for others that ugly people have to go through . . .; what a splendid and magnificent gift!" (211:138–39). It is symptomatic of dandyism that D'Albert in Gautier's *Mademoiselle de Maupin* should yearn for beauty as an avenue to power. Free of the need to persuade ("before you have spoken"), and be pleasant ("lovable," "polite concern"), beauty would empower him automatically to *plaire en déplaisant*. Unlike the honnête homme, then, the dandy values extraordinary physical beauty as a universally accepted sign of superiority, as a "privilege comparable to nobility . . . it is recognized everywhere and often worth more than good fortune and talent," writes Balzac. "Beauty need only be seen to triumph, all it has to do is exist" (19:IV, 355). Accordingly, dandies in fiction are often possessed of a beauty found only in works of art. Lucien de Rubempré compares favorably with the Apollo of Belvedere, and Gautier's Fortunio with the supreme visions of Phidias, but Sue's Marquis de Létorière surpasses even these incomparable works of art: "All the treasures of ancient statuary, so they say, could not rival the harmonious beauty of his form" (491:35).[66]

Such hyperbolic beauty has traditionally been the province of the "feminine." In an esthetics of power, it must therefore be conjoined with signs of the "masculine": "If a person combined supreme strength and supreme beauty, if he had Hercules' muscles under Antinoüs' skin, what more could he want?" asks D'Albert. "I am convinced that with those two assets and the soul that I have, in three years' time, I could rule the world" (211:139). A topos of dandyism, this androgynous compound conveys an ambiguous message that contains a contradiction between what is perceptible and sensed, apparent and hidden. Henri de Marsay, for example, has "a girlish beauty, soft and feminine," which is belied by the aura of remarkable power he exudes (19:IV, 614; V, 295). The Marquis de Létorière, who could be mistaken for a woman, hides "beneath that enchanting exterior . . . muscles of steel, and the courage of a lion" (491:35).[67] And Barbey's Marmor de Karkoël conceals the potential savagery of a sleeping tiger beneath his velvet skin (38:I, 205). In all these examples, the "feminine" elements connote softness and charm (*plaire*), the overdetermined signs of the "masculine" bespeak hardness and violence (*déplaire*).

The signs of the dandy's enormous power are invariably localized in his eyes, the mirror of his soul. In *Les Diaboliques*, the eyes of the Vicomte de Brassard "didn't bother to scrutinize, they penetrated" (38:I, 24). This phallic eye, which goes far beyond the honnête homme's effortless penetration, cuts through the receiver's surface like "a drawn sword" (200:188), rapes him/her with a savage swiftness that is concretized in a series of animalistic metaphors: *oeil fauve, oeil d'aigle, de tigre*. As Gautier says of his dandy, Onuphrius, "his lynx-like eyes . . . seemed to peer into the depths of their hearts" (210:61). Elsewhere, it is a *lion*'s eye that terrorizes or a Medusa's head that petrifies the victim:

> The savage sparkle of his lion's gaze . . .
> Made you perforce shiver and pale.
> The boldest would lower their lids
> Before this Medusan eye that could turn them to stone (205:27).

Nineteenth-century writers found convincing explanations for this ocular magic in Mesmer's then popular psychophysiological theories of magnetism. A powerful will—so goes Balzac's version—flashes from the eye like an electric charge and "mesmerizes" everything that stands in the way of genius (22:117). That dandies in the works of Sue, Gautier, and du Terrail exercise this faculty automatically over everyone confirms Balzac's statement: "this magnetic power is the final goal of elegant life" (p. 100).[68]

The haunting power of the proverbial evil eye serves as a metonymy for the uncanny ability of the dandy's looks to rivet and transfix (51:II, 310). "If you had seen him once, you could never forget him," Gautier commented in describing Delacroix's savage and exotic face (207:202). Equally unforgettable is the fascination inspired by the impassive marble face of Sue's Lord Falmouth, reminiscent of a vampire or some other "fantastic creation" (489:I, 182–83). The "unpleasantness" contained in these signifying surfaces occasionally fledges out into a type of ugliness which, as Ronteix put it, echoing the seventeenth-century *mondains*, has "a *je ne sais quoi* which is more lively and piquant than beauty" (432:25). But the perverse impact that the seme *déplaire* could have on *l'art de plaire* can be measured by the terrifying ugliness of Barbey's dandy-hero, Mesnilgrand: "He was *incredibly* ugly! his pale and ravaged face . . . , his flat, leopard-like nose, glaucous eyes slightly lined with blood, like those of very fiery horses, bore an expression before which the most sarcastic women . . . stopped being sarcastic. . . . Having seen him once, you never forgot him" (38:I, 267–68). The negative animalistic connotations in this portrait comprise a powerfully invasive language that Barbey calls *une expression*. For Barbey, the most effective set of bodily signs do not spell beauty, with its boring similarity, or ugliness which, although polysemic, allows but a limited number of variants. Since facial traits are sealed in an inflexible geometry, they can produce relatively few individual combinations. Only *expression* or physiognomy—Barbey's analog for what the seventeenth century knew as *mine*—can generate an indefinite number of variations or achieve "a permeation of the soul through the regular or irregular, pure or distorted lines of the face" that will transform facial geometry into a powerful and original idiolect (I, 338).[69]

Like the face, hands can have a superior and menacing language of their own. "If you have white hands . . . they'll slit your throat to a chorus of 'Long live the common man! Death to the nobles!'" exclaims Balzac (22:103). Lucien de Rubempré discovers that he is suspect to peasants because his hands bespeak the religious, princely, or ministerial status of one who "does nothing" (19:IV, 882). By that token, the "sign" of the patrician hand could exact obeisance from others (pp. 485–86); and so Gautier could understand why Balzac preferred to be complimented on his hands rather than on his writing (206:155). The dandy's hands were, in fact, to be unveiled and displayed like some rare *objet d'art*. Marmor de Karkoël, writes Barbey, "had drawn from a perfumed leather case, white and well sculpted hands which a courtesan would have thanked God for if she had been blessed with them, and he dealt cards around the circle with a prodigious speed as stunning as the virtuoso movements of Liszt's fingers" (38:I, 206–7).[70] In what is more than a metaphor, Baudelaire analyzed the hand's harmony of color and line and labeled it a system (51:II, 423).

In various combinations, the parts of the body, its attitudes and movements, could be made to display what Balzac called "all the physical nobility of the aristocrat" (19:VII, 730). Sue's Rodolphe, when not incognito in the Parisian underworld, exudes a princely aura "in the poetic ideality of the word" (492:167). And Edgar Allan Poe, immersed in the hideous vulgarity of the American landscape, still possessed an aristocratic physiognomy, said Baudelaire, that "marked" his gestures and demeanor (51:II, 310). The semiology of these two aspects of self-representation are examined in Balzac's eighty-five-page essay, *Théorie de la démarche.* Scrutinizing the signs transmitted by different kinds of character, profession, habits, and style of life, he formulates the "laws" which govern the elegance and eloquence of the body. He contends that the face should be motionless, held slightly to the left, neither raised (a sign of pride and combativeness) nor lowered (a sign of poverty and shame). Conversely, the body, rather than immobile (a sign of contemplativeness and intellectuality) should favor infrequent, effortless, majestic gestures that connote wealth, leisure, and nobility. Because mechanical and staccato movements betray the professional man condemned to a monotonous repetition of a single activity, because sharp angles and rigid lines are disharmonious, the aristocratic body should blur transitions and aim for an "exquisite roundness" (22). The several Balzacian dandies who illustrate these precepts display an ease and nonchalance reminiscent of the *ancien régime*; "that's what they used to call having *un grand air*," explains Balzac (19:VII, 726). Whereas the honnête homme questioned the benefits of *la grande mine*, the dandy strives to emit *un air hautain* (38:I, 125, 268). Some even prefer an air of stiffness as a sign of English seriousness and dignity. According to Barbey, the dandy lives "on his dignity as if he were impaled on it, a fact which—however supple he may be—hampers somewhat his freedom of movement and makes him stand straighter than is comfortable" (IX, 311, #25).[71] Like *l'air hautain*, this stiffness partook of the esthetics of power rather than of persuasion; Gavarni, noted the brothers Goncourt, dominated others specifically by "the stiffness of his physiognomy and of his character" (225:71, 73). Stiffness or ease, then, could communicate different but equally significant messages. With the body and the face, as with dress and adornment, the individual signifier mattered less than the connotations of superiority that could be inscribed on the surface of the self-as-art.

Elegance: The Poeticity of Dress and Adornment

A seventeenth-century neologism, for which Méré took personal credit, elegance became a nineteenth-century synonym for dandyism itself. In Balzac's *Traité de la vie élégante*, a more inclusive companion work to *Théorie de la démarche*, bearing, costume, manners, and speech comprise the four main elements that go into the exteriorization of the self. These substances determine an individual's "external translation," to use the term of Chapus, Balzac's imitator, in his *Théorie de l'élégance* (122:41); in collaboration, they constitute what Balzac himself calls "a kind of organized system" (22:81) by which every individual can be decoded and classified: "Talk, walk, eat or dress and I will tell you who you are" (p. 58). Elegance, "the index of a perfected nature," predicates "the perfection of palpable objects" which emanate either directly or indirectly from the emitter (pp. 58, 60). The latter objects, which include food, servants, horses, carriages, furnishings, and domicile, are secondary signs in the system: "Although these accessories of life all carry the same stamp of elegance with which we mark everything that emanates from us, they seem somehow removed from the seat of intelligence, and should occupy only a secondary rank in the vast theory of elegance" (p. 74). Nonetheless, all signifiers that can be infused with spiritual connotations will convey a self-reflexive "poetic" message (p. 59). The dandy who incarnates "the principle of the elegant life . . . a sublime concept of order and harmony, whose purpose is to infuse poetry into material things," emerges as a living work of art (p. 59).[72]

In Balzac's exemplary analysis, dress is treated as the most profound of the four categories of elegance. Not only do we dress before we act or speak, he argues, but our speech and actions are products of the way we dress (p. 74). Sartorial perfection must be the foundation of the elegant life (pp. 105–6); whence the dandy's principal identification as "a man who prides himself on a supreme elegance in his attire" (162:[1835], s.v.). Anything but an ephemeral amusement (22:97), this mode of ornamentation contains the makings of a science. If the body, so Chapus maintains, were to be perceived as a geometric form—an inverted cone—then the art of dress could become an exact science in which the value of each sartorial sign could be permanently determined (121:80–81). The prevailing tendency, however, was to view the body not as an abstract form, but as an unfinished object of nature which dress, as a force of art and culture, must complete (21:II, 50). In a more metaphysical refraction of this attitude, the body partakes of a corrupt nature that dress has to redeem: "Fashion must therefore be considered . . . a sublime deformation of nature, or rather, a permanent and successive attempt at the reformation of nature," insisted Baudelaire; even children and savages understand "the high spirituality of dress" and reveal "by their naïve aspiration toward brilliance, many-colored plumage, shimmering fabrics and the superlative majesty of artificial forms, their loathing for reality" (51:II, 716).[73] These instinctive, spontaneous efforts to remedy a deficient nature represent the common denominator by which one can measure the achievement of the conscious artisans of modern heroism—Eugène Lami, Gavarni, Constantin Guys, and the dandy (II, 494, 687, 694–97).

With his art of dress, the dandy saw himself as inaugurating "a completely new order of distinction and aristocracy" (122:156–57). This was a particularly difficult task, since the Revolution had banished all automatically significant sartorial signs of distinction. "In the past," Ronteix pointed out, "each estate had its own distinct costume: the revolution eliminated this old practice. These days a duke dresses like a lawyer. . . . Our rank and status in society is no longer inscribed in the embroidery of the clothes we wear" (417:28). In what constitutes an early nineteenth-century topos, prerevolutionary clarity is contrasted with postrevolutionary confusion: "Today all the different styles of dress are mixed together; the various elements of attire have been stripped of their privilege" (415:222). In the area of male dress, at least, sartorial signifiers were now both fewer in number and sharply diminished in signifying force. This was an age when men's costume, as compared to the continued ornamentation of women, was designed to express a serious, work-oriented, democratic spirit. A generalized sobriety had muted the expressive sartorial language of the past. "How then can we recognize one another in all this uniformity?" asks Balzac. "By what external sign can we distinguish the rank of each individual?" (21:II, 476). Nothing demonstrated this egalitarian uniformity more clearly than the unornamented black garb that dominated male fashion from the 1830s onward. Pitiful and prosaic, as Gautier characterized it (210:58–59), this "uniform" seemed to provide no substance on which to base meaningful distinctions. But the creative mind will always find poetic connotations where none exist. Thus in fiction, the dandy's black garb became a sign of his profound seriousness and his *Weltschmerz* (487:1282). Drawing on the traditional associations of the color black, dandy-writers further depicted this costume as the vehicle for society's consuming ideas: "we are all dressed in black like so many people in mourning," observed Balzac (21:I, 345). In a similar vein, Baudelaire wrote that "the black suit and coat have . . . their own poetic beauty which expresses the spirit of the times. . . . We are all commemorating a burial" (51:II, 494).[74]

Among the Jeunes-France, however, there was widespread rebellion against the prosaic tyranny of black. Each member of this group, according to Gautier, "sought to call attention to himself through some sartorial peculiarity" (207:74), and donned what were decoded as costumes rather than clothing; Nestor Roqueplan, in Banville's opinion, looked "like a touring actor" (29:332). Gautier, whose pale green pants banded in black velvet and gray top coat lined in green satin may have launched this theatrical mode, revealed the underlying intent of his celebrated, often imitated, scarlet vest: to display contempt for established codes, to irritate and scandalize the philistines with "a piece of cloth of a most unusual, aggressive, and piercing shade" (207:91). Since this kind of effect was based on the principle of antithesis to a uniform thesis, it could and did generate a variety of sartorial signifiers. Those reminiscent of the "aristocratic" *ancien régime*, however, were especially frequent: "These precious idols constitute . . . a costumed resurrection of the annals of France. . . . At the Tuileries, you see pageboy haircuts from the reign of Charles VI, and from the era of Louis XIII and XIV, velvet doublets, lace and open-work collars, cavalier hats, short coats, ribbons, and rosette-trimmed shoes" (326:67). In an effort to go beyond mere imitation of an idealized past, certain dandy-groups mixed various prerevolutionary styles and collectively communicated a baffling array of mixed messages:

Their dress was not French. You would have been hard pressed to say precisely to what century and nation it belonged. One man had a trimmed black beard à la Francis I, the second a goatee and

close-cropped hair à la Saint-Megrin, a third a kingly beard like
Cardinal Richelieu; the others, still too young to possess this
important accessory, made up for it by the fullness of their head of
hair. One man had a black velvet doublet and skin-tight pants like
a medieval archer; another was dressed like a member of the
National Convention but with the pointed felt hat of the
Renaissance fop; still another had donned a dandy frock coat, with
a highly stylized cut and a fraise à la Henry IV. . . . It seemed that
they had all randomly and blindly taken from the hand-me-downs
of the centuries whatever they needed to create, as best they could,
a complete wardrobe. (210:215–16)

Such poetic juxtapositions were hardly accidental, since their
components recur in both fiction and nonfiction. In *Les Jeunes-
France*, for example, Elias Wildmanstadius displays all the trappings of the medieval knight, complete with a "merovingian"
hairdo and full beard (210); and in his *Histoire du romantisme*,
Gautier explains the significance of anachronistic beards: in 1830,
"there were only two in France: the beard of Eugène Dévéria and
the beard of Pétrus Borel! To sport a beard took a truly heroic
courage, sangfroid, and disdain for the masses! . . . We could thus
think of it as providing something novel, singular, and even
somewhat shocking" (207:21). Any sign, in fact, which classified
the emitter as *un flamboyant* and not *un grisâtre*, in Gautier's
terminology, conveyed the desired message; "the word 'artist*
excused everything," he adds, "and each person more or less
obeyed his own whim" (p. 93). The dandy did not merely invoke
the word, he emulated the achievements of artists, down to the
costumes depicted in masterful portraits. "Like all artists,"
Gautier says of his hero Onuphrius, " . . . he strove to imbue our
pitiful clothes with a colorful style and a less prosaic turn. He
modeled himself after a beautiful Van Dyck which he had in his
atelier; and he resembled it so perfectly you couldn't tell the two
apart. You would say that he was the portrait come out of its
frame or the mirror reflection of the painting" (210:58–59).[75]
　　Outside the radical Jeunes-France, however, the majority of
dandy-writers articulated a sartorial code that was closer in spirit
to *l'art de plaire*. They rejected *caprice* in theory, if not always in
their personal practice, in favor of apparent conformity to sar-

torial norms. Balzac, whose personal eccentricities were known (203:13), insisted, like a seventeenth-century *mondain*, that beyond fashion lies caricature, not heroism or artistry, and that profuse colors and excessive ornamentation are crude and tasteless (22:94, 95, 111–12). Barbey, who also personally favored *un habit de caprice* (142:27), endorsed this shift from the blatant to the subtle, which paralleled Brummell's own sartorial evolution: "He toned down the colors of his clothes, simplified their cut"; his style became "more intelligent than dazzling" (38:IX, 253, 251). Baudelaire in 1846 and Huysmans in 1884 were to trace the very same development in dandyism itself: "[the] eccentrics who were all too visible with their markedly violent colors . . . are satisfied today with the nuances of style and cut even more than those of color" (51:II, 494). This evolution reflected a widespread preference for subtle simplicity as the more persuasive sign of elegance: for Baudelaire, "sartorial perfection consists . . . in absolute simplicity, which is, in fact, the best way of being distinctive" (II, 710); or in Barbey's paradox: "everything was simple and *dandy*, as Brummell understood the term, in other words *unnoticeable*" (38:I, 125). More precisely, this imperceptibility furthers the dandy's desire to be "recognized by his own kind and not recognized by the populace" (22:112). It excludes from the circuit of communication the masses who are, by definition, insensitive to those nuances which allow members of the secret society to spot each other in a crowd (21:II, 34).[76]

"There are masonic signs, are there not?" asks Balzac, "by which *les gens comme il faut* recognize one another" (22:91). As a signifying system, dandyism contained a plethora of such nonverbal pointers. Beyond the subtleties of line and cut, it was the mode of inscription of the sartorial signifier, rather than its brute content, which conveyed secret meanings, in dandyism as in honnêteté. "It isn't the clothing but a certain way of wearing it that defines dress," insists Balzac as he develops the topos that a person's manner permeates even the most anodyne detail: "A man's mind can be divined by the way he holds his cane" (pp. 108, 35). Since the same tradesmen may supply both the artistocrat and his rank imitators in postrevolutionary society, it is that unique "turn," that indefinable "way of wearing our clothes," echoes

Raisson, "that accounts for their effect" (415:27). On these grounds, Barbey rejects Carlyle's famous definition of the dandy as "a clothes-wearing man": "he is not a suit of clothes walking all by itself! On the contrary, it is a certain way of wearing it that creates dandyism." The sartorial signifier is always eclipsed by the weight of the spiritual signified: "the clothes don't count *at all.* They are almost *nonexistent*" (38:IX, 307–8).[77]

Of all the signifiers in the dandy's sartorial repertory, the cravat was upheld as the foremost "symbol of the aristocratic superiority of his mind" (51:II, 710). The object of two substantial analyses—Raisson's *De la cravate considérée dans ses attributions morales, littéraires, politiques, militaires, religieuses* (1828) and Balzac's *De la cravate considérée en elle-même et dans ses rapports avec la société et les individus* (1830)—it represented the only sartorial signifier whose form the emitter must personally constitute. The cravat thus served as the synecdoche for originality in an egalitarian world. "The French became complete equals in their rights as well as in their dress," writes Balzac. ". . . From that moment on . . . the cravat . . . was called upon to reestablish the obliterated nuances of dress. It became the criterion by which we could distinguish the elegant from the uncouth. . . . A man is only as good as his cravat," he continues, ". . . by his cravat man is revealed and made known" (21:11, 47–48). In a more hierarchical sense, whereas the masses hang a cord around their necks, whereas even most beings who understand its significance are mere imitators, the dandy alone can express his vision of ideal beauty through the sculpture of the cravat (p. 49). For Raisson, this article is thus "the mark of genius" (415:227).[78]

In addition to the cravat, the idiolect of dandyism forged several other synecdoches that fulfilled the need to exhibit "as a sample of one's power, a sign designed to inform bystanders of one's position in the great pecking order" (22:46). Balzac compared to the *talons rouges, mouches,* and snuff of the *ancien régime* (p. 47) such signs as boots, sporting accoutrements, and lemon-yellow gloves (preferably from Bodier or Boivin) which were used by dandies to encode their membership in a caste; *gant jaune, corsaire à gants jaunes,* and *daim* (the leather out of which his gloves were made) became metonyms for the dandy. Another was the vest, owned and exhibited in hyperbolic quantity and diversity. In Charles Grandet's vast and "ingenious" collection, "some were gray, white, black, or scarab-colored, gold-flecked, spangled or chiné, reversible, with shawls, stand-up or turned back collars, and some had gold buttons or fastenings to the neck" (19:III, 509). One salon, in Balzac's ironic description, based its inclusions and exclusions on such signs as the books one had written, the carriage one owned, or the vests one wore (II, 106).[79] There was no irony, however, in de Marsay's explanation of the significance inherent in a vest, a glove, or a cravat, and of the dialectic of power in which such objects were inscribed: "Do you think it a small matter to have the right to enter a salon, survey everyone over the top of your cravat or through a lorgnon, and to have the capacity to scorn the most superior man if he is wearing an outmoded vest?" (V, 287). From Balzac to Barbey, the lorgnon magnifies the lion's eye, and becomes the lens through which he projects his contempt: "A mortal fear seized [Lucien de Rubempré] . . . when de Marsay eyed him; the Parisian *lion* then let his lorgnon drop in such an extraordinary manner that Lucien felt he had been struck by the blade of the guillotine" (IV, 624). That de Marsay wields his lorgnon at close range—precisely when he does not need to—confirms the nonfunctional, semiotically charged effect of the gesture. Yet another potent accessory sign was the recently imported cigar, to which the dandy claimed addiction. Balzac noted in *Physiologie du cigare*, that it could shoot smoke "at people's faces, something they did not find in any way amusing" (21:II, 440). In a less aggressive vein, Baudelaire saw in the cigar a symbol of aristocratic self-absorption and aloofness (51:I, 667).[80]

In the dandy's system, every ornament, every object, was tapped for its potential significance and its special contribution to the overdetermination of the intended message. "This ensemble, rigorously required by the principle of unity," assures Balzac, "makes all of the accessories of life interdependent" (22:82). With an almost pedantic insistence, a dandy in Sue's *Mystères de Paris* defines the range of his arsenal of signs: "From my stable to my table, from my dress to my house . . . I strove to make my life an example of taste and elegance" (492:562). In this system of values, food loses its utilitarian or functional properties and is elevated to the status of esthetic spectacle: "the chef d'oeuvre of a great artist" (487:II, 1357). Like Gautier's D'Albert, who cannot even ingest ordinary fare (211:140), the dandy-hero of Baudelaire's *La Fanfarlo* describes in detail "the requisite alimentary system for creatures of the elite" (51:I, 574)—the heavy burgundies, the exotic spices, truffles, and rare meat—a predilection of English origin, like the oxtail soup, haddock, roast beef, ale, and Stilton cheese savored by Des Esseintes. In a further deviation from bourgeois norms, Des Esseintes's home constitutes an artistic recreation of the most austere and vulgar abodes. Magnificent fabrics and furnishings are used to transform his bedroom into a monk's cell "which looked real but which, of course, was not" (266:98). His dining room becomes a ship's cabin, with an aquarium containing mechanical fish and water whose colors vary with the season and atmospheric conditions. A similarly motivated preference of art(ifice) over nature, of fantasy over reality, dominates the habitat of Gavarni who, according to the brothers Goncourt, loved secret doors and ingenious gadgets: "The mechanic in Gavarni, who was always attracted by the secret tricks of white magic and the machinations of sleight-of-hand, had designed a whole series of contraptions for his dwelling, which thus resembled a stage set à la Robert Houdin" (225:124). Gautier's Ferdinand ingeniously conjoins Louis XIII furniture and oriental objects—"daggers, pipes, narghiles, tobacco pouches, and a thousand other mummeries" (210:85). Whatever the style(s) the aim was the same: "a fantastic world in which everything is poetic" (205:33).[81]

Poetry, superiority, power. The dandy's elegance, in all its varied manifestations, produced the first to prove the second and to derive the third. In Musset's words, "Adornment is a weapon" (367:I, 240). Within the context of sartorial "uniformity," the dandy unearthed and forged the tools that gave him a power which others, even outsiders, had to acknowledge. Seeing Maxime de Trailles for the first time, the neophyte Rastignac is dumbfounded by "the superiority which dress gave this dandy" (19:II, 894); and Charles Grandet, arriving in Saumur "with all of the superiority of a fashionable young man," strikes Eugénie as "a creature descended from some seraphic region" (III, 508, 511). The dandy's reward for his efforts was to partake of "the royalty of fashion" (III, 91), and at the apex of the paradigm, to become the *arbiter elegantiarum* whose innovations mark him as a prophetic leader, always to be followed by an ignorant throng. "The intelligent, enlightened minds walk ahead and show the way," Balzac wrote in *Physiologie de la toilette*; "the masses follow willy-nilly more or less quickly; they adopt what is good but often use it unawares, without any understanding of what they are doing" (21:II, 52, 82). Contemptuous of the ignorant in the self-possessed splendor of his elegant body, the dandy was the incarnation of *l'art de plaire en déplaisant.*[82]

The Meaning of Manners

"Those minds which view things only from the most trivial angle," Barbey declared in his treatise, "have supposed that dandyism was above all the art of dressing, a felicitous and audacious tyranny in matters of dress and superficial elegance. That is most definitely true, but it is much more than that. Dandyism is a whole way of being, and man does not live by the physical or visible things alone. It is a way of being, comprised entirely of nuances" (38:IX, 229). Like all exemplary dandies, argued Barbey, Brummell had achieved eminence primarily by his "ineffable manners": their subtle nuances could never be articulated and surely not imitated, but their effect was faultless (p. 234). The importance of such nuances, Balzac speculated, derived from the abolition of traditional distinctions by the Revolution; hereafter, "atmospheric mutations" alone could distinguish the behavior of the aristocrat (21:II, 34). By that very token, however, the most minute flaw could undermine the entire strategy: "a single dissonance, as in music, negates the art itself" (19:IV, 613).[83]

Within the dandy's system of manners, gentlemanly civility and insinuating politeness were regarded by some writers as the essential units of significance. Chapus and Mortemart Boisse agree with Balzac that "an impolite man is the leper of the fashionable world" (22:73). In practice, however, those who display an appealing politeness interject subtle negative signs that produce a mixed message; Senanges, in Ancelot's *L'Homme du monde*, for example, exhibits the most refined manners, but his mien conveys counterindicating signs that discourage any effort to approach him (8:586, 600). Exaggerated politeness, in particular, served to scramble the messages of *plaire* and *déplaire* by creating an anachronistic effect which disquieted the bourgeois (29:74); Gautier's Ferdinand, by combining excessive gallantry with condescending respect, forces others to blush or bite their tongues (210:61). This perversion of traditional politeness often proved to be more humiliating and cruel than outright insolence. Insolence, conversely, needed the norm of traditional courtesy as the line from which to deviate. Like linguistic contexts which allow measurement of stylistic *écart*, a fixed set of behavioral expectations provided the backdrop for the cultivation of social singularity. Lucien Leuwen soon discovers the effectiveness of this strategy: at first civil and polite, he learns that the vulgar will show respect in direct proportion to his insolence (487:I, 1029). For Barbey, however, insolence is a crude and obvious version of impertinence, a quality which requires a most delicate balance: "The child of Nimbleness and Aplomb—traits which seem mutually exclusive—Impertinence is also sister to Grace with which it must stay united. Each is enhanced by its contrast to the other. Isn't it in fact true that without Impertinence, Grace would resemble a dull blonde and that without Grace, Impertinence would be an all too piquant brunette? For each to fulfill its potential they must be intermingled" (38:IX, 257).[84] With this synthesis of opposites, this perfect blend of seasonings, the dandy offends and conquers simultaneously. Thus Henri de Marsay "conquers the right" to be impertinent because of his graceful manners, and becomes the undisputed leader of the dandies, "the illustrious impertinents," of *La Comédie humaine* (19:IV, 614; II, 874). From Balzac to Baudelaire, the dandy is praised for "the most admirable," "the most irreproachable impertinence" (IV, 784; 51:II, 631–32).

Dandyistic impertinence was all the more effective stylistically because it emanated from a backdrop of total composure. Repressing powerful emotions, like the honnête homme before him, the dandy valorized *le flegme*, which Philinte had recommended to Alceste. In the nineteenth-century corpus, however, what is invariably called *le flegme brittanique* represents a positive sign in the French dandy's eyes, a negative one in the receiver's. Gavarni, according to the Goncourt biography, "took an instinctive liking to things and customs that shock people on the continent, and, by a somewhat paradoxical bent of mind, he believed that British coldness, reserve, and phlegm, that temperament which is opposite, contrary, and repugnant to ours, had an austere charm" (225:220–21). In French dandyism, the "pose" of indolence and apathy conveys the "charming" message that one has experienced it all, and therefore, is above it all (38:IX, 309, #11). It identifies the other as a bore and affirms the dandy's absence from a circuit of communication which curtails his autonomy. Interest in the other betokens imperfection in the self—this was the logic behind Brummell's apathy: "his indolence," Barbey explains, "did not allow him to get excited, because to get excited is to feel passion; to feel passion is to want something badly; and to want anything badly is to show that one is inferior" (p. 256).[85]

Beyond this lethargic impassivity, *l'air anglais* included a *sang-froid*, which was literalized to mean iciness, the antithesis of the hot-blooded French prototype. Here again Brummell served as a model; his elegant *froideur* surrounded him in a protective armor that "made others believe he was invulnerable" (p. 314, #32). The chilling manner which is cultivated by French dandies from Julien Sorel to Barbey's Robert de Tressignies, sometimes to the point of steely glaciality (487:I, 484; 38:I, 348), mystifies and shocks, and thereby can be counted among those "captivating airs which constitute beauty" (51:I, 659). More often, however, the icy and the lymphatic, which designate two different kinds of water, are combined with fiery passion on an axis that differentiates the displayed from the concealed. In this topos, a "stagnant," glacial manner reveals to the perceptive observer enormous subjacent passion (38:I, 210); in the case of Poe, Mérimée, and Delacroix, Baudelaire noted, "the very same mantle of ice cloaked . . . an ardent passion" (51.II, 758). As an esthetic presence, the dandy generates the sustained tension between ice and a fire willfully contained: "The beauty of the dandy derives above all from his cold air which is the product of unshakable resolve never to feel emotion; it resembles a latent spark which we can sense, and which could glow but refuses to" (II, 712).[86]

To dominate the self is to dominate the other. To want the other is to be wanting. "To love, even in the least spiritual sense of the term, that is, to desire, is always to be dependent, to be slave to one's desire," insisted Barbey. "The most tenderly embracing arms are still chains" (38:IX, 246). Like the honnête homme, the dandy was never to fall passionately in love; Stendhal's characters, who are the exception, experience fear of ridicule and deception, even shame and degradation. In contrast to honnêteté, however, it was part of the dandyistic idiolect to express an inability to love: "When it comes to love," de Marsay proudly declares, "I became as atheistic as a mathematician" (19:III, 218). That Brummell was not known to have had a mistress struck Barbey as a unique case among men who are "born to seduce" (38:IX, 245), and who have always indulged in extra- and nonmarital affairs; but his avoidance of love was perfectly consistent with basic dandyistic principles: "The moment a dandy falls in love, he is no longer a dandy. Dandyism stops at love" (33:II, 177). In more attenuated terms, Baudelaire subscribed to the same notion: "Love is the natural occupation of idle men, but the dandy does not consider love a special goal" (51:II, 710).[87]

The manifest indifference, incapacity, or refusal to love overlay a fear of subordination, of castration, that finds its logical expression in the dandy's misogynism. Overturning the pedestal on which courtly love placed the lady, rejecting the Romantic ideal of the Madonna, the dandy dismissed woman as "a bundle of stupid nonsense" (19:V, 286), and even as an animal devoid of soul, the incarnation of human depravity (51:I, 682–83, 693–94, 697–98). As mistress, she was a slave, an instrument of sexual pleasure, "a delightful pillow for sleeping, yawning and making love" (211:194; 38:XI, 45), or often just another status symbol: "You have a stylish woman just as you have a fine horse, a necessary item in a young man's array of luxuries" (482:6), an accessory, an ornament, an "object" that can "fill out his stylish appearance" (210:98). For Rastignac, a society woman is "the diamond that a man uses to cut open all the windows when he does not have the golden key that opens all the doors" (19:III, 15)—not even an object of pure value, but a mere cutting tool, a means of penetration, an instrument of aggression.[88]

Himself a work of art, the dandy will valorize women only as a mediating agency through which to further his quest for beauty. The female's resemblance to a favorite painting as the source of desire is a topos from Balzac to Barbey: Henri de Marsay pursues Paquita Valdès because she is the reincarnation of *La Femme caressant sa chimère*, while Barbey's Robert de Tressignies is obsessed by the prostitute who resembles Vernet's *Judith* and a courtesan by Veronese. Conversely, Gautier's D'Albert envisages an ideal woman who is the synthesis of his favorite paintings and sculptures, and judges real female forms accordingly: "How is the arm? Pretty good. —The hands have a certain delicacy. —What do you think of the foot? The ankle lacks nobility and the heel is common. But the breast is well placed and well shaped, its line is serpentine, even undulating, the shoulders are soft, plump and attractive. —Yes, this woman would serve as a tolerable model, you could perfect a number of her proportions. —We'll love her" (211:191). D'Albert, a latter-day Pygmalion, rejects this particular female form because he cannot mold it to perfection; but ultimately, he finds in Rosalinde the realization of his artistic ideal and thus a source of erotic stimulation: "the painter full satisfied, the lover regained the upper hand" (p. 367). Samuel Cramer, for whom desire is "above all an admiration and appetite for beauty" (51:I, 577), disdains La Fanfarlo's exquisite nude body, preferring to make love with her in her stage costume and makeup. Like D'Albert, Samuel has attained that peak of esthetic (i.e., dandyistic) sensibility "where beauty itself no longer suffices unless seasoned by perfume, adornment, et cetera" (447:131).[89]

Although the dandy judges the female as he wishes to be viewed—a work of art—he never relinquishes his superordinate position. In a reversal of the sexual dynamics of courtly love, he rejects the role of Werther in favor of Don Juan and thinks of love "the way a general plans out his maneuvers" (482:233). With this militaristic model of sexual conquest in mind Julien Sorel engineers the seduction of the awesome Mathilde de la Môle. With similar intent, Raimbaud de Maulevrier in Barbey's *L'Amour impossible* resolves "to attack the vanity of . . . this fortress which was impregnable to love. She will not love me the more for it," he muses as he contemplates the icy Mme de Gesvres, "but she will succumb . . . coldly and elegantly still wearing her armor" (38:IX, 109). Like the archetypal Don Juan, the dandy loses interest once assured of conquest: "Because he triumphed so easily," observed Balzac, "de Marsay was bound to be bored with his triumphs. . . . Like so many rulers, he had finally come to implore fortune for some obstacle to overcome, some enterprise that would require the deployment of his inactive moral and physical powers" (19:V, 284–85). The need for ever more challenging obstacles leads to what is encoded as perverse eroticism, which ends, as it originates, in dissatisfaction. Marsay's extravagant fantasies and ruinous tastes bring him no gratification until he meets the lesbian Paquita Valdès, a mysterious, alluring but attainable synthesis of the satanic and the divine, the ugly and the beautiful. That he allows her to dress him in female clothes in a reversal of sexual roles does not mean, however, that he has abandoned the will to dominate; this "surrender" serves, rather, to raise the stakes of sexual combat with an opponent capable of challenging his strength and thus of renewing his desire. Barbey's Marigny describes an identical source of pleasure: "I had a fancy for slavery. In our liaison, I was the odalisque and she the sultan. . . . I felt pleasure seeing her . . . imperiousness even in my arms; a shaking lioness whose wrath was so like her caress" (38:V, 165). Through role inversion, the dandy aspires to a kind of singular experience which Gautier's D'Albert brings into sharp focus: "In moments of sexual pleasure, I would gladly have changed roles, for it is most frustrating never to experience the effect one produces " (211:95).[90] In this search for sexual doubleness, the dandy reveals his desire to be both the emitter and the receiver of a self-contained communication system. The ultimate goal of this sexual quest is thus hermaphroditic unity: "One cannot imagine anything more ravishing than those two perfect bodies harmoniously fused . . . which form a single beauty superior to both . . . ; for someone who worships form exclusively, can there be a more captivating uncertainty?" (pp. 201–2). With its incomparably artistic form, its unique ambiguity and bivalence, the hermaphrodite not only translates the dandy's "perverse" sexuality, it exemplifies the means and the message of dandyism. It was the global implications of this concept that writers had in mind when they compared the dandy, in nonsexual contexts, to the androgyn: for Jouy in the 1820s (277:I, 337), for Barbey in the 1840s, dandies were "androgyns, no longer of myth but of history" (38:IX, 278). But it was Lemaître, in his essay on Barbey (1889), who brought out the fullest implications of the relation between androgyny and *l'art de plaire en déplaisant*: "This sovereignty of manners which he elevates to the stature of other types of royalty he usurps from women, who alone seemed born to exercise that power. He dominates in a woman's way and even with a woman's means. And he gets women themselves and, what is even more surprising, men to accept this usurpation of functions. The dandy has something antinatural and androgynous about him by which he can be infinitely seductive" (301:IV, 58).[91]

A Dandy Idiolect

Brummell's "effect on others," wrote Barbey, "was even more immediate than any which language alone can create. He produced that effect by his intonation, look, gesture . . . even his silence. This is one possible explanation for the few words he left" (38:IX, 257). Another explanation was that conversation, although praised by some as "the unique pleasure of superior beings," had ceased to be an art in nineteenth-century society. Brummell was "a consummate conversationalist," insisted Barbey, but even in fashionable circles, "his mind, which required mental sparks from others to reach full blaze, had nothing to work with" (p. 271). In France, good talk, like so many other aristocratic pastimes, had gone out with the Revolution: "There has never been a more barren time for the art of conversation" (121:137). Valorizing the past to condemn the present, Balzac wonders where he can find those conversations which had formerly made Paris "the capital of the spoken word" (21:I, 350); in his novels, the circle of Mlle des Touches represents "the last retreat where the old French esprit has found refuge" (19:III, 208–9). The topos of the progressive disappearance of *l'esprit français* served not only to condemn society's egalitarianism and materialism, but also to underscore the dandy's superiority without ever subjecting him to communication with others. Silence, which had been a form of courtesy for the honnête homme, expresses here a particularly contemptuous message: "*Le fashionable* seems to say: . . . There is no point in speaking to you; you would never understand me" (432:82–83). In Brummell's case, silence, enlisted as a technique in the esthetics of power, was "one more means of creating an effect—the coquettish teasing of creatures confident of their appeal who know precisely how to kindle desire" (38:IX, 312, #26).[92]

Despite the inclusion of speech among the principal categories of elegance, the art of conversation occupies little space in the treatises on dandyism. The authors of some texts continue to pay lip service to the *art de plaire*, but *déplaire* has clearly become the order of the day. The dandy's "jargons" or "elegant dialects," whose popularity is attested by Balzac (19:V, 230; 21:II, 38), contained "particular modes of pronunciation" (364:29) that subverted ideals of clarity and purity. The *incroyable*, for example, was known for replacing *ch* by *s* and *g* by *z*; *le cocodès* was prone to "lisp and simper"; and the dandy of the 1850s would omit a syllable, drop a final vowel or *s*—the aristocratic version of the linguistic law of least effort (295:s.v.). These instances of phonetic deviance served to singularize the dandy, and were calculated to mystify and alienate the outsider, and to confront him, at yet another level, with his own ignorant inferiority. Parallel effects were achieved semantically through recourse to anglicized parlance and most especially to the idiolects of the lower classes and the underworld, which the Romantics had espoused in their revolt against the "purity" of the French classical idiom. In *Des mots à la mode*, Balzac enumerated some of the hyperboles—*cassant, remarquablement, étourdissant, culminant, outrageusement*, and *ravissant*—which, in an echo of *préciosité*, were included among the secrets of fashionable language (21:II, 38); to this list the Jeune-France idiolect added: *phosphorescent, transcendental, pyramidal, stupéfiant, foudroyant*, and *annihilant* (210:87). That adjectives such as *ineffable, monumental, délirant, mirifique* (21:II, 33–38) were used to describe a material signifier like a vest surely offended linguistic purists but pointed to the spiritual connotations ascribed to signs of elegance. In the esthetics of dandyism, however, such a lexicon was ultimately a weapon, which needed continual sharpening if its full power was to be tapped: "A man who knows the latest linguistic fashions is armed with immense power. He has the right to eye disdainfully the fool who asks him the meaning of a word, to laugh in his face; exclaim: 'What! you don't know that word?'; explain it with cruel condescension; submit him to a lecture; prove to everyone that the man is backward, etc., etc. . . . Not speaking as others do, a man who possesses the secret of fashionable language has the pleasure of hearing others say: Mr. X. has a certain way of expressing himself . . . I don't know, but his conversation has something *distinguished* about it . . ." (II, 34).[93]

With language, as with the other elements of dandyism, innovation and eccentricity, paradox and hyperbole numbered among the techniques that created a contrast to an established norm. As a speaking subject, the dandy sought to strike, wherever possible and profitable, an opposing, paradoxical stance that would singularize him (432:82–83). Thus he spoke mockingly of serious matters and seriously of frivolous ones "so that you never know where you stand when you listen" (38:XIII, 77). Maximizing the "power of the monosyllable," he could manifest his disdain nonchalantly, apathetically in an occasional, incidental word, or crush his interlocutor under the dead weight of a lapidary phrase (I, 188, 271). Or he could submerge the would-be emitter in an endless monologue, the kind of one-way communication that Baudelaire described as "a kind of fraternity founded on contempt" (51:II, 313). As with the quantity of signs, their quality could vary with powerful and disturbing effects. The conversation of Ancelot's Count de Senanges was piquant and witty at one moment, and the next, crushingly sarcastic (8:600, 611). Similarly, as Baudelaire observed, Edgar Allan Poe knew "the art of ravishing, stimulating thoughts and fantasies, lifting the spirit from the mire of routine," but just as often overwhelmed his listeners with his absolute cynicism (51:II, 313).[94]

Cynicism, sarcasm, and irony constituted the primary units of significance in the dandy's speech. However cruel, it was never crude—its deadly sting was tempered and concealed by appealing signs, a combination designed to elicit admiration and inspire respect, even to force others' connivance in their own humiliation. Always the prototypical dandy, Brummell concealed his savage irony beneath a seductive nonchalance that drove others to expose their most hidden and grotesque defects, thereby stimulating a bored, sadistic society and enhancing his own unique prestige (38:IX, 255). The power of this exemplary irony was one which Barbey understood: "It envelops a man with a sphinxian air which is as disquieting as danger. Brummell possessed this air and used it to terrorize everyone's egos even as he flattered them" (p. 255), he concluded, encapsulating the amalgam of *plaire* and *déplaire* that defines the esthetic strategy of dandyism. It remained for Aloys de Synarose, one of Barbey's fictional heroes modeled on Brummell, to push this art to its outer limits of perfection: "An eternal irony dictated his words, an irony so profound that nothing in the softness of his voice or the courtesy of his language revealed its mystery. . . . You experienced it the same way as, when listening to the harmonica—that celestial music! ineffable pleasure!— you feel you are about to faint" (XI, 40).[95]

The dandy's devastating irony, bewildering alternations in conversational style, the minimal or excessive quantity of his speech, his "impure" and incomprehensible idiom replete with neologisms, these were among the signs that were designed to offend, as the conversation of the honnête homme strove to beguile. No less pronounced were the contradictions between the manner(s) of the honnête homme and the dandy—civility and impertinence, affability and glaciality, animation and indolence. Beyond the extensive list of binaries that the juxtaposition of units of significance in other paradigms would provide, the four basic semiological categories in the systems of honnêteté and dandyism revealed different hierarchical structures that placed a premium on manners and speech in one instance, body and dress in the other. And from a systemic perspective, the signs emerged as more uniform in the seventeenth century and more varied in the nineteenth century, when they were subjected to less intensive metalinguistic analysis.

While such oppositions pinpoint obvious differences, they

overlook the more meaningful similarities between the honnête homme and the dandy. If the two systems valorized some of the same specific signs—hidden beauty which included ugliness, a patrician air and graceful ease, understated elegance, phlegmatic calm and a total composure that rejected passionate love and the female which symbolized that enslavement—both systems, even where distinctively dissimilar, predicated poeticity, like all texts, on deviations from codes and contexts, deviations that were subtle in the honnête homme's case and blatant in the dandy's. Because the seventeenth-century noble emphasized the body and its ornamentation, the honnête homme deemphasized them, only to have the dandy reemphasize them in opposition to postrevolutionary values. Because the noble lacked *politesse*, the honnête homme glorified it; because the nineteenth-century bourgeois believed in being polite, the dandy preferred impertinence. Because the noble spoke impurely, the honnête homme cleansed and purified the language that the dandy was determined to contaminate and impurify. That one wished to *plaire* and the other to *plaire en déplaisant* confirms a common purpose—to seduce like Circe—while it reveals the subtle but determining shifts in the strategic semes that could realize that goal—from seduction to satanism, mystery to mystification, ravishing surprise to stunning fear, persuasion to paralysis and petrification. In that process, the signifiers and signified changed, but not on the ultimate connotational level: each sign signified first and always the superior man. To achieve that end the honnête homme and the dandy utilized the same basic means: the transformation of every pertinent element of body, dress or ornamentation, manner, manners, and speech into a system of poetic signs, laden with secret, nondiscursive meanings, that aimed to extract a powerful response from the receiver and reflect autotelically back on the superiority of the emitter.

That the honnête homme and the dandy devoted their energies to transforming the self into a work of art might seem gratuitous to a Gidean, absurd to an existentialist, frivolous to a puritan.[96] But it is precisely in appropriating what we deem to be the insignificant and injecting it pervasively and profoundly with significance that the artistic feat of the honnête homme and the dandy can be measured. Jules Lemaître wrote of the dandy in 1889, though his remarks apply equally to the honnête homme: "From an ensemble of insignificant and useless practices he fashions a craft which bears his personal stamp, and which appeals and seduces in the manner of a work of art. He confers on minute signs of costume, bearing and language, a meaning and a power they do not naturally possess. *In short, he makes us believe in what does not exist.* He 'reigns by his airs,' as others do by talent, strength or wealth. He creates out of nothing a mysterious superiority . . . whose impact is as great as those superiorities that men have categorized and recognized" (301:57–58). Overturning the traditional notions of merit (p. 57), the honnête homme and the dandy "made something out of nothing" and thereby revealed the arbitrariness inherent in all systems: "Because he makes something with nothing, because his inventions consist of perfectly superfluous nothings which have worth only by the personal meaning he gave them, he teaches us that things have no value except the one we attach to them, and thus, that 'idealism is truth'" (pp. 58–59). Both the honnête homme and the dandy evinced a strong belief in the connections between signifier and signified that the artistic sensibility can create, and as such, in idealism as the true principle of poetry. Instead of accepting the existing order of things and signs, they strove to unearth and manifest the artistic within the mundane, the spiritual in the material, and in Baudelaire's terms, "the serious in the frivolous" (51:II, 710).[97] It is, of course, on an "other scene," behind the scene of self-representation, that the honnête homme and the dandy forged the signs of artistocracy that fashion the self-as-art. An understanding of that essential process (which, from a sequential perspective, antedates the product) requires a shift of focus from the circuit of communication between the emitter and the receiver to the internal mechanisms of production—from the *phénotexte* to the *génotexte* (283:280 ff.). Underlying and determining the signs in the system, the process of production is the deep structure that contains the final meaning of the honnête homme and the dandy.

CHAPTER FOUR

THE PROCESS AND ETHICS
OF PRODUCTION

The ideal you envisage is noble, but
are you a noble enough stone to be
made into such an image?

Nietzsche, *The Gay Science*

"This game is no longer a game but a truth," insists the eponymous hero of Rotrou's *Saint-Genest*, "in which by my actions I
am represented . . . I, the object and the actor of my *self*" (IV.vii).
In the play of signs that constitutes the poetic representation of
self—performance, for Rotrou's dramatic actor—a single subject
subsumes the dual functions of artist ("actor of my self") and
work of art ("object"). In honnêteté and dandyism, as in acting,
however, special complexities inevitably attend the creative act,
since the producer and the product inhabit the same being. To
isolate the steps in the performative process of honnêteté and
dandyism, and to approximate the sequence by which the self-as-
artist produces the self-as-art, requires the elaboration of a
theoretical model. Viewed as finished performances, the honnête
homme and the dandy, we might say, mark the culmination of a
process that predicates a doer who has successfully put to the test
his intention, knowledge, and capacities (*vouloir*, *savoir*, *pouvoir*).
Such an approach is consistent with the more complex model of
"potential human doing" provided by the six actants which
Greimas has developed for the understanding of narrative structures (236:172 ff.). According to the Greimasian scheme, the artist-
doer as "actor" fulfills the actantial function of the Sender
(*Destinateur*) or "the bestower of the Good." But since his goals
are preeminently self-reflexive, he also acts as the Receiver

(*Destinataire*) or ultimate "obtainer of the Good." As Sender, he determines the achievement of the object of desire, the self-as-art, which marks the passing of a test (*épreuve*) on the part of the subject, the natural, pre-performative self. The terminal predicative relation between Subject (*St*) and Object (*O*)—superposition (*O/St*), elimination (*O/St̸*), or transformation (*St* → *O*)—lies at the core of the problematics of production in both honnêteté and dandyism. Although the "choice" among these possible relations depends in part on those supportive or hindering actantial factors in the process that Greimas calls Helper (*Adjuvant*) and Opponent (*Opposant*), the primary actors in the production of the self-as-art are the artist-doer, the natural self and the artistic object.[1]

Nature, Artifice, and the Ideal Artifact

In honnêteté as in dandyism, it is Sender who generates the process of production; it is his esthetic values and perception of the Subject as a datum of nature that determine the particular predicative procedures required for the creation of the as yet nonexistent Object. In the seventeenth century, of course, Nature and naturalness have more to do with the effects of Art than with its origins. Nature in its raw or primitive form, however, is often characterized as uncouth, unappealing, vulgar, brutal (172:183, 395:337). It is this negative nature that Méré has in mind when he writes to a pupil: "I don't know who gave you the idea that everything that seems natural should be appealing; you don't realize that nature is made up of good and evil, beauty and ugliness, appealing as well as unappealing objects and that no sight is more widespread or more natural than that of the *malhonnête homme*" (339:224). Although the ambivalence of the term *nature* has maintained itself to this day, during the last third of the seventeenth century its sense as an esthetic denominator was sharpened by the addition of positive qualifiers—"the most perfect and polished nature" (p. 224), for example—or the celebrated cliché *la belle nature*, which became the pivotal concept in the classical doctrine of imitation. To form and formulate the model of *la belle nature*, so we read in a typical passage from Méré, "we must observe and select the most beautiful, appealing and captivating elements that we can find, not only in physical [nature] but also in the intellectual, the intelligible, the invisible or the spiritual" (p. 224)—no easy task, since the "most captivating elements" are often the most obscure (418:57). Nor does mere selection suffice. In Rapin's words, the artist must go "a little farther than nature" (85:151) to correct and reform its defects, supplement its deficiencies, remedy its disorder and irregularities (15:310). The goal of art and of the artist, according to Perrault's rehearsal of this esthetic commonplace, is ultimately to "apprehend the idea of the beautiful, which not only brute nature but even *la belle nature* itself have never attained; this is the ideal on which he must model his work, and he must use nature only as a means to achieve it" (395:337).[2]

The seventeenth-century theoreticians on art and honnêteté knew full well that the model for their ruminations on *la belle nature* went directly back to Plato. "Someone will undoubtedly say," writes Méré in *De la vraie honnêteté*, "that I am conceiving ideas that no one has ever seen, like the Republic of the divine Plato or the Orator of the most eloquent of the Romans. . . . It is true that we see so very few [true *honnêtes gens*] that we don't really know how we would react to them" (340:III, 78–79). Honnêteté, he admits, *is* "a pure idea . . . all we ever see is its shadow and outward appearance" (339:522). Its immutable essence must be sought beyond the natural sphere "which can be apprehended by our senses," in that "invisible world of infinite extension [where] we can uncover the reasons and the principles underlying reality, the most hidden truths . . . the authentic models, and the ideal forms of everything that we seek" (pp. 124–26). Because no single honnête homme can ever be the perfect incarnation of honnêteté—"the most perfect model cannot encompass everything" (340:III, 98)—because the imitation of even such a model would produce nothing more than an imperfect reflection of an imperfect reflection, twice removed from the pure idea of honnêteté, Méré insists that "we must model ourselves solely on ideas of perfection" (III, 148). Sharing Plato's optimism, however, Méré maintains that "excellent workers" can perhaps achieve this perfection: "sometimes we come so close to perfection that we can rejoice in the same way as if we had really found it, and perhaps we do find it occasionally, and should be more confident" (II, 81, 83). And yet, since we can never be certain of reaching or holding on to perfection (II, 101), and such presumption predicates against success (I, 54), Méré repeatedly urges the honnête homme to push his capacities to their outer limits and come "as close as we can" to the idea of honnêteté (II, 93).[3]

With this transcendent ideal as his model, the Sender calls upon the power of artifice as the principal Helper in transforming the natural self (*St*) into a work of art (*O*). The lie which can produce artistic truth, artifice must be wrought so deftly and delicately that it will allow us to "carry off with an appealing air those things that come naturally to us," writes Méré (340:III, 74), building on the paradox of the *artifice agréable* that was central to French classical esthetics. As summed up by La Bruyère, it consists in awareness of the nonnatural origins of what seems natural: "How much art it takes just to achieve the effects of nature! so many rules, so much time, attention and effort to dance with the same freedom and grace with which we have learned to walk" (286:355–56, #34). The overt message of artifice, on the other hand, would connote affectation, a falseness that is destructive of nature, instead of an artistic fiction that perfects it (80:10). The terminal predicative function of artifice, then, is to produce its own invisible disguise. The proverbial *Ars est celare artem* is the intertextual reference in La Bruyère's statement and in Méré's reflections as well: "Not that we can ever put too much art or artifice in anything we do . . . but neither the one nor the other should be obvious" (340:II, 109). For visible signs of artifice undermine all claims to superiority: "If art does not take us in adroitly, we feel contempt for it, and the artist looks ridiculous" (III, 108). To avoid such ridicule—the ungainly, unesthetic bumbling that seventeenth-century comedy exposes—the artist calls upon yet another "dissimulated artifice" (I, 143), that "pleasant deception" (II, 34) known as *négligence*: with the help of "a certain *négligence* which conceals artifice and confirms that we give no thought to anything we do" (188:20), the Sender can display the kind of naturalness which is the mark of great art.[4]

A century later, preromanticism initiated an anti-classical valorization of primitive and untutored nature. By 1830, however, what had become the esthetics of identity began to yield to yet another esthetics of opposition, of which dandyism was a primary manifestation. "Shut up, you ugly beast," so Gautier begins his assault on nature in the preface to *Les Jeunes-France* (210:ix), before he goes on to revile it as stupid and thoughtless, and natural human needs as ignoble and disgusting (211:23). In Baudelaire's vision, nature, not merely restrictive, becomes malevolent and criminal: "Nature . . . *compels* man to sleep, to drink, to eat. . . . It is also nature which incites man to kill his brother, to eat him, to imprison him, to torture him. . . . It is that unfailing nature which has created parricide and cannibalism, and a thousand other abominations. . . . Picture, analyze everything that is natural, all the actions and desires of the purely natural man, you will find nothing but horrors" (51:II, 715); from this perspective, nature is to art as sin is to virtue (pp. 527, 660 ff., 718). At best, it may function as a dictionary from which the artist takes elements that he must reform, in both the moral and plastic senses of the term, by giving them "a completely new physiognomy" (p. 747). At bottom, nature is nothing more than an incoherent mass which serves as a stimulus (*incitamentum*) to produce the form and order that it lacks (p. 752). For Baudelaire, therefore, art must be essentially supernatural or nonnatural (pp. 715–18) and its primary aim must be to protest *against* nature (218:254).[5]

In Gautier's extreme version, art emerges as nothing less than antinatural (212:27). Under such a dispensation, artifice becomes the very message of the artistic product, and when transmuted into the esthetic principle of "the artificial," signifies "a creation which owes its existence entirely to art and from which nature is completely absent" (p. 39). To Gautier, no creation exemplified this ideal more fully than Baudelaire's *Rêve parisien*, a poem in which nothing lives or breathes, no blade of grass, leaf, or flower disturbs the implacable symmetry of fictitious forms invented by art (p. 40). In the behavior and attitudes of the notorious dandy, Nestor Roqueplan, he saw an equally strenuous rejection of nature: his life was a "crusade against the sun, against the countryside . . . against nature which he tolerated only in paintings" (207:175). When art becomes the only reality, nature must seem false; Gautier's Tiburce reaches the point "where he no longer finds nature true" (213:160). In a more aggressive protest against nature, his dandy-hero,

Fortunio, replaces the natural world beyond his windows with man-made dioramas, which allow him to (re)create his surroundings daily; "which country," his valet asks him, "would you like us to serve you today?" (p. 143). The last word in the dandy's desire to go "against the natural grain" is Des Esseintes's: there is no moonlight, he argues, that electric light cannot reproduce, no cascade that hydraulics cannot equal to perfection, no rock, no flower, which man cannot fabricate (266:52). Going beyond imitation and re-production, Des Esseintes's olfactory experiments, wherein he blends fragrances associated with diverse seasons, landscapes, and sites, create a synthetic world which exists nowhere in nature. The era of nature is over, he proclaims, as he inaugurates the reign of artifice.[6]

The dandy's life was to be "an artificial existence" (210:207). An object of beauty, he represented the antithesis of nature and the female, nature's archetypal symbol, the incarnation of appetite in Baudelaire's (in)famous formulation: "The female is the opposite of the dandy . . . the female is famished and she wants to eat, thirsty, and she wants to drink. She is in heat and wants to be fucked. . . . The female is *natural*, that is to say, abominable" (51:I, 677). The same antithesis underlies the opposition between the artificiality of social existence and the human (i.e., natural) needs that Barbey describes with faultless dandyistic logic: "When a person is dying of hunger, he abandons the affectations of the society he lives in and returns to human life: he ceases to be a dandy" (38:IX, 274). But as Barbey's statement also implies, the dandy's need to transcend nature, to realize what Sartre has called "the dream of an anti-Nature" (447:133), leads to an inevitable confrontation with the incontrovertible limitations of human nature. Gautier's dandy-hero, Tiburce, refuses to accept those limits, "suppresses nature, the world and life" (213:197), and thus mysteriously disappears from the text itself. Exploring his own attraction for *L'Idéal artificiel*, as he first entitled *Le Poème du hashish*, Baudelaire admired the ability of hallucinogens to produce "the enchanting spectacle of one's own corrected and idealized Nature," but ultimately rejected the "diabolical" drug which he feared would drag him down "even lower than his real Nature" and finally push him to suicide (51:I, 397, 409, 436–38). At the terminal point of the corpus of dandyism, the death of Des Esseintes's turtle, whose gem-encrusted shell produces the optical illusion of an ambulatory swarm of flowers, serves him as a final warning. Although he regards his capacity to be nourished by rectal injections as the crowning achievement in artificiality, the decisive "insult thrown in the face of old Nature whose uniform requirements would be forever abolished" (266:256), Des Esseintes's utter debilitation imposes a choice: death or abandonment of his "artificial paradise."[7]

The dandy's yearning for perfect artificiality, like the aspiration of the honnête homme to perfect naturalness and a perfected nature, must inevitably fall short of its sublime goal. The ideal, at one and the same time, stimulates action and defies fulfillment. The quest for the absolute, insists Baudelaire, produces *Les Plaintes d'un Icare*, the tormented feeling of being bogged down in "the ditch of the Ideal" (51:I, 143, 342). In Gautier's rendition, the dandy's sights are firmly set on the unattainable regions of Platonic forms: "Birds in the sky, lend me, each of you, a feather," begs D'Albert, ". . . so that I may make myself a pair of wings and fly high and fast through unknown regions . . . where I may forget that I am *me* and live a strange, new life . . . farther than the world's last isle, over the frozen ocean, beyond the pole where the aurora borealis trembles, into that impalpable kingdom where the divine creations of poets alight and the models of supreme beauty [reign]" (211:239). The failure of this Icarian venture evokes the combined imagery of the companion Platonic myth of the cave and of the doctrine of reminiscences in Rosette's analysis: "Something irresistible calls and attracts him, something that is neither of this world nor in this world . . . and like the heliotrope in a cave, he twists and turns to face a sun that he cannot see. He is one of those men whose soul was not immersed long enough in the waters of Lethe before it was attached to his body; his soul retains, from the heavens whence it came, reminiscences of eternal beauty which trouble and torment it; it remembers that it once had wings, but now all it has is feet" (p. 155). In the end, however, D'Albert finds consolation in the contemplation of immaculate human forms, most especially of hermaphrodites, those Platonic symbols of a primordial human oneness, which conserve "as in a Greek temple, the precious gift of form" (p. 315). Although palpable and material, such forms transcend nature and represent, in D'Albert's eyes, "the purest symbolization of eternal essence—beauty" (p. 315).[8]

D'Albert, in his own right, was a model for Samuel Cramer, the hero of Baudelaire's *La Fanfarlo*, who adores a beautiful human form for its "material harmony." But this "absolute materialism," Baudelaire emphasizes, "[is] not far from the purest idealism" (51:I, 577) since a material form *qua* form is the product and the sign of a subjacent spirituality: "In and of itself, every idea is endowed with an immortal life, just like a person. All forms, even those created by man, are immortal. Because form is independent of matter and it is not molecules that constitute form" (I, 705). In this essentially Platonistic conception of form, matter does not compromise the autonomy of the spiritual principle. On the contrary, its interconnection with spirit points to a modified conception of nature as the Helper rather than the Opponent of poetic production. For Baudelaire, as for Balzac, the Swedenborgian theory of correspondences provided a modern re-writing of the Platonic theory of participation: "It is this admirable, this immortal instinct for the beautiful that causes us to consider the earth and its spectacles as a glimpse, a *correspondence* of Heaven" (II, 113–14); "form, movement, number, color, fragrance—everything in the *spiritual*, as in the *natural*, realm is significant, reciprocal, correlative, *correspondent*" (II, 133). From within the metaphysic and esthetic of *correspondence*, the dandy cannot be viewed as the mere sum of his carefully assembled parts, but, in the same way as a poetic text, as corresponding to and standing for something that, objectively speaking, does not exist on his material (textual) body: he represents "the supreme incarnation of the idea of the beautiful in material life" (II, 326). On an even more global level, the dandy exemplifies, like every work of art, the collocation of the relative and the absolute, the body and the soul, the many and the one. A symbol of modernity, "the transitory, the ephemeral, the contingent" (II, 695), the self-as-art is the "titillating envelope" which alone makes the "divine *gâteau*" of absolute beauty digestible on earth (II, 685).[9]

The theoretical bridge between ideality and poetic reality does not span the gap between nature and art, nor does it identify the process which, in practice, allows the passage from one to the other.

Process and Ethics of Production

The broad outlines of this process are implicit, however, in Baudelaire's acknowledgment of the exigencies of nature, the acceptance of its "uncontrollable law" (I, 438), that will enable the Sender to combine bread with wine, the natural self with the symbol of the transformative spiritual principle, so as to produce finally "a third person . . . the superior man, who derives equally from the other two" (I, 387). The power of this transformative principle may be gauged by the dramatic comparison between two women, the one natural, the other supernatural: "One of them was a rustic matron, disgustingly healthy and virtuous, with no allure, no expression in her eyes, in short, owing everything she was to brute Nature . . . the other was one of those beauties who dominate and haunt our memory, who adds to her profound and original charm all the eloquence of dress, in control of her every movement, with a queenly self-awareness, a speaking voice like a finely tuned instrument and thought-filled eyes from which flow only what she wills" (II, 319). Although of female gender, this perfectly controlled instrument of seduction, the product of sustained artifice, incarnates the dandyistic ideal. For identical reasons, Baudelaire could see Emma Bovary as a transform of man and artist, not only because she is active and imaginative, rather than "femininely" passive and sentimental, but chiefly because of her "immoderate taste" for all artificial means of seduction—dress, perfumes, makeup—"in a nutshell: dandyism, exclusive love of domination" (II, 82). Among all the available instruments of the transformative principle, none achieves the passage from subject to object more dramatically or more radically than makeup, a metonym for the entire process of making oneself *up*, making up for one's natural deficiencies, or better, making oneself *into* what one naturally is not. In his *Eloge du maquillage*, Baudelaire offers an exalted vision of the alchemical powers of ordinary rice powder: "Its purpose and result is to eliminate the blemishes that nature has scandalously sown on the complexion, and to create in the skin's texture and color an abstract unity, a unity which . . . makes a human being immediately resemble a statue, that is to say, a divine and superior being" (II, 717). In this series of binaries—blemishes/abstract unity, nature/statue, human/divine—lies the passage of the test and the terminal appearance of the ideal artifact. The point of departure was a material cosmetization of a defective nature: the point of arrival the creation of a beautiful signifying surface that can proclaim its complete and irreversible triumph over nature. Thus makeup "does not have to hide, or avoid making its presence felt; on the contrary, it can be displayed, if not with affectation, at least with a kind of candor" (II, 717). Before the matter of artifice has been subsumed into the spirituality of art, however, only the initiated should be privy to the secret workings of the transformative process. Could it be otherwise, Baudelaire asks rhetorically: "Do we let the crowd into the ateliers of the wardrobe mistress and the stage designer, or into the actress's dressing room? Do we show the public . . . the mechanisms of theatrical machines? Do we explain the retouchings and the variants worked out during rehearsals? . . . Do we reveal the rags, the makeup, the pullies or the chains, the corrections or the error-filled proofs, in short, all the horrors that constitute the sanctuary of Art?" (I, 185).[10] When this other "scene" becomes *the* scene, the revelation of the stumbling, trial-and-error process of production destroys the artistic illusion and undermines the preeminence of the artist over the masses who incarnate nature at its worst. The locus of production is the sanctuary which must remain hidden until the rite of performance can begin. It is here that the artist (as Sender) will determine whether the transformation of Subject into Object can take place at the deepest level—whether "I is another"—or whether performance partakes of appearance that serves to hide the immutable being of the natural self.

Actants, Actors, and Masks: "L'être et le paraître"
"I am convinced that on many occasions it is useful to regard what we do as theater," writes Méré, "and to imagine that we are performing a role in a stage play" (340:III, 158). Throughout the corpus of honnêteté, this histrionic capacity is stressed as a means of concealing defects, or of protecting the self "against the traps that others are always setting for us, trying to make us look like fools" (286:244, #88). Because it is a necessary precaution, Guéret does not criticize individuals who hide the natural self behind the mask, provided they do so "exclusively to defend themselves

against the stratagems of others" (246:55–56). By and large, however, this is a moral universe where the mask, far from requiring justification, is, as in Nietzsche, proof of aristocracy (385:292, 497–98). Bellegarde argues, in fact, that the superior man should never let the mask slip: "There are times when we relax our guard, when we don't always feel like constraining ourselves in order to hide our faults and weaknesses. . . . The discoveries that others make in such instances destroy their regard for our merit" (60:406). With Marmet, this indifference to the "immorality" of masquerading reaches paradigmatic heights: "Try . . . to cover up your faults; you should at least seem virtuous and pretend to be, so that people will think that you are; it is far better to be a hypocrite than to be known as a scoundrel" (329:151). In this perspective, the mask can be used not only to conceal, as the redundant *cacher* and *couvrir* confirm, but also to dissimulate. Following the example laid down by Castiglione, writers on honnêteté, starting with Refuge, hail dissimulation as "the *chef d'oeuvre* of prudence and judgment" (421:177–78) and, by replacing ethical with esthetic values, rank it with *souplesse* and *insinuation* among the primary qualities for the performance of honnête sociability.[11]

"To be a good actor in life is a very rare talent," observed Méré; "a great deal of intelligence and judgment are needed if we are to do it to perfection. . . . To do always what is required both in our gesture and in our tone of voice, and to carry it all off so skillfully that it produces the proper effect, that, in my view, is a masterpiece" (340:III, 157). This degree of artistry presupposes the self-distantiation of the actor, the dispassionate evaluation of one's own performance "by the same standards that one would use for a stranger" (p. 126). Such objectivity with respect to the self affords an indispensable emotional detachment, "prevents us from taking anything too seriously, and gives us a freedom of speech and action that we don't have when we are fearful and anxious" (p. 158). But if it is essential that the honnête homme know how to act, it is equally essential that he be more than a mere actor. On the stage, genuine emotion on the actor's part constitutes a grotesque intrusion of reality; on the stage of life, however, authentic feeling may never be entirely absent. Those who lack it strike Méré as "good actors" rather than *honnêtes gens* (339:482). Of a man who feigned friend-ship, he wrote: "I felt that he was more of an actor than an honnête homme; that made him unbearable" (pp. 484–85).[12]

The true honnête homme must bring to his performance some trace of genuine feeling from the natural self so that it will not be "a vain charade" (340:III, 158). The precise means of measuring the presence of this "genuine feeling" becomes, therefore, a central question: "When I happen to meet someone, I know full well how to figure him out. Although he may say good things and behave as gracefully as one would want, I do not draw immediate conclusions. Often it is merely borrowed language or a role someone is playing. I carefully note whether everything comes from within, whether there are any inconsistencies. In short, I am less attentive to apparent polish and propriety than to certain indications of intellectual depth and breadth" (I, 45). Despite his confidence, Méré's criteria are not foolproof. Contradictions can be perceived, the quality of the mind may be determinable, but neither criterion guarantees that "everything comes from within." In his posthumous essays, where he tackles the problem of *être* and *paraître* once again, Méré contends that honnêteté is genuine when the qualities of the persona come from the heart but he describes *l'être* in relative rather than absolute terms: "The courtesies of a *galant homme* have more to do with reality than appearance" (III, 82). Nor is he on firmer ground when he equates authenticity with the ability to *plaire* (p. 133) or with universal criteria of what is right and reasonable: "To distin-guish true honnêteté from the spurious, we must be sure that it contains nothing that is not genuine, nothing that would not be right and reasonable everywhere on earth" (p. 93). In the end, Méré reverts to a simplistic equation: "To appear honnête one must in fact be honnête, for external appearances are only images of internal acts" (p. 141).[13]

Ultimately, the most valid criterion proposed by Méré is consistency. Like Montaigne, he believes that when an individual displays the persona of an honnête homme "everywhere and with all sorts of people" (I, 77), in private as well as in public, then it no longer partakes of playacting: "When one is even more of an honnête homme privately than publicly, that is an infallible sign of genuine superiority" (III, 93). Although "infallible" may by hyperbolic, Méré insists that honnêteté is genuine if it functions so consistently as to become a reflexive response to any appropriate stimulus: "I hear people say . . . that it is desirable to act like an honnête homme in the *grand monde*, but that in private, when no one is looking, they should not take the trouble, because it would be too demanding. Those who share this view have neither honnêteté nor discernment. . . . Honnêteté . . . is one of those things which could not exist without manifesting itself every time that duty or decorum required it: so that an honnête homme cannot help acting in an honnête manner, any more than a man of great valor can help acting resolutely, if the occasion calls for it. They have no choice in such matters" (pp. 89–90). With his enormous idealism, Méré was convinced that this reflexive capacity for honnêteté could be acquired and that the role could be internalized in the same way as a physical or moral habit. The "complete habituation" (p. 107) which he posed as a goal for the honnête homme is identical in function with what Pascal called "a second nature that destroys the first" (393:514, #126).[14] It is, then, theoretically possible to "make honnêteté a part of one's nature" (340:III, 74), to eliminate the dichotomy between nature and art, person and persona, *l'être* and *le paraître*.

Méré's faith in human ability to resolve the ontological dilemma of the binary was rare. Most seventeenth-century writers considered the gap between *paraître* and *être* and the status of the artistic Object as surface appearance to be the central and most obsessive problem in honnêteté. "People don't take the trouble to be honnêtes hommes, they simply try to act the part," declared Bellegarde; "most men are artificially honnêtes . . . their honnêteté is merely counterfeit" (61:119, 77–78). "What do you say to the fact that all individuals put on a face and a façade and that they substitute what they *want* to be for what they really are?" asks Marie de Hautefort. "I thought and said so a long time ago: everyone is masquerading as someone else, and better disguised than at the court spectacles, for no one can be recognized. It seems really quite strange that the *arte di parer honesta* is everything and that being honnête is nothing" (293:270). Anything but strange, in Pascal's view, this dichotomy is rooted in our profound desire to deny our essential nothingness by creating the imaginary being we would like to be: "We are not satisfied with the life that is in us and in our own being: we want to live an imaginary life in the minds of others, and to that end we strive to *paraître*. We work unceasingly to embellish and preserve this imaginary being and neglect the true one. . . . A great sign of the nothingness of our being" (393:602–3, #806). Instead of narrowing the distance between *paraître* and *être*, the demands of the artistic self foreclose the amelioration of the real self and even feed its natural perversity. Since genuine transformation can only come from a suprahuman order, according to Pascal, honnêteté must necessarily partake of *paraître*. Thus, although a theorist like Mitton recognizes that "nature is corrupt and that men are opposed to honnêteté," he cannot eliminate the natural self or transmute it, he can only conceal it (pp. 584, #587; 588, #642). Sharing some of Pascal's pessimism, La Rochefoucauld emphasized the negative consequences that the preoccupation with *le paraître* has upon *l'être*: "the desire to appear *habile* often prevents us from becoming *habile*, because we think more about the way we appear to others than we do about actually being the way we should be" (294:378, #238). The final recourse, then, is the pursuit of those qualities which will function harmoniously with our inner being as we can understand it: "We must try to find out what our natural [air] is, never abandon it, and perfect it as much as we can. . . . I do not mean that we should be prisoners of ourselves to the point where we are not free . . . to take on useful or necessary qualities with which Nature did not endow us . . . but these acquired qualities must have a certain rapport and connection with our natural qualities, which will extend and augment them slowly and imperceptibly . . . we must join and blend them together and never let them appear separate" (pp. 507–8). This incremental and synthesizing process, which, as Starobinski has observed, produces a musical consonance "between the *outside* of the person and the presumed *inside*" (475:223), blurs the lines of demarcation between *l'être* and *le paraître*. In a further effort to (con)fuse the boundaries between nature and art, the honnête homme must deftly admit to his imperfections: "Spurious *honnêtes gens* are those who conceal their faults from others and from themselves; genuine *honnêtes gens* are those who know all their faults and admit to them" (294:429, #202); but as La Rochefoucauld knew only too well, "certain faults, if well displayed, shine brighter than virtue itself" (p. 450, #354). Because absolute perfection is no more possible than absolute change, only that performance which contains traces of the natural self, along with its defects, can sustain repeated tests of authenticity. Used in this way, the self will serve as the Helper and not the undermining Opponent in the artistic process.[15]

Whether the natural subject is estheticized or the esthetic object is naturalized, habitualized, either procedure mediates the disjunction between *être* and *paraître* in seventeenth-century aristocracy and cancels the equation honnête homme/actor. Analogously, at the culminating point of the nineteenth-century corpus the hero of *A rebours* is what he appears to be. Like Méré, Baudelaire wrestled with the dilemma of the binary and concluded that "man ends up resembling what he would like to be" (51:II, 684). Although resemblance is not the same as being, most dandy-writers regarded the resolution of the binary as impossible, but furthermore, as undesirable. For Barbey, the quintessential Englishness of dandyism precluded the possibility of its naturalization in France; as he put it succinctly, "mimicry is not similarity" (38:IX, 224). And yet, according to Barbey, even Brummell's prototypical dandyism partook of *le paraître*: only at the piteous end of the Beau's life did dandyism, "stronger than his reason, penetrate the whole man" (p. 317, #42).[16] Madness, rather than oneness, attends that merger of *paraître* and *être* which destroys both. Paradoxically, the continuing dichotomy guarantees the efficacy of *le paraître* in dandyism. For the dandy's persona comprises a series of antitheses—effeminacy/virility; politeness/ hostility; glaciality/ passion—which are structured by the binary *paraître*/*être*. Since binaries such as these are in fact part and parcel of *paraître*, the self-as-art in dandyism consistently provokes the audience to search out the genuine self in a maze of receding mirrors. Exploiting the binary, the dandy mystifies by both revealing and concealing, affirming and denying, through *le paraître*, the presence and the absence of *l'être*.

Whereas the honnête homme, like a chameleon, adjusts his persona to different contexts, the dandy, "one of those Proteuses with a thousand shapes" (405:II, 299), demonstrates his worth by the multiplicity of his roles and disguises. In Eugène Sue's works, for example, Rodolphe sustains three identities simultaneously, one in the aristocratic world to which he belongs and two in the underworld (492), while the Marquis de Létorière undergoes three complete transformations—from coarse hunter to poor scholarly poet to romantic adolescent (491). That the identities of such metamorphoses (i.e., coarse hunter) were often antithetical to the dandyistic persona was decoded as proof of inordinate powers; Stendhal, who more than any other writer dramatized the dandyistic addiction to multiple masks, described the "privileged man" as one who can transform himself regularly into an ideal being and its antithesis, a brute animal (485:1526). Because this passion for multiple incarnations was linked to a quest for omnipotence, the dandy proudly claimed for himself the dual function in the spectacle that he offers the world: "To describe the perfection of the genre in which I excelled," wrote Stendhal, "I could say that I played . . . the kind of part that Molière might have written: I was at one and the same time author and actor" (p. 622). Such productions and performances become a powerful weapon in the hands of the dandy, and a deep source of pleasure. "I am convinced that certain people enjoy the pleasure of imposture," declared Barbey. "There is a frightful, intoxicating joy in the idea of lying and deceiving, in the thought that only *we* know who we are and that we are putting on a show in which society plays the fool; the pleasure of being able to look down on others compensates us for the production costs. People who wear their *heart on their sleeve* can't imagine the solitary joys of hypocrisy" (38:I, 225). Starting with Julien Sorel, the dandy countervalorizes hypocrisy, not merely as a means to artistic ends—this was the sole function of dissimulation in honnêteté—but as a challenge to mediocrity, a sign of heroism, and ultimately, a principle of spiritual joy (477:204, 220).[17]

"Look good on the outside!" Vautrin exhorts Lucien de Rubempré, "hide the seamy side of your life. . . . Display your beauty, your charm, your intelligence, your poetry. . . . Then no one will ever accuse you of marring the scenery of that great stage they call the world" (19:IV, 1024–25). Unlike Vautrin, the dandy often clings to his mask(s) out of fear of appearing ridiculous in the eyes of a hostile, trap-filled world: "Have I played my part well?"

Julien Sorel wonders anxiously until the moment of his death, when he doffs the mask and assumes his natural self (487:I, 299). In fiction, this natural "substance" is valorized by the authorial persona as precious and devalued by the dandy as dangerous and shameful. "There is a kind of *idée fixe* which we always feel *beating* inside of us," admits the hero of Sue's *Arthur*, ". . . it is, above all, this ever palpitating spot which we must perhaps conceal most skillfully from others. . . . Because this is usually where the weakness lies, the wound, the unfailingly vulnerable point in our nature" (489:II, 2–3). Whence the need to silence the emotions and passions which could impair his performance and transform him from impenetrable Object to defenseless Subject. "Mortally afraid of revealing what is in his heart" (487:I, 952), Julien Sorel, like Lucien Leuwen, wants to "kill off his humiliating sensitivity" (p. 471). The maturation of the dandyistic self presupposes, in fact, the gradual demise of the sensitive Romantic self; the Balzacian neophyte—Rastignac, Rubempré, Grandet—is desensitized as he is dandified: "his heart grew cold, contracted, and dried up" (19:III, 632). Thus a consummate dandy like the Count de Senanges can instantaneously extinguish the sparks of feeling that remain in his heart. Baudelaire, who characterized passion as "something *natural*, even too natural . . . not to scandalize . . . the supernatural regions of Poetry" (51:II, 114), expressed a basic principle of the nineteenth-century aristocracy when he recognized that the dandy "aspires to insensitivity" (II, 691). He found in Valmont, Laclos's *roué*, "a trace of sensitivity which made him inferior to la Merteuil," the female dandy in whom "everything human is calcinated" (II, 73).[18] Whereas the honnête homme enlisted the civilized and civilizing emotions of the natural self in the production of the object, and distinguished himself from the actor by the presence of some genuine feeling, the dandy, disdaining "all emotion as inferior" (38:I, 30), erects a rigid barrier between the natural and the artistic self and strives to destroy the first in order to insure the invulnerability of the second. Whatever the price, dandies are to exemplify the heroism of those rare individuals who live and breathe, "their head laced into a mask" (I, 225).

Process and Ethics of Production

Self-Overcoming: The Process of Askesis

"We must control our speech, tone of voice, gestures, actions, everything," declares Méré. "Some people are in control of one area and not of another. We must control everything" (78:XXXII[1925], 438). In honnêteté, as in dandyism, the quality of production and the level of performance demand unremitting control over every element of the natural self. This sustained, arduous process is well described by the Neitzschean term self-overcoming, *Selbst-Überwindung* (381:201, #257), in which the Sender becomes the taskmaster or the superego of a resistant subject. "If our passions try to turn us away from the dictates of honnêteté," Méré maintains, "we must restrain them severely" (340:III, 88). In this and other texts, the expressions "to compose, constrain, and restrain ourselves" figure as recurrent metaphors for control over a restive nature, for that systematic mastery of the self in which seventeenth-century writers, beginning with Faret, located the practical means and heroic ends of honnêteté: "Let us, then, master our selves and learn how to control our own feelings if we wish to win others over. For it would not be right to presume to conquer the will of so many *honnêtes gens* at court if we had not first learned to overcome our own" (188:69). And at the end of the century, Bellegarde stresses an identical need for "mastery of oneself and of one's passions"; this is "the mark of an extraordinary merit," one which requires "greatness of soul, firm resolve and an outlook far beyond that of the common people" (61:78–79).[19]

The elitist vision of self-mastery in honnêteté was stoic in inspiration and even in formulation. Accordingly, and with very few exceptions, the *mondains* understated the difficulties involved in achieving perfect self-mastery: "At first, we will feel some constraint, but not for long" (340:III, 89), insisted Méré; or, as he wrote elsewhere, "this activity is neither painful nor disagreeable" (II, 85). Well equipped to handle the passions of the natural self as well as the whims of fortune, the honnête homme could say with Saint-Evremond, "I have, in fact, made myself virtually insensitive: my soul [is] indifferent to the most trying events" (439:III, 33). But this stoic strain was generally absorbed into an eclectic Epicureanism, in the influential tradition of Montaigne. Saint-Evremond's position was typical: he viewed Seneca's austere concept of virtue as a doctrine of poverty and death (438:I, 158–59) that was antithetical and inimical to the aristocratic ethic. "You will allow refined people to call pleasure what uncouth and coarse people call vice," he countered, "so do not found your virtue on those old-fashioned ideas with which savage nature had imbued primitive men" (III, 14). To this "savage nature," Méré and La Rochefoucauld opposed "true virtue: . . . it appears, the way Socrates' did, without artifice and with a simple, natural air. . . . But inauthentic *honnêtes gens*, like inauthentic religious people, are only concerned with appearances: and I believe that in questions of morality, Seneca was a hypocrite and Epicurus a saint" (339:86–87).[20] This was not, of course, the kind of vulgar Epicureanism that the church had condemned as "shameful debauchery" (p. 86). What Méré and La Rochefoucauld had in mind was that liberated, composed feeling of inner peace that the ancients knew as *ataraxia*. Here again, Saint-Evremond provides a subtle description of this rational and "natural" state of spiritual pleasure: "the thought of seeing myself free and my own master gives me the spiritual pleasure that Epicurus spoke of: I mean that delightful indolence which is not a painless and pleasureless state, but a delicate feeling of pure joy that comes of a conscience at rest and a mind at peace" (438:IV, 21). Although Saint-Evremond criticized Epicurus' seventeenth-century partisans—most notable Gassendi, Bernier, and Sarasin—for ascribing to the apologist of pleasure a morality as abstemious as stoic virtue (III, 429), the prevailing austere view of Epicurus, originating in Seneca himself, accounts for the particular collocation of Epicurean and stoic strains in honnêteté. Whatever individual interpretations of Seneca and Epicurus they advanced, theorists of honnêteté collectively rejected impossible goals that produce nothing but pain and failure, and sought to integrate perfect mastery of the self with the essential spiritual pleasure inherent in *l'art de plaire*. As Starobinski has put it, "this involves . . . a maximum of moral discipline . . . without forsaking the pleasure principle" (475:217–18). The doctrine of honnêteté places an ethic of repression at the service of an esthetic of seduction. The end goal is the achievement of human happiness, the telos of human action (339:86). "Honnêteté is desirable only because it brings happiness to those who have attained it, and those who approach it," proclaims Méré (pp. 317–18). "The best minds of the past agree that this is the chief source of happiness, and I believe they are right" (p. 522).[21]

Judged outwardly, the dandy might appear to have no other preoccupation "than to chase after happiness" (51:II, 709). But an obsessive ennui and contempt for humanity number among the factors which confirm Baudelaire's view of dandyism, as "a kind of cult of the self, that can do without seeking happiness through others" (p. 710). In rebelling against his society's values, the dandy did express a type of hedonism. "Instead of giving a Monthyon prize for virtue," argued Gautier, "I would rather, like Sardanapalus, that great but badly misunderstood philosopher, give a large reward to the man who would invent a new pleasure; for enjoyment strikes me as the goal of life and the only useful thing in the world" (211:24). As the evocation of Sardanapalus suggests, however, the dandy's purported hedonism overlays a deep-rooted pessimism. Gautier is pointing to a *Schadenfreude,* "the gaiety of despair" (38:I, 265), a frenzied attempt to escape anxiety and ennui. "At the hollow sound of the past crumbling into nothingness / Let us all, the lost children of this critical age, / Dance gaily at the edge of the gaping abyss" (210:1–2).[22]

More often, the dandy's need for distance from the horror of existence and the odiousness of others took the form of *ataraxia,* "an almost complete quietude" (432:28) that replicated Baudelaire's image of Parnassian beauty as a statue-like woman, motion- and emotionless (51:I, 22). This stillness, comparable to the "serenity of the heroic figures in classical statuary," was to constitute a contrast to the context, to symbolize, as Barbey put it, "the calm of antiquity in the midst of contemporary agitation" (38:IX, 328, 309, #11). Barbey, however, also stressed the difficulty and the pain involved in wearing and bearing the "cruel, horrible mask" of the dandy (p. 224). To show signs of this "painful constraint" (p. 273), to voice his suffering—"If you knew what a task it is to bear this casualness as close to the heart as I do" (p. 314, #32)—is to destroy the artistic illusion and abandon performance. And so, Barbey continues, "these boudoir stoics drink the blood that flows behind their masks and remain masked" (p. 314, #32). In the striking oxymoron, *boudoir stoics,* the act of violence/violation committed against the self occurs in the very place where the dandy transforms himself into a work of art. At the same time, what Barbey and others call dandyistic stoicism should rightly be termed asceticism: for whereas the Senecan sage feels little pain achieving self-mastery, the Christian ascetic equates superiority with a capacity for suffering modeled after the Christian martyr. Thus the silent suffering of Barbey's Aloys de Synarose emerges as a prideful *Imitatio Christi:* "biting my heart as it reached my lips and pushing it back down into my breast as it was about to escape, drinking my tears inwardly, oh! what a bitter brew! . . . But pride was the column that I leaned against . . . the stake to which *they* had bound me and which prevented me from giving in. Like Jesus beneath the bloody scourge, I did not succumb under their blows" (XI, 36). Instead of merely accepting suffering as a necessary stage in his re-production and performance, this same dandy is depicted as the instigator of a metaphorical *auto da fé*: Aloys "impassively watched his heart burn, the way Scaevola watched his hand burn. Suffering, for him, was living, fulfilling his vocation as a man. Even if he could have escaped the pain on a team of horses, he would have refused to mount them!" (p. 50).[23] Self-consumption is the precondition to self-consummation. In the baptism of fire, the dandy-martyr is (re)born.

This metaphoric line extends the familiar Romantic vision, never absent from the dandy's consciousness, of the superior man as messianic in spirit and outlook. The religious component, at the very least, is systematically manifest in discussions of the substance and form of the dandyistic (secret) society. For Eugène Sue, dandyism is "a kind of brotherhood whose rules . . . must be as strictly observed as those of the Trappist order" (489:III, 122). In Baudelaire, the monastic/ascetic model, no longer a passing simile ("a kind of brotherhood"), assumes the full power of sustained metaphor: "The most rigorous monastic rule, the irresistible order of the *Old Man of the Mountain*, who made his intoxicated disciples commit suicide, was no more despotic nor more blindly obeyed than this doctrine of elegance and originality which likewise imposes on its ambitious and humble sectarians, men who are often filled with spirit, passion, courage, and

repressed energy, the terrible formula, *Perinde ac cadaver!*"
(51:II, 711). Imposed by a tyrannical superego, this symbolic
death of the natural self is the condition sine qua non for rebirth
into the highest spiritual order. It must be experienced in full consciousness of its grandeur if one is to achieve salvation (I, 683) and
thus must rightly constitute, Baudelaire writes, echoing De
Maistre, a voluntary sacrifice: "Dandies. . . . Theory of sacrifice.
Justification of the death penalty. The sacrifice is complete only
with the *sponte sua* of the victim. A man condemned to death,
whom the executioner fails to kill, whom the people set free, but
who returns to the executioner" (50:1212). "For the sacrifice to be
perfect there must be agreement and joy on the part of the victim"
(51:I, 683). In the "sacrament of suicide" (I, 664), the annihilation
of the natural self, Baudelaire saw beatific joy—the ultimate
manifestation of the principle of pleasure-in-pain—and hailed "the
eternal superiority of the dandy" (I, 682).[24]

"Strange spiritualism!" Baudelaire exclaimed, " . . . all the
complicated material requirements to which [dandies] submit
themselves, from their irreproachable attire at all hours of the day
and night to the most perilous athletic feats, are merely a gymnastics designed to strengthen the will and discipline the soul" (II,
710). In Baudelaire's statement, we find the underlying meaning of
the elements that enter into the production of the dandy as well as
of the honnête homme. The "complex material requirements" to
which the Sender submits the subject represent, at a deeper level,
what Nietzsche too called "a gymnastics of the will" for
"strengthening" the soul (385:483). The means that serve to conquer others thus have the more profound function of conquering
the self and elevating it to a higher order of being, like those
rigorous *Spiritual Exercises* devised by Saint Ignatius for the
Christian ascetic (267). They are obstacles imposed by superior
individuals on themselves in the quest for a moral perfection,
whose attainment is its own pleasurable reward. This connection
between difficulty and pleasure, which has always distinguished
exemplary beings, as Nietzsche recognized (385:58, 81; 383:349,
#305), is underscored in a passage from *Les Liaisons dangereuses*,
which Baudelaire cites: "The most difficult or the gayest course is

the one that I always take, and I never blame myself for a good action so long as it exercises or amuses me" (51:II, 74). The apparent antitheses here—difficult/gay, exercise/amuse, blame/ good action—are, in fact, synonyms in the code of superior beings like the dandy and the honnête homme; the true antithesis is pleasure or happiness achieved "without expending the least effort, by stupidly following the instinct [of the] . . . heart" (p. 73). Whether inspired by ascetic, stoic, or Platonic models, this ethic, which structures the process of production in dandyism and honnêteté, exemplifies the ideal of *askesis*—exercise, rigorous training, self-discipline, self-restraint. Like an athlete, *askètès*, the seventeenth- and nineteenth-century artistocrat trains and disciplines body and mind, senses and spirit, through arduous effort of the will and unremitting practice of self-imposed rules.[25]

"It would be very strange if the body were capable of instruction and the mind were not," observed Méré. "Could it be that for learning how to ride a horse properly teachers and practice are infallibly effective, but that for becoming an honnête homme the one and the other are useless and even harmful?" (340:I, 69). Méré's rhetorical question is rooted in the vision of the self-as-art as the final product of an extended *askesis*. This *disciplina voluntatis* (385:81) requires testing out the most effective techniques and refining them through endless practice: "when we want to *plaire*," writes Méré, "we seek the proper means. If the first does not succeed, we try another and by dint of continuous reflection and self-improvement, we become honnêtes hommes" (340:II, 22–23). To achieve the technical agility that distinguishes masters from novices predicates, furthermore, a tireless search for nuances that "are infinitely varied . . . excellent workers discover so many ways of doing things well that they seldom do anything in the same manner" (p. 17). The underlying urge to self-perfection must necessarily enlist the virtue of self-dissatisfaction: "the best workers are not satisfied with what they do . . . the greater their excellence, the greater their modesty" (p. 112); genuine honnêteté "is never so self-satisfied that it does not sense something beyond what has already been done" (I, 76).[26] This steady, unremitting *askesis*, the process of ever higher ascent to ever higher levels of performance, will end only with death. And "if we never died," fantasizes Méré, "we would not stop being honnêtes hommes, in fact, we would perfect ourselves even more" (I, 75). The enduring striving for perfection depends solely on the power of desire (II, 49), just as self-overcoming, self-transformation, in both the esthetic and ethical senses, is fundamentally a feat of will: "Intelligent people can improve themselves easily. . . . They need only will it so" (p. 64).[27]

"By the pure and free exercise of the will, great poets, philosophers, and prophets achieve a state where they are both cause and effect, subject and object" (51:I, 398). Recognizing that the "exercise of the will" lies at the core of all superior systems of production, Baudelaire found proof in dandy-artists, like Poe and Delacroix, of the "most admirable willpower" (II, 590): "Not only did [Poe] expend considerable efforts to subjugate the fugitive demon of time to his will . . . he insisted . . . that the true poet must be the master of his memory, the ruler of words, the compass of his own feelings" (II, 331). This is the very same kind of will-power and creative spirit which Baudelaire found in Mme de Merteuil's assertion: "I say: my principles . . . I created them, and I can state that I made myself what I am. . . . I am the fruit of my own labor" (II, 74). Because such willpower and self-discipline demand concentration of the most "self-centered" and virtuous sort (II, 761), the laziness which "vaporizes" Samuel Cramer's resolve ultimately disqualifies him from the enterprise of dandyism (I, 553). That is equally true of the dissipation of the weakly Lucien de Rubempré (19:IV, 906; V, 697), whose creator Baude-laire regarded as "the theoretician of the will" (212:59). For Balzac, it was de Marsay's remarkable willpower that accounted for his perpetual successes: "What he wanted, he *did*" (19:V, 229–300). In the age of Napoleon, when willpower was the prime mover in the will to power, the dandy from Julien Sorel onwards formulates his code as a combination of moral and military logis-tics. Baudelaire discovered the same passion for "strategies, rules, and methods" in Laclos's dandyistic masterminds (II, 69), and in the dandy artists he most admired—Poe (II, 273) and particularly Delacroix, whose needs he compared to Stendhal's: "Another similarity to Stendhal was his predilection for simple formulas, brief maxims concerning the right way to live. Like all people whose fascination with method is that much greater because their passionate, sensitive nature seems averse to it, Delacroix loved to make up little catechisms of practical ethics . . . ; sound, sturdy, simple, and demanding maxims that serve as armor and shield for a person whom the destiny of genius throws into perpetual battle" (II, 758). No one understood better than Baudelaire that the dandy's passion for constricting formulas is directly proportioned to the passionateness of the natural self. Numerous entries in his journal, *Mon coeur mis à nu*, bear the titles *Hygiène*, *Conduite*, *Méthode*, *Morale* (I, 668–75), and define self-imposed disciplines with visible fervor: "Henceforth I swear that I shall adopt the following rules as the eternal rules of my life . . . " (p. 673).[28]

For Baudelaire, as for other theorists of dandyism, all the rules of *askesis* are subsumed in the single idea, *work*. Under the heading, *Morale*, in his *Manuel du fashionable*, Ronteix insists that "it takes as much labor to become a perfect *élégant* or *fashionable* as to rise to the highest rank in the sciences or the arts" (432:131). The archmoral precept of Daniel D'Arthez, in Balzac's *Illusions perdues*, applies to all who search for perfection: "suffer courageously and put one's faith in work" (19:IV, 662). Baudelaire, who hailed the "power of the idée fixe," noted obsessively in his journal: "work all day long," "work fortifies us," "the more we work, the better we work and the more we want to work" (51:I, 688–73). Although Delacroix, one of his idols, seemed to produce effortlessly, work was, in fact, also his religion: "I can work endlessly and without any hope of reward," declared the dandy painter. "I have experienced many passions, but it is only in my work that I have felt perfectly happy" (II, 633, 763). Here lay the difference between sublime spirits, like Delacroix and Poe, and those who, like the hashish addicts, would never achieve the spiritual renaissance that is the ultimate product of work: "Those unfortunate creatures who . . . have refused redemption through work, look to black magic for a way of soaring instantly into a supernatural existence . . . while we, the poets and philosophers, have regenerated our souls through incessant work and contemplation; through the assiduous exercise of our will and the enduring nobility of our intentions we have created for ourselves a garden of true beauty" (I, 441).[29]

Modes of Cognition: "*L'esprit de géométrie et l'esprit de finesse*"

"Unless you have a truly perverse nature," wrote Méré, "you can make yourself into an honnête homme as easily as you wish, so long as you have the knowledge required to achieve perfection; for the heart readily conforms to the guidelines of reason" (340:III, 144). In Méré's vision of the process of production, the natural self poses no obstacles to the dictates of the will, but instead, in good Cartesian fashion, favors and advances the dominant goals of reason. However, since proper exercise of the will (*vouloir*) predicates mastery of the "knowledge required" (*savoir*), Méré never ceases to emphasize the importance of arduous intellectual effort for acquiring every quality in the system of the self-as-art: "there is no such thing as too much application, too much reflection" (339:429). Whether it be eloquence, *le bon air*, or *les agréments*, "you can apply yourself to this kind of endeavor all of your life and become more accomplished day by day" (340:II, 66). Like its individual parts, the total performance of *l'art de plaire* constitutes "a never-ending study" and demands "never-ending application in which you make constant progress if you have taken the right path" (339:405, 667).[30]

The "right path" to honnêteté, an image which dominates Descartes's *Discours de la méthode*, included knowledge of the body of laws that governed seventeenth-century social and esthetic praxis. In a world where the esthetic was as socialized as the social was estheticized, the notion of *bienséance* also regulated individual self-representation. As the source of esthetic harmony between the parts and the whole, the whole and the social context, *la bienséance* involved, in the words of Rapin, "everything that goes against the rules of the times, of custom, of feeling, of expression" (418:67). The least fault committed against what is *bienséant* "can badly hinder those who want to *plaire* and be loved" (340:II, 51), warns Méré, expressing one of the topoi of honnêtetê. In his view, however, the existing rules for *quod decet* were not the most desirable: "there are, of course, some rules that must be observed, although they may not be the best, or the ones we would have chosen at the outset. . . . They can't be ignored because people have become used to them over a long period of time" (339:216–17). Accepting only the indispensable rules, the honnête homme is to expend great effort "to make them his own" (340:III, 144) so that they will not mar the desired effect: "the most casual rule always cramps one's style, thus making it less free and less appealing" (339:217). Even more important, the existing rules do not begin to encompass the enormously subtle art of determining what is most fitting, which would literally comprise an "infinite number of precepts" (103:89). No code of *bienséance*, including the most detailed, can ever prescribe infallible rules for the performance of honnêteté: "it is impossible to give hard and fast rules: besides the fact that it concerns things that are in constant flux, it also depends on certain external circumstances that are never exactly the same" (340:I, 96).[31]

Méré's reflections on *bienséance* illustrate a pervasive attitude toward the efficacy of the rules and methods of others in the production of honnêteté: "it is neither rules nor maxims nor even knowledge of facts that really accounts for the success of 'good workers' and great men. Such things can certainly contribute to excellence . . . but even when you have them you may never get beyond mediocrity" (II, 78). Méré's statement, however, raises significant epistemological questions: can the desired elements in the product be referred back to a preexistent code, theory, or method? If it exists, is this collective body of law articulable? If it is not, what mode of cognition can be utilized to discover the optimal process that will produce the self-as-art? In a partial answer to those questions, La Rochefoucauld maintains that *l'agrément*, like the other qualities of *l'art de plaire*, involves "a symmetry, whose rules we do not know" (294:436, #240). Pascal went even further: "It is not that I don't believe that the *art de plaire* has rules every bit as certain as the rules of demonstration, and that a person who knows and applies them perfectly will succeed with equal certainty in making others love him. . . . But I maintain, and it's perhaps my own inadequacy that makes me think so, that it can't be done" (393:356). Far from being peculiar to Pascal, this inability is widely acknowledged in the corpus of honnêteté, not as an admission of deficiency, but as proof of superiority over the rule-bound "technicians" (340:I, 47). Thus although seventeenth-century theorists approached honnêteté like so many *esprits de géométrie*, promising principles and procedures and implying thereby the teachability of the subject, actual attainment of the ideal is the ultimate function of the more rarefied *esprit de finesse*. Méré, the probable source of Pascal's celebrated distinction, speaks of two kinds of endeavor, "one which is concerned only with art and the rules; [the other] . . . which aims exclusively at an instinctive and mental grasp of those things that cannot fail to *plaire* in each particular area" and expressed his clear preference for the second (II, 109). He dismissed *l'esprit mathématique* as fit for "small minds and half-baked scholars" (339:111–12) and extolled *la justesse du sentiment* which "gets right to the heart of those higher forms of knowledge that never lead us astray" (340:II, 126–27). This he called *l'esprit métaphysique*.[32]

As Méré and Pascal make abundantly clear, this "natural feeling" (339:114) does not refer to an emotion of the natural self, but rather, to the hyperacuity of superior beings who can "immediately see a thing at a glance, and not through a gradual reasoning process" (393:576, #512). It is also what La Rochefoucauld means by *l'esprit fin:* "he has subtle thoughts and can see those that are the most difficult to perceive" (294:528). This periphrase for intuition (<*intueor* = to see) which echoes the Platonistic cliché, "the eye of the soul" (401:II, 368, #540), predicates a strong distinction between merely discursive and supradiscursive "knowing." "I have . . . many inner feelings that guide me more reliably than my reason," says Méré; "these are the obscure counsels of my instinct or of an indwelling spirit," he adds, evoking the image of the Platonic daemon, "that lets me sense the difference between right and wrong" (339:9). For Méré, every single element in the elaboration of the self-as-art is the product of this superior sense. Thus only those "who sense the most subtle nuances which can be perceived in *la bienséance*" can hope to bring it to perfection (340:II, 51). The same "feeling" determines the artistic worth of conversation: "if we are to attain the highest eloquence, we can never be too sensitive to the *agréments* and the *bienséances*" (339:624). Likewise, proper deportment requires "an exquisite feeling" (340:II, 120), and consummate manners, the ability "to feel just where the proper limits are" (p. 104). Finally, to discern the nuances of *l'art de plaire* "we need great accuracy of taste and feeling" (p. 102).[33]

Often used as a metonym for the entire range of "feeling," taste provides an alternative mode of knowledge to the crude rules devised by others. The honnête homme is to "prefer his taste to run-of-the-mill rules, when [he] is certain that his taste is good" (339:122). The product of keen intuition, good taste is qualitatively different from the random tendencies of the natural self. "Those who are guided exclusively by their inclination," writes Bellegarde, "usually have bad taste because they are like animals who act only on instinct and impulse" (58:10). To signal the radical difference between good taste and untutored nature, Bellegarde reintroduces the concept of reason: *le bon goût*, he maintains, "is the result of an unerring, enlightened reason, that always takes *the* right course" (p. 10). The very same synthesis of method and vision ("unerring/enlightened") underlies Bouhours's definition of good taste as "a kind of instinct of right reason that moves it along swiftly" (281:44–45). As the perfect compound of the primary cognitive binary—reason and intuition—good taste ranked high among the faculties required for the production of honnêteté: "Delicacy of taste . . . is absolutely necessary for understanding the true value of things, for selecting their most outstanding elements, expressing them in the way that suits them best, and for showing them in their best light, the way they should be seen" (340:II, 127); thus "there is nothing so rare or that we should try harder to attain than to have taste, and to have fine taste" (p. 91). La Rochefoucauld spoke even more pointedly to the rareness of this quality: "There are some people who, by a kind of instinct of unexplained origin, . . . always make the right choice. . . . In such people everything acts in concert. This harmony allows them to make sound judgments and gives them a true idea of things" (294:516–17). As the phrases "the right choice" and "a true idea" suggest, the concept of *the* good taste was rooted in Platonic thought, and accordingly, was considered an acquirable quality with *the* right method. Underscoring the need for *askesis*, Méré claimed that the honnête homme "[can] gradually make his taste good by looking at things that *are* good" (340:II, 92), "by modeling himself on people whose taste is excellent" (p. 128), and by giving the matter "much care and reflection" (339:219). In what only appears to be a contradiction in terms, Méré would found honnêteté itself on a marriage between taste and method, *finesse* and *géométrie*. His final advice: "to transform *le bon goût* into a science or a habit" (340:II, 128).³⁴

Two centuries later, when the first Romantic generation pitted the "natural" Shakespeare against the canonical Racine, some dandy writers took strong exception to methodizing art and fabricating what Balzac called "a corpus of Aristotelian rules, a veritable code à la Boileau." Even an artifact like the cravat, he maintains, "thrives only on originality and naturalness; imitation, subjection to rules takes away its color, its warmth, its life. . . . A cravat must be put on spontaneously, instinctively, and inspirationally. A properly knotted cravat is one of those marks of genius that can be felt and admired, but not analyzed or taught. . . . The cravat is romantic in its very essence; the day it is subjected to general rules, fixed principles, it will cease to exist" (21:II, 49). Rules are destructive of art and can only govern the inartistic: fashion is defined in the monthly magazines—"it can be studied and learned"; elegance, however, "is an instinct. It must be felt and sensed" (II, 252). The superior man has "a feeling for the elegant life" (22:50), an intuitive sense closely related to *tact*, the nineteenth-century equivalent to good taste—"(the intelligence of our senses, perhaps!) which always leads us to choose truly beautiful or good things. . . . It is an exquisite tact; only constant practice will allow us suddenly to discover connections, foresee consequences, sense the right place and the real meaning of objects, words, ideas and people" (p. 59). In *Théorie de la démarche* Balzac calls this faculty that all creative beings possess *observation:*

All human inventions are the result of an analytical observation in which the mind moves with incredible speed from one insight to another. . . . [The great scientist], the great painter and the great

musician are all observers. . . . But these sublime birds of prey, who
rise to great heights and still retain a gift for seeing clearly the
things of this earth, . . . have, as it were, a purely metaphysical
mission. . . . They are carried away in the bold flight of their genuis
and in their ardent search for truth toward the simplest formulations. They observe, judge and leave behind principles that meticulous men prove, explain and comment upon. . . . Also required is a
kind of vision that makes phenomena come together, a logic that
sorts them out, a perspicacity that sees and deduces, a deliberateness that insures they will never discover one point on a circum-
ference without observing all the others, and a speed that goes from
toe to head in a single leap. (pp. 148–49)[35]

In Balzac's conception of *observation*, as in seventeenth-century
analyses of good taste, we find a conjunction of intuition and
reason for creative production. What is more, the perfection of
this syncretic faculty and that of tact requires the same *askesis*
that underlies the development of a habit of elegance—constant,
even "immoderate" training (21:I, 354). In his treatise, however,
Balzac reveals the problematics of (and his own resistance to) a
habit and a science of elegance in an imaginary dialogue between
Brummell and his companion, William Crad——k. Every aristocracy is distinguished by "the feeling for elegance" and "the taste
that serves to put a poetic stamp on life," admits Crad——k, and
yet, since aristocratic children do not possess this capacity at birth,
the "privilege" of elegance can only derive from "upbringing and
practice" (22:70). He believes in principle that elegance "should be
accessible to all through practice," and concludes that "application can teach a rich man to wear boots and trousers as well as we
do" (pp. 70–71). Brummell, on the other hand, is opposed to
removing "the barrier which separates elegant from vulgar life"
for fear of compromising the elite's exclusive superiority (pp.
70–71). Reaching a compromise, Brummell and his friend agree to
ban such types as shopkeepers, businessmen, and humanities
professors from the ranks of elegant men, but to allow all others
"the hope [of] attaining [it] . . . through practice" (pp. 71–72).
Only this possibility can provide a justification for a formal
treatise on elegance such as Balzac's. Thus, despite his initial mis-
trust of codes and legislations, Balzac finally concedes that

elegance is "at one and the same time, a science, an art, a habit, a feeling" (p. 107).[36]

Balzac's romanticist hesitations concerning the conjunction of *géométrie* and *finesse* are completely absent in Baudelaire. "I pity those poets who only follow their instincts" (51:II, 793), he writes, in flat opposition to the early Romantic image of the inspired poet. He rejects "pure sentiment" (49:IV, 70), the kind of sensibility that is devoid of intellect and will (51:II, 690), in favor of imagination, which he hails as the queen of faculties (pp. 82, 619–20). A "visionary faculty" (pp. 692–94), a source of illumination (p. 655), which "perceives immediately . . . the intimate and secret connections among things, the correspondences and the analogies" (328–29), imagination is also "the most scientific of faculties" (49:I, 368): "It is analysis, it is synthesis. . . . It decomposes all of creation, and, with materials gathered and rearranged according to rules whose origin can be found only in the depths of the soul . . . it produces a sensation of novelty" (51:II, 620–21). "Quasi-divine," profoundly religious (pp. 620–23), imagination encompasses all the separate operations of intuition and reason: "The sensitivity of imagination . . . knows how to judge, compare, avoid this, seek out that, rapidly, spontaneously. It is from this sensitivity, generally called *Taste*, that we derive the ability to avoid the *bad* and find the *good* in poetical matters" (p. 116). Baudelaire's esthetic posits an ascent from the first rumblings of poetic sensibility to the certainty and predictability of science. Just as true artists "invariably . . . want to analyze their art, discover the hidden laws underlying what they have produced and draw from this study a series of precepts whose divine goal is infallibility in poetic production" (p. 793), dandyism, following the same itinerary, may be viewed as a "passion . . . become doctrine" subject to its own rigorous laws (pp. 709–10). This desire to imbue art with "the precision and rigorous logic of a mathematical problem" (p. 335) was what Baudelaire prized in the poetic production of the dandy Edgar Allan Poe: "He often said . . . that originality is a matter of apprenticeship, which does not mean something that can be transmitted through instruction. The accidental and the incomprehensible were his two great enemies . . . his genius, although ardent and agile, was passionately taken up with analysis, schemes, and calculations. . . . The partisans of poetic frenzy will perhaps be revolted by [his] cynical maxims; . . . It will always be useful . . . to point out to mundane people the kind of labor that is needed to produce that object of luxury called poetry" (212:25).[37]

The "je ne sais quoi"

As epistemological constructions, the theories of dandyism and honnêteté betray the same desire to methodize art, to endow the creative process with the power and certainty of mathematical reasoning. This urge stands in sharp contradiction with the repeatedly admitted inability to chart the proposed method in discursive terms, to communicate its rules to the uninitiated, to instruct the incompetent. The product and performance are a matter of evidence, they testify to the existence of an antecedent power and process (*vouloir, savoir, pouvoir*), but the words can never be found to reproduce their essence. The captivating conversational style of an honnête homme, for example, "usually consists in things so delicate that, although we may sense them, we can hardly say what they are" (340:I, 39). *Urbanité*, which participates in the same arcane order, "is one of those things that are more easily sensed than explained" (339:305); so with *le bon goût*—"it is easier to feel it than to express it" (340:II, 128). The authors of the many manuals which purport to teach honnêteté all agree that there will always and inevitably remain "something unexplainable that is easier to discern when seen in action than when described in words" (I, 77).[38]

Renaissance and classical esthetics had a special expression for this essential, inexpressible "something": *le je ne sais quoi*. The existence of a linguistic signifier to denote all esthetic effects that defy linguistic description conveyed a double message, however: the inability to put a sublime essence into words, on the one hand, and on the other, the conviction of one's personal awareness of its presence. As Leibnitz noted, the *je ne sais quoi* involves a significant perception, since it is "possible . . . to recognize the thing represented," but it lacks distinction as an act of cognition, "since the thing cannot be distinguished from all others by sufficient marks and observations" (300:449). In what constitutes the most extensive seventeenth-century commentary on *le je ne sais quoi*, Bouhours insists that it can be known only by its effects and that all the terms which have been used to define it—"those impressions, penchants, instincts, feelings, affinities"—are nothing but flim-flam: "When we have said all that and a thousand other things besides, we have said nothing. It would no longer be a *je ne sais quoi* if we knew what it was; its nature is to be incomprehensible and unexplainable" (79:196).[39]

Although Méré purported to believe that "certain people know its cause and origin" (339:568), he, along with the other writers on honnêteté, continued to regard *le je ne sais quoi* as the impenetrable "explanation" of the self-as-art. The countenance of an honnête homme, for example, radiates "a merry and insinuating *je ne sais quoi*" (340:III, 144), and his body, "a certain secret, charming *je ne sais quoi* that we cannot describe" (454:IV, pt.1, 89). Like his manner, his *urbanité* brings together "a courteous and polished *je ne sais quoi*, a *je ne sais quoi* that is at the same time bantering and flattering" (339:305). In conversation, his voice has "a gentle and tender *je ne sais quoi* that touches the heart" (454:IV, pt.3, 857), or "one that has an appealing, casual *je ne sais quoi*" (III, pt.2, 852–53), and his verbal style, according to Méré, has a "*je ne sais quoi* [that is] pure and noble," "refined," "natural," "subtle and lofty," "precise and insinuating" (340:I, 11, 89; II, 92, 125; III, 136). The global pertinence of this sign of the ineffable also dominates Scudéry's analysis: "this *je ne sais quoi galant* which permeates the entire person of its possessor—his mind, his words, his actions or even his clothing—puts the finishing touch on *honnêtes gens*, makes them lovable and causes others to love them" (453:X, pt.2, 468). Bouhours said both the first and the last word on the subject when he insisted that the presence of the *je ne sais quoi* could remedy all defects and that its absence could invalidate all virtues: "Thus, the most reasonable and certain thing one can say about it is that the greatest qualities are powerless without it, and that it needs only itself to produce the most powerful effects. A person may be attractive, witty, lively, anything you like, and it won't matter; if the *je ne sais quoi* is missing, all those fine qualities might just as well be nonexistent, because there is nothing striking or stirring about them. They are like hooks without bait and without lure, arrows and darts without points. But, on the other hand, whatever our defects may be, whether of mind or body, if we have this single quality we will captivate others unfailingly; in fact everything we do will be captivating. The *je ne sais quoi* is a cure-all" (79:197).[40]

Two centuries later, we find Balzac and Chapus expressing the same idea, in somewhat more sophisticated language, about the dandy: he exercises "the indefinable, the mysterious secret of seduction and ascendancy over others" (121:212–13), he exemplifies that "magnetic capacity [to carry us off] into his sphere by means of an unexplainable power" (22:99). For Balzac, the *oisif* stands out from ordinary men by his *savoir-vivre*, his *élégance*, and *je ne sais quoi* (p. 57); this is also the distinctive sign of *la race*, "an air of grandeur, a proud countenance, in a word, everything that has been so rightly called the *je ne sais quoi*" (19:IV, 611; V, 735). Henri de Marsay identifies this indispensable quality with those numerous nuances which women, the "intuitive sex," perceive far better than men: "it has to do with a person's air, bearing, the sound of his voice, the way he looks at you, his gestures, a number of little things that women see and to which they attach a certain meaning that escapes us" (III, 359–60); the androgynous dandy, of course, can invariably perceive this ineffable "something" "without which the greatest talent will never be recognized" (VIII, 893). Even though Barbey objected to its impreciseness (32:13), he still resorted to the *je ne sais quoi* after acknowledging that dandyism "is almost as difficult to describe as to define" (38:IX, 229). Brummell, he wrote, "was born to reign by means of very positive faculties, although one day, in frustration, Montesquieu called them a *je ne sais quoi* instead of saying what they are. That was the way Brummell dominated his society. . . . He was king by the grace of Grace" (p. 275).[41]

Barbey's association of *le je ne sais quoi* and grace rehearses a tendency that is as old as the two terms themselves. During the Italian Renaissance, neo-Platonic estheticians, the first users of the *non so che*, traced the expression back to the indefinable grace or charm that the Greeks had called *charis*, that Cicero referred to as *venustas* or *suavitas*, and Quintilian as *gratia*.[42] Firenzuola, for example, defines grace as a "splendor . . . born of a secret proportion and a measure, which is not in our books, which we do not know, nor even imagine, and [which] is, as one says of things that we do not know how to express, *un non so che*" (354:139). Extending the relevance of this concept to the self-as-art, Castiglione devotes the entire first book of the *Cortegiano* to the problems posed by "supreme grace," the semantic equivalent of the *non so che*: "You have repeated several times," says Cesare Gonzago to Count Canossa,

> . . . that the Courtier must accompany his actions, his gestures, his habits, in short, his every moment, with grace [*con la grazia*]. And it strikes me that you require this in everything as that seasoning without which all the other properties and good qualities would be of little worth. And truly I believe that every one would easily let himself be persuaded of this because, by the very meaning of the word, it can be said that he who has grace finds grace. But since you have said that this is often a gift of Nature and the heavens . . . those men who are born as fortunate and as rich in such treasure . . . have little need, it seems to me, of any teacher in this, because such benign favor from heaven lifts them, almost in spite of themselves, higher than they themselves had desired, and makes them not only pleasing but admirable to everyone. Therefore I do not discuss this, it not being in our power to acquire it of ourselves. (113:40–41)

The quality at issue here is not a property of the natural self, but signals, rather, a "benign favor of heaven," "a little ray of divinity," in Faret's terms (188:18–19), a supranatural force functionally analogous in terrestrial matters to grace in the religious sphere. The *yo no sé* of Juan de la Cruz, the "celestial *je ne sais quoi*" of Marie de Gournay (77:189–90) refer to the same abstruse spiritual essence, in a literal religious context, that Bouhours was to evoke metaphorically, as he reaches what one critic has called the metaphysical point of honnêteté (282:28): "Grace itself, that divine grace . . . which works such admirable effects in the soul . . . , which triumphs over the obduracy of our hearts without compromising the freedom of our will, which rules our nature by adapting to it, which makes itself mistress of the will while leaving it mistress of itself, this grace, what else is it, I ask, but a supernatural *je ne sais quoi* that can neither be explained nor understood. The Church Fathers tried to define it and called it a profound and secret vocation, an impression of the spirit of God, a divine unction, an all-powerful sweetness, a victorious pleasure, a holy concupiscence, a covetous desire for the true Good: in other words, a *je ne sais quoi* which can readily be felt but which cannot be expressed in words and about which we would do well to say nothing" (79:211–12).[43]

The tradition which identified *le je ne sais quoi* as the secular equivalent of religious grace was not forsaken in the century that was to proclaim the death of classicism and God. For dandy-writers, like Paul de Musset, only "the magic of the *je ne sais quoi*, the omnipotence of the *je ne sais quoi*" could explain how certain persons of quality managed to overcome their natural defects: "we see dwarfs, stutterers, and hunchbacks among them, but the dwarf of the *grand monde* is debonair, the stutterer speaks trippingly, the hunchback carries his hump nobly . . . even the ignoramus lets fly his anachronism like a man of good society and the imbecile bumbles along gracefully, looks for the right words, but stops in the middle of a sentence, like a perfect gentleman. Such is the prestige . . . of the male *je ne sais quoi*" (391:418, 424). Instead of using this sign, Balzac borrows terms for grace from "scholastic theology" (22:97) to distinguish three orders of elegance. The lowest belongs to the "methodist of elegance," who possesses *sufficient grace:* "neither gracious nor unpleasant, you will never hear him use an indecorous word or see him lapse into bad form" (97–98). Above him stands the recipient of *essential grace*, in whom "everything is gracious, fresh, choice, even poetic," but whose obvious egotism "seduces without captivating" (p. 98). At the apex of the paradigm, we find the person gifted with *divine and concomitant grace*, whose faultless and effortless speech, manners, manner, and dress exact a love befitting divine beings: "you will love him irresistibly. You will take him as your model and make him an object of worship" (p. 100).[44]

The Religion of Art
When Gautier declared that "in literature as in theology, good works are nothing without divine grace" (212:12–13), he provided the basic formula for the production of the self-as-art—grace and

good works or *le je ne sais quoi* and *askesis*. This notion is, of course, a rewriting of the most ancient of critical topoi in which levels of creative activity—divine/human—and their terrestrial analogs—natural/artificial—have always been counterposed only to be conjoined in a higher synthesis. No analysis of artistic production, no discussion of the origins of beauty, has ever taken place outside this or some similar binary confrontation. Greek rhetorical theory opposed *physis* to *techné*, as Horace was to do with *Natura* and *Ars* in a debate which continued unabated in honnêteté and dandyism. In Méré's terms, the honnête homme constitutes "the masterwork of an excellent nature and consummate art" (340:I, 111); he is endowed with an excellent, beautiful, rich *naturel* or *génie* (<*ingenium*), which has nothing whatever to do with untutored nature, but which he makes every effort to refine and perfect (II, 36–37). For Boileau, it is the "perfect alliance" between nature and art which produces "sovereign perfection" (72:391). Two centuries later, Baudelaire termed the rare union of nature and art "poetic health" (51:I, 331), and ultimately, genius itself: ". . . he must constantly perfect his natural talents, refine them with care, find new effects in them; he must push his own nature to its outer limit" (p. 751). Just as asketic exercises, "a set of rules required by the very constitution of a spiritual being," enhance the power of originality (pp. 749–50), so too do the inspiration and enthusiasm of a sublime writer, like Edgar Allan Poe, stimulate him to "sharpen unceasingly his genius as a practicing poet" (p. 334).[45]

As Baudelaire's views suggest, the model for the ritual opposition and complementarity of discrepant modes of creativity must be sought in the mythic equation of the poet as *vates* or bard, a divine surrogate, like Amphion or Orpheus, infused with *pneuma* (in-spir-ation), inhabited by the *theos*, filled, as it were, with en-thus-iasm, partner in God's breath and mysteries. The arch-example of the priest-as-poet, of course, is found in the Pythian oracle who spoke Apollo's wisdom in perfect poetic meters. When Cicero and Quintilian speak of the rhetor's "gift of divinity" (131:I, 141), or his priest-like dedication,[46] they are referring to this venerable critical cliché. Throughout the ages, whenever the need arose to account for extraordinary esthetic phenomena, writers have gone irresistibly to the more exalted level in the paradigm—nature, birth, talent, genius—to underscore the poet's transcendent being, i.e., his divinity. This is the weighty tradition that underlies Chapus's ostensibly innocuous remark, "One is born elegant" (121:28), and Barbey's etiological explanation of the birth of his dandy-hero: "You cannot make yourself into a Brummell. Either one is or isn't. . . . He had his divine right and his raison d'être like all other kings. . . . [He] was one of the rarest individuals who had simply taken *the trouble to be born*" (38:IX, 217). *Poetae nascuntur.* . . . "Inspired" by fashionable arbiters, like Fox and Sheridan, Brummell went on to develop his gifts in a unique manner: "One of the future dandy's first impressions, then, was to feel the inspiration of those strong, charming men flowing over him. They were like the Fairies, bestowing gifts upon him; but they gave him only half of their powers, the most ephemeral of their faculties. It is certain that by seeing and hearing those spirits . . . the young Brummell developed the faculties which were in him" (p. 242). In more global terms, Baudelaire rehearses the same topos when he speaks of dandies as "creatures of election" endowed by nature with special gifts (51:II, 309, 743, 751); they harbor within them a "faculty of dandyism" (I, 697), a poetic potentiality which comes of "gifts from heaven that work . . . cannot bestow" (II, 712). Herein lay the difference between *minores*, like Hégésippe Moreau, who lacked the willpower and the asketic capacity to use "grace, the gratuitous gift," which he possessed (II, 160), and a figure of genius like Poe, whom Baudelaire envisioned in a Christ-like posture, at the "center of the instruments of the Passion" (49:II, 315–16). Because Poe was a dandy as he was a poet, the following comment applies to him and to his unique kind in both of these capacities: "Strange spiritualism," wrote the author of *Bénédiction* and *La Beauté* in his essay on dandyism, "for those who are, at one and the same time, its priests and its victims" (51:II, 711).[47]

Vigny's celebrated declaration, "Art is the modern religion, the modern spiritual belief" (515:II, 1058), is only partly accurate. The accent on modernity obscures the great antiquity of this idea, which extends the classical topos of the divine madness of the poet that Plato described in the *Phaedrus*, in Chapelain's words, as "an extraordinary light of the soul by which the god seems to draw the poet to him" (204:460). Like such poets, honnêtes hommes from Faret to Méré possess "something divine or some special genius" (188:83), the "kind of genius [that] is suffused with grace" (340:III, 130). In the deepest, most spiritual sense, then, *honnêtes gens* are to the manner born (p. 104): "This predisposition . . . comes to us at birth, it is a present from heaven, it is a natural light which cannot be acquired" (II, 79). Such was the explanation that Méré advanced for the greatness of men like Julius Caesar, who attributed to the gods what was in fact most admirable in themselves (p. 79). No wonder then that Méré, who was no more religious in the literal sense than he believed Caesar to have been, maintained that *dévotion* and honnêteté point in the same direction, follow "the same path" (III, 101);[48] or that he stated in absolute seriousness that the *art de plaire* leads to union with Christ: "the best and perhaps the only way to find salvation is to be appealing (*plaire*) to Him" (II, 29). By the same logic, *déplaire* becomes the cardinal sin: "It is a sin to *déplaire* when you can prevent it . . . and the 'scandal' that our Savior forbids under pain of the harshest punishments consists in nothing other than to *déplaire* or to cause ennui" (p. 29). In Christ's exhortation that the believer should cut off the hand or foot which would "scandalously" deny him the kingdom of heaven (Mat. xviii. 7–9), Méré finds an exact analog for the rigor with which the honnête homme should view his faults—the obstacles to *plaire*—in strict conformity with notions of good and evil, or *ce qui sied bien et mal* in the system of honnêteté (pp. 29–30). Although he does not utter the word, divine grace, in Méré's scheme, is ultimately equated to the mysteries of *agréments*: "When I wonder that the Lord loves one person and hates another without our being able to say why, the only reason I can think of is that he sees a wealth of *agréments* in one of them that he does not find in the other" (p. 29). Méré argues further that Christ "loved everything done *de bonne grâce*, like those wonderful fragrances with which he was anointed" (p. 28). Not surprisingly, he cites a number of biblical examples to show that Jesus preached *la bienséance* (pp. 28–29), and in what becomes the final step in this progression, he ascribes to the honnête homme the Christ-like mission of elevating fallen nature to the heights of moral and spiritual perfection: "One honnête homme is enough to inspire good behavior in the most wicked people on earth, and to make the members of a crude, barbarous court want to become *honnêtes gens*" (p. 31). It is precisely because of this priestly function that honnêteté alone, concluded Méré, "can make us happy in this life and the next" (p. 93).[49]

In a similar effort to pronounce artistocracy a substitute religion, dandy-writers from Balzac to Huysmans stressed the "similarity between our doctrines and those of Christianity" (22:97). Balzac, in fact, devotes the second half of his treatise to the "rigorous dogma" that "governs the world of elegance as it controls the Catholic universe" (pp. 79, 84). Elegance, like Christianity, has its capital sins and cardinal virtues: simplicity, harmony and cleanliness; their mysterious concordance produces a unity as "indivisible as the Trinity" (p. 80). As with any religion, moreover, elegance needs its spiritual leader, what Barbey was to call the "Dandy-priest" (38:IX, 218),[50] who can guide the "catechumens" to the altar (22:71–72). More often, however, the dandy usurps the religious function as an instrument of power over those whom he despises. At the culminating moment of French dandyism, we witness the supremely arrogant, but entirely logical, spectacle of Des Esseintes appointing himself dandy-pope: "He had a vaulted chamber built in which to receive his tradespeople: they would enter, sit next to one another in church pews, and then he would climb into the pulpit and preach a sermon on dandyism, exhorting his bootmakers and tailors to conform religiously to his briefs on matters of style, threatening them with monetary excommunication if they did not follow to the letter the instructions contained in his monitories and bulls" (266:39). This performance, however, is no mere public role playing designed to awe the profane; it is the acting out of an inner calling, a vocation which is concretized in the fabrication of Des Esseintes's abode. The bedroom that he transforms into a monk's cell, with its "clerical-yellow" walls, priedieu, cathedral candelabra, cenobite bed, and El Greco, stands as a symbol of dandyism itself, which strove to fashion, with the available materials of production, a religious domain. This retreat dramatizes the spiritual fervor that underlies the surface frivolity of the dandy's public pose. Thus, it is no accident that Huysmans' text should close with the annunciation

215

of the pilgrimage, which Des Esseintes will launch, in search of kindred souls to share his passion and his mission. But it was Baudelaire, the most catholic of dandy-writers, who, as always, had the ultimate word: "In truth, I was not completely wrong in considering dandyism a kind of religion" (51:II, 711).[51]

AFTERWORD

The knot of causes in which I am entangled
recurs and will create me again.

Nietzsche, *Thus Spoke Zarathustra*

"There are only three types of people who deserve respect: the priest, the warrior, the poet" (51:I, 684).[1] In Baudelaire's personal paradigm for excellence, we find the three prototypes that converged and merged in the literary representation of the dandy and the honnête homme: the warrior-aristocrat who ventures from his exclusive citadel to dominate society; the artist who meticulously fashions an autotelic, poetic system of signs; and the consecrated priest of a demanding, lifelong spiritual ideal. Whatever inescapable differences exist between the honnête homme and the dandy, as reflections and determinants of the codes and values of their particular epochs, both types emerge as variants of an aristocratic impulse that has persistently haunted the human imagination.

There is, perhaps, no clearer instance of the aristocratic self as both a synchronic and a diachronic typology, in the specificity of its sameness-in-difference, than the dual portrait bequeathed us by the seventeenth and nineteenth centuries of Antoine Nompar de Caumont, Duc de Lauzun (1632–1723). Regarded by posterity, in Barbey's words, as "a dandy before the dandies" (38:IX, 276),[2] Lauzun was hailed as the model of the honnête homme by Louis XIV's first cousin, to whom he was briefly betrothed. "I am doing nothing contrary to my conscience or my reputation. He is a perfect honnête homme": these are the words that Mlle de Montpensier claims to have used in defense of her scandalous decision to marry a man who had risen from mere colonel to favorite of the king (358:XLIII, 258). When, under pressure from his intimates, Louis XIV withdrew his approval and forbade the marriage, she

Afterword

argued her case from a position that was to govern her portrayal of her paramour: "[I beg] Your Majesty . . . to allow me to marry the most eminent honnête homme in your kingdom" (p. 278). Although this vision of Lauzun was to change radically after his extended imprisonment, the predominant characterization in her *Memoirs* brings together all the major elements in the typology of the honnête homme as the incarnation of *l'art de plaire*: "I told him that he was like the gardens at Enghien, that people were enchanted with him every time they looked at him, that his beauty was both inimitable and unfathomable" (p. 316). The most handsome and beautifully attired man at court, Lauzun does everything with an *air de grandeur* that makes him seem "the master of one and all" (p. 148). Whether on the battlefield or in the salon, his performance is effortless: "what would have seemed difficult for anyone else, came naturally to him" (p. 104). None can imitate the *civilité* or honnêteté of his manners (p. 343), or the *agrément* of his conversation (pp. 126, 136), which is always "astonishingly effective, so great is his natural eloquence" (p. 158). Because he is so consistently astonishing and superior, "there were times," admits La Grande Mademoiselle, ". . . when I thought that he deserved far more than I could do for him; and I had ample reason to feel this way, since all of France shared my opinion, such was his reputation for being in all ways unique" (p. 144).[3]

" 'I am intelligent, I am courageous,' he said about himself," writes La Bruyère in his thinly disguised portrait of Lauzun, "and everyone repeated after him, 'He is intelligent, he is courageous' " (286:246, #96). If La Bruyère emphasized Lauzun's ability to beguile, he also suggested the ambivalence that this personage aroused in his contemporaries: "the words 'cute,' 'appealing,' 'rare,' 'wondrous,' 'heroic,' were used to praise him; and their contraries have since been used to vilify him: an equivocal, mixed, involved character; an enigma, an all but insoluble problem" (#96). Seventeenth-century writers filled the interpretative space marked out by Lauzun's dramatic rise and fall with a plethora of images and judgments that ranged from the relatively positive (Bussy-Rabutin, Sévigné, Saint-Simon) to the decidedly negative (La Rochefoucauld, Choisy, La Fare). Some found him unattractive, ungroomed or uncultured, insolent, caustic, or cruel, but all agreed that Lauzun was altogether too ambitious, as his own

218

motto might have implied: "I will rise as high as any man can go" (358:XLIII, 42). Bussy saw him as a schemer, challenged by the unprecedented feat of marrying the king's cousin (99:II, 200), but Bussy was also the only commentator to defend his aspirations as heroic: "Like another Caesar, he wants to rise above his destiny, and show, as did the great Roman emperor, that his great heart is as capable of fearlessly resisting the onslaughts of misfortune as he is of gracefully accepting the fruits of success" (p. 243). Lauzun's Caesarism was not the kind, however, that his contemporaries wished to associate with honnêteté: his *amour propre* was not "under control" (244:55); he fell victim to *hubris* as he tried to "carry his bold flight too high" (p. 276). Consumed by the "gnawing worm of ambition" (440:VII, 367), he allowed his unrestrained narcissism to manifest his most offensive inclinations: "Inwardly contemptible but outwardly dignified, he would go to any lengths to curry favor with the King" (p. 367).[4]

Even his most relentless critics agreed with Montpensier, however, that Lauzun was altogether extraordinary, so much so that only esthetic terms, rather than ethical ones, could accommodate his perplexing uniqueness. Thus, as she thinks of Lauzun's "elevation," Montpensier rushes off to reread her Corneille (358:XLIII, 143–45), while Sévigné actually applies to him a Cornelian alexandrine: "Polyeucte has a noble name, and comes from a line of kings" (461:I, 186). In this climate, the subsequent reversal of Lauzun's fortunes logically became "the perfect subject for a tragedy, according to all the rules of the genre" (p. 184). And in 1689, when Lauzun reversed his fortunes once again (by helping the Queen of England escape during the revolution that cost James II his throne), when he regained his lost honors and rose to the ranks of Duke of France and English Knight of the Garter, Sévigné was prompted to declare: "the second volume of M. de Lauzun's epic is fine indeed, and worthy of the first" (III, 305). "Here is a wonderful subject for a novel or a tragedy," she wrote, "but especially, a wonderful subject for endless discussion and debate" (I, 183). The nineteenth century was to prove Sévigné right.[5]

"Those who witnessed these remarkable events did not understand the wonder and beauty of Lauzun's behavior," insisted Paul de Musset in his two-volume novel, *Lauzun* (1835), and went on to compare his hero's life to a five-act Cornelian tragedy and to rank his exploits above any described in fiction (370:II, 13, 275). Barbey, who devoted the entire second half of his treatise on dandyism to Lauzun, whom he called "the Englishman from France," regarded Montpensier's suitor as "the greatest artist in seduction that the world has ever seen. . . . It took nothing less than the will of Louis XIV to overthrow this masterpiece" (38:IX, 283, 300). In the syncretic portrait of the seventeenth-century dandy that emerges from the works of Musset, Stendhal, Roger de Beauvoir, Dumas, and Barbey, Lauzun is credited with a genius for elegance equal to Turenne's for war or Mignard's for painting (57:II, 14–15, 163, 169), and a power so unrivaled that he continues to lay down the laws of fashion from his cell at Pignerol. His noble, beautiful face and deceptively delicate exterior, like that of "a girl in disguise" (38:XIII, 375), conceal "a man of steel" (IX, 301), and an eye "that sees everything and is upset by nothing" (370:I, 78; 482:80). Although able to charm anyone and everyone (38:IX, 287), he never stooped to servility, as seventeenth-century writers wrongly claimed (370:II, 284). On the contrary, his aim was always to be special, unique (38:IX, 289), to deviate from social norms "in some strange and unexpected way" (370:I, 150–51), to defy the sanctified rules of court etiquette right under His Majesty's nose (II, 313). With his "incredible facility for adopting a thousand shapes" (II, 17), this consummate strategist assumed a tantalizing respectfulness with Montpensier (38:IX, 292), or an unsettling gravity with flighty courtiers (370:II, 287); "he had an equal knack for winning people's hearts with his appealing manners, or for crushing his enemies under the weight of his ironies" (I, 17). Because of his habitual sarcasms, which terrorized fools (370:II, 296), and his mystifying array of masks (57:II, 119), Lauzun, more hated than loved, was slavishly courted (II, 13–14; 370:II, 285). Musset depicts him as an irresistible Don Juan who is dissipated and racked by ennui, but ever hopeful that his next adventure will not leave him as dissatisfied as the others (II, 30, 97, 104, 315). In Barbey's version of the "Machiavellian" affair with Montpensier, the sadistic Lauzun "takes her spellbound heart and nails it to his person" with "unheard-of cruelties" (38:IX, 283, 298, 302). With equally extraordinary mastery over the self, he never once emerges from "the tortoise-shell of hypocrisy in which he encloses himself"; "Célimène and Tartuffe combined," Lauzun is "satanically admirable," the incarnation of *l'art de plaire en déplaisant* (p. 297).[6]

The two traits that were inimical to the seductive strategy of the honnête homme—vanity and ambition—were central to the systematic nineteenth-century countervalorization of Lauzun. "His . . . was the most terrifying egotism that has ever existed since the egotism of the Romans," declared Barbey. ". . . He had the merciless vanity, the tiger-like vanity of the dandy" (p. 282). In Musset's novel, this vanity reflects the essential elements in the Napoleonic legend—the quasi-miraculous rise to power of the self-made man: "Instead of being a Caumont, I would rather have been born in some garret, so that future historians, writing about this period, might include a chapter entitled: a man rose up from the depths of the masses and by his cunning alone became one of the royal family" (370:I, 329). But marriage to the king's cousin is only a means to the possession of "a kingdom where I may be the absolute ruler" (p. 158). On a symbolic level, there is a drive to conquer every height "which does not bear my footprints . . . the peak of the mountain I am climbing can hardly even be seen" (p. 111). In this titanic climate, the stratagems of Louis XIV are child's play: "Haven't I put into practice . . . tactics that are a thousand times more sophisticated than those used to rule a kingdom?" (II, 249). The king, in fact, feels personally threatened by Lauzun's keen mind, valor, and seductiveness, and sets out to destroy him (I, 202–3); Musset speculates that Lauzun may really have been the legendary Man in the Iron Mask (II, 168). Ignoring, rationalizing, or denying his apparent failures, dandy-writers transform Lauzun into a symbol of success, the realization of the paradigmatic nineteenth-century fantasy of power. The occasional seventeenth-century speculation that he and Montpensier may have secretly married is unanimously accepted in the nineteenth century as literary fact. Even his incarceration is presented as part of a deliberate and successful strategy: "It is absolutely essential for me to be imprisoned for a few weeks so that I may emerge more radiant than Christ on Easter night" (I, 208). Musset evokes the image of Christ once again, as he identifies Lauzun with the

221

archetypal hero from whom death always recoils: "Twenty times did death leap down upon him and dig its claws into his finest garments; but just as it was about to cut into his flesh, death drew back each time, filled with awe, like the Magdalene who dropped her outstretched arms . . . when the Lord said to her: *Noli me tangere.* It was written that this man would use up all the possibilities that one life can hold" (II, 280).[7]

Musset's belief that this dandy *Übermensch* had exhausted the possibilities of human greatness is not fundamentally different from La Bruyère's own conclusions about Lauzun: "No one got more out of his life than he did. . . . Nothing passed him by" (286:243, #96). The hint of opprobrium contained in this remark has no place in Musset's pervasive glorification of Lauzun, as he goes on to emphasize his essential similarity and his superiority to the Marquis de Vardes, an exemplary honnête homme: "He seemed to have a make-up just like Lauzun's. His pretty face, his mocking wit, his ambition and talent for manipulating people through flattery, made him resemble the King's favorite in more than one respect; and yet he lacked a *je ne sais quoi de grand* that put Lauzun in a class that Vardes could never reach. . . . The difference between the two of them was the same as between two pieces of fruit from the same tree; they look identical, but one of them is delicious and succulent, while the taste of the other is ordinary" (370:I, 103). If we disregard his personal preference, Musset's image of two different fruits from the same tree, generically identical but subtly different, provides an accurate analogy for honnêteté and dandyism themselves as variant outgrowths of the timeless aristocratic impulse.[8]

Dandyism, Baudelaire observed, is "a very ancient institution, since in Caesar, Cataline, Alcibiades, we have outstanding examples; it is also a universal institution since Chateaubriand found it in the forests and the lakefronts of the New World" (61:906). With the notable exception of Cataline, these were, of course, the very same examples that Méré and other *mondains* had alleged in their desire to prove the universality of honnêteté as an ideal of human greatness: "I consider [Caesar] the greatest man in the world," Méré had written, "and what pleases me even more, I find it hard to imagine a more perfect honnête homme" (340:I, 26).

When it came to Alcibiades, whom writers on honnêteté, following Montaigne's example, considered the ultimate *galant homme* (355:II.xxxvi, 735-36), Méré spoke of him as he would a contemporary: he had that "inexpressible brilliance that made him stand out wherever he went" (340:II, 42); and because of his protean suppleness and capacity for *insinuation*, his company was always sought after "by the most accomplished *honnêtes gens* and the most beautiful women of his time" (III, 73). With these suprahistorical examples as proof, Méré could argue with perfect conviction that "honnêteté, when developed to perfection, is always the same wherever it is found, although differences in time and social station may create a very different impression" (I, 75). In his posthumous essays, he even denied these apparent differences: "The subtle qualities of any one century belong in every age" (III, 83). In substance and in form, then, Méré envisaged honnêteté as a universal phenomenon, linking past, present, and future, bridging court, town, and countryside: "the ways of honnêteté have their place in every court on earth, from one end of the globe to the other; but this place is not limited to courts, it can even be found in the wilderness. Neither changes in surroundings, nor the passage of time, nor even variations in customs can make any significant difference" (p. 93). Thus, even though Caesar and Alcibiades had come and gone, Méré, Baudelaire, and their contemporaries knew, like Nietzsche, that there is in the human landscape, an "eternal recurrence of the same" (386:217 ff.).[9]

"A dandy the likes of Brummell will never be seen again," Barbey wrote of his own prototype, "but men *like* him, ... no matter what livery they are made to wear, will always be with us. Of that we can be sure" (38:IX, 278). The "aristocratic instinct" will be found even in the most patently democratic civilizations, because "it is not a social phenomenon, but a fact of human nature" (35:36). More precisely, dandyism "is rooted in human nature at all times and in all places ... because vanity is universal" (38:IX, 281). The kind of vanity in which Barbey located the artistocratic impulse, like the more concealed but equally fundamental *amour-propre* of the honnête homme, cannot be dismissed as vainglorious, no matter what the Bible may tell us. Nor in its modern, Freudian name—narcissism—should it be

223

viewed as essentially pathological—a fixation on the female principle (the Mother) that emerges as homo-erotic or auto-erotic perversion (199:XIV, 73–102). For the narcissism that motivated the (gyno)system of the honnête homme and the dandy—and of all those whom Baudelaire called "the family" (49:III, 114)—rejected the mire of self-reflection, that "luminous abyss in which Narcissus-like, [a man] admires his face" (51:475); rather, it strove persistently, even obsessively upward to the Apollonian heights of self-creation and self-perfection. This particular type of narcissism, which Nietzsche considered "one of the most weighty and significant of qualities" (38:228, #10), may be the prime mover of all forms of creativity, the generative impulse of the artistic function, which Freud recognized was inaccessible to psychoanalysis (199:XI, 136).[10] Out of this irreducible drive was wrought and rewritten the sublime vision of humanity which the honnête homme and the dandy illustrate. Imprinted on the poetic text of the body, that vision still endures today, permanently inscribed in the body of work left behind.

NOTES

INTRODUCTION

1. Throughout this study, references will be documented by a number, which corresponds to a specific item in my bibliography, volume, where necessary (in roman numeral), and page. Unless otherwise indicated, all translations from the French are my own. The original quotations (with spelling modernized) will be given in the notes.

2. This gaming impulse or play can be interpreted either as the sublimation of warring or the desublimation of the sacred (the priestly). For various theories of play, see Huizinga (264), Benveniste (67), Caillois (107), and Ehrmann (176).

3. "La langue est un système de signes exprimant des idées, et par là, comparable à l'écriture, à l'alphabet des sourds-muets, aux rites symboliques, aux formes de politesse, aux signaux militaires, etc., etc. Elle est seulement le plus important de ces systèmes. On peut donc concevoir *une science qui étudie la vie des signes au sein de la vie sociale* . . . ; nous la nommerons *sémiologie*. . . . Elle nous apprendrait en quoi consistent les signes, quelles lois les régissent."

4. For a definition of the poetic function, see Jakobson (457:350–77).

5. ". . . un souverain mépris pour l'argile dont nous sommes pétris [qui] . . . confine au péché"; "Les peintures du visage confèrent à l'individu sa dignité d'être humain; elles opèrent le passage de la nature à la culture, de l'animal stupide à l'homme civilisé."

6. "[Il] était, en effet, le plus honnête homme du monde, allant au devant des occasions d'obliger, ami sincère et effectif, plein de politesse et de mesure, fait pour plaire également à la cour et à la ville."

7. It is, perhaps, for similar reasons that a number of nineteenth-century novels are situated in the first half of the seventeenth century: Alexandre Dumas's *Les Trois mousquetaires*, *Le Vicomte de Bragelonne*, *La Christine*, *Vingt Ans après*; Alfred de Vigny's *Cinq Mars*, *La Maréchale d'Ancre*; Sainte-Beuve's *Marion Delorme*. For a list of articles written during the 1830s on the first half of the seventeenth century, see 273:220 ff.

8. "Il fallait vivre sous Louis XIV; on passait son temps à la cour, dans la meilleure compagnie du monde, avec Mme de Sévigné, le duc de Villeroy, M. le duc de Saint-Simon, et l'on n'était avec les soldats que pour les conduire au feu et accrocher de la gloire, s'il y en avait." See also Stendhal (482:190; 487:I, 762).

9. "Je me console avec le siècle de Louis XIV de toutes les sottises du siècle présent." "J'aime le luxe et même la mollesse/Tous ses plaisirs, les arts de toute espèce/ La propreté, le goût, les ornements:/ Tout honnête homme a de tels sentiments."

10. ". . . toutes les qualités agréables qu'un homme peut avoir dans la vie civile."

11. "[Il] n'a point voulu corriger les vices, mais les ridicules . . . voulant exposer à la risée publique tous les défauts opposés aux qualités de l'homme aimable, de l'homme de

Notes: 1. Pre-Texts and Prototypes

société; après avoir joué tant d'autres ridicules, il lui restait à jouer . . . le ridicule de la vertu."

12. See Magendie (323:384–86), Zévaco (527:3), Villey (514:340–41). An exception will be made for *Les Caractères* (1688–1694). La Bruyère's portraits and criticisms signal the dissolution of the dream of honnêteté. The sublime vision of life is undermined by traditional moral considerations.

13. " . . . le travail de connaissance vise une vérité approximative, non une vérité absolue. Si la science descriptive prétendait dire *la* vérité, elle contredirait à sa raison d'être. . . . L'imperfection est, paradoxalement, une garantie de survie."

1. PRE-TEXTS AND PROTOTYPES

1. "On ne s'imagine Platon et Aristote qu'avec de grandes robes de pédants. C'étaient des gens honnêtes et, comme les autres, riant avec leurs amis." " . . . changer sans peine et son extérieur et sa façon d'agir"; " . . . le faisait toujours souhaiter parmi les plus honnêtes gens et les plus belles femmes de ce temps." On Alcibiades' "protean suppleness," see also Refuge (421:127–28), Faret (188:70), and Marmet (329:263).

2. "Tout s'est poli et raffiné sous ce règne, tout était savant et ingénieux en cette cour, depuis Auguste jusqu'à ses valets." " . . . le plus honnête homme de son temps." " . . . l'homme qui plaisait, et à qui les gens polis et spirituels tâchaient de plaire. . . . Son goût réglait celui des autres; . . . on affectait de se donner·son tour, et de prendre autant qu'on pouvait son caractère." On Maecenas, see also Balzac (24:I, 317–19); on Augustus, Saint-Evremond (438:II, 327–52). Méré was one of the few not to consider Augustus an honnête homme (340:II, 66–67).

3. "Ce qu'il appelle afféterie, mollesse, dissolution, s'appelle gaieté, galanterie, délicatesse."

4. See Seneca 460:I, 49, 89; II, 103, 151; 459:I, 289, 427, 429; II, 115, 121; III, 109.

5. " . . . cette urbanité que les mots de civilité, de galanterie, et de politesse n'expliquent qu'imparfaitement." " . . . ce don . . . que Cicéron affectait et qui est d'autant plus difficile à acquérir qu'il fait le caractère le plus essentiel et la partie principale qui constitue l'honnête homme." On "Roman urbanity," see also Chalesme (117:180–81); Méré (340:III, 121); Vaumorières (511:I, 26,28).

6. See Cicero 131:III, 141; 133:465; Quintilian 413:IV, 373, 499, 513.

7. Like other writers, Méré objected to the grandiloquent style and tone of Cicero's works: "Les pédanteries des dix livres qu'il a faits déshonoreraient un honnête homme" (78:[1924]89). Notwithstanding his characterization of Cicero as a pedant, a bourgeois specialist (340:I, 75), Méré was greatly influenced by the Roman's concepts, as his texts reveal. See Boudhors's extensive notes to this effect in Méré's *Oeuvres complètes* (340).

8. "On a entièrement abandonné l'ordre gothique, que la barbarie avait introduit pour les palais et pour les temples; on a rappelé le dorique, l'ionique et le corinthien. . . . De même on ne saurait en écrivant rencontrer le parfait, et s'il se peut, surpasser les anciens que par leur imitation. Combien de siècles se sont écoulés avant que les hommes, dans les sciences et dans les arts, aient pu revenir au goût des anciens." For an unusually positive

Notes: 1. Pre-Texts and Prototypes

view of the evolution of the French language during the Middle Ages, see Bouhours (79:102–15).

9. On the seventeenth-century passion for tourneys, see Edelman (175b:111–23); he can also be consulted for seventeenth-century readings, interpretations and rewritings of medieval texts. See in particular Bussy-Rabutin's purported translation of the letters of Héloïse and Abelard, in which the middle-aged medieval monk is transformed into a young, seventeenth-century courtier (100:II, 166 ff.). Chapelain's *De la lecture des vieux romans* underwent a rewriting in Sarasin's *S'il faut qu'un jeune homme soit amoureux* (445:139 ff).

10. French writers were sustained in this endeavor by other Italian texts, notably Guazzo's *Civil conversatione* (1574), a utilitarian and moralistic rewriting of the *Cortegiano*. On the influence of Italian treatises, other than Castiglione's, on honnêteté, see Toldo (504) and Magendie (323). Both also examine in detail on the less influential contributions of Spanish texts. Gracián's work, particularly *El Héroe* and *Oraculo manual*, became familiar to the cultivated French reader through Bouhours's *Entretiens d'Ariste et d'Eugène* (1671), but by this date could contribute little to the formulation of honnêteté. Only La Rochefoucauld and especially La Bruyère clearly seem to have consulted Gracián. For an analysis of Gracián's influence on La Bruyère, see van Delft (152).

11. Castiglione uses the term *onesta* far less often than Faret does *honnête*. And he uses the term in its original moral sense more often than in the social. In the latter instances, he seems to distinguish social acts motivated by virtuous intentions from those that are not. Cf. 114:45, 50, 141, 165–66, 171, 303–05, 429, 439–40, 488–90.

12. " . . . les qualités les plus nécessaires . . . que doit posséder celui qui se veut rendre agréable dans la cour." "Le plus que l'on y peut mettre sans beaucoup s'incommoder est le meilleur, et c'est une des plus utiles dépenses, qui se fassent à la cour. . . . [Elle] leur ouvre des portes qui bien souvent sont fermées à la grande condition." " . . . une médiocre teinture des plus agréables questions qui s'agitent quelquefois dans les bonnes compagnies."

13. " . . . le bréviaire des honnêtes gens." " . . . le grand maître aussi bien que le grand exemplaire de la noblesse." Bourgeois writers of the first half of the century were not oblivious to Montaigne. Passages in Faret's and Bardin's treatises are reminiscent of the *Essais* (cf. 188:xxxvi–vii; 323:336); Grenailles's *L'Honnête garçon* (1642) cites or summarizes Montaigne frequently (240:I, 189–93; II, 54, 59–61, 103–04, 154–58, 174–77). But as Boase has written, the bourgeois took "isolated ideas without adopting anything of the outlook of the *Essays*" (71:313).

14. "Les hommes de la société et familiarité desquels je suis en quête, sont ceux qu'on appelle honnêtes et habiles hommes; l'image de ceux-ci me dégoûte des autres. C'est à le bien prendre de nos formes la plus rare, et forme qui se doit principalement à la nature." For this and the following passages from the *Essais*, I generally follow, and only occasionally alter, the translation of Donald Frame (*The Complete Essays of Montaigne*. 3 vols. New York: Anchor Books, 1960).

15. "Le port de sa robe, et quelque façon externe qui pouvait n'être pas civilisée à la courtisane . . . sont choses de néant . . . au dedans c'était l'âme la plus polie du monde." " . . . la délicatesse et obligation à certaine façon particulière"; " . . . personnage à tous patrons et formes de perfection"; " . . . à peine bons à un seul pli."

16. "Composer nos moeurs est notre office, non pas composer des livres, et gagner non pas des batailles et des provinces, mais l'ordre et tranquillité à notre conduite. Notre

Notes: 1. Pre-Texts and Prototypes

grand et glorieux chef d'oeuvre c'est vivre à propos." "Mon métier et mon art, c'est vivre."
On life as art, see also Montaigne, I.xxvi, 167; II.xxxvii, 764; III.xiii, 1088.

17. " . . . le plus fructueux et naturel exercice de notre esprit"; " . . . plus doux que
d'aucune autre action de notre vie." "Je reçois et avoue toutes sortes d'atteintes qui sont de
droit fil . . . mais je suis par trop impatient de celles qui se donnent sans forme. . . . Tout
un jour je contesterai paisiblement si la conduite du débat se suit avec ordre. Ce n'est pas
tant la force et la subtilité que je demande, comme l'ordre. . . . Comme en un concert
d'instruments, on ouït pas un luth, une épinette et la flûte, on ouït une harmonie en globe,
l'assemblage et le fruit de tout cet amas." " . . . la gentillesse et la beauté me remplissent et
occupent autant ou plus que le poids et la profondeur."

18. "Moulant sur moi cette figure, il m'a fallu si souvent dresser et composer pour
m'extraire, que le patron s'en est fermi et aucunement formé soi-même."

19. "Outre ce profit que je tire d'écrire de moi j'en espère cet autre que s'il advient que
mes humeurs plaisent et accordent à quelque honnête homme avant que je ne meure, il
recherchera de nous joindre."

20. On Montaigne's praise of Seneca, see also II.xvii, 621. On his opposition to
Cicero's style, see I.xl, 243; II.x, 389. The seventeenth century had very different responses
to Montaigne's style; they ranged from the very positive (Camus, Pascal and Saint-
Evremond) to the negative (Balzac, Mitton, Méré). Mitton was actually bent on rewriting
the *Essais* to improve their style (71:303). For their comments see Boase (71) and Villey
(514).

21. "Les grâces . . . qui coulent sous la naïveté et la simplicité échappent aisément à
une vue grossière comme la nôtre; elles ont une beauté délicate et cachée; il faut la vue nette
et bien purgée pour découvrir cette secrète lumière."

22. "Me peignant pour autrui, je me suis peint en moi de couleurs plus nettes que
n'étaient les miennes premières. Je n'ai plus fait mon livre que mon livre m'a fait." "Elle
me sert aucunement de règle. . . . Cette publique déclaration m'oblige de me tenir en ma
route, et à ne démentir l'image de mes conditions."

23. The precepts contained in the anonymous *Bienséance de la conversation entre les
hommes* (1618), written for the nobility, reveal the current state of manners: " . . . ne pas
hurler en bâillant, ne pas regarder dans son mouchoir, ne pas arroser de sa salive le visage
de l'interlocuteur, ne pas se préparer en présence d'autrui à satisfaire les besoins intimes"
(323:160–61). According to all accounts, the court atmosphere was hardly more sophisticated (323:1–13, 31–111).

24. " . . . le rendez-vous de ce qu'il y a de plus galant à la cour et de plus poli parmi
les beaux esprits de ce siècle." "On ne croit point être du monde qu'on n'ait été connu
d'elle."

25. "Celui qui est né roturier peut renaître gentilhomme, et remplir sa vie de lumière,
malgré l'obscurité de son origine." "Les auteurs . . . servent à étendre leur empire et à conserver leur réputation et leur puissance: ce qui se fait réciproquement entre elles et les
auteurs."

26. "On y parle point savamment, mais on y parle raisonnablement, et il n'y a lieu au
monde où il y a plus de bon sens et moins de pédanterie." "[Elle] n'ignore presque rien de ce
qui mérite d'être su; mais elle le sait sans faire semblant de le savoir; et on dirait à l'entendre
parler . . . qu'elle ne parle . . . que par le simple sens commun, et par le seul usage du
monde."

Notes: 1. Pre-Texts and Prototypes

27. *Stances écrites de la main gauche sur un feuillet qui regardait un miroir mis au dedans de la couverture des tablettes.* "Tout le monde était sans proférer une parole, en admiration de tant d'objets qui étonnaient en même temps les yeux et les oreilles." See also Tallemant des Réaux (497:I, 445–46).

28. See Debu-Bridel (148:207–8). Lathuillère maintains that "avec les précieux l'honnêteté devient une qualité mondaine" (296:592).

29. The satirical works which seem to have popularized the term *précieuse* were all written during the decade 1650–1660: Scarron, *L'Epître chagrin* (1652); d'Aubignac, *Relation véritable du royaume de coquetterie* (1655); Saint-Evremond, *Le Cercle* (1656); de Pure, *La Précieuse* (1656–1658); and Molière, *Les Précieuses ridicules* (1659). Since Somaize's *Dictionnaire des précieuses* (1660) applies the term to *la société mondaine* as a whole, it ceases to have a specific significance. By 1667, Torche used the past tense to describe "une secte ridicule qu'on appelait la secte des précieuses, qui avaient introduit des mots nouveaux et des manières bizarres" (505:2). And if Molière still uses the term in *Critique de l'Ecole des femmes* and *L'Impromptu de Versailles* (1663), by 1672, he speaks of *Les Femmes savantes,* as had Chapelain and Balzac in the 1620s, to describe female pedants. Contrary to what Mongrédien's *Les Précieux et les précieuses* would suggest, the noun form for a male does not seem to have existed in the seventeenth century. The abstract *la préciosité* is not to be found before 1671—"l'honnêteté et la préciosité d'un long veuvage" (461:I, 405), where it has positive connotations. No evidence suggests the actual existence of a movement called *préciosité.*

30. "Certaines personnes du beau sexe, qui ont su se tirer du prix commun des autres, et qui ont acquis une espèce et un rang tout particulier." "Il n'y a point de roturiers dans leur empire, les sciences et la galanterie n'ayant rien que d'illustre et de noble." "Quand dans une compagnie il ne se trouve qu'une seule précieuse, elle est dans un ennui et un chagrin qui la fatiguent fort, elle baille, ne répond à tout ce qu'on lui dit, et si elle y répond, c'est tout de travers pour faire voir qu'elle ne songe pas à ce qu'elle dit. . . . S'il arrive dans cette compagnie une autre précieuse, elles se rallient ensemble . . . ce sont les emportements à rire au nez des gens les plus insupportables du monde."

31. "Laissez-nous faire à loisir le tissu de notre roman." "Il faut nécessairement qu'une précieuse parle autrement que le peuple, afin que ses pensées ne soient entendues que de ceux qui ont des clartés au-dessus du vulgaire." The available documents show no trace of a distinct idiolect. According to F. Brunot, the number of neologisms created by *précieux* circles was small and rarely used in their novels and poetry, although they may have been more widespread in conversation. The expressions in Somaize's dictionary and *Les Précieuses ridicules* seem ridiculous, argues Brunot, only because they are quoted out of context (92:III, pt.1, 66–74).

32. "Elles penchent la tête sur l'épaule, font des mines des yeux et de la bouche, et ont une mine méprisante et une certaine affectation en tous leurs procédés." "C'est un artifice naturel, par lequel la machine du visage en change absolument la disposition, comme le théâtre change de scène pour représenter divers sujets, ou pour plaire à ses spectateurs. Ainsi, quoique l'âme soit toujours en même situation et dans la même fierté le faux semblant ne laisse pas de porter quelque marque de douceur sur le visage."

33. " . . . il disait souvent d'excellentes choses, mais je sentais qu'il était plus comédien qu'honnête homme; cela me le rendait insupportable." In his letters, *Propos,* and essays, especially *De la justesse,* Méré chastized the style of Voiture's much heralded letters and

Notes: 1. Pre-Texts and Prototypes

pointed out his consistent disregard for correct usage. Other *mondains*, however, usually praised Voiture; Bussy-Rabutin and Sévigné took exception to Méré's criticisms (340:I, 172; 461:II, 511–15).

34. On Wellington's dandyism for example, see Chateaubriand (126:II, 76).

35. Despite his knowledge of English philosophy, Voltaire spoke only rarely of British reasonableness, nor did he stress British coldness, which was to figure so prominently in the dandy's typology (522:96, 730). Voltaire's characterization, even with its potential contradictions, is a distillation of an earlier cliché (see Ascoli, *La Grande Bretagne devant l'opinion française au xviie siècle* [12]).

36. "Tout le monde a la passion des chevaux, des chiens, de étoffes, des voitures venant d'Angleterre . . . un élégant serait honteux de se fournir ailleurs." "En voilà où en est l'urbanité, le bon goût, l'élégance des manières dans le pays de François Ier, de Lauzun et de Richelieu."

37. Pichot unearths "le type de ces fats manqués" in Shakespeare himself and cites Hotspur's harangue (*Henry IV, Part I*, I.iii, 33–69) against the elegant, perfumed lord who disdains the "slovenly corpses on the battlefield" (397:287).

38. "Rien ne réussissait à Londres comme l'insolence." " . . . ses formes graves, son originalité naturelle, son indépendance et sa dignité pour affecter ces grâces frivoles qui jusqu'ici avaient fait exclusivement partie du caractère français. Elle ne cache pas son admiration pour les agréments parisiens; elle les croit indispensables pour le bonheur de la vie. Sans doute les deux sexes se façonnent passablement sur le modèle qu'ils ont sans cesse sous les yeux; mais ils restent imitateurs et perdent leur physionomie nationale." "Les anglais de la nouvelle race sont infiniment plus frivoles que nous."

39. "On nous juge par nos habits plutôt que par nos qualités . . . si un homme n'est pas mis à la dernière mode, il doit se contenter d'occuper la dernière place dans l'estime du bon monde." " . . . à se faire lacer et serrer dans un corset, à arranger les plis d'une cravate qui vous étrangle comme si vous étiez au pilori, à se faire huiler la tête, à se peindre la figure, et tout cela pour ne pas avoir l'air d'un homme comme il faut." "Souvent ils ont à la bouche un curedent, une paille qu'ils ont ramassée dans leur écurie, ou pour se donner un air militaire, une [sic] cigare allumée dont la fumée semble indiquer qu'il ne se trouve dans l'intérieur de leur tête que vide, vapeur et brouillard. Quelquefois vous voyez ces héros de taverne et d'écurie, placés nonchalamment sur un cheval fermant un oeil et approchant une lorgnette de l'autre, ayant sur le bras un bâton tordu, emblème parfait de leur esprit."

40. See Vigny (515:I, 238–39) and Stendhal (486:154, 164, 167, 168). Pichot's ten-volume prose translation (1819–1821) is often more "Byronic" than the original, and was disavowed by Byron (183:22). The eight-volume fourth edition (1822–1825) was the most widely read.

41. Stendhal's Octave de Malivert, the hero of *Armance*, provides one of the earliest examples of the synthesis between Byronism and dandyism. Closer to Harold than to Conrad, this inactive noble shares the Byronic hero's misanthropy, somber melancholy, terrifying outbursts and impassive coldness. The mysterious air he cultivates, the criminal tendencies to which he confesses, are designed both to fascinate others and to prevent discovery of his "monstrous" secret, his impotence. Doomed to solitude, Octave discovers to his own horror that he loves Armance: he takes the heroic route, and commits suicide in Greece, the site of Byron's own death. In addition to his Byronic traits, however, Octave

Notes: 1. Pre-Texts and Prototypes

attaches particular importance to his elegant manners: "Que me fait l'esprit d'un homme? Ce sont ses manières qui peuvent me donner la tristesse" (487:I, 102). Octave displays an 'English' haughtiness and disdain for the French nobility, a class that he considers insipid and effete. To his surprise, he is all the more respected for his impertinence and is viewed as "un être rebelle" destined for a glorious future (p. 64).

42. "Nous admirions fort les prouesses du jeune lord et ses bacchanales nocturnes dans l'abbaye de Newstead avec ses jeunes amis recouverts de frocs de moine . . . ; ces banquets . . . nous semblaient la suprême expression du dandysme, par l'absolue indifférence pour ce qui cause l'épouvante du genre humain."

43. "Ses chevaux, son tilbury, ses gens en livrée, faisaient de lui l'objet de l'envie de . . . tous les jeunes gens de Nancy et des environs. . . . Sa noire mélancolie, lorsqu'il était seul dans la rue, ses distractions, ses mouvements d'impatience avec apparence de méchanceté, passaient pour de la fatuité de l'ordre le plus relevé et le plus noble. Les plus éclairés y voyaient une imitation savante de Lord Byron, dont on parlait encore beaucoup à cette époque."

44. "Il passa la Manche avec un vers brutal du Don Juan de Lord Byron." This verse (XI.lxxviii) deals with the nemesis of celebrated careers: "Where's Brummel? Dish'd. Where's Long Pole Wellesley? Diddled." Balzac does introduce Brummell in his treatise of 1830 as the ultimate authority on elegance (22).

45. " . . . il fut le dandysme même." "Il était un grand artiste à sa manière; seulement son art n'était pas spécial, ne s'exerçait pas dans un temps donné. C'était sa vie même. . . . Il plaisait avec sa personne, comme d'autres plaisent avec leurs oeuvres."

46. Although Matoré's lexical classifications for various periods are, in my view, reductionist, his concept of *le mot clef* is useful to my purpose (see 334).

47. Semantic mutability, it should be noted, does not negate the concept of synchrony, that is, the specific state of a linguistic system; since it always reflects some unit of time, a synchrony can never be absolutely static; it is inevitably a microdiachrony. See Saussure (448:142–43) and Jakobson (270:75).

48. "Je ne puis souffrir qu'on dise qu'un tel est honnête homme, et que l'un conçoive sous ce terme une chose et l'autre une autre. Je veux qu'on ait une idée particulière de ce qu'on nomme *le galant homme, l'homme de bien, l'homme d'honneur, l'honnête homme* . . . Ne vous amusez pas à former vos définitions sur l'usage du parler; car la plupart des termes deviennent synonymes par là. . . . Je définis . . . peut-être bien, peut-être mal; mais enfin je veux fixer mes idées."

49. " . . . plutôt de fâcheux négotiateurs, que des gens de bonne compagnie"; " . . . qui ne sont ni avares ni ambitieux . . . n'ont guère pour but que d'apporter la joie partout." See La Bruyère 286:93–94, #11; 215, #2; 216, #10; 218–19, #18; 238, #72.

50. "Un bel esprit pense toujours noblement; il produit des choses claires, agréables et naturelles; il les fait voir dans leur plus beau jour, et il les pare de tous les ornements qui leur conviennent; il entre dans le goût des autres, et retranche de ses pensées ce qui est inutile, ou ce qui peut déplaire." "Comme ce titre a été donné à un nombre infini de mauvais poètes et d'auteurs ennuyeux, on s'en sert plus souvent pour tourner les gens en ridicules, que pour les louer."

51. "Je ne prétends pas ici de former un honnête homme, je suppose qu'il l'est déjà, et qu'il n'a besoin que de conduite pour arriver à sa fin." "On peut bien dire qu'un homme est

de grande qualité comme de grande naissance, l'usage le veut ainsi, mais de confondre sous ce mot de qualité l'avantage d'être fils d'un grand Prince avec celui d'être bien fait, d'être brave, ou d'être honnête homme, on s'en garde bien quand on entend ce qu'on dit."

52. " . . . digne d'être proposé pour modèle lorsqu'on veut définir le véritable homme d'honneur." "Vous n'avez qu'à bien paraître ce que vous êtes, pour être reconnu pour un fort honnête homme . . . vous êtes franc et sincère, et vous avez la franchise d'un vrai homme d'honneur qui ne sent rien en son âme qu'il ait intérêt de cacher." "La plupart de ces gens d'honneur ont je ne sais quoi de rigide qui ferait préférer les insinuations d'un fourbe à une si austère fidélité. Je remarque dans ces hommes . . . une gravité qui vous importune, ou une pesanteur qui vous ennuie." Other critical portraits of the *homme d'honneur* are to be found in Molière's characterization of Alceste (*Le Misanthrope*) and Don Carlos (*Dom Juan*).

53. *Honnête homme* and *homme de bien* are also treated synonymously in Bardin's *Le Lycée* and Grenailles's *L'Honnête garçon*.

54. "Il y a deux morales qui se contredisent formellement, la morale de Jésus-Christ et la morale du monde. Parcourons les maximes de l'une et de l'autre, nous n'en trouverons point entre lesquelles il ne se rencontre une contrariété absolue." "On pourrait être fort homme de bien et fort mal-honnête homme. Il ne faut qu'être juste pour être homme de bien, et pour être honnête homme il se faut connaître à toutes sortes de bienséances, et les savoir pratiquer. Il me semble aussi qu'on pourrait être le plus honnête homme du monde sans être le plus juste."

55. "Nous voyons moins d'honnêtes gens que d'habiles: plus de bon sens dans les affaires, que de délicatesse dans les entretiens." "La distance qu'il y a de l'honnête homme à l'habile homme s'affaiblit de jour à l'autre et est sur le point de disparaître. L'habile homme est celui qui cache ses passions, qui entend ses intérêts, qui y sacrifie beaucoup de choses, qui a su acquérir du bien ou en conserver. L'honnête homme est celui qui ne vole pas sur les grands chemins, et qui ne tue personne, dont les vices enfin ne sont pas scandaleux." "C'est le rôle d'un sot d'être importun: un homme habile sent s'il convient ou s'il ennuie." "Le jeu produit de bons effets quand on s'y conduit en habile homme . . . jouant toujours en honnête homme, on gagne quelquefois plus en perdant, qu'on ne perd." "De la sorte que le monde considère ce qu'on appelle être habile homme, on dirait que cette qualité ne se montre qu'à s'établir puissament; mais elle consiste beaucoup plus à trouver le bonheur de la vie." "[Etre habile] consiste à nous bien servir des choses qui dépendent de nous pour vivre plus heureusement."

56. "1. metable en ce dont il se mêle: praeclarus, insignis, praestans; 2. honnête, de belle humeur et de bonne convention; 3. garnement: improbus, nequam, nebulo; 4. arrogant: arrogans, praesidens." "Je voudrais que les hommes eussent pour les dames ces déférences que les honnêtes gens doivent avoir, et qu'ils fussent toujours devant elles dans un esprit d'honnêteté et de galanterie." "On dit que *c'est un homme galant* pour dire qu'il a de la bonne grâce et qu'il cherche à plaire aux dames par ses manières complaisantes et honnêtes, et on dit *c'est un galant homme* pour dire qu'il fait les choses avec honneur et qu'il sait bien se tirer de toutes sortes d'affaires." "D'autres disaient que . . . c'était un composé où il s'entrait du je ne sais quoi ou de la bonne grâce, de l'air de la cour, de l'esprit, du jugement, de la civilité, de la courtoisie et de la gaieté, le tout sans contrainte, sans affectation, et sans vice. Avec cela il y a de quoi faire un honnête homme à la mode de

Notes: 1. Pre-Texts and Prototypes

la cour. Ce sentiment fut suivi comme le plus approchant de la vérité, mais on ne laissait pas de dire que cette définition était encore imparfaite, et qu'il y avait quelque chose de plus dans la signification de ce mot, qu'on ne pouvait exprimer." "Un galant homme n'est autre chose qu'un honnête homme un peu plus brillant ou plus enjoué qu'à son ordinaire"; " . . . la différence n'en est pas si grande, que l'on s'y puisse beaucoup tromper."

57. In the infrequent instances when Méré used *homme d'honneur*, he did not give the term strong moral connotations, nor did he assimilate it to *honnête homme*. See 340:I, 80; III, 90; 78:XXX (1923), 520. For Méré's negative characterization of *bel esprit*, see 340:I, 57–95.

58. " . . . un homme poli et qui sait vivre," "Honnête homme . . . comprend encore toutes les qualités agréables qu'un homme peut avoir dans la vie civile. . . . Quelquefois on appelle aussi honnête homme un homme en qui on ne considère alors que les qualités agréables et les manières du monde. En ce sens, honnête homme ne veut dire autre chose que galant homme, homme de bonne conversation, de bonne compagnie," "Honnête (comis, urbanus) qui a de l'honnêteté, de la civilité et de l'honneur (l'honnête homme est celui qui ne se pique de rien)."

59. "Il n'y a plus, à proprement parler, des fats, de ces fats transcendants, qui brillaient dans la société, dictaient des lois sur la parure et les modes, subjugaient les femmes, imposaient aux hommes, dont la jeunesse s'empressait de copier les manières et d'imiter le ton." " . . . [est] le signe d'un incontestable pouvoir conquis sur le peuple femelle. Un homme aimé par plusieurs femmes passe pour avoir des qualités supérieures." "Intriguées par le dédain du fat, . . . stimulées pour son affectation à prétendre qu'il était impossible de le faire sortir de son marasme, et piquées par son ton de sultan blasé, les femmes le recherchaient encore plus vivement qu'à son arrivée." "D'un fat, par un fat, à des fats."

60. " . . . un homme du monde, qui n'a ni vertus ni principes, mais qui donne à ses vices des dehors séduisants, qui ne les ennoblit qu'à force de grâce et d'esprit."

61. "Il se mettait bien . . . mais il avait beaucoup de prétentions, et l'élégance n'en laisse jamais soupçonner."

62. "Ainsi qu'on le voit, le nom même qu'ils portèrent accuse l'influence française. Leur grâce aussi était comme leur nom. Elle n'était pas assez indigène, assez mêlée à cette originalité du peuple . . . à cette force intime qui devait plus tard la pénétrer." "Ne mettez pas sous cette expression de 'beau' . . . rien du frivole, du mince, et de l'exigu . . . car vous n'auriez pas la notion juste de mon vicomte de Brassard, chez qui, esprit, manières, physionomie, tout était large, étoffé, opulent, plein de lenteur patricienne, comme il convenait au plus magnifique dandy que j'aie connu, moi qui ai vu Brummel devenir fou et d'Orsay mourir."

63. The *macaroni* of the 1760s, whose name originated from the Macaroni Club of London, affected the tastes and fashions of continental society; the *buck* was known as a fop and a ladies' man. Among the infrequent references to these two terms in the corpus of dandyism, see 38:IX, 242; 408:20.

64. " . . . toutes les actions, à tous les moments de la vie: c'est l'art de s'habiller, de manger, de marcher, de parler, d'aimer, de dormir. . . . En un mot, c'est l'art de vivre." "Une énorme cravate, un air niais; un vaste lorgnon stupidement dirigée sur quelque face bouffie, et voilà un dandy, goddam!" " . . . un meuble de boudoir, un mannequin

Notes: 1. Pre-Texts and Prototypes

extrêmement ingénieux . . . , mais un être pensant . . . , jamais." "Le fashionable, sachez-le bien, n'est pas l'homme poli; c'est le triomphe du bizarre, du singulier, sur le naturel. Le fashionable anglais-pur-sang doit avoir un facile dédain des hommes et des choses. . . . Il ne doit jamais s'émouvoir, sourire affectueusement, être heureux ou malheureux . . . [sa réserve] envers tout le monde doit être taciturne, hautaine, insolente." See also Gautier (213:137); Barbey (38:IX, 267).

65. The texts that herald the lion's ascendancy include: Barbey's *Les Lions d'autrefois*, 1840 (36); Guichardet's *Le Lion de contrebande*, 1840 (247); Dériège's *La Physiologie du lion*, 1842 (158); Soulié's *Le Lion amoureux*, 1852 (468); and Gozlan's *Le Lion empaillé*, 1848 (230).

66. M. de Cernay "était fort curieux de lions de toute espèce; et dès qu'il arrivait à Paris un Arabe, un Persan, un Indien, un étranger de quelque distinction, M. de Cernay se le faisait aussitôt présenter. Etait-ce pour attirer encore davantage attention par ces voyants et étranges acolytes?" "Les femmes aiment prodigieusement ces gens qui se nomment pachas eux-mêmes, qui semblent accompagnés de lions, de bourreaux et marchent dans un appareil de terreur. Il en résulte chez ces hommes une sécurité d'action, une certitude de pouvoir, une fierté de regard, une conscience léonine qui réalise pour les femmes le type de force qu'elles rêvent toutes." " . . . les dandies qui naguère l'avaient mystifié . . . les lions de cette époque." " . . . les princes du dandysme: ce sont les élus parmi les élus, c'est la fine fleur du monde élégant et fashionable." In a similar vein, Barbey writes that M. de Marigny "a quelque chose de si mâle, de si *léonin* diraient les écrivains de ce temps-ci, dans l'esprit et dans la physionomie que l'amour qu'il [ressent] . . . doit être la plus énivrante attestation qu'on est bien puissant, puisqu'on a pu le subjuguer" (38:VI, 17). For examples of the use of the jaguar and the tiger, see Gautier (213:7, 135; 207:204) and Barbey (38:V, 78–79; IX, 282).

67. " . . . n'était pas *gentleman-like* . . . sifflait les linottes du dandysme." "[c'est] l'homme d'honneur même qui, par les convenances, est retenu dans les limites de bonne conduite et de bienséance que la religion n'atteindrait pas; car il y a bien des choses que ferait un prêtre et que jamais ne pourrait faire un galant homme." "Ce mot anglais *gentleman* ne signifie pas gentilhomme dans une acception aristocratique, mais homme parfaitement bien élevé et de très bonne compagnie, de quelque condition qu'il soit." " . . . appartenait à ce dandysme sobre qui râpe ses habits avec du papier de verre pour leur ôter l'éclat endimanché et tout battant neuf si cher au philistin et si peu désirable pour le vrai gentleman." "Nous avons des gentlemen, des dandies, des seigneurs qui prêchent l'évangile du savoir vivre."

68. "Du lion au gandin, il y a un abîme; mais quel autre abîme entre le gandin et le petit crevé! au moins le dandysme, avec sa raideur hautaine, avait-il une certaine grandeur." " . . . un jeune homme que son élégance excessive et son air prétentieux rendent ridicule." *Le snob* has been omitted from this survey of the semantic field of dandyism because the term rarely appears in French literature before 1885. Admittedly, under the influence of Guiffrey's translation of Thackeray's *The Book of Snobs* (1846) in 1857, the term can be found in Taine's essay on Thackeray (1858) with the observation, "Nous n'avons pas le mot parce que nous n'avons pas la chose" (494:164, 179). In his dictionary (1867), Delvau also cites *snob*: "fat, ridicule, vaniteux dans l'argot des gens de lettres qui ont emprunté ce mot au *livre des snobs* de Thackeray, comme si nous n'avions pas déjà le

mot sous une douzaine de formes" (154:s.v.). But as E. Carassus has observed in *Le Snobisme et les lettres françaises*, it is only in 1884 that *le snobisme* "conquiert vraiment son état civil et se développe" (110:111). He traces the development of the concept from 1884 to 1914. On *snob* see also D'Ormesson (167:443–59), Jullian (278), Fatta (189), Voivenel (519:154 ff.). *Le décadent* and *l'esthète* as types do not appear prior to 1885. On the former, see Carter (111); on the latter, Lethève (307).

2. SELF-ASSERTION AND THE METAPHORS OF WAR

1. "... l'empire et l'ascendant qu'on veut prendre sur son esprit"; "il secouerait le joug par honte ou par caprice."

2. "L'on ne doit pas vouloir vaincre à quelque prix que ce soit comme les princes barbares, mais comme les héros d'une manière qui plaise et même aux vaincus." "... assiéger les esprits," "réduire l'esprit des autres," "gagner les personnes comme on veut." "... ce grand art de manier les coeurs et de gagner les inclinations [est] le chef d'oeuvre de l'esprit humain." For Méré's use of *gagner* see 340:I, 9, 51; II, 46, 72, 106, 130; III, 79–80; cf. *vaincre* I, 52; II, 130.

3. "... le sujet de toutes nos conversations: chacun s'est rendu partisan de l'un ou de l'autre."

4. "Ne fallait-il pas qu'il eût le coeur bien vaste, et l'esprit d'une grande étendue, pour songer à des choses dont les conquérants ordinaires font si peu de cas?" "... [il] me paraît le plus grand homme du monde, et ce qui m'en plait davantage, j'ai de la peine à imaginer un plus honnête homme."

5. "[Il] est aussi grand poète qu'Homère; il écrivit de la poésie tout comme Homère a lancé des batailles." Musset regarded Goethe and Byron as "les deux plus beaux génies du siècle après Napoléon" (367:III, 73).

6. "... tous les matins, comme sous l'Empire la ressource de l'héroïsme en action." "... les épais bataillons de la tourbe aristocratique ou bourgeoise.... L'exemple de Napoléon ... apparut à Lucien qui jeta ses calculs au vent en se les reprochant." "... comme Napoléon, à toujours livrer bataille en sachant qu'une seule défaite était le tombeau de sa fortune." On a less epic scale, Balzacian dandies are sometimes called *corsaires*. The term, borrowed from Byron, is used to characterize Maxime de Trailles as "le plus habile, le plus renardé ... de tous les corsaires à gants jaunes, à cabriolet, à belles manières qui naviguèrent, naviguent et navigueront sur la mer orageuse de Paris" (19:VI, 806). The term *condottiere*, which refers to a self-made man whose fortunes thrived during the Italian Renaissance (87:13–17, 82, 279), is also used frequently to describe dandies in *La Comédie humaine* (19:II, 32, 591; V, 592–93; VI, 151, 839).

7. "Les miracles de ses armes ont ensorcelé la jeunesse en nous apprenant à adorer la force brutale. Sa fortune inouïe a laissé à l'outrecuidance de chaque ambition l'espoir d'arriver où il était parvenu." On the military as the noble métier in the seventeenth century, see Méré (340:I, 11; III, 142), Saint-Evremond (438:III, 258–59), and Bussy-Rabutin: "Lorsque j'entrai dans le monde, ma première et ma plus forte inclination fut de devenir honnête homme, et de parvenir aux grands honneurs de la guerre" (323:840).

Notes: 2. Self-Assertion and Metaphors of War

8. "La magnanimité méprise tout pour avoir tout." "Cette honnêteté qui a été l'idole des sages païens n'est rien dans le fond qu'un amour-propre plus intelligent et plus adroit que celui du commun du peuple." ". . . se voyant exclus de la violence ouverte, ils sont réduits à chercher d'autres voies, et à substituer l'artifice à la force, et ils n'en trouvent point d'autre que de tâcher de contenter l'amour propre de ceux dont ils ont besoin, au lieu de le tyranniser." ". . . le moi est haïssable: vous Miton le couvrez, vous ne l'ôtez pas pour cela." As Port Royal explained, "le mot *moi* dont l'auteur se sert . . . ne signifie que l'amour-propre" (393a:541, #5).

9. ". . . celui qui ne se pique de rien." The writers on honnêteté who use this definition include Mitton (244:56), Méré (340:I, 146–47; II, 45), Vaumorières (511:I, 24), and La Bruyère (286:349, #20).

10. "[le] fruit de cette vanité qu'on a trop flétrie." For Barbey, there is basically no difference between vanity and *fatuité*: "Quand la vanité est satisfaite et qu'elle le montre, elle devient de la fatuité" (38:IX, 223). Some dandy-writers, however, like the *mondains*, stressed the need for artfully concealing the more offensive aspects of vanity (416:320–21). Balzac, who censured the dandies' vanity as "le fil principal de ces pantins" (19:V, 276), described elegance, by comparison, as "un habile développement de l'amour-propre; tout ce qui révèle trop fortement la vanité y produit un pléonasme" (22:9).

11. ". . . des représentants de ce qu'il y a de meilleur dans l'orgueil humain." ". . . les derniers représentants de l'orgueil humain." ". . . l'homme . . . accoutumé dès sa jeunesse à l'obéissance des autres hommes."

12. "Ils étaient devenus, comme le Roi le voulait, autant de capucins, capables seulement d'obéissance."

13. ". . . déclassé par les hasards de la naissance et de la vie, mais naturellement aristocrate." "Le Dandysme apparaît surtout aux époques transitoires où la démocratie n'est pas encore toute puissante, où l'aristocratie n'est que partiellement chancelante et avilie. Dans le trouble de ces époques, quelques hommes déclassés, dégoûtés, désœuvrés, mais tous riches de force native, peuvent concevoir le project de fonder une espèce de nouvelle aristocratie."

14. "Rends-toi toujours conforme . . . à l'usage du pays où tu seras car autrement tu passerais pour fol ou pour misérable." "Le plus sûr c'est de l'honorer et de le craindre et de n'en parler qu'avec admiration." Only during the latter part of Louis XIV's reign, when the country is financially and psychically exhausted by war, does criticism of the king emerge on the published page, most notably in Saint-Simon (440).

15. ". . . je veux qu'on me distingue." ". . . quand on est du monde, il faut bien que l'on rende/Quelques dehors civils que l'usage demande." "Oui, je vois ces défauts, dont votre âme murmure/Comme vices unis à l'humaine nature;/Et mon esprit enfin n'est pas plus offensé/De voir un homme fourbe, injuste, intéressé,/Que de voir des vautours affamés de carnage,/Des singes malfaisants, et des loups pleins de rage." I owe the last two translations to Richard Wilbur (Molière, *The Misanthrope and Tartuffe*. New York: Harcourt, Brace & World, 1965).

16. "Nous devons quelque chose aux coutumes des lieux où nous vivons, pour ne pas choquer la révérence publique, quoique ces coutumes soient mauvaises. Mais nous ne leur devons que de l'apparence: il faut les en payer, et se bien garder de les approuver dans son cœur, de peur d'offenser la raison universelle qui les condamne." "C'est encore une

Notes: 2. Self-Assertion and Metaphors of War

marque d'un bon fonds d'esprit, de n'être abusé ni des modes, ni des coutumes, de ne décider de rien à moins que de bien voir ce qu'on décide, et de compter pour peu de chose l'autorité de qui que ce soit, quand on voit . . . qu'elle choque le bon sens." See also Méré (340:III, 94–95; 339:37); Marmet (329:261); J. de Caillières (106:21).

17. Huysmans' Des Esseintes, perhaps the only dandy who lives isolated and apart from society, is ultimately forced to choose between reintegration and a progressive debility that will lead to death (266).

18. " . . . les limites extérieures des convenances." " . . . se joue de la règle et pourtant la respecte encore. Il en souffre et s'en venge tout en la subissant; il s'en réclame, quand il y échappe; il la domine et en est dominé tour à tour." " . . . caprice dans une société classée et symétrique."

19. "Ce qu'il y eut de plus caractéristique dans notre Bohème ce fut notre révolte ouverte contre tous les préjugés, je dirais presque contre toutes les lois. Réfugiés là comme dans une citadelle d'où nous faisions des sorties belliqueuses, nous nous moquions de tout. . . . Nous nous étions mis hors la loi."

20. See Balzac (19:I, 9); Barbey (35:93–94, 207; 38:XII, 23, 24, 134–35; XIV, 306, 309, 310, 314, 324).

21. " . . . faire de l'opposition, . . . n'est-ce pas s'emphilistiner quelque peu? On oublie à chaque instant qu'injurier une foule, c'est s'encanailler soi-même." "Croule donc, société!"

22. " . . . machinations bienfaisantes"; " . . . roueries charitables." "Je puis maintenant me promener incognito, faire des actions basses et me livrer à la crapule comme les simples mortels."

23. "Si vous vouliez devenir mon élève je vous ferais arriver à tout. Vous ne formeriez pas un désir qu'il ne fût à l'instant comblé. . . . On vous réduirait toute la civilisation en ambroisie." There is one notable instance of power achieved through criminality in the corpus of dandyism. In the works of Ponson du Terrail (403–406), the aristocratic Sir Williams assumes the dandyistic exterior when it furthers his vast plan of revenge against his brother, as does Rocambole, the street urchin he trains to help him implement that plan. That there is no deep bond between Sir Williams and Rocambole, each of whom entertains the thought of betraying the other, is secondary to what primarily distinguishes them from Rastignac or Lucien: criminality is their dominant mode, dandyism only the means, the obverse of the Balzacian dandy.

24. Julien Sorel's rise stops only when he commits the unpremeditated (and undandyistic) crime of passion that allows society to take revenge on his audacity. Victurnien d'Esgrignon, who becomes a forger in desperation, is one of the few Balzacian dandies incapable of sustaining the necessary outward conformity to the law (19:IV, 334 ff.).

25. " . . . au-dessus de toutes les lois." "Tu peux . . . te placer au-dessus des lois générales, . . . des convenances adoptées. . . . Moi, j'appartiens à la masse. Je dois jouer le jeu selon les règles de la société dans laquelle je suis forcé de vivre." See also Lucien's confession to Vautrin (19:IV, 514).

26. "Je me suis souvent étonné comme on abandonne à la bourgeoisie des plaisirs qui ne devraient être destinés que pour les personnages de notre qualité." "Les humeurs d'un gentilhomme sont toutes différentes de celles d'un marchand." " . . . l'air grossier et peu noble, l'air qui sent le palais, la bourgeoisie, la province et les affaires." "Tout ce qui tient

du métier déplaît." "Je ne puis comprendre comme un docte . . . homme est toujours si insipide dans ses sentiments, si difforme du publique, si opposé à l'honnête homme." " . . . leurs civilités, leurs compliments, et leurs formes d'écrire n'ont rien qui se ressemble."

27. Scudéry finds the provincials' presence on a coach ride to Rouen so asphyxiating that she fabricates an imaginary conversation with members of her circle to regain in mind, if not in body, the aristocratic citadel she has left (249:I, 92–97). Two centuries later, Fromentin's d'Orsel feels like a caged bird in the stifling atmosphere of the provinces (200:51).

28. " . . . les moeurs des villes, et leurs façons de faire ne sont pas nobles; le grand monde ne les peut souffrir." " . . . il faut considérer la cour et le grand monde séparément, et ne pas ignorer que la cour, ou par coutume, ou par caprice, approuve quelquefois des choses que le grand monde ne souffrirait pas. Qui veut bien juger de celles du grand monde, et même de celles de la cour, il est nécessaire de pénétrer ce qu'en pourraient dire les plus honnêtes gens de toutes les cours, s'ils étaient assemblés, pour en connaître la juste valeur." "Même à la cour, où tout semble si galant et si poli, la plupart ne comprennent le mérite que dans un certain degré: ce qui se montre au dessus, les passe ou les éblouit." See also Méré (340:III, 114–17, 125, 127, 131; 78:XXXII [1925], 455); Saint-Evremond (438:III, 121–22). Even Bellegarde, who believed that attendance at court was rewarded by "cette teinture de politesse qui relève infiniment le naturel quelque riche qu'il soit," had to admit that some individuals could spend their entire life there and never be anything but uncouth and unpolished (61:402).

29. The views of Méré and others force us to reconsider the principal role that critics have ascribed to *la cour et la ville* in setting the standards of French classicism. See, e.g., Auerbach (17:133–79) and Gossman (227:232–33).

30. *Le cabinet*, for example, which derives from *secretius cubiculum*, according to Richelet, is "[un] petit endroit qu'on met souvent au bout d'une galerie . . . un petit lieu . . . où l'on se retire pour converser" (426:s.v.); in the definition of the Académie Française it is "[un] lieu de retraite pour travailler ou converser en particulier" (162 [1694]:s.v.).

31. "En cet état, leurs âmes étaient, sans doute, bien disposées pour recevoir les inspirations d'Apollon. . . . Toute la troupe s'en ressentit: tout le palais en fut rempli et s'il est vrai ce qu'on en conte, la Poésie passant l'antichambre, les salles et les garderobes même, descendit jusqu'aux offices; . . . un grand laquais fit pour le moins six douzaines de vers burlesques. Mais nos héros et nos héroïnes ne s'attachèrent qu'aux madrigaux; jamais il n'en fut tant fait ni si promptement. A peine celui-ci venait-il d'en prononcer un, que celui-là en sentait un autre qui lui fourmillait dans la tête. Ici on récitait quatre vers, là on en écrivait douze. Tout s'y faisait gaîment et sans grimace." " . . . ce n'était que défis, que réponses, que répliques, qu'attaques, que ripostes."

32. So exposed did this activity become that it served as food for satire. See Sorel's *Description de l'île de portraiture, et de la ville des portraits* (1659).

33. " . . . communs à toute sorte de personnes, n'étant pas moins pratiqués par les valets que par les maîtres, et sont aussi faciles aux ignorants et grossiers qu'aux savants et subtils." " . . . ne peuvent plaire qu'à des personnes de bonne condition, nourries dans la civilité et la galanterie, et ingénieuses à former quantité de discours et de réparties, pleines de jugement et de savoir, et [qui] ne sauraient être accomplis par d'autres."

34. "Ce leur serait un sujet de mauvaise raillerie quoiqu'il n'y ait rien de meilleur ni de plus réel." "Il faut plaire . . . surtout aux honnêtes gens et pour les autres ne t'en mets pas en

Notes: 2. Self-Assertion and Metaphors of War

peine." "C'est être véritablement honnête homme que de vouloir être toujours exposé à la vue des honnêtes gens."

35. "... une de ces assemblées sans choix, où la porte est ouverte à tout le monde, et où l'on voit quelque fois cent personnes qu'on ne vit jamais, et qu'on ne voudrait jamais voir, et où l'on voit aussi tout ce que l'on connaît de gens fâcheux et incommodes." "... des sociétés établies où les honnêtes gens se pussent retirer commodément."

36. "Cet espace mis entre une classe et toute une capitale, n'est-il pas une consécration matérielle des distances morales qui doivent les séparer? Dans toutes les créations, la tête a sa place marquée." On the Faubourg Saint-Germain, see also Barbey (38:I, 129, 232; IX, 194); on la Chaussée d'Antin, see Stendhal (487:I, 88); Balzac (19:II, 962; 21:II, 149); Mortemart-Boisse (364:8).

37. The English Jockey Club was established c.1750 "to enable its members to hold their own against the rabble ... without more intrusion than was absolutely unavoidable on the part of the profane vulgar" (347:64). On Le Jockey, founded in France in 1833 by Lord Seymour for the purpose of encouraging equestrian sports, see Beauvoir (55:284); Dériège (158:12, 69); Musset (367:III, 1105).

38. "... le perron est envahi par les barbares, c'est-à-dire les gens de la Bourse." On Tortoni's see also Musset, "Mardoche," xx (367:I, 93); Barbey (38:I, 336, 375; XIII, 286, 297, 330, 334, 346). Other dandy haunts include the Café de Paris and the Café Anglais; see Barbey (38:I, 97, 336; XIII, 321–22); Jollivet (275:98–105); and d'Ariste (10:passim).

39. "Sachez donc ... qu'il y a de certaines heures et de certains lieux où les fashionables doivent être vus." "L'univers est là. De l'autre côté du ruisseau ce sont les Grandes Indes." "... le centre du monde, la fin de tout, le but suprême de tant d'efforts, le dernier mot de tant d'ambitions."

40. "Le fashionable ... n'a de prix qu'autant qu'il est vu ... si on était huit jours sans le voir, il serait oublié." "... il ne doit pas songer à voir, à admirer, mais à être vu, à être admiré." "... le vrai héros s'amuse tout seul."

41. "... perpétuellement armé contre le succès des autres." "Déjà plus d'une fois il avait pu craindre que le sceptre de la mode ne lui échappât; et il ressentait un violent dépit dès qu'il voyait paraître dans la société quelque jeune homme doué de tous les avantages que les années lui devaient bientôt enlever à lui-même."

42. "Le mérite ne fait pas toujours des impressions sur les plus honnêtes gens; chacun est jaloux du sien jusqu'à ne pouvoir souffrir aisément celui d'un autre." "... agitation sans désordre." "... ce précepte semble choquant, mais il est très souvent nécessaire." "Je vois d'ordinaire que de s'abandonner à ce qu'on appelle *des amis*, le succès n'en est pas heureux." "... un honnête homme ne hait rien tant que d'être à charge à qui que ce soit, et même à ses meilleurs amis." "... il n'y a quasi personne qui n'ait de l'ingratitude pour les grandes [obligations]."

43. "On ne trouve que fort peu de ces excellents maîtres d'Honnêteté.... Il faut donc essayer de les découvrir de soi-même, ou par les sentiments des personnes qui jugent bien, et se former sur les plus accomplis." "L'école du monde est plus capable que toute autre chose, de former l'esprit, et de donner cette teinture de politesse qu'on n'acquiert qu'en voyant souvent des personnages polis."

44. "On ne se lassera point de le répéter, ce qui fait le Dandy, c'est l'indépendance. Autrement il y aurait une législation du Dandysme, et il n'y en a pas." "... serait dandy

qui voudrait, ce serait une prescription à suivre, voilà tout." " . . . mais tout cela est dominé par la fantaisie." " . . . les Dandys, de leur autorité privée, posent une règle au-dessus de celle qui régit les cercles les plus aristocratiques . . . et ils parviennent à faire admettre cette règle mobile, qui n'est, en fin de compte, que l'audace de leur propre personnalité." " . . . une caste hautaine," "[une] caste provocante." " . . . en dehors des lois [qui] a des lois rigoureuses auxquelles sont strictement soumis tous ses sujets, quelles que soient d'ailleurs la fougue et l'indépendance de leur caractère."

45. "Aujourd'hui, grâce au ciel et à la révolution, c'est par son mérite seul qu'on s'assigne un rang dans la société." "Il n'est pas nécessaire, parce que vous êtes duc, que je vous estime; mais il est nécessaire que je vous salue. Si vous êtes duc et honnête homme, je rendrai ce que je dois à l'une et à l'autre de ces qualités. Je ne vous refuserai point les cérémonies que mérite votre qualité de duc, ni l'estime que mérite celle d'honnête homme. Mais si vous êtes duc sans être honnête homme . . . je ne manquerai pas d'avoir pour vous le mépris intérieur que mériterait la bassesse de votre esprit." "Ce n'est en effet que le coeur et l'esprit qui donnent les vrais avantages. . . . Tout le reste, n'est qu'une vaine apparence." Examining the dialectical relationship between the heart and mind, Méré argued that the heart implements the creative visions of the mind in one instance (340:I, 55) and elsewhere, that the mind merely ornaments the primary virtues of the heart (III, 78, 94). "Je ne vois rien de si beau que la noblesse du coeur et la hauteur de l'esprit; c'est de là que procède la parfaite honnêteté que je mets au-dessus de tout, et qui me semble à préférer, pour l'heur de la vie, à la possession d'un royaume." See also Méré (339:481); Somaize (467:I, 171); Scudéry (141:II, 102); Tallemant des Réaux (497:I, 485).

46. Although it could be argued that the overwhelming majority of seventeenth-century texts also use pseudoclassical anthroponyms and do not distinguish semantically the aristocrat from the nonaristocrat (i.e., Philinte and Alceste), the fact remains that the literature of this period is essentially written by aspiring or recognized *honnêtes gens* for aspiring or recognized *honnêtes gens* about the ideal of honnêteté, and thus reflects a closed and exclusive world with strikingly homogeneous tastes and values.

47. " . . . des mortifications à s'entendre appeler Chardon, quand il voyait n'entrer dans les salons que des hommes portant des noms sonores enchâssés de titres." "Le Mascarille moderne . . . appelle cela faire revivre l'ancienne monarchie. . . . Le Mascarille date de la Restauration; mais il a pullulé d'une manière alarmante. Toute la nation française s'emmascarille, et, à force d'être égaux, nous allons tous être gentilshommes."

48. " . . . la noblesse de nature," "la noblesse de condition." "Il était profondément aristocrate. Il ne l'était pas seulement de naissance, de caste, de rang social; il l'était de *nature*, comme il était *lui*, et pas un autre, et comme il l'eût été encore, aurait-il été le dernier cordonnier de sa ville. Il l'était enfin, comme dit Henri Heine, 'par sa grande manière de sentir,' et non point bourgeoisement, à la façon des parvenus qui aiment les distinctions extérieures."

49. "La pauvre condition de Socrate ne l'empêchait pas de pouvoir être aussi libéral qu'Alexandre qui possédait tant de trésors et de royaumes." "L'honnêteté est bien au dessus de cela."

50. " . . . un crédit indéfini pourrait lui suffire." " . . . l'homme élevé dans le luxe [qui] n'aspire pas à l'argent comme à une chose essentielle . . . il abandonne cette grossière

passion aux mortels vulgaires." " . . . les facultés les plus précieuses, les plus indestructibles, et sur les dons célestes que le travail et l'argent ne peuvent conférer."

51. "Il faut qu'on n'en puisse [dire] ni 'il est mathématicien,' ni 'prédicateur,' ni 'éloquent,' mais 'il est honnête homme'! Cette qualité universelle me plaît seule." " . . . ne sont appelés ni poètes, ni géomètres, etc. mais ils sont tout cela et juges de tous ceux-là." " . . . le plus honnête homme serait le moins prêt à s'y hasarder."

52. "En un temps . . . où les hommes se laissent abrutir par l'idée exclusive d'utilité, je crois qu'il n'y a pas grand mal à exagérer un peu en sens contraire." " . . . taillables et corvéables, faits pour l'écurie, c'est-à-dire pour exercer ce qu'on appelle des professions." "[C'est] de l'essence du fashionable de ne jamais travailler." " . . . l'homme habitué au travail ne peut comprendre la vie élégante." " . . . sera ce qu'il voudra être. . . . Je ne m'étonnerais pas de le trouver un jour ministre des affaires étrangères. Rien ne lui résiste." " . . . une puissance grondante, et sans emploi"; " . . . un Hercule sans emploi."

53. "Prendre une pensée dans un filon dans son cerveau . . . la poser devant soi, et du matin au soir, un ciseau d'une main, un marteau de l'autre, cogner, tailler, gratter et emporter à la nuit une pincée de poudre pour jeter sur son écriture, voilà ce que je ne pourrai jamais faire." " . . . l'homme des belles oeuvres ratées"; " . . . le Dieu de l'impuissance."

54. " . . . ils se sont divertis à faire leurs lois et leur politique, ils l'ont fait en se jouant." "Je ne m'attache pas à mettre dans un ordre bien exact tout ce que j'écris en cet ouvrage, ni à séparer par des distinctions étudiées les sujets qui me viennent dans l'esprit . . . les règles si visibles ne conviennent qu'aux maîtres de profession, et je n'en suis pas un: je n'ai pour toute méthode, qu'un ordre naturel, et même selon mon caprice ou mon goût." See also Bellegarde (58:7). " . . . rien du poète . . . et tout de l'honnête homme."

55. "Il écrivit donc, sans prétention d'auteur . . . ce tout petit livre, uniquement pour se faire plaisir à lui-même et aux trente personnes, ces amis inconnus, dont on n'est pas très sûr, et qu'on ne peut guère, sans fatuité, se vanter d'avoir à Paris." " . . . [un livre] essentiellement inutile et absolument innocent, [qui] n'a pas été fait dans un autre but que de me divertir et d'exercer mon goût passionné de l'obstacle."

56. " . . . une exception: son oisiveté est un travail, et son travail un repos." " . . . les oisifs ne seront plus des fétiches, mais de véritables dieux." See also Ronteix (432:134), Gautier (211:252), and Baudelaire's *homme de loisir* (51:I, 689).

57. "Pourquoi donc trouverait-on si mauvais que pouvant obtenir de la paresse ce bienheureux repos, qui est un si grand plaisir, je n'en jouisse pas paisiblement? Pourquoi, dis-je, me blâmera-t-on de la louer, et de l'aimer et de préférer l'oisiveté au travail? car y a-t-il rien de si doux que de n'avoir rien à faire et que de pouvoir faire tout ce qu'on veut?" "Un galant homme oisif est un philosophe, qui ne fait rien parce qu'il n'y a rien au monde qui soit digne de l'occuper; c'est un homme qui cherchant la sagesse par un autre chemin que le commun des hommes, cherche seulement les plaisirs, sans se mêler ni du bien public, ni de cent choses qui font tout ce tracas de la vie, et qui se trouve plus heureux . . . que les ambitieux qui sont toujours diligents ne se le trouvent au milieu de tous les honneurs qu'ils acquièrent par des travaux continuels." "Il y a toujours eu de certains fainéants sans métier, mais qui n'étaient pas sans mérite, et qui ne songeaient qu'à bien vivre, et qu'à se produire de bon air. Ce pourrait bien être de ces sortes de gens, que nous est venu ce mot si essentiel: et ce sont d'ordinaire des esprits doux et des coeurs tendres; des gens fiers et civils;

Notes: 2. Self-Assertion and Metaphors of War

hardis et modestes, qui ne sont ni avares ni ambitieux . . . : Ils n'ont guère pour but, que d'apporter la joie partout, et leur plus grand soin ne tend qu'à mériter de l'estime, et qu'à se faire aimer."

58. "En un même temps, en un même jour on peut se divertir et s'ennuyer d'une même chose. Les longs plaisirs cessent de l'être." "Les hommes s'ennuient enfin des mêmes choses qui les ont charmés dans leurs commencements: ils déserteraient *la table des Dieux*, et *le nectar* avec le temps leur devient insipide." " . . . il n'y a rien de pareil à l'ennui qui les dévore." "Rien n'est si insupportable à l'homme que d'être dans un plein repos, sans passions, sans affaires, sans divertissement, sans application." " . . . son néant, son abandon, son insuffisance, sa dépendance, son impuissance, son vide. Incontinent, il sortira du fond de son âme, l'ennui, la noirceur, la tristesse, le chagrin, le dépit, le désespoir." On the meaning of *repos* in the *Pensées* as well as on the general significance of the concept in seventeenth-century French literature, see Stanton (90:79–104).

59. Pascal himself mentions Damien Mitton on three separate occasions (393:612, #853; p. 588, #642; p. 584, #597). Demorest suggests that the model for Pascal's "homme sans religion" may be either Mitton or Méré, or "Un représentant de l'Honnêteté qu'il anime d'individualité" (156:217–20). On the connection between ennui and honnêteté see also Esprit (184:I, 216–17).

60. " . . . surtout qu'il se garde de témoigner jamais de chagrin."

61. "Pour vivre heureux, il faut faire peu de réflexions sur la vie; mais sortir souvent comme hors de soi, et . . . se dérober à la connaissance de ses propres maux. Les *divertissements* ont tiré leur nom de la *diversion* qu'ils font faire des objets fâcheux et tristes . . . : ce qui montre assez qu'il est difficile de venir à bout de la dureté de notre condition, par aucune force d'esprit; mais que, par adresse, on peut ingénieusement s'en détourner." " . . . si l'on se divertit avec un peu de soin, et beaucoup de négligence, on se guérit insensiblement." In Méré's letters, the cycle of *divertissement* > *repos* > *ennui* appears within the spatial alternations of city (*divertissement*) and country (*repos*, *ennui*). Fleeing the diversions of Parisian life, he seeks the country, only to fall into a negative *repos* and an oppressive ennui: "On devient triste et chagrin dans une longue solitude, et pour l'ordinaire on y gagne un autre mal, et quelque fois plus fâcheux que le premier" (339:418). Although he perceives the vicious cycle in which he is caught, Méré begins to yearn once again for *divertissement*: "Si le monde a ses dégoûts, la retraite a les siens, et plus pesants et plus tristes" (pp. 432–33). See also Saint-Evremond (438:IV, 287). In the first half of the century, Guez de Balzac was no less emphatic about his need for *divertissement*: "Depuis que je suis au monde, je me suis perpétuellement ennuyé . . . c'est pourquoi si je veux être joyeux il faut nécessairement que je me trompe moi-même et ma félicité dépend tellement des choses de dehors que sans la peinture, la musique et quantité d'autres divertissements . . . je n'ai pas assez de quoi m'occuper ni de quoi me plaire."

62. "Le Dandysme est le produit d'une société qui s'ennuie." "Condamnés au repos par les souverains du monde, livrés aux cuistres de toute espèce, à l'oisiveté et à l'ennui, les jeunes gens voyaient se retirer d'eux les vagues écumantes contre lesquelles ils avaient préparé leurs bras. Tous ces gladiateurs frottés d'huile se sentaient au fond de l'âme une misère insupportable." " . . . je ne sais quel . . . besoin impérieux d'occuper mon esprit inquiet et toujours mécontent, de chercher . . . quelque accident imprévu qui me put sortir de cette morne et douloureuse apathie qui m'écrasait." "Sais-tu quel est mon plus grand

souci? c'est de tuer l'ennui. Celui qui rendrait ce service à l'humanité serait le vrai destructeur des monstres. Le vulgaire et l'ennuyeux! toute la mythologie des païens grossiers n'a rien imaginé de plus subtil et de plus effrayant. Ils se ressemblent beaucoup, en ce que l'un et l'autre sont laids, plats et pâles, quoique multiformes, et qu'ils donnent de la vie des idées à vous en dégoûter dès le premier jour où l'on y met le pied. De plus ils sont inséparables, et c'est un couple hideux que tout le monde ne voit pas. Malheur à ceux qui les aperçoivent trop jeunes! Moi, je les ai toujours connus." " . . . une dénégation de toutes choses du ciel et de la terre, qu'on peut nommer désenchantement, ou si l'on veut *désespérance*." " . . . ménagerie infâme de nos vices"; " . . . ferait volontiers de la terre un débris/Et dans un bâillement avalerait le monde."

63. " . . . les gens d'esprit de cette intéressante époque ont volé aux sots la faculté de s'ennuyer qu'ils possédaient seuls autrefois." "Vous avez la mine d'un trappiste . . . vous outrez le principe de la gravité. . . . L'air triste ne peut être de bon ton; c'est l'air ennuyé qu'il faut. Si vous êtes triste, c'est donc quelque chose qui vous manque, quelque chose qui ne vous a pas réussi. *C'est montrer soi inférieur*. Etes-vous ennuyé, au contraire, c'est ce qui a essayé vainement de vous plaire qui est inférieur."

64. "Le dandy est blasé, ou il feint de l'être, par politique et raison de caste." " . . . c'est l'ennui des après-midi. On est sans emploi, on fait mal plutôt que de ne rien faire." See Gautier (210:51, 219; 211:179). Other manifestations of sadism in the corpus of dandyism include the recurrent Englishman whose chief pleasure is attending well-performed executions (Borel [76:77–83]; Villiers de l'Isle-Adam [516:88–113]), and the English doctors who carry out lethal experiments on a young woman (407:416–17). On dandiacal sadism, see Praz (407:123–87).

65. " . . . l'émotion de cette autre vie que l'on trouve au fond des breuvages, qui bat plus fort, qui tinte et qui éblouit." See Gautier's "Le Club des Haschichiens" (215:467–99; 212:57–69); see also Musset's translation/adaptation of De Quincey's work, *L'Anglais mangeur d'opium* (367:III, 3–64); Barbey (38:XIV, 264); and Mickel's study on the influence of opium and hashish on French Romantic literature (345).

66. " . . . n'échappe qu'à moitié . . . [à] l'ennui de cette existence oisive." "C'est le fond de tout et pour tous, à plus forte raison pour une âme de Dandy . . . dont on a dit bien ingénieusement mais bien tristement aussi: Ils rassemblent autour d'eux tous les agréments de la vie, mais, ainsi qu'une pierre qui attire la mousse, sans se laisser pénétrer par la fraîcheur qui la couvre." " . . . le héros de l'élégance oisive—le héros dandy." Cf. Baudelaire: "Le spectacle de la vie élégante . . . prouv[e] que nous n'avons qu'à ouvrir les yeux pour connaître notre héroisme" (51:II, 495). See also Lemaître (301:IV, 60–61).

67. "[il est] peut être plus glorieux de se vaincre soi-même que de vaincre les autres."

3. THE SELF-AS-ART

1. "On connaît de certains gens qui sont les plus beaux ouvrages du monde." " . . . on dirait alors qu'elles imitent les règles des grands peintres, pour nous donner des tableaux parfaits." " . . . son air et ses manières avec sa figure . . . ses tons et ses paroles avec ses pensées et ses sentiments." " . . . une espèce d'architecture"; " . . . toute entière comme un tableau."

Notes: 3. The Self-As-Art

2. "... un portrait qui marche"; "... artiste en tout"; "... il plaî[t] avec sa personne comme d'autres plaisent avec leurs oeuvres." See also Barbey (38:IX, 274). "... n'ont pas d'autre état que de cultiver l'idée du beau dans leur personne." Baudelaire repeatedly emphasizes the similarities between the artist and the dandy. In fact, the only difference he recognizes is that the artist has an obsessive desire to see, to feel and to experience, whereas the dandy is blasé or pretends to be for symbolic reasons (51:II, 689, 745). On the dandy as work of art, see also Sue (492:561–62); Camus (108:72); Starobinski (478:233).

3. See, however, Saussure's *Anagrammes* (476).

4. See in particular Todorov (503), Erlich (182), Matejka (333), Lucid (318).

5. Todorov and Ducrot have clearly expressed the problem. "La sémiotique est, d'une certaine manière, écrasée par la linguistique. Ou bien *on part des signes non-linguistiques* pour y trouver la place du langage (c'est la voie de Peirce); mais ces signes se prêtent mal à une détermination précise ou, lorsqu'il le font, se révèlent d'importance mineure, ne pouvant en rien éclairer le statut du langage (ainsi le code de la route) ou bien *on part du langage*, pour étudier les autres systèmes de signes (c'est la voie de Saussure), mais alors on risque d'imposer à des phénomènes différents le modèle linguistique, l'activité sémiotique se réduisant dès lors à un acte de dénomination (ou de renomination)... Le malaise ne vient pas de l'absence d'un sens non-linguistique; celui-ci existe bien; mais de ce qu'on ne peut en parler qu'en termes linguistiques, qui sont pourtant incapables de saisir ce qu'il y a de spécifique dans les sens non-linguistique. Une sémiologie construite à partir du langage (et on n'en connaît pas d'autre, pour l'instant), doit renoncer à l'étude du problème central de tout système sémiotique, qui est celui de la signification: elle ne traitera que de la significa-tion linguistique, la substituant subrepticement à son véritable objet. La sémiotique du non-linguistique est court-circuitée non au niveau de son objet (qui existe bien), mais à celui de son discours qui vicie de verbal les résultats de son travail" (170:120–21).

6. "Une chose au moins est sûre," writes Benveniste, "aucune sémiologie du son, de la couleur, de l'image ne se formulera en sons, en couleurs, en images. Toute sémiologie d'un système non-linguistique doit emprunter le truchement de la langue, ne peut donc exister que dans et par la sémiologie de la langue" (69:130).

7. There is, after all, a decided difference between the propositions "system X is a lan-guage" and "system X can/should be studied as a language" (174:22, 27), a fact which Mounin seems to ignore in his attack on Barthes (365:189–99). In the extended introduction to the *Eléments de sémiologie* which appeared in book form, as compared to the version published in *Communications* IV, Barthes emphasizes the need for a *translinguistic* approach, a term he never fully clarifies (41:80–82). Although Kristeva speaks of the contributions that mathematics and logic can make to achieve this translinguistic perspec-tive, there is, as yet, little evidence that this approach would be more fruitful (see 283:110–13).

8. The bivalent function of clothes was already apparent to Sorel in the seventeenth century, who writes in *Lois de la galanterie* that dress does not simply exist "pour cacher le corps... mais encore pour l'ornement" (323:35). See also Simmel (465:339, 344).

9. On the semiology of objects, see *Communications* XIII (388).

10. "... dont la poésie brille bien plus dans sa personne que dans ses oeuvres" (51:I, 553).

Notes: 3. The Self-As-Art

11. Jakobson has also spoken of the "esthetic function" (271:123), a term preferred by Mukarovsky (333:275) and Eco (173:124 ff.), among others.

12. Mukarovsky regards this "foregrounding" of the sender as integral to art (333:235). In this perspective, the conative function—the sender's expression of will or desire with respect to the receiver—must be closely integrated in the poetic function. The only function that Jakobson associates with the sender, however, is the expressive or emotive, which "aims at a direct expression of the speaker's attitude toward what he is speaking about. It tends to produce an impression of a certain emotion whether true or feigned" (272:354). This is an unduly narrow perception of the function of the sender.

13. Most researchers, including Jakobson (272:366) and Riffaterre (429:29), insist on permanence or durability of form as a precondition of art or the poetic function, a traditionalistic notion which would logically exclude from either classification certain surrealist experiments and pop happenings, not to speak of oral literature or the dance unless recorded in writing, on tape, or on film.

14. Part of the inadequacy of Jakobson's approach to the poetic function is that it fails to treat the work of art as a totality. For a critique of Jakobson's analysis of the poetic function, see Mounin (372:64–69). When Jakobson, along with Lévi-Strauss, approached a text as a totality, a system (i.e., Baudelaire's *Les Chats*), they assumed, as Riffaterre demonstrated in his counter-analysis of the same sonnet, that all linguistic structures are ipso facto poetic structures, and thus failed to deal with the poeticity of the text. See Jakobson (271:401–17); and Riffaterre (429:307–64).

15. Whereas Mounin contends that art only involves expression or transmission (365:15), I would agree with Riffaterre and Lotman that it comprises a system of communication (429:138, 316:31, 33). I see no reason to reject the concept of communication in favor of signification, as Barthes does in his definition of the domain of semiology (41:169). Communication and signification are not mutually exclusive; they are, to the contrary, "strictly intertwined" in semiological processes (174:9).

16. See Eco (174:228–37). For Lotman, painting, music and other art forms are systems which do not have signs in the linguistic sense of the term (318:193–97). Even these systems, however, are based on conventions which function in ways comparable to the relation between the signifier and signified in language. See 333:249 ff.

17. The signifying units are what Riffaterre calls the marked, as opposed to the unmarked, elements of a text (429:31–37).

18. See Barthes for an analysis of what he calls the problem of arthrology in semiology (41:130). The problem is not peculiar to secondary systems, however. Saussure, for example, never resolved to his own satisfaction the question of the unit of significance in language (448:144–58).

19. For Barthes's analysis of this phenomenon, which he calls "le champ de dispersion," see 41:159.

20. As Barthes observes, most semiological systems reveal this type of relative motivation, or represent mixed types which combine the arbitrary with the motivated (41:122–26).

21. For purposes of simplification, I am excluding architecture and sculpture here, because time (and thus, linear sequence) is involved in a full survey of their forms.

22. See also Delas and Philliolet (150:74, 174); Todorov (501:426 ff.).

Notes: 3. The Self-As-Art

23. Lotman has insisted that the artistic text is characterized by boundedness, that is, contains a beginning and an end (however open-ended or fragmented it may intentionally appear to be [316:92–97, 299–300]). Although the validity of this notion could be questioned, it is worth noting that the boundedness of the self-as-art is only defined by the boundaries of finite human life, during which the poetic system could, theoretically, always function.

24. I have studiously avoided labeling the system of the artistocratic self primarily metaphoric or metonymic. That vague distinction, which Jakobson used to differentiate various types of texts (sonnet vs. epic; poetry vs. prose [270:61–67]), strikes me as reductionist and useless when confronting the complexities of any poetic system, although critics continues to make it a staple of their work.

25. "Il me semble que dans le dessein de se rendre honnête homme et d'en acquérir la réputation le plus important consiste à connaître en toutes les choses les meilleurs moyens de plaire et de les savoir pratiquer." "Sous quelque forme qu'elle se montre elle plaît toujours, et c'est à cela principalement qu'on la peut reconnaître." "L'un avait toute sorte d'agréments . . . et il semblait avoir dans son naturel, de quoi plaire à tous les hommes. L'autre avait tant de belles qualités qu'il pouvait s'assurer d'avoir de l'approbation dans tous les lieux où l'on fait quelque cas de la vertu. Le premier . . . ne manquait jamais de s'attirer les inclinations. Le second avait quelque fierté, mais on ne pouvait pas lui refuser son estime. Pour achever cette différence: on se rendait avec plaisir aux insinuations de celui-là, et on avait quelquefois du chagrin de ne pouvoir résister à l'impression du mérite de celui-ci." "Ceux qui n'ont rien trouvé de plus aimable que la vertu n'avaient pas senti de ces grâces si piquantes qui paraissent dans votre personne et dans vos moindres actions. C'est un enchantement secret qui confondrait la plus haute sagesse."

26. ". . . étonner, ravir un spectateur"; ". . . le prendre par les entrailles." "*Le Cid* du poète français, ayant plu . . . ne serait-il point vrai . . . qu'il est arrivé à son but, encore que ce ne soit pas par le chemin d'Aristote, ni par les adresses de sa Poétique? Mais vous dites, Monsieur, qu'il a ébloui les yeux du monde, et vous l'accusez de charme et d'enchantement . . . vous me confessez vous-même que si la magie était chose permise, ce serait une chose excellente. Ce serait à vrai dire une belle chose de pouvoir faire des prodiges innocemment, de faire voir le soleil quand il est nuit, d'apprêter des festins sans viande ni officiers, de changer en pistoles les feuilles de chêne et le verre en diamants. C'est ce que vous reprochez à l'auteur du *Cid*, qui vous avouant qu'il a violé les règles de l'art, vous oblige de lui avouer qu'il a un secret qui a mieux réussi que l'art même; et ne vous niant pas qu'il a trompé toute la cour et tout le peuple, ne vous laisse conclure de là, sinon qu'il est plus fin que toute la cour et tout le peuple, et que la tromperie qui s'étend à un si grand nombre de personnes est moins une fraude qu'une conquête." The basic principle of seventeenth-century esthetics, *plaire* represents from Corneille to Boileau, in literature as in the other arts, "la grande règle et pour ainsi dire la seule" (291:I, 11). See also Bray (85) and Borgerhoff (77:passim).

27. ". . . [les] choses de montre . . . ne sont bonnes qu'à jeter de la poudre aux yeux"; ". . . suspect de je ne sais quoi de faux." "Cette aimable reine d'Egypte avait peu d'éclat . . . elle n'était pas si belle que d'abord on en fût surpris; mais quand on venait à la considérer, c'était un charme: et ce fut par ses manières délicates qu'elle tint César trois ou quatre ans, comme enchanté." ". . . comme une belle enchanteresse charme ses amants."

Notes: 3. The Self-As-Art

28. "... s'insinue, se communique insensiblement"; "... un poison lent ... un charme de magie." "... il sait connaître et suivre l'esprit et l'humeur de ceux avec qui il traite, et en ménageant leurs intérêts, il avance et il établit les siens." The extended impact of *insinuation* is underscored in Pascal's evaluation of the style of Montaigne and Epictetus (393:596, #745). "... certains détours, assaisonnés de certaines complaisances propres à mener insensiblement l'esprit de celui, aux sentiments duquel il semble qu'on défère." "... gagner la première place ... dans le coeur et dans l'esprit de ceux qui vous approchent." "... ces agréments secrets, dont on ne peut découvrir la cause. [Ils] sont aussi les plus dangereux. Ce sont les personnes qui les ont qui tiennent le plus au coeur. On ne les saurait oublier, parce qu'elles plaisent toujours."

29. "C'est le visage qui domine au maintien extérieur, puisque c'est lui qui prie, qui menace, qui flatte, et qui témoigne nos joies et nos tristesses, et dans lequel on lit nos pensées, devant que notre langue ait eu le temps de les exprimer. Les yeux sur tout font bien cet office de la parole, et c'est par eux que notre âme s'écoule bien souvent hors de nous, et qu'elle se montre toute nue à ceux qui la veillent pour lui dérober son secret." "Tâche de composer ton visage d'une telle manière, qu'en tout temps, en tous lieux, et en toutes sortes de rencontres il ne puisse paraître de ton âme que les sentiments qui te sont les plus favorables et les plus avantageuses."

30. "... qui promet quelque chose de grand ... un homme qui n'est pas un grand seigneur, et qui se trouve assez malheureux pour en avoir la mine, doit essayer de s'en défaire, parce que d'abord on s'y trompe, et qu'ensuite on vient à le mépriser." "Vous reluisez trop ... que je ne voudrais; et vous devriez vous en corriger." On *la mine* see also Méré (340:I, 90; II, 148; 78:XXIX [1922], 220). For La Bruyère, *la mine* revealed wealth and station as clearly as the signs of a verbal text: "le plus ou le moins de mille livres de rente se trouve écrit sur les visages" (286:141, #53).

31. "... l'adresse et le tour de l'esprit qui font presque tout pourvu que la personne n'ait rien de choquant." "La Beauté, pour le moins la grande et l'extrême ... pourrait être inutile et même nuisible parce qu'elle étouffe et qu'elle accable.... D'ailleurs on s'ennuie aisément de n'avoir devant les yeux que même chose et cette sorte de beauté se présente toujours également: quand on l'a vue une fois on n'y découvre plus rien qui surprenne." "... qu'on ne ... découvre qu'à peine ... qui se cache comme sous un voile," "... couverte d'un nuage."

32. "... un grand fond d'agréments ne se peut épuiser, il en sort toujours de nouveaux qu'on n'avait pas aperçus. C'est ce qui ranime et qui fait qu'on ne s'en lasse point." "... l'homme du monde le mieux fait et le plus beau"; "... ce qu'il avait de moins admirable." "Ce qui le mettait au-dessus des autres était une valeur incomparable, et un agrément dans son esprit, dans son visage et dans ses actions que l'on a jamais vus qu'à lui seul." "... il arrive même souvent qu'un homme contrefait a meilleure grâce qu'un autre qui semble fait à peindre."

33. "... gagnait les sens extérieurs en un instant, et donnait passage jusqu'à l'âme, par la qualité de ses gardes qui d'abord se laissaient prendre." "... [C']est un assaisonnement qui rend agréable jusqu'au moindre geste de la personne.... C'est la beauté de l'action et du repos, qui se fait connaître par cette juste proportion, que le corps conserve durant qu'il se remue ou qu'il se repose; enfin, c'est *un certain air* plein d'appas naturels, et sans artifice,

247

qui accompagne toutes les postures de la personne qui agit ou qui est sans rien faire, de sorte que la vue s'y arrêtant, l'esprit à même temps y donne une tacite approbation." ". . . ravit les yeux et les coeurs de tout le monde." ". . . avait en lui de quoi faire six honnêtes gens . . . on ne pouvait pas dire pourtant que ce fut un honnête homme. . . . Il ne faisait rien avec grâce." ". . . plus belle encore que la beauté." On *la grâce* see also Bouhours (80:12); Méré (340:II, 39); La Rochefoucauld (294:534); Furetière (202:s.v. *grâce*).

34. "Celui qui se mêle d'une chose . . . difficile s'y doit pourtant prendre de manière si dégagée, qu'on en vienne à s'imaginer qu'elle ne lui coûte rien." "Quoique le soin soit deviné, pourvu qu'il ne soit pas visible, il ne peut nuire car c'est l'empressement qui déplaît." "Le bon air se montre d'abord, il est plus régulier, et plus dans l'ordre. L'agrément est plus flatteur, et plus insinuant, il va droit au coeur, et par des voies plus secrètes. Le bon air donne plus d'admiration, et l'agrément plus d'amour." "Le premier et le plus commun est celui qui cherche la pompe et l'éclat: l'autre est plus modeste et plus caché. Le premier a beaucoup de rapport avec la beauté, et je trouve qu'il lasse aisément; mais cet autre qui se montre moins à découvert, plus on le considère plus on l'aime. Il y a toujours dans le premier je ne sais quoi de faux et quelque espèce d'illusion; le dernier est plus réel, quoique plus imperceptible; et je vois qu'il approche de l'agrément . . . [celui-ci] plaît davantage à ceux qui ont le goût fait."

35. "Que d'histoires et d'angigorniaux boutont ces messieux-là les courtisans! je me pardrais là dedans pour moi; et j'étais tout ébobi de voir ça. . . . Ils ant des chemises qui ant des manches où j'entrerions toute brandis, toi et moi. En glieu d'haut-de-chausse, ils portont un garde-robe aussi large que d'ici à Pâques: en glieu de pourpoint, de petites brassières, qui ne leu venons pas jusqu'au brichet; et, en glieu de rabats, un grand mouchoir de cou à réziau, aveuc quatre grosses houpes de linge qui leu pendont sur l'estomaque. Ils avont itou d'autres petits rabats au bout des bras, et de grand entonnois de passement aux jambes, et parmi tout ça, tant de rubans, tant de rubans, que c'est une vraie piquié. Ignia pas jusqu'aux souliers qui n'en soient farcis tout depis un bout jusqu'à l'autre; et ils sont faits d'une façon que je me romprais le cou aveuc." I am indebted to Donald Frame for the translation of this passage (Molière, *Tartuffe and Other Plays*. New York: New American Library. 1967). "[Les courtisans] ont une physionomie qui n'est pas nette, mais confuse, embarrassée dans une épaisseur de cheveux étrangers qu'ils préfèrent aux naturels et dont ils font un long tissu pour couvrir leur tête: il descend à la moitié du corps, change les traits, et empêche qu'on ne connaisse les hommes à leur visage."

36. "On se récrie enfin contre une telle ou une telle mode, qui cependant, toute bizarre qu'elle est, pare et embellit pendant qu'elle dure, et dont l'on tire tout l'avantage qu'on en peut espérer, qui est de plaire. Il me paraît qu'on devrait seulement admirer l'inconstance et la légèreté des hommes, qui attachent successivement les agréments et la bienséance à des choses tout opposés; qui emploient pour le comique et pour la mascarade, ce qui leur a servi de parure grave et d'ornements les plus sérieux; et que si peu de temps en fasse la différence." On the monarchy's efforts to legislate apparel, see La Bédollière (285:83–84); Du Bled (168:296–303); Magendie (323:40 ff.).

37. ". . . cette mode qui étant autorisée par les plus approuvés d'entre les grands et les honnêtes gens sert de loi à tous les autres." "L'un et l'autre excès choque, et tout homme bien sage/Doit faire des habits ainsi que du langage,/ N'y rien trop affecter, et sans empressement,/ Suivre ce que l'usage y fait de changement." I am indebted to Donald

Notes: 3. The Self-As-Art

Frame for the translation of this passage (*op. cit.*). ". . . de se faire remarquer à quelque prix que ce soit." "La bizarrerie des habits fait soupçonner avec raison celle des moeurs." See also Faret (188:91–93); Guez de Balzac (24:292); Chalesme (117:207–08); Marmet (329:262); La Bruyère (286:395, #11).

38. ". . . il avait une manière de s'habiller qui était toujours suivie de tout le monde, sans pouvoir être imité." "C'est à peu près comme une dame qui paraît avec de beaux habits et de riches parures qu'elle ne prend pas la peine d'ajuster curieusement. Ce peu de soin qui sent la grandeur, témoigne assez qu'elle ne les admire point. Je trouve aussi que le plus beau linge et le plus blanc sied mieux lorsqu'il est un peu foulé que s'il n'avait pas un pli." In contrast to the texts on the honnête homme, some novels, anecdotal histories and memoirs underscore the obsession with costume that *les grands* manifested, among them Louvois: "il s'enfermait dans une chambre des journées entières avec le Marquis de Villeroi pour savoir où un ruban irait le mieux sur son habit" (409:56). And according to Tallemant des Réaux, "Changer tous les jours d'habits et de plumes, c'est la marque la plus ordinaire à quoi l'on reconnaît dans Paris les gens de qualité" (351:101). See also Magendie (324: 274 ff.). It goes without saying that vulgarians were noted for trying to impress and for being impressed by sartorial signs. In Molière's *Les Précieuses ridicules*, the valet Mascarille advertises his perfumed gloves, his wig, the cost of his plumes, and the excessive length of his *canons* (sc. ix), and the two pitiful provincials, like the two peasants in *Dom Juan* (II.i), are duly impressed. Méré satirized the populace's inability to distinguish between genuine and counterfeit sartorial signs: "Si le peuple voit un homme brillant de faux or et de fausse broderie, il croit volontiers que c'est un grand seigneur" (340:III, 117).

39. ". . . je n'en connus jamais un seul à qui l'éclat et la magnificence aient réussi." ". . . rien de trop éclatant qui pût attacher la vue ou la pensée." On sartorial simplicity see also Faret (188:91); Méré (340:III, 86; 339:668–69); La Bruyère (286:96, #17); Vaumorières (511:II, 8).

40. "Les manières, que l'on néglige comme de petites choses, sont souvent ce qui fait que les hommes décident de vous en bien ou en mal: une légère attention à les avoir douces et polies prévient leurs mauvais jugements. Il ne faut presque rien pour être cru fier, incivil, méprisant, désobligeant: il faut moins pour être estimé tout le contraire."

41. ". . . simples lois de bienséance, dont l'obligation naît du consentement des hommes qui sont convenus entre eux de blâmer ceux qui y manqueraient. C'est de cette manière que nous devons à ceux avec qui nous vivons les civilités établies entre les honnêtes gens quoi qu'elles ne soient point réglées par des lois expresses." "Quand on n'est pas persuadé par les sens qu'on est aimé et considéré il est difficile que le coeur le soit ou qu'il le soit vivement. Or, c'est la civilité qui fait cet effet sur les sens, et par les sens sur l'esprit: Et si l'on y manque, cette négligence ne manque point de produire dans les autres un refroidissement qui passe souvent des sens jusqu'au coeur." The semiological and semantic differences between *civilité* and *politesse* are often hard to discern in the literature of honnêteté: Furetière, for example, uses both *poli* and *honnête* to define *civilité* (202:s.v.); for Bellegarde, "l'empressement à faire plaisir, la politesse, la civilité" are the primary qualities of honnêteté, but he does not pinpoint the differences between them (58:30). ". . . a plus de fond et plus d'étendue que la civilité qui n'en a que l'apparence." See also La Rochefoucauld's subtle distinction between the two (294:442, #260). ". . . un homme poli et qui sait vivre"; ". . . cette belle science . . . dont la politesse fait la principale partie." "On n'est pas sûr de plaire avec un grand esprit, de

beaux talents, de grandes manières mais on ne peut se défendre des charmes d'une véritable politesse."

42. "Cet art semble avoir un peu de sorcellerie; car il instruit à être devin, et c'est par là qu'on découvre un grand nombre de choses qu'on ne verrait jamais autrement . . . il faut ici pénétrer ce qu'on n'a point dit, et bien souvent ce qu'on tient de plus secret." ". . . rien ne se passe dans le coeur ni dans l'esprit qu'il n'en paraisse quelque marque sur le visage ou dans le ton de la voix, ou dans les actions, et quand on s'accoutume à ce langage il n'y a rien de si caché ni de si brouillé qu'on ne découvre et qu'on ne démêle." ". . . une science qui s'apprend comme une langue étrangère, où d'abord on ne comprend que peu de chose." "Le personnage . . . d'un honnête homme . . . se doit transformer par la souplesse du génie, comme l'occasion le demande"; "il se trouve bien quelques naturels si souples, qu'ils se tournent comme ils veulent selon les occasions, et que tout leur réussit; mais c'est une merveille d'en rencontrer."

43. "Quiconque sait complaire peut hardiment espérer de plaire." "On se plaît bien avec les personnes qui font tout ce qu'on veut, sans qu'on les en avertisse." ". . . fine et délicate . . . [qui] doit paraître libre et fondée sur la raison si l'on veut qu'elle produise les effets que l'on est bien aise d'en espérer." On the limits of the honnête homme's complaisance see Faret (188:55, 70). "[Il faut] de la complaisance . . . qui cède sans faiblesse, qui loue sans flatterie, qui s'accommode avec jugement et avec innocence, aux temps, aux lieux et aux personnes: et qui sans affectation, et sans bassesse, rende la société agréable, et la vie plus commode, et plus divertissante. . . . Il faut donc s'il est possible trouver . . . cette honnête complaisance qui plaît, qui ne nuit à personne, qui pare l'esprit, qui rend l'humeur agréable . . . et qui s'accommodant avec la justice et la générosité, devient le charme secret de la société de tous les hommes."

44. ". . . cette vertu nous apprend à compâtir aux faiblesses des uns, à supporter les caprices et les bizarreries des autres, à entrer dans leurs sentiments pour les ramener à la raison par des voies douces et insinuantes . . . par un véritable désir de plaire." On this manipulative capacity, see also Faret (188:70); Scudéry (454:III, pt.2, 743); Chalesme (117:169–75); La Rochefoucauld (294:505). "Ce chagrin philosophe est un peu trop sauvage./Je ris des noirs accès où je vous envisage . . . /Je vous dirai tout franc que cette maladie,/Partout où vous allez donne la comédie." I am indebted to Donald Frame for the translation to this passage (Molière, *The Misanthrope and Other Plays*. New York: New American Library, 1968). ". . . [il n'y a] rien de plus malhonnête en compagnie, que d'être recueilli et comme enfoncé en soi-même."

45. ". . . il faut donner au monde quelque signe de pensée ou de sentiment dans la moindre chose qui se présente, autant que la bienséance le permet." Carefully wrought, masterfully emitted, such signs of emotion can determine the success or failure of the honnête homme's goals, as La Rochefoucauld observed: "Tous les sentiments ont chacun un ton de voix, des gestes et des mines qui leur sont propres et ce rapport, bon ou mauvais, agréable ou désagréable, est ce qui fait que les personnes plaisent ou déplaisent" (294:438, #255). ". . . la joie honnête et spirituelle"; "une humeur douce, enjouée et même plaisante"; "[cet] accès facile et gai." ". . . juste tempérament"; ". . . de grands charmes pour se faire aimer."

46. "Les galants de l'antiquité avaient une grande repugnance pour la sujétion. . . . Ils se gardaient la liberté de passer d'un sexe à l'autre à leur fantaisie. L'amour des femmes

Notes: 3. The Self-As-Art

aurait amolli le courage des grands hommes . . . la grandeur d'âme des magnanimes en eût pu être affaiblie." "Il faut . . . ne s'attacher pas trop fortement, ni trop longtemps auprès d'une dame, car tu pourrais en être le divertissement, au lieu qu'une semblable occupation doit être comme le divertissement d'un honnête homme."

47. "L'amour n'est pas seulement une simple passion comme partout ailleurs, mais une passion de nécessité et de bienséance: il faut que tous les hommes soient amoureux et que toutes les dames soient aimées. Nul insensible parmi nous; on reproche cette dureté de coeur comme un crime à ceux qui en sont capables; et la liberté de cette espèce est si honteuse que ceux qui ne sont point amoureux font du moins semblant de l'être." The honnête homme is never represented as a married man: the rare comments on this bourgeois institution are far from positive (e.g., Méré 340:I, 175). La Bruyère is an exception; see his apologia for marriage (286:415–16, #33–35). ". . . pour la galanterie, je crois qu'elle est toute dans son esprit, car il la cache et la montre quand il veut, et il en est si absolument maître qu'on ne peut pas croire que cela soit autrement. Ce n'est pas qu'il ne fasse et ne dise cent choses que l'amour fait dire et faire; mais selon moi, il les dit et les fait trop bien."

48. ". . . le peuple orne l'amour de ces faux brillants qu'il idolâtre parce qu'il ne les connaît pas, et les suit jusque dans le précipice où ils le conduisent, au lieu que les honnêtes gens l'en dépouillent pour le revêtir des vrais ornements qu'il mérite et le mettre en cette perfection qui fait le bonheur de ceux qui savent aimer." ". . . sans toutes les façons qu'on y fait, l'amour ne serait pas ce qu'elle est. Les cérémonies font la principale beauté de beaucoup de choses." ". . . [le] grand nombre de gens qui se mêlent d'une chose qu'ils n'entendent pas." ". . . faire d'illustres conquêtes et . . . ne perdre pas les amants qu'elles ont assujettis . . . le principal honneur de nos belles est de retenir dans l'obéissance les esclaves qu'elles ont faits." "Il y a une égale nécessité d'être amant et malheureux."

49. "Il n'y a rien de plus injuste que de faire l'amour pour se rendre malheureux, et que d'aimer si fort qu'on cesse d'être aimable et qu'on ne puisse jamais se faire aimer." ". . . elle m'ordonna pour la divertir de faire semblant que je mourais d'amour pour elle."

50. ". . . aussi agréables pour les autres que pour celles qu'ils aiment; c'est la chose du monde la plus rare, que de trouver un amant qui le soit de bonne grâce." ". . . donne un charme inexplicable à tout ce que l'on fait ou à tout ce que l'on dit." "Je soutiens qu'il n'y en a jamais eu qui ait eu l'air galant, qui ait fui l'entretien des personnes de mon sexe; et si j'ose dire tout ce que je pense, je dirais encore qu'il faut même qu'un homme ait eu du moins une fois en sa vie, quelque légère inclination amoureuse, pour acquérir parfaitement l'air galant . . . il faut qu'il ait eu le coeur un peu engagé . . . il faut avoir aimé ou avoir souhaité de plaire pour l'acquérir." "Comme les dames sont naturellement ennemies de toutes sorte de rudesse, il est difficile qu'un homme qui les fréquente veuille continuellement offenser la délicatesse de leur esprit. Au contraire, il s'accoutume insensiblement à leur vouloir plaire, de sorte qu'il accommode à la douceur de leur entretien et de leur manière d'agir ce qu'il peut avoir de trop choquant dans son langage ou dans sa contenance." ". . . nécessaires pour s'achever dans l'honnêteté." On the essential role of women in forming an honnête homme, see Scudéry (454:III, pt.2, 1382); F. de Caillières (103:23); Méré (340: I, 18).

51. "Il y a . . . des airs, des tons et des manières qui font souvent ce qu'il y a d'agréable ou de désagréable, de délicat ou de choquant dans la conversation; le secret de

s'en bien servir est donné à peu de personnes." ". . . tout cela n'est pas ce qu'on doit appeler conversation. Tous ces gens-là peuvent bien parler de leurs intérêts et de leurs affaires; et n'avoir pas cet agréable talent de la conversation qui est le plus doux charme de la vie." ". . . le plus grand plaisir des honnêtes gens"; "le plus exquis que puissent goûter des personnes délicates."

52. "Il faut parler le langage des honnêtes gens du pays où l'on est et fuir également celui du peuple bas et grossier, celui des sots beaux esprits, et celui qu'ont certains gens qui tenant un peu de la cour, un peu du peuple . . . et beaucoup de la ville est le plus bizarre de tous." On diction and accent, see also Méré (340:I, 21; II, 125). On the court's vulgar practices in this regard, see Vaugelas (510:II, 162–63).

53. "On se doit bien garder de représenter une chose dégoûtante, ou qui donne une fâcheuse idée, et se ressouvenir que lorsqu'on s'étend sur un sujet, qui déplaît, on se rend presque aussi désagréable que le sujet même. Les mieux faits de la cour ont grand besoin de cet avis." See also Méré (340:III, 131). "Il n'y a pas moins d'éloquence dans le ton de la voix que dans le choix des paroles."

54. ". . . qui persuade par douceur, non par empire." On language as painting, see Méré (340:II, 105; III, 134) and Bellegarde (58:92–93). "Les beautés d'éclat en fait de paroles, sont pour l'ordinaire de fausses beautés, qui . . . déplaisent d'abord aux personnes de bon goût. Je vous conseille . . . de n'en aimer que les plus modestes, qui semblent se cacher sous un voile, et de là vient qu'on les cherche quand on les connaît, et que plus on les considère plus on les aime . . . en les examinant on y découvre des grâces qui ne se montrent pas si vite, et . . . on les trouve plus aimables en effet qu'en apparence." "Quoi que ce langage éblouisse les ignorants et les dupes, je puis assurer qu'il est aussi peu du monde que celui du peuple, et que jamais les grands princes ou les honnêtes gens ne l'ont parlé." On the contempt for grandiloquence see also Pascal (393:594, #728) et Méré (340:I, 157–58). ". . . le peuple et les gens du commun en sont charmés; mais les honnêtes gens ne les peuvent souffrir." "Diseur de bon mots, mauvais caractère." On *bons mots* see also Méré (340:I, 63; II, 116; III, 121).

55. ". . . je ne sais quel tour naturel." ". . . être éloquent sans le paraître." ". . . un ordre secret et naturel"; "[un] ordre bien déguisé"; ". . . [un] faux agrément"; "une pauvre invention . . . qui sied mal aux honnêtes gens." "La vraie éloquence se moque de l'éloquence."

56. "Pour . . . rencontrer heureusement sur les plus petits sujets, il faut trop de manières, trop de politesse, et même trop de fécondité; c'est créer que de railler ainsi, et faire quelque chose de rien." "Pour éviter l'apparence d'un flatteur ordinaire, et pour donner quelque agrément aux louanges qui presque toujours ont je ne sais quoi qui dégoûte, on fait bien d'y chercher de l'adresse et de l'esprit, et de les rendre plus piquantes que douces. Il ne faut pourtant pas que l'assaisonnement ait rien de fâcheux, au contraire, il faut inventer de secondes louanges plus avantageuses que les premières, mais sous quelque apparence de dépit, et cela se fait en déguisant, et reprochant les choses que les personnes qu'on veut obliger sont bien aises d'avoir."

57. ". . . une moquerie d'enjoûment qui n'a rien de malin, ni d'injuste et qui ne choque personne." ". . . moquerie douce . . . piquante . . . et caressante"; "le même effet que le sel ordinaire dans un ragoût." "Beaucoup de choses font rire qu'on n'aime point, mais tout ce qui plaît se fait aimer."

Notes: 3. The Self-As-Art

58. "... l'auditeur sera comme forcé de se rendre." On the power of speech to penetrate "dans la plus secrète partie de l'homme" see Balzac (90:64). On conversation as synchronization see Scudéry (454:IV, pt.2, 400 ff.). "Une des choses qui fait que l'on trouve si peu de gens qui nous paraissent raisonnables et agréables dans la conversation, c'est qu'il n'y a quasi personne qui ne pense plutôt à ce qu'il veut dire, qu'à répondre précisément à ce qu'on lui dit; et que les plus habiles, et les plus complaisants, se contentent de montrer seulement une mine attentive, au même temps que l'on voit dans leurs yeux et dans leurs esprits un égarement et une précipitation de retourner à ce qu'ils veulent dire, au lieu de considérer que c'est un mauvais moyen de plaire ou de persuader les autres, de chercher si fort à se plaire à soi-même; et que bien écouter et bien répondre c'est une des grandes perfections qu'on puisse avoir." "... il sert quelquefois à approuver et à condamner; il y a un silence moqueur; il y a un silence respectueux." "... le langage du silence." "Il faut donc que celui qui veut plaire emploie beaucoup moins sa dextérité à faire connaître les lumières de son esprit, qu'à faire paraître celui des autres, et à relever avec choix et avec délicatesse les choses qu'ils ont bien faites ou bien dites. Le sacrifice qu'il semble faire en cela de ses intérêts est un détour ingénieux et qui lui fait faire beaucoup plus de progrès dans leur estime et dans leur amitié, que tout ce qu'il pourrait dire de plus merveilleux." "... celui qui sorte de votre entretien content de soi et de son esprit, l'est de vous parfaitement."

59. "Quand on excelle à parler, on pourrait écrire de même ... l'on ne peut savoir bien écrire sans savoir bien parler. Mais il arrive que ceux qui ne s'attachent qu'à bien écrire ont pour l'ordinaire en parlant une manière languissante et presque éteinte. ... Cette douceur de langage qu'ils affectent, leur fait perdre peu à peu l'usage naturel." "Quand on voit le style naturel on est tout étonné et ravi, car on attendait de voir un auteur et on trouve un hommme." [La] règle est l'honnêteté."

60. "D'Orsay plaisait si naturellement et si passionément à *tout le monde*, qu'il faisait porter son médaillon jusqu'à des hommes! tandis que les Dandys ne font porter aux hommes que ce que vous savez, et *plaisent aux femmes en leur déplaisant*." "Il déplaisait trop généralement *pour ne pas être recherché*. Ne reconnaît-on pas là le besoin d'être battues qui prend quelquefois les femmes puissantes et débauchées?"

61. "Telle tache peut n'être que la conséquence indivisible de telle beauté. ... Effacez l'une, vous effacez l'autre." "Là même où [Baudelaire] déplaît, il l'a voulu ainsi d'après une esthétique particulière et un raisonnement longtemps débattu." Cf. Baudelaire's "la jouissance de la laideur" as an esthetic principle (51:I, 548). "... le plaisir aristocratique de déplaire."

62. "... la coquetterie des hommes puissants peut être très médiocre et paraître irrésistible." "... l'art de plaire et de séduire au plus haut degré." "... la tournure d'un vieux fat qui suit encore les modes." In Nerval's adaptation of *Faust*, Mephistopheles materializes as *un élégant*, "avec l'habit écarlate brodé d'or, le petit manteau de satin empesé, la plume de coq au chapeau, une épée longue et bien affilée" (374:I, 67). See also Estève (185:203).

63. "... ces êtres privilégiés en qui le joli et le redoutable se confondent si mystérieusement." On another, more comic register, mystery became mystification, particularly among the Jeunes-France. According to Gautier, Jules Vabre "faisait les farces les plus énormes et mystifiait les bourgeois avec l'aplomb de Panurge" (207:36). "... il versait à doses parfaitement égales la terreur et la sympathie, et il en composait le philtre

magique de son influence." On the esthetics of fear, see Chateaubriand (124:230, 298 ff.), and Hugo (263:XII, 233–34, 269); and among dandies, Balzac (19:V, 299–300; VI, 61; VII, 727), and Gautier (215:156–57). "Le plus beau des étonnements c'est l'épouvante." "Mon cher . . . les hommes . . . comme moi, n'ont été faits, de toute éternité, que pour étonner les hommes . . . comme toi." ". . . la satisfaction orgueilleuse de ne jamais être étonné."

64. "Vous n'avez par compris votre siècle . . . : *faites toujours le contraire de ce qu'on attend de vous.* Voilà, d'honneur, la seule religion de l'époque. Ne soyez ni fou, ni affecté, car alors on attendrait de vous des folies et des affectations, et le précepte ne serait plus accompli." "Un des caractères des Dandys, c'est de ne jamais faire ce qu'on attend d'eux." ". . . produire toujours l'imprévu"; "toujours la singularité." ". . . en dehors d'une certaine exquise originalité." ". . . le besoin ardent de se faire une originalité." On originality, see also Baudelaire (51:II, 167, 178, 697). Cf. Furetière (1690): "On appelle ironiquement original un homme qui a quelque chose d'extravagant, de singulier et de ridicule dans ses manières ou dans son esprit" (202:s.v. *original*). See also Smith (466:109 ff.).

65. "Le Beau est toujours bizarre. Je ne veux pas dire qu'il soit volontairement, froidement bizarre, car dans ce cas il serait un monstre sorti des rails de la vie. Je dis qu'il contient toujours un peu de bizarrerie, de bizarrerie naïve, non voulue, inconsciente, et que c'est cettte bizarrerie qui le fait être particulièrement le Beau. . . . Cette dose de bizarrerie qui constitue et définit l'individualité . . . joue dans l'art (que l'exactitude de cette comparaison en fasse pardonner la trivialité) le rôle du goût ou de l'assaisonnement dans les mets, les mets ne différant les uns des autres, abstraction faite de leur utilité ou de la quantité de substance nutritive qu'ils contiennent, que par *l'idée* qu'ils révèlent à la langue." Cf. Barbey, who located the dandy's esthetic strategy midway between originality and eccentricity (38:IX, 250). "Il n'y a pas de hasards dans l'art, non plus qu'en mécanique. Une chose heureusement trouvée est la simple conséquence d'un bon raisonnement. . . . Un tableau est une machine dont tous les systèmes sont intelligibles pour un oeil exercé." "L'idée que l'homme se fait du beau s'imprime dans tout son ajustement, chiffonne ou raidit son habit, arrondit ou aligne son geste, et même pénètre subtilement à la longue, les traits de son visage. L'homme finit par ressembler à ce qu'il voudrait être." ". . . le costume, la coiffure et même le geste, le regard et le sourire (chaque époque a son port, son regard et son sourire) forment un tout d'une complète vitalité."

66. "Etre beau, c'est-à-dire avoir en soi un charme qui fait que tout vous sourit et vous accueille: qu'avant que vous ayez parlé tout le monde est déjà prévenu en votre faveur et disposé à être de votre avis; que vous n'avez qu'à passer par une rue, ou vous montrer à un balcon pour vous créer, dans la foule, des amis ou des maîtresses. N'avoir pas besoin d'être aimable pour être aimé, être dispensé de tous ces frais d'esprit et de complaisance auxquels la laideur vous oblige . . .; quel don splendide et magnifique." ". . . [un] privilège semblable à celui de la noblesse . . . elle est partout reconnue et vaut souvent plus que la fortune et le talent; elle n'a besoin que d'être montrée pour triompher, on ne lui demande que d'exister." "Tous les trésors de la statuaire antique n'offraient, dit-on, rien de comparable à la beauté harmonieuse de ses formes." On the dandy's beauty, see also Balzac (19:IV, 270, 272); Gautier (213:121).

67. "Celui qui joindrait à la beauté suprême la force suprême, qui, sous la peau d'Antinoüs, aurait les muscles d'Hercule, que pourrait-il désirer de plus? Je suis sûr qu'avec ces deux choses et l'âme que j'ai, avant trois ans, je serais empereur du monde!" Antinoüs

Notes: 3. The Self-As-Art

is the beautiful young Greek (c. 110 A.D.) who became Hadrian's favorite, and was honored after his death by cult, festivals, and statues. "... une beauté de jeune fille, beauté molle, efféminée." "... sous cette enveloppe charmante ... des muscles d'acier, un courage de lion."

68. "... ne se donnaient pas la peine de scruter, et ils pénétraient." "On eût dit que son regard de lynx ... plongeait au profond de leur coeur." On these animalistic metaphors, see also Balzac (19:IV, 614); Ponson du Terrail (405, II, 55; III, 218); Barbey (38:I, 92; V, 78–79; IX, 33); Baudelaire (51:II, 760, 692); Richard (424:81–83). "Son regard de lion et la fauve étincelle ... /Vous faisaient frissonner et pâlir malgré vous./—Les plus hardis auraient baissé la paupière/Devant cet oeil Méduse à vous changer en pierre." "... ce pouvoir magnétique est le grand but de la vie élégante." On this magnetic power, see Sue (492:30; 491:36); du Terrail (405:II, 55, 69; III, 36, 135, 542); Gautier (215:25, 337 ff.).

69. "... on ne pouvait [l']oublier quand on l'avait vu." See also Baudelaire (51:II, 760). "... je ne sais quoi de plus spirituel, de plus piquant que la beauté." "Il était rudement laid! mais son visage pâle et ravagé ... son nez épaté de léopard, ses yeux glauques, légèrement bordés d'un filet de sang, comme ceux des chevaux de race très ardents, avaient une expression devant laquelle ... les plus ricaneuses ne ricanaient plus.... Qui l'avait vu une fois ne l'oubliait plus." See also Barbey (38:I, 204; XI, 37). "... une immersion de l'âme à travers les lignes correctes ou incorrectes, pures ou tourmentées du visage."

70. "Avez-vous les mains blanches ... vous êtes égorgé aux cris de 'Vive Jacques Bonhomme! Mort aux seigneurs!'" On hands as a sign of *race* see Du Bled (168:304). "... avait tiré de leur étui de chamois parfumé, des mains blanches et bien sculptées à faire la religion d'une petite maîtresse qui les aurait eues, et il donnait les cartes ... avec un mouvement circulaire d'une rapidité si prodigieuse, que cela étonnait comme le doigté de Liszt."

71. "C'est ... ce qu'on appelait autrefois avoir *un grand air*." On this, see also Balzac (22:84–85, 96; 19:III, 508; IV, 617; 21:II, 50). On *l'air hautain* or *l'air de domination*, see Ronteix (432:2, 114); Baudelaire (51:I, 659). "... [vit] toujours sur l'idée de dignité comme sur un pal, ce qui—si souple qu'on soit—gêne un peu la liberté des mouvements et fait tenir par trop droit." "... la raideur de sa physionomie et de sa nature."

72. "... une sorte de système organisé." "Parle, marche, mange ou habille-toi et je te dirai qui tu es." "... l'indice d'une nature perfectionnée"; "la perfection des objects sensibles." "Quoique ces accessoires de l'existence portent également le cachet de l'élégance que nous imprimons à tout ce qui procède de nous, ils semblent en quelque sorte éloignés du siège de la pensée et ne doivent occuper que le second rang dans cette vaste théorie de l'élégance." "... le principe de la vie élégante est une haute pensée d'ordre et d'harmonie, destinée à donner de la poésie aux choses." Cf. Méré (78:XXXI [1924], 494). With the exception of Balzac's *Traité de la vie élégante*, Chapus's *Théorie de l'élégance* and Mortemart-Boisse's *La Vie élégante à Paris*, *l'élégant* and *le dandy* are equated in the nineteenth-century corpus (cf. chapter 1, p. 56). In his esthetic paradigm, Barbey situates the notion of elegance between those of grace and beauty: "L'élégance est plus que la grâce et moins que la beauté, mais elle se compose néanmoins de beauté et de grâce; pourquoi ne serait-elle pas, par exemple, la notion de la beauté, réalisée dans les petites choses et élevée grâce à la grâce au-dessus de la simple notion du joli?" (32:13). Absolute beauty may be more impressive and intoxicating, but elegance, "beauty in miniature," born of fantasy and imagination, is ultimately, for Barbey, the most captivating.

Notes: 3. The Self-As-Art

73. ". . . un homme qui se pique d'une suprême élégance dans sa toilette." To the ritual of dressing, the French dandy, like Brummell, consistently devotes two hours. See Ronteix (432:114); Stendhal (487:I, 805); Balzac (19:V, 25); Gautier (211:58); Barbey (38:XIII, 117). "La mode doit donc être considérée . . . comme une déformation sublime de la nature, ou plutôt comme un essai permanent et successif de réformation de la nature." ". . . la haute spiritualité de la toilette"; ". . . par leur aspiration naïve vers le brillant, vers les plumages bariolés, les étoffes chatoyantes, vers la majesté superlative des formes artificielles, de leur dégoût pour le réel."

74. ". . . tout un nouvel ordre de distinction et d'aristocratie." ". . . chaque état avait son costume spécial: la révolution a passé son niveau sur ce vieil usage. Le pair de France se met aujourd'hui comme l'avoué . . . l'on ne porte plus écrit sur la broderie de son habit le rang et l'état qu'on tient dans le monde." On the dandy's contempt for sartorial egalitarianism, see Kempf (280:171). "Tous les costumes aujourd'hui sont confondus; les diverses parties de la toilette sont déchues de leurs privilèges." On this confusion, see Ronteix (432:7-8); Chapus (122:20-21). "Nous sommes tous vêtus de noir comme des gens qui portent le deuil de quelque chose." ". . . l'habit noir et la redingote ont . . . leur beauté poétique, qui est l'expression de l'âme publique. . . . Nous célébrons tous quelque enterrement."

75. ". . . chercher à se signaler par quelque singularité de costume." ". . . un morceau d'étoffe d'une nuance si insolite, si agressive, si éclatante." On Gautier's predilection for costumes, see Du Bled (168:304-5). "Ces chères idoles nous forment . . . une palingénésie habillée des annales nationales . . . [on rencontre] aux Tuileries, les cheveux coupés carrément à la Charles VI, les pourpoints de velours, les cols de dentelle et les guipures, les chapeaux à la cavalière, les manteaux courts, les canons et les souliers à rosettes de Louis XIII et de Louis XIV." "Leur costume n'était pas le costume français et l'on eût été fort embarrassé de désigner précisément à quelle époque et à quelle nation il appartenait. L'un avait la barbe noire taillée à la François Ier, l'autre une pointe et les cheveux en brosse, à la Saint-Mégrin, un troisième une royale, comme le cardinal Richelieu; les autres, trop jeunes encore pour posséder cet accessoire important, s'en dédommageaient par la longueur de leur chevelure. L'un avait un pourpoint de velours noir et un pantalon collant, comme un archer du moyen-âge; l'autre un habit de conventionnel, avec un feutre pointu de raffiné; celui-ci une redingote de dandy, d'une coupe exagérée et une fraise à la Henri IV . . . l'on eût dit qu'ils avaient pris au hasard et les yeux fermés, dans la friperie des siècles, de quoi se composer, tant bien que mal, une garde-robe complète." ". . . il n'y en avait que deux en France: la barbe d'Eugène Dévéria et la barbe de Pétrus Borel! il fallait pour les porter un courage, un sang-froid et un mépris de la foule vraiment héroïques. . . . Nous pouvions donc chercher de ce côté-là quelque chose de nouveau, et singulier et même d'un peu choquant." ". . . le mot *artiste* excusait tout et chacun suivait à peu près son caprice." "Comme tous les artistes . . . il cherchait à donner à nos pitoyables vêtements un galbe pittoresque, une tournure moins prosaïque. Il se modelait sur un beau Van Dyck qu'il avait dans son atelier, et vraiment il y ressemblait à s'y méprendre. On eût dit le portrait descendu du cadre ou la réflexion de la peinture dans un miroir."

76. "Il éteignit les couleurs de ses vêtements, en simplifia la coupe"; ". . . plus intelligent qu'éclatant." ". . . [les] excentriques que les couleurs tranchées et violentes

256

Notes: 3. The Self-As-Art

dénonçaient facilement aux yeux . . . se contentent aujourd'hui des nuances dans le dessin, dans la coupe, plus encore que dans la couleur." See also Huysmans (266:39, 164). This evolution is confirmed in studies of nineteenth-century costume. From decade to decade the principal formal modification involves the length and width of the pants, coat, collar, and top hat. The dramatic style of the 1830s—skin-tight pants, cinched waist, full skirt, padded shoulders and wide, stand-away lapels—is slowly replaced by a looser, less sensual style that tends to hide the body. "La perfection de la toilette consiste . . . dans la simplicité absolue, qui est, en effet, la meilleure manière de se distinguer." "Tout était simple et *dandy* comme l'entendait Brummell, c'est-à-dire *irrémarquable*." ". . . reconnu par les siens et méconnu par la foule."

77. "N'existe-t-il pas pour les gens comme il faut des signes maçonniques à la faveur desquels ils doivent se reconnaître?" "La toilette ne consiste pas tant dans le vêtement que dans une certaine manière de le porter." "L'esprit d'un homme se devine à la manière dont il porte sa canne." Brummell, according to Barbey, was concerned that his tailors not take credit for his own celebrity (38:IX, 252). ". . . ce n'est pas un habit qui marche tout seul! au contraire, c'est une certaine manière de le porter qui crée le Dandysme . . . l'habit n'y est pour rien. Il n'*est* presque *plus*."

78. "Les Français devinrent tous égaux dans leurs droits, et aussi dans leur toilette . . . . Dès lors . . . la cravate . . . fut appelée à rétablir les nuances entièrement effacées dans la toilette, elle devint le critérium auquel on reconnaîtrait l'homme comme il faut et l'homme sans éducation. . . . Tant vaut l'homme, tant vaut la cravate. . . . c'est par elle que l'homme se révèle et se manifeste."

79. ". . . comme un échantillon de sa puissance, un signe chargé d'instruire les passants de la place où [l'on] perche sur le grand mât de cocagne." On the dandy as *un gant jaune* et al., see Dériège (158:10–11); Stendhal (487:I, 953); Balzac (22:49; 19:V, 15; VII, 726; X, 628; 21:II, 34); du Terrail (485:III, 228, 276); Barbey (38:I, 203, 309, 336, 375). ". . . il y en avait de gris, de blancs, de noirs, de couleur scarabée, à reflets d'or, de pailletés, de chinés, de doubles, à châle ou droits de col, à col renversé, de boutonnés jusqu'en haut, à boutons d'or." On the dandy's vest, see also de Beauvoir (53:71). On the dandy's carriage, see Balzac (22:49; 21:II, 34; 19:II, 900–01).

80. "Crois-tu que ce ne soit rien aussi que d'avoir le droit d'arriver dans un salon, d'y regarder tout le monde du haut de sa cravate, ou à travers un lorgnon, et de pouvoir mépriser l'homme le plus supérieur s'il porte un gilet arriéré?" "Un froid mortel saisit [Lucien de Rubempré] quand de Marsay le lorgna; le lion parisien laissa retomber son lorgnon si singulièrement qu'il semblait à Lucien que ce fût le couteau de la guillotine." On the lorgnon, see also Barbey (38:XI, 19) and Kempf (280:35). ". . . à travers la physionomie des gens que cela n'amuse nullement." On the cigar, see Dériège (158:20); Balzac (21:II, 439–40); Mortemart-Boisse (364:373).

81. "Cet ensemble rigoureusement exigé par l'unité rend solidaires tous les accessoires de l'existence." "Depuis mon écurie jusqu'à ma table, depuis mon habit jusqu'à ma maison . . . je voulus que ma vie fût comme un enseignement de goût et d'élégance." ". . . le système d'alimentation nécessaire aux créatures d'élite." "Le mécanicien qu'était Gavarni, toujours un peu attiré par les ressorts cachés de la magie blanche et la mécanique de l'escamotage, avait imaginé pour son logis toute une série de *trucs* qui en faisaient un

Notes: 3. The Self-As-Art

intérieur à la Robert Houdin" (French conjurer and magician, 1805–1871, celebrated for his optical illusions and mechanical devices). "... un monde fantastique/... où tout est poétique."

82. "La parure est une arme." "Les esprits intelligents et éclairés marchent en avant et indiquent la route; la masse les suit bon gré mal gré plus ou moins vite; elle adopte ce qui est bien et le pratique souvent à son insu sans le comprendre."

83. "Les esprits qui ne voient les choses que par leur plus petit côté ont imaginé que le Dandysme était surtout l'art de la mise, une heureuse et audacieuse dictature en fait de toilette et d'élégance extérieure. Très certainement c'est cela aussi; mais c'est bien davantage. Le Dandysme est toute une manière d'être, et l'on n'est pas que par le côté matériellement visible. C'est une manière d'être entièrement composée de nuances." "Une seule dissonance est, comme en musique, une négation de l'art lui-même."

84. "... l'homme impoli est le lépreux du monde fashionable." On polite manners see also Chapus (121:154); Mortemart-Boisse (364:20–25); and Sue (489:I, 172, 176). "Fille de la Légèreté et de l'Aplomb—deux qualités qui semblent s'exclure—elle est aussi la soeur de la Grâce, avec laquelle elle doit rester unie. Toutes deux s'embellissent de leur mutuel contraste. En effet, sans l'Impertinence, la Grâce ne ressemblerait-elle pas à une blonde trop fade, et sans la Grâce, l'Impertinence ne serait-elle pas une brune trop piquante? Pour qu'elles soient bien ce qu'elles sont chacune, il convient de les entremêler."

85. "... se prenait de goût pour les choses et les habitudes qui choquent les gens du continent, et, par une pente un peu paradoxale de son esprit, la froideur, la réserve, le flegme brittanique, ce caractère opposé, contraire, antipathique à notre caractère national, lui semblait un charme sévère." On *le flegme*, see also Sue (489:I, 72, 76); Barbey (38:IX, 253, 312, #29). "Son indolence ne lui permettait pas d'avoir de la verve, parce qu'avoir de la verve, c'est se passionner; se passionner, c'est tenir à quelque chose; et tenir à quelque chose, c'est se montrer inférieur." On the dandy's impassivity, see also Balzac (19:V, 713); Sue (489:I, 182–83); Barbey (38:IX, 240, 254).

86. "... le même manteau de glace recouvr[ait] ... une ardente passion." "Le caractère de beauté du dandy consiste surtout dans l'air froid qui vient de l'inébranlable résolution de ne pas être ému; on dirait un feu latent qui se fait deviner, qui pourrait mais qui ne veut pas rayonner." On dandyistic *froideur*, see also Sue (489:I, 139, 145); Barbey (38:IX, 316, #38); Baudelaire (51:II, 335).

87. "Aimer, même dans le sens le moins élevé de ce mot, désirer, c'est toujours dépendre, c'est être esclave de son désir. Les bras les plus tendrement fermés sur vous sont encore une chaîne." On the dandy's fear of love, see Stendhal (487:I, 778, 906; II, 1351); Sue (489:I, 238). "En fait d'amour je devins athée comme un mathématicien." "Dès qu'un dandy est amoureux, il n'est plus dandy. Le dandysme finit à l'amour." Elsewhere, Barbey defined *le fat* as "l'homme qui ne met pas toute sa gloire à les aimer [les femmes], et dont la vanité n'est pas la très humble servante de la leur" (38:IX, 41). On the dandy's contempt for the bourgeois institution of marriage, see Ancelot (9:9) and Balzac (19:III, 87–88, 90). Balzac's Paul de Manerville is literally ruined by his marriage. Baudelaire's Samuel Cramer simply ceases to be a dandy when he marries. "... L'amour est l'occupation naturelle des oisifs. Mais le dandy ne vise pas à l'amour comme but spécial."

88. "On a une femme à la mode comme on a un joli cheval, comme chose nécessaire

au luxe d'un jeune homme." ". . . le diamant avec lequel un homme coupe toutes les vitres, quand il n'a pas la clef d'or avec laquelle s'ouvrent toutes les portes."

89. "Comment est le bras? Assez bien. —Les mains ne manquent pas de délicatesse. —Que pensez-vous de ce pied? Je pense que la cheville n'a pas noblesse, et que le talon est commun. Mais la gorge est bien placée et d'une bonne forme, la ligne serpentine est assez ondoyante, les épaules sont grasses et d'un beau caractère. —Cette femme serait un modèle passable, et l'on en pourrait mouler plusieurs proportions. —Aimons-la." ". . . le peintre satisfait, l'amant reprit le dessus." ". . . où la beauté elle-même ne suffit plus si elle n'est assaisonnée par le parfum, la parure et cetera." At the extreme point of the dandy's objectification of women, Des Esseintes hires a female ventriloquist for the sole purpose of projecting her voice onto a chimera and a sphinx, and thrills to hear her utter the Flaubertian dialogue he has taught her (266:145).

90. ". . . comme un général au succès de ses manoeuvres." ". . . d'attaquer par la vanité . . . cette forteresse imprenable à l'amour. Elle ne m'aimera pas davantage, mais elle succombera . . . froidement, élégamment et dans sa cuirasse." "En triomphant aussi facilement, de Marsay devait s'ennuyer de ses triomphes; aussi depuis environ deux ans s'ennuyait-il beaucoup. . . . Il en était venu, comme les souverains, à implorer du hasard quelque obstacle à vaincre, quelque entreprise qui demandât le déploiement de ses forces morales et physiques inactives." "J'eus la coquetterie de l'esclavage. Je fus l'odalisque de notre liaison et elle en fut le sultan. . . . Cela me plaisait de la voir . . . impérieuse jusque dans mes bras; lionne frémissante dont le courroux était si près de la caresse." "Aux instants de plaisir j'aurais volontiers changé de rôle, car il est bien impatientant de ne pas avoir la conscience de l'effet qu'on produit." See also the inversion of roles that marks the brief encounter between Des Esseintes and the acrobat, Mlle Uranie (266:140–43).

91. "Il ne se peut rien imaginer de plus ravissant au monde que ces deux corps tous deux parfaits, harmonieusement fondus ensemble . . . qui n'en forment plus qu'une [beauté] supérieure à toutes deux . . .: pour un adorateur exclusif de la forme, y a-t-il une incertitude plus aimable?" It should be noted that in *Mademoiselle de Maupin*, Gautier also becomes an apologist for lesbianism—Maupin and Rosette—and homosexuality—D'Albert and Théodore (211:150, 380). However, homosexuality becomes an important theme in French literature only post-1885 (110:passim). ". . . [des] androgynes de l'Histoire, non plus de la Fable." "Cette royauté des manières qu'il élève à la hauteur des autres royautés humaines, il l'enlève aux femmes, qui seules semblaient faites pour l'exercer. C'est à la façon et un peu par les moyens des femmes qu'il domine. Et cette usurpation des fonctions, il la fait accepter par les femmes elles-mêmes, et, ce qui est encore plus surprenant, par les hommes. Le dandy a quelque chose d'anti-naturel, d'androgyne, par où il peut séduire infiniment." On androgynism in *fin de siècle* literature, see Carter (111:passim).

92. "Son action sur les autres était plus immédiate que celle qui s'exerce uniquement par le langage. Il la produisit par l'intonation, le regard, le geste, l'intention transparente, le silence même; et c'est une des explications à donner du peu de mots qu'il a laissés." ". . . son esprit qui avait besoin pour s'enflammer de l'étincelle de l'esprit d'autrui, demeurait sans ressource." "Jamais époque ne fut plus stérile dans l'art de la conversation." ". . . le dernier asile où se soit réfugié l'esprit français d'autrefois." On the dandy's love for good talk and his inability to find it see Raisson (416:51); Balzac (21:II, 14); Barbey (38:V,

Notes: 3. The Self-As-Art

33–34; IX, 186, 315, #37; XIV, 235); Baudelaire (49:IV, 312; 51:II, 109). "Le fashionable ... a l'air de dire, vous n'êtes pas à la hauteur du siècle. Il est inutile que je vous parle, vous ne me comprendriez pas." ". . . un moyen de plus de faire effet, la coquetterie taquine des êtres sûrs de plaire et qui savent par quel boût s'allume le désir."

93. "Un homme au courant de *la mode des mots* se trouve armé d'un immense pouvoir. Il a le droit de toiser assez impertinemment le niais qui lui demande la significa-tion d'un mot; Ou de lui rire au nez; De s'écrier: 'Quoi! vous ne savez pas ce mot-là?' De lui expliquer avec une condescendance cruelle; De lui faire subir une dissertation; De prouver à tout le monde que ce monsieur est en arrière . . . etc., etc. . . . L'homme qui possède le secret du langage à la mode, ne parlant pas comme un autre, a le bonheur d'entendre dire de lui: Monsieur un tel a une certaine manière de s'exprimer. . . . Je ne sais, mais sa conversation a quelque chose de *distingué*. . . . " Cf. dandy-writers who extol *l'art de plaire* in conversation: Balzac (22:98–100); Raisson (416:119); Chapus (121:141–164). On the dandy's use of lower-class idioms or the jargon of criminals, see Balzac (19:III, 193); Chapus (121:150); in *Les Voleurs*, Vidocq attests to this dandyistic usage (513). The dandy was also reputed to have a particular mania for the idiom of artists (210:87) and utilized the expression, "il y a de la poésie là-dedans," in what seemed to Degleny a most indiscriminate fashion: "Qui de nous n'a entendu cette plate bêtise appliquée à toutes les circonstances, et dans toutes les occa-sions? On contemple la misère sans émotions, le vice sans dégoût, le crime sans effroi: pourquoi non? *Il y a de la poésie là dedans*" (335:50). The dandy was not merely displaying aristocratic composure in the face of sordid, criminal or immoral phenomena, he was emit-ting a linguistic sign that underscored his self-definition as poetic in all aspects of life. Balzac concurred: "Aujourd'hui que la poésie n'est plus dans les livres, la mode veut que l'on voie de la poésie partout" (21:II, 36).

94. ". . . de façon qu'on ne sache jamais où l'on en est quand on écoute." On the dandy's monosyllabic speech, see Ronteix (432:77–78); Barbey (38:IX, 311, #25).. ". . . une espèce de fraternité basée sur le mépris." ". . . l'art de ravir, de faire penser, de faire rêver, d'arracher les âmes des bourbes de la routine."

95. "Elle jette sur un homme l'air de sphinx qui préoccupe comme un mystère et qui inquiète comme un danger. Or, Brummell la possédait et s'en servait de manière à transir tous les amours-propres, même en les caressant." "Une éternelle ironie dictait ses paroles, ironie si profonde que, dans la mollesse de sa voix et la courtoisie de son langage, rien n'en trahissait le secret. . . . On sentait cela comme, en entendant l'harmonica—musique céleste! plaisir inénarrable!—on sent que l'on va s'évanouir."

96. As Sartre writes of Baudelaire's dandyism: "l'exercice trop utilitaire du métier artistique devient le pur cérémonial de la toilette, le culte du beau qui produit des oeuvres stables et durables se change en amour de l'élégance, parce que l'élégance est éphémère, stérile et périssable; l'acte créateur du peintre ou du poète, vidé de sa substance, prend forme d'acte strictement gratuit, au sens gidien, et même absurde" (447:167–68).

97. "D'un ensemble de pratiques insignifiantes et inutiles il fait un art qui porte sa marque personnelle, qui plaît et qui séduit à la façon d'un ouvrage de l'esprit. Il commu-nique à de menus signes de costume, de tenue et de langage, un sens et une puissance qu'ils n'ont point naturellement. *Bref, il fait croire à ce qui n'existe pas.* Il 'règne par les airs,' comme d'autres par les talents, par la force, par la richesse. Il se fait, avec rien, une supériorité mystérieuse . . . dont les effets sont aussi grands que ceux des supériorités

classées et reconnues par les hommes." "Comme il fait quelque chose avec le néant, comme ses inventions consistent en des riens parfaitement superflus et qui ne valent que par l'opinion qu'il en a su donner, il nous apprend que les choses n'ont de prix que celui que nous leur attachons, et que 'l'idéalisme est vrai.'" "... [la] gravité dans le frivole."

4. THE PROCESS AND ETHICS OF PRODUCTION

1. "Ce jeu n'est plus un jeu mais une vérité/ Où par mon action, je suis représenté ... moi-même, l'objet et l'acteur de moi-même." In Greimas's analysis, a single actor, like the honnête homme or the dandy, can represent syncretically several actants (234:256). Subsequent to the initial presentation of his actantial model, Greimas refined the concept of *épreuve* with those of competence/performance, terms which I will also use (235:117–18).

2. "Je ne sais qui vous a mis dans l'esprit que tout ce qui paraît naturel doit plaire; vous ne songez pas que la nature est composée de bien et de mal, de beau et de laid, d'objets agréables comme d'objets fâcheux, et qu'on ne voit rien de plus fréquent ni de plus naturel que d'être malhonnête homme." See also La Calprenède (287:I, 2). Seventeenth-century estheticians also used the term *beau naturel* as a synonym for *belle nature* (194:106). Less often, the negative acceptation is described as "pure or ordinary" nature: see Perrault (395:337), and Champaigne (194:116). "Il faut observer et choisir tout ce qu'on peut découvrir de plus beau, de plus aimable et de plus charmant, non seulement dans la [nature] sensible mais encore dans l'intellectuelle ou l'intelligible ou l'invisible ou la spirituelle." See also Champaigne (194:114–15); Nicole (376:2); Perrault (395:337). "... attraper l'idée du beau à laquelle non seulement la pure nature, mais la belle nature même ne sont jamais arrivées; c'est d'après cette idée qu'il faut qu'il travaille, et qu'il ne se serve de la nature que pour y parvenir."

3. "Quelqu'un ne manquera pas de dire que je me forme des idées qu'on n'a jamais vues, comme la République du divin Platon ou l'Orateur du plus éloquent des Romains. ... Il est vrai que nous voyons si peu de ces gens-là, qu'on ne sait pas bien comme on s'en trouverait." On the rareness of the honnête homme see also Méré (340:I, 44; III, 69–71, 77); Mitton (244:55–56). "... une pure idée [dont] ... on n'en voit que l'ombre et l'apparence." "... qui tombe sous la connaissance des sens"; "... ce monde invisible et d'une étendue infinie [où] l'on peut découvrir les raisons et les principes des choses, les vérités les plus cachées ... les vrais originaux et les parfaites idées de tout ce qu'on cherche." Although Leibnitz questioned his Platonism (300:II, 952), Méré repeatedly expressed his belief in a transcendental model for the ideal modes of honnêteté (e.g., 340:II, 101). "... on ne se doit former ... que sur les idées de la perfection." On this idea of perfection, see also II, 36, 115; III, 89, 98, 148, 160; 339:122–23, 600, 705; 78:XXXII(1925), 499. "... il arrive quelquefois qu'on approche tant de la perfection, qu'on s'en peut réjouir comme si on l'avait trouvée, et peut-être qu'on la trouve en quelque rencontre, et qu'on n'y devrait pas être si défiant." For a general analysis of Platonist influences on French classical esthetics, see Brody (88).

4. "... faire d'un air agréable ce qui nous est naturel." On artifice as the source of artistic truth, see La Fontaine (291:I, 215); La Rochefoucauld (294:441, #282); Boileau (*Art*

Notes: 4. Process and Ethics of Production

poétique, III, 1–4). "Combien d'art pour rentrer dans la nature! combien de temps, de règles, d'attention et de travail pour danser avec la même liberté et la même grâce que l'on sait marcher." "Ce n'est pas qu'on ne puisse avoir trop d'art ni trop d'artifice en quoi que ce soit . . . mais il ne faut pas que l'un ni l'autre se montre." On hidden artifice, see also Méré (340:I, 47; II, 74; III, 108); cf. Faret (188:20). ". . . si l'art ne trompe adroitement, on le méprise et l'ouvrier paraît ridicule." On *le ridicule* (the Aristotelian τό γελείων), see e.g., Molière (349:I, 660–61, 679). ". . . une certaine négligence qui cache l'artifice et témoigne que l'on ne fait rien que comme sans y penser."

5. "La nature . . . *contraint* l'homme à dormir, à boire, à manger. . . . C'est elle aussi qui pousse l'homme à tuer son semblable, à le manger, à le séquestrer, à le torturer. . . . C'est cette infaillible nature qui a créé le parricide et l'anthropophagie, et mille autres abominations. . . . Passez en revue, analysez tout ce qui est naturel, toutes les actions et les désirs du pur homme naturel, vous ne trouverez rien que d'affreux." In Baudelaire's view, the early nineteenth-century cult of nature was a "signe évident de l'abaissement général" (51:II, 660), an anathema to all spiritual beings (49:I, 322–23). On art as the reformation of nature, see also Baudelaire (51:I, 302, II, 716).

6. ". . . une création due toute entière à l'art et d'où la nature est complètement absente." ". . . croisade contre le soleil, contre la compagne . . . contre la nature qu'il n'admettait que dans les tableaux." See also Gautier (197:6), and Musset (367:II, 283). "Quel pays voulez-vous qu'on vous serve aujourd'hui?" Despite his hatred for contemporary society, the dandy extolled its industrial objects as a triumph of artifice over nature: "Nous acceptons la civilisation telle qu'elle est, avec ses chemins de fer . . . ses machines, ses tuyaux de cheminée," wrote Gautier; "le monde antique peut être balancé par un monde nouveau, tout resplendissant d'acier et de gaz" (216:202–03). See also Baudelaire (51:II, 666–67). In this perspective, we can see the logic underlying Des Esseintes's preference for the locomotive over the female (266:53).

7. "La femme est le contraire du dandy. . . . La femme a faim et elle veut manger; soif, et elle veut boire. Elle est en rut et elle veut être foutue. . . . La femme est *naturelle*, c'est-à-dire abominable." "Quand on meurt de faim, on sort des affectations d'une société quelconque, on rentre dans la vie humaine: on cesse d'être dandy." ". . . le spectacle enchanteur de sa propre nature corrigée et idéalisée." ". . . insulte jetée à la face de cette vieille nature dont les uniformes exigences seraient pour jamais éteintes." Des Esseintes manifests here the dandy's contempt for his own body, which he regards as a hindrance to the attainment of his spiritual (artificial) ideal. As Starobinski has noted, the dandy tries to "s'absenter de son corps," but remains trapped in it (478:67–68).

8. "Oiseaux du ciel, prêtez-moi chacun une plume . . . afin que je m'en fasse une paire d'ailes pour voler haut et vite par des régions inconnues . . . où je puisse oublier que je suis moi, et vivre d'une vie étrange et nouvelle . . . plus loin que la dernière île du monde, par l'océan de glace, au-delà du pôle où tremble l'aurore boréale, dans l'impalpable royaume où s'envolent les divines créations des poètes et les types de la suprême beauté." "Quelque chose l'attire et l'appelle invinciblement qui n'est pas de ce monde ni en ce monde . . . et comme l'héliotrope dans une cave, il se tord pour se tourner vers le soleil qu'il ne voit pas. C'est un de ces hommes dont l'âme n'a pas été trempée assez complètement dans les eaux du Léthé avant d'être liée à son corps, et qui garde du ciel dont elle vient des réminiscences d'éternelle beauté qui la travaillent et la tourmentent, qui se souvient qu'elle a eu des ailes,

Notes: 4. Process and Ethics of Production

et qui n'a plus que des pieds." See also Théodore's version of the myth of the cave (211:157–58) and D'Albert's comments on the Platonic model (p. 63). ". . . la plus pure symbolisation de l'essence éternelle—la beauté."

9. ". . . Le matérialisme absolu n'était pas loin de l'idéalisme le plus pur." "Toute idée est, par elle-même, douée d'une vie immortelle comme une personne. Toute forme créée, même par l'homme, est immortelle. Car la forme est indépendante de la matière, et ce ne sont pas les molécules qui constituent la forme." "C'est cet admirable, cet immortel instinct du Beau qui nous fait considérer la Terre et ses spectacles comme un aperçu, comme une *correspondance* du Ciel"; "tout, forme, mouvement, nombre, couleur, parfum dans le *spirituel*, comme dans le *naturel*, est significatif, réciproque, converse, *correspondant*." See also Baudelaire (51:I, 430). For Balzac's Swedenborgian theories, see 19:VI, 627 and especially X, 268–72, 380 ff., 494–515. ". . . [la] suprême incarnation de l'idée du beau dans la vie matérielle." See also Baudelaire (51:II, 716). As Balzac had observed in seeking for elegance "les lois du beau idéal" (22:145), the dandy can reproduce in his cravat "ce type sans pareil qu'il avait dans l'esprit" (21:II, 49). On the internal model which the artist uses to create the artistic object see Chapus (122:32); Barbey (38:XVI, 77, 154), and Baudelaire (51:II, 454–58). For Baudelaire every work of art represents a combination of the relative and the absolute: "Je défie qu'on découvre un échantillon quelconque de beauté qui ne contienne pas ces deux éléments" (II, 685). In contrast to Plato, Baudelaire, like Gautier, refuses to equate the beautiful, the true, and the good (pp. 111–12): beauty transcends and subsumes all other Platonic ideals (pp. 333–34). On Baudelaire's Platonism, see Eigeldinger's study (178), to date the best, but still very inadequate treatment of the subject.

10. "L'une, matronne rustique, répugnante de santé et de vertu, sans allure et sans regard, bref, ne devant rien qu'à la simple nature . . . l'autre, une de ces beautés qui dominent et oppriment le souvenir, unissant à son charme profond et originel toute l'éloquence de la toilette, maîtresse de sa démarche, consciente et reine d'elle-même, une voix parlant comme un instrument bien accordé, et des regards chargés de pensée et n'en laissant couler que ce qu'ils veulent." "[Elle] a pour but et pour résultat de faire disparaître du teint les taches que la nature y a outrageusement semées, et de créer une unité abstraite dans le grain et la couleur de la peau, laquelle unité . . . rapproche immédiatement l'être humain de la statue, c'est-à-dire, d'un être divin et supérieur." Gautier's attitude toward make-up is closely related to Baudelaire's: "De même que les peintres habiles établissent l'accord des chairs et des draperies par des glacis légers, les femmes blanchissent leur peau, qui paraîtrait bise à côté des moirés, des dentelles, des satins, et lui donnent une unité de ton préférable à ces martelages de blanc, de jaune et de rose qu'offrent les teints les plus purs. Au moyen de la poudre de riz, elles font prendre à leur épiderme un mica de marbre, et ôtent à leur teint cette santé rougeaude qui est une grossièreté dans notre civilisation, car elle suppose la prédominance des appétits physiques sur les instincts intellectuels. . . . Peut-être même un vague frisson de pudeur engage-t-il les femmes à poser sur leur col, leurs épaules, leur sein et leurs bras, ce léger voile de poussière blanche qui atténue la nudité, en lui retirant les chaudes et provocantes couleurs de la vie. La forme se rapproche ainsi de la statuaire, elle se spiritualise et se purifie. Parlerons-nous du noir des yeux, tant blâmé aussi? Ces traits marqués . . . sont comme les coups de force que les maîtres donnent aux chefs d'oeuvre qu'ils finissent" (168:326–27). "Mène-t-on la foule dans les ateliers de l'habilleuse et du décorateur, dans la loge de la comédienne? Montre-t-on au public . . . le mécanisme des

trucs? Lui explique-t-on les retouches et les variantes improvisées aux répétitions . . . ? Lui révèle-t-on toutes les loques, les fards, les poulies, les chaînes, les repentirs, les épreuves barbouillées, bref, toutes les horreurs qui composent le sanctuaire de l'art?" In an even stronger echo of the attitudes of the *mondains* toward artifice as a productive medium, rather than an esthetic end in itself, Balzac labeled as ridiculous those artists who, like inept mechanics, "laissent apercevoir les ressorts, les contrepoids et les coulisses"; the primary goal of elegance, he maintains, is to conceal the means (22:83).

11. "Je suis persuadé qu'en beaucoup d'occasions il n'est pas inutile de regarder ce qu'on fait comme une comédie et de s'imaginer qu'on joue un personnage de théâtre." ". . . contre les pièges que l'on y tend sans cesse pour faire tomber dans le ridicule." "Il y a des moments que l'on se relâche et où l'on est pas toujours d'humeur à se gêner, pour cacher ses défauts et ses faiblesses. . . . Ces nouvelles découvertes détruisent l'estime qu'on avait de notre mérite." "Tâche . . . de couvrir tes défauts; il faut de moins paraître vertueux, et feindre de l'être pour être estimé tel; et il vaut encore mieux être hypocrite que d'être connu pour un méchant homme." In his lengthy review of the French texts influenced by the *Cortegiano*, Toldo concludes that dissimulation is "la première règle qui s'impose" (504:84). This attitude reaches its crowning expression in Acetto's *Della dissimulazione oneste* (1641), which endorses dissimulation, not only as a defensive device but as a pleasurable quality, the source of which lies in triumph over the natural self (see 1:39, 69–70). On dissimulation see also Refuge (421:177–78); Scudéry (455:359–384; 141:II, 398–99); Rousset (435:224–25).

12. "C'est un talent fort rare que d'être bon acteur dans la vie, il faut bien de l'esprit et de la justesse pour en trouver la perfection; . . . de faire toujours ce qu'il faut tant par l'action que par le ton de la voix, et de s'en acquitter d'une manière si juste, que la chose produise l'effet qu'elle doit, cela me paraît un chef d'oeuvre." Analyzing the tones, gestures and manners that best express the thoughts and feelings we wish to convey, La Rochefoucauld comments: ". . . c'est ce qui fait les bons et les mauvais comédiens et c'est ce qui fait aussi que les personnes plaisent ou déplaisent" (294:317, #74). ". . . empêche d'avoir rien trop à coeur, et donne ensuite une liberté de langage et d'action, qu'on n'a point quand on est troublé de crainte et d'inquiétude." ". . . je sentais qu'il était plus comédien qu'honnête homme; cela me le rendait insupportable." See also La Bruyère (286:264–65, #50); Bellegarde (61:120).

13. ". . . une vaine apparence." "Quand il m'arrive d'en rencontrer quelqu'un je le sais bien démêler, et quoique j'entende dire de bonnes choses, et que j'en voie faire qui ont toute la grâce qu'on peut souhaiter, je ne conclus pas pour cela. Ce n'est bien souvent qu'un langage emprunté, ou qu'un personnage qu'on joue. Je prends garde si tout vient du fond, et si rien ne se dément: Enfin je ne regarde pas tant à ce qui me paraît de poli et de régulier, qu'à de certaines choses qui témoignent que l'esprit va loin, et qu'il est de grande étendue." "Pour être civil en galant homme, il faut l'être plus en effet qu'en apparence." "Pour démêler la vraie honnêteté d'avec la fausse, on se doit assurer qu'elle n'a rien que de bien réel; rien qui ne soit juste et raisonnable en tous les endroits du monde." "Pour le paraître, il faut l'être en effet; car les apparences du dehors ne sont que les images des actions intérieures."

14. "Quand on est encore plus honnête homme en particulier qu'en public, c'est une marque infaillible qu'on ne l'est pas médiocrement." See also Méré (340:I, 77; III, 89–90).

Notes: 4. Process and Ethics of Production

"J'entends dire . . . qu'il est à désirer de paraître honnête homme dans le grand monde; mais qu'en des lieux à l'écart, où qui que ce soit ne nous observe, ils ne jugent pas à propos de l'être, et qu'il en coûterait trop. Ceux qui sont de cet avis, n'ont ni honnêteté ni discernement. . . . L'honnêteté . . . est une de ces choses qui ne sauraient subsister, sans se produire toutes les fois que le devoir ou la bienséance le veut: de sorte qu'un honnête homme ne se peut empêcher de faire une action honnête, non plus qu'un brave d'une extrême valeur d'en faire une déterminée, si l'occasion le demande. Ils n'ont point, pour ce regard, de franche volonté." On honnêteté as "une parfaite habitude," see also Méré (340:I, 45, 53; II, 128; III, 110; 78:XXX[1923], 79). ". . . une seconde nature qui détruit la première."

15. "On ne se met pas en peine d'être honnête homme, on tâche seulement de le paraître; la plupart des hommes ne sont honnêtes que par artifice . . . toute leur honnêteté n'est que contre-faite." "Que dites-vous . . . de ce que chacun se fait un extérieur et une mine qu'il met en la place de ce que l'on veut paraître au lieu de ce qu'on est? Il y a longtemps que je l'ai pensé et que j'ai dit que tout le monde était en mascarade, et mieux déguisé qu'à celle du Louvre, car l'on n'y reconnaît personne. Enfin que tout soit *arte di parer honesta* et non pas l'être, cela est pourtant bien étrange." Commenting on the widespread art of the written portrait in circles of honnêteté, Sorel observed: "Ils voulaient tous que leur portrait fût fait sur ce qu'ils paraissaient être, non pas ce qu'ils étaient effectivement" (351:138). See also Rousset (435:219). "Nous ne nous contentons pas de la vie que nous avons en nous et en notre propre être. Nous voulons vivre dans l'idée des autres d'une vie imaginaire, et nous nous efforçons pour cela de paraître. Nous travaillons incessamment à embellir et conserver notre être imaginaire, et négligeons le véritable . . . grande marque du néant de notre propre être." ". . . la nature est corrompue et que les hommes sont contraires à l'honnêteté." ". . . le désir de paraître habile empêche souvent de le devenir, parce qu'on songe plus à paraître aux autres qu'à être effectivement ce qu'il faut être." "Il faut essayer de connaître [l'air] qui nous est naturel, n'en point sortir, et le perfectionner autant qu'il nous est possible. . . . Je ne prétends pas . . . nous renfermer tellement en nous-même que nous n'ayons pas la liberté . . . de joindre à nous des qualités utiles ou nécessaires que la nature ne nous a pas données . . . mais ces qualités acquises doivent avoir un certain rapport et une certaine union avec nos qualités naturelles, qui les étendent et les augmentent imperceptiblement . . . il faut les unir et les mêler ensemble et qu'ils ne paraissent jamais séparés." "Les faux honnêtes gens sont ceux qui déguisent leurs défauts aux autres et à eux-mêmes; les vrais honnêtes gens sont ceux qui les connaissent parfaitement et les confessent." ". . . il y a de certains défauts qui, bien mis en oeuvre, brillent plus que la vertu même."

16. ". . . l'homme finit par ressembler à ce qu'il voudrait être." ". . . singerie n'est pas ressemblance." ". . . plus fort que sa raison, pénétré l'homme tout entier."

17. "Pour exprimer la perfection du genre dans lequel j'ai excellé, je pourrais dire que j'ai joué . . . un rôle tel que Molière aurait pu l'écrire, en étant en même temps auteur et acteur." On the dandy's addiction to masks in the quest for power, see Gautier (211:195); Sue (492:282); Goncourt (225:174–75). "Je suis convaincu que pour certaines âmes il y a le bonheur de l'imposture. Il y a une effroyable, une énivrante félicité dans l'idée qu'on ment et qu'on trompe; dans la pensée qu'on *se* sait *seul soi-même*, et qu'on joue à la société une comédie dont elle est dupe, et dont on se rembourse les frais de mise en scène par toutes les

Notes: 4. Process and Ethics of Production

voluptés du mépris. Les natures *au coeur sur la main* ne se font pas l'idée des jouissances solitaires de l'hypocrisie." On dissimulation, see Gautier (211:196–97); Baudelaire (51:II, 757–58).

18. "Ayez de beaux dehors! . . . cachez l'envers de votre vie. . . . Mettez en dehors votre beauté, vos grâces, votre esprit, votre poésie. . . . Dès lors vous ne serez plus coupable de faire tache sur les décorations de ce grand théâtre appelé le monde." "Il est une sorte d'*idée fixe* que l'on sent pour ainsi dire *battre en soi* à toute heure . . . c'est surtout ce point toujours palpitant qu'il faut peut-être le plus habilement déguiser à la connaissance de chacun . . . car ordinairement là est la faiblesse, la plaie, l'endroit infailliblement vulnérable de notre nature." ". . . une frayeur mortelle de laisser deviner ce qui se passait dans son coeur"; ". . . tuer cette sensibilité si humiliante." ". . . son coeur se refroidit, se contracta, se déssécha." ". . . chose *naturelle*, trop naturelle même . . . pour ne pas scandaliser . . . les régions surnaturelles de la Poésie"; "aspire à l'insensibilité." ". . . un reste de sensibilité par quoi il est inférieur à la Mertueil . . . tout ce qui est humain est calciné." To feel passion is to lose one's status as a work of art: in Barbey's terms, "si on était passionné on serait trop vrai pour être dandy" (38:IX, 310, #16). Because he has utter contempt for emotion, the Sender in dandyism often ridicules the natural self; as Barbey noted of his hero, Robert de Tressignies, "le dandy se moquait de l'homme" (I, 375). Some dandies, among them Samuel Cramer, are so thoroughly imbued with what Baudelaire calls "la faculté comédienne" (51:I, 555) that they verify the physical signs of emotion in the mirror to observe their effect: "Se sentait-il effleuré et chatouillé par la gaieté, il fallait se le bien constater et notre homme s'exerçait à rire aux éclats. Une larme germait-elle dans le coin de l'oeil à quelque souvenir, il allait à sa glace se regarder pleurer" (p. 378).

19. "Il faut être maître de sa parole, du ton de sa voix, de son geste, de son action et de toutes choses. Il y a des gens qui le sont en une chose et qui ne le sont pas en une autre. Il faut l'être en tout." "Si nos passions nous veulent détourner de ce qu'elle nous ordonne, rebutons-les sévèrement." For expressions such as *se concerter* et al., see Méré (340:III, 158); Vaumorières (511:II, 6); Bellegarde (58:25; 60:406). "Soyons donc maîtres de nous-mêmes, et sachons commander à nos propres affections si nous désirons gagner celles d'autrui. Car il ne serait pas juste de prétendre à la conquête des volontés de tant d'honnêtes gens qui sont à la cour si premièrement nous n'avions appris à surmonter notre volonté propre." ". . . être toujours le maître de soi et de ses passions"; "la marque . . . d'un mérite extraordinaire . . . il faut avoir pour cela de la grandeur d'âme, de la fermeté, et des vues au-dessus de celles du peuple." See also Caillières (103:214). La Rochefoucauld is perhaps the only writer to regard self-mastery as a sign of tepid passion rather than heroic force (294:419, #122).

20. "Nous y sentirons d'abord quelque contrainte, mais elle ne sera pas longue." ". . . je me suis rendu en effet presque insensible; mon âme [est] indifférente aux plus fâcheux accidents." For rare examples which stress the difficulties involved in self-mastery, see Faret (188:72); Bellegarde (58:25); La Bruyère (286:182–83, #25). On the honnête homme's superiority to the whims of fortune, see also Méré (340:I, 76; III, 89, 146, 148, 159–60). "Trouvez bon que les délicates nomment plaisir ce que les gens rudes et grossiers ont nommé vice, et ne composez pas votre vertu des vieux sentiments qu'un naturel sauvage avait inspiré aux premiers hommes." ". . . la véritable vertu: . . . elle se montre sans artifice et d'un air simple et naturel, comme celle de Socrate. Mais les faux honnêtes gens aussi bien que les

Notes: 4. Process and Ethics of Production

faux dévots ne cherchent que l'apparence: et je crois que dans la morale Sénèque était un hypocrite et qu'Epicure était un saint.'' This tendency to criticize Seneca and to regard the sage as an unattainable ideal of perfection may reflect the strong Jansenist attack on stoicism. See Spanneut (470:311–17); Pascal (393:146 ff.); Nicole (375:II, 260–88); among secular writers on honnêteté, Balzac (24:I, 433; II, 315–16); La Rochefoucauld (294:490, #589); La Bruyère (186:290–91, #3); Saint-Evremond (439:III, 419–20).

21. ''. . . la réflexion de me voir libre et maître de moi me donne la volupté spirituelle du bon Epicure: j'entends cette agréable indolence qui n'est pas un état sans douleur et sans plaisir; c'est le sentiment délicat d'une joie pure, qui vient du repos de la conscience, et de la tranquillité de l'esprit.'' On the *mondains'* conception of Epicurean pleasure, see also Saint-Evremond (439:III, 426); Méré (339:85–87). Cf. Montaigne (355:I.xx, 80; III.iii, 807; III.v, 799; III.xiii, 1086 ff.). Seneca, whose independent brand of stoicism included several epicurean principles, had emphasized the sobriety of Epicurus' notion of pleasure (e.g., 460:II, 129–31; 183–89). Montaigne also insisted on the similarity between stoic and Epicurean principles (355:I.xx, 91 ff.; I.xxxiii, 216; I.xxxix, 241–42; II.x, 392–93; II.xi, 400); see also Sayce (449:142–67). Of course, this does not diminish the importance of Platonic principles in honnêteté; Sainte-Beuve, in fact, spoke of the collocation of Epicurean and Platonic principles in Méré (441:III, 123). Although Plato tends to regard pleasure as the proper criterion of art, he does speak of the avoidance of pain and the quest for pleasure as teleological principles in *The Laws*, where he defines the good and the just as the most pleasurable of goals (#657–63). ''L'honnêteté . . . n'est à souhaiter que parce qu'elle rend heureux ceux qui l'ont et ceux qui l'approchent.'' ''Les meilleurs esprits des siècles passés demeurent d'accord que c'est en cela principalement que la félicité consiste, et je crois qu'ils en jugent bien.'' See also Méré (340:I, 34, 76; II, 93; III, 79, 99).

22. ''. . . de courir à la piste du bonheur.'' See also Barbey (38:I, 18; IX, 276–77). ''. . . une espèce de culte de soi-même, qui peut survivre à la recherche du bonheur à trouver dans autrui.'' ''Au lieu de faire un prix Monthyon pour la récompense de la vertu, j'aimerais mieux donner, comme Sardanapale, ce grand philosophe que l'on a si mal compris, une forte prime à celui qui inventerait un nouveau plaisir; car la jouissance me paraît le but de la vie, et la seule chose utile au monde.'' See also Sue (489:II, 98–99). ''Nous tous, enfants perdus de cet âge critique/Au bruit sourd du passé qui s'écroule au néant/Dansons gaiement au bord de l'abîme béant.''

23. ''. . . sérénité comparable à celle des héros de la statuaire antique.'' ''. . . le calme antique au sein des agitations modernes.'' ''Si tu savais quel travail c'est de porter cette nonchalance aussi près du coeur que je la porte.'' On the difficulty of wearing the mask, see also Sue (489:I, 238); Balzac (19:IV, 388). ''. . . ces stoïciens de boudoir boivent dans leur masque leur sang qui coule et restent masqués.'' See also Enault (391:185). Most critics, however, tend to dismiss the dandy's pain by calling him a ''stoic of frivolity'' (e.g., 167:443–59). ''. . . mordant mon coeur jusque sur mes lèvres et le ravalant dans ma poitrine quand il allait s'en échapper; buvant mes larmes au dedans, amer breuvage! . . . Mais l'orgueil était la colonne où je m'adossais . . . le poteau auquel *ils* m'avaient lié et qui m'empêcha de fléchir. Comme Jésus, dans la flagellation sanglante, je ne tombai pas sous leurs coups.'' ''Il se regardait, impassible, brûler le coeur, comme Scaevola se regardait brûler la main. Souffrir, pour lui, c'était vivre, c'était remplir sa vocation d'homme. Il aurait eu des chevaux de poste pour fuir la douleur qu'il eût refusé de les monter!''

Notes: 4. Process and Ethics of Production

24. "... une sorte de confrérie dont les règles [sont] ... d'une observation aussi rigoureuse que celle de l'ordre des trappistes." "La règle monastique la plus rigoureuse, l'ordre irrésistible du *Vieux de la Montagne*, qui commandait le suicide à ses disciples enivrés, n'étaient pas plus despotiques ni plus obéis que cette doctrine de l'élégance et de l'originalité, qui impose, elle aussi, à ses ambitieux et humbles sectaires, hommes souvent pleins de fougue, de passion, de courage, d'énergie contenue, la terrible formule: *Perinde ac cadaver!*" According to Persian and Syrian legends, the Old Man of the Mountain drugged his young disciples with hashish (whence their name, *assassins*) and introduced them into paradisiacal gardens which so convinced them of his power to grant them eternal bliss that they committed suicide in his name. "Dandies.... Théorie du sacrifice. Légitimation de la peine de mort. Le sacrifice n'est complet que par le sponte sua de la victime. Un condamné à mort qui, raté par le bourreau, délivré par le peuple, retournerait au bourreau." This quotation, which appears in the 1958 edition of Baudelaire's *Oeuvres* (50), was omitted from the 1975 edition of his *Oeuvres complètes* (51). "Pour que le sacrifice soit parfait, il faut qu'il y ait assentiment et joie de la part de la victime."

25. "Etrange spiritualisme! ... toutes les conditions matérielles compliquées auxquelles [les dandys] se soumettent, depuis la toilette irréprochable de toute heure du jour et de la nuit jusqu'aux tours les plus périlleux du sport, ne sont qu'une gymnastique propre à fortifier la volonté et à discipliner l'âme." The Ignatian exercises represent a way of preparing the soul to rid it of secular *affecciones*, a term usually translated as "attachments," but what they accomplish is, of course, mastery over the self. "Le parti le plus difficile ou le plus gai est toujours celui que je prends, et je ne me reproche pas une bonne action, pourvu qu'elle m'exerce ou m'amuse." "... sans se donner la moindre peine, en suivant tout bêtement l'instinct [du] ... coeur." The concept of *askesis* appears in Plato's *Republic* (VII.536), but takes on more austere implications in the *Timaeus* (#69–71); it recurs among the stoics (Epictetus, above all) and is then appropriated by Christianity and gives rise to the ascetic tradition. See Lalande (292:s.v.; 180:63 ff.). The relevance of the concept of *askesis* for honnêteté has been noted by Bray (164:503) and for dandyism by Sartre (447:22) and Camus (108:72).

26. "Cela serait bien étrange que le corps fût capable d'instruction, et que l'esprit ne le fût point. Quelle apparence, que pour être bien à cheval, l'exercice et les maîtres fissent leur effet sans y manquer, et que pour se rendre honnête homme l'un et l'autre fût [*sic*] inutile et même nuisible?" In Caillières's formulation: "Il faut ... travailler ... à acquérir ... la discipline nécessaire à notre condition et au personnage que chacun de nous se propose de représenter dans le monde" (103:179). "Lorsqu'on veut plaire, on en cherche les moyens. Que si le premier réussit mal, on a recours à un autre, et par une suite de réflexions et à force de se corriger on se rend honnête homme." "... les nuances vont à l'infini et les excellents ouvriers découvrent tant de moyens pour bien faire les choses, qu'ils ne refont que bien peu d'une même manière." "... les meilleurs ouvriers ne sont pas contents de ce qu'ils font ... plus on excelle plus on est modeste"; "... n'est jamais si satisfaite d'elle-même qu'elle ne sente quelque chose au delà de ce qu'elle fait." See also Méré (340:II, 81; III, 115; 339:15, 65; 78:XXIX [1922], 91). Pride is no less pernicious a sin than sloth in the *askesis* of honnêteté: "Il ne faut pas douter que celui qui pourrait ne pas être désagréable, et qui demeure comme il est, ne commette pas un grand péché de paresse" (340:II, 29). For La Rochefoucauld, laziness was the most diabolical of passions because it held the promise of absolute tranquillity (294:496, #630; see also pp. 380–81, #253; p. 439, #266).

Notes: 4. Process and Ethics of Production

27. "... si l'on ne mourait point, on ne laisserait pas d'être honnête homme, et même on y pourrait faire un plus grand progrès." In honnêteté, writes J. de Caillières, "pour y réussir heureusement, il faut commencer de bonne heure, c'est une entreprise haute, longue et difficile qui mérite toute notre application" (106:314). "Quand on a de l'esprit on se corrige aisément ... il ne faut que le vouloir."

28. "Les grands poètes, les philosophes, les prophètes ... par le pur et libre exercice de la volonté parviennent à un état où ils sont à la fois cause et effet, sujet et objet." "Non seulement [Poe] a dépensé des efforts considérables pour soumettre à sa volonté le démon fugitif des minutes heureuses.... Il affirmait ... que celui-là seul est poète, qui est le maître de sa mémoire, le souverain des mots, le registre de ses propres sentiments." "Je dis: mes principes.... Je les ai créés, et je puis dire que je suis mon ouvrage.... *Je me suis travaillée.*" "Il pouvait ce qu'il voulait." See also Barbey (38:IX, 316, #38). "Un autre trait de ressemblance avec Stendhal était sa propension aux formules simples, aux maximes brèves, pour la bonne conduite de la vie. Comme tous les gens d'autant plus épris de méthode que leur tempérament ardent et sensible semble les en détourner davantage, Delacroix aimait à façonner de ces petits catéchismes de morale pratique ... ; maximes saines, fortes, simples et dures, qui servent de cuirasses et de bouclier à celui que la fatalité de son génie jette dans une bataille perpétuelle." "Je me jure à moi-même de prendre désormais les règles suivantes pour règles éternelles de ma vie...."

29. "... il faut autant de travail pour devenir un élégant parfait ou *fashionable* que pour parvenir au premier rang dans les sciences ou dans les arts." "... souffrir courageusement et se fier au travail." "... travailler toute la journée"; "le travail nous fortifie"; "plus on travaille, mieux on travaille et plus on veut travailler." "Je puis travailler sans cesse et sans aucun espoir de récompense.... J'ai connu plusieurs passions, mais ce n'est que dans le travail que je me suis senti parfaitement heureux." "Ces infortunés qui ... ont refusé la rédemption par le travail, demandent à la noire magie les moyens de s'élever, d'un seul coup à l'existence surnaturelle ... tandis que nous, poètes et philosophes, nous avons régénéré notre âme par le travail successif et la contemplation; par l'exercice assidu de la volonté et la noblesse permanente de l'intention, nous avons créé à notre usage un jardin de vraie beauté." See also Gautier (212:25–28), and his own definition of the Parnassian work esthetic in the poem *L'Art:* "Sculpte, lime, cisèle/Que ton rêve flottant/Se scelle/Dans le bloc résistant" (vv. 52–55).

30. "A moins que d'avoir un naturel bien pervers, on se rend aussi honnête homme qu'on veut, quand on a les connaissances nécessaires pour l'être en perfection: car le coeur s'accommode aisément aux choses que la raison lui conseille." "Vous ne sauriez trop étudier, trop méditer." "... on se peut appliquer toute sa vie à cette sorte d'étude et s'y rendre de jour en jour plus accompli." "une science infinie ... une étude infinie où l'on fait incessamment du progrès quand on en prend le bon chemin." On the theme de "l'étude infinie," see also Méré (340:I, 53; II, 23, 27, 49; III, 69, 136, 139, 144; 339:1–2).

31. "... tout ce qui est contre les règles du temps, des moeurs, du sentiment, de l'expression." "... peut extrèmement nuire aux personnes qui veulent plaire et se faire aimer." See also Méré (340:II, 29; III, 70, 139; 339:459, 511–12); Bellegarde (61:467); Furetière (202:s.v. *honnête*). "Il y a bien quelques règles qu'on doit observer, quoique ce ne fussent peut-être pas les meilleurs que d'abord on eût pu choisir ... on ne s'en peut dispenser, parce que le monde s'y trouve accoutumé par un long usage." "... la règle la plus aisée contraint toujours le style, et par conséquent le rend moins libre et moins agréable."

Notes: 4. Process and Ethics of Production

See also Méré (340:III, 84); Saint-Evremond (438:III, 60). Méré maintained that very rare individuals, like Socrates, were "above" the rules of *bienséance* (340:II, 51). "... il est impossible d'en donner des règles bien assurées; car outre qu'elle s'occupe sur des sujets qui changent de moment en moment, elle dépend encore de certaines circonstances, qui ne sont quasi jamais les mêmes."

32. "Ce ne sont pas les règles ni les maximes, ni même les sciences qui font principalement réussir les bons ouvriers et les grands hommes. Ces choses-là peuvent beaucoup servir pour exceller ... mais on peut les avoir et ne rien faire que de fort commun." "... une symétrie dont on ne sait point les règles." "Ce n'est pas que je ne croie qu'il y ait des règles aussi sûres pour plaire que pour démontrer et que qui les saurait parfaitement connaître et pratiquer ne réussit aussi sûrement à se faire aimer. ... Mais j'estime, et c'est peut-être ma faiblesse qui me le fait croire, qu'il est impossible d'y arriver." "... étude, l'une qui ne cherche que l'art et les règles; [l'autre] ... qui n'a pour but que de rencontrer par instinct et par réflexions ce qui doit plaire en tous les sujets particuliers." "... entrer d'abord en des connaissances plus hautes et qui ne trompent jamais." The letter in which Pascal acknowledged his debt to Méré for the distinction between *l'esprit de finesse* and *l'esprit de géométrie* is lost, but the Chevalier's answer clearly suggests its contents: "Vous m'écrivez à cette heure que je vous ... ai tout à fait désabusé [des mathématiques] et que je vous ai découvert des choses que vous n'eussiez jamais vues si vous ne m'eussiez connu." But he is far too grateful, insists Méré, as he chastizes Pascal's inability to free himself from the limited perspectives of *l'esprit de géométrie*: "Il vous reste encore une habitude que vous avez prise en cette science à ne juger de quoi que ce soit que par vos démonstrations qui le plus souvent sont fausses. ... Je vous avertis aussi que vous perdez par là un grand avantage dans le monde, car lorsqu'on a l'esprit vif, et les yeux fins on remarque à la mine et à l'air des personnes qu'on voit quantité de choses qui peuvent beaucoup servir. ... Vos nombres ni ce raisonnement artificiel ne font pas connaître ce que les choses sont, il faut les étudier par une autre voie, mais vous demeurez toujours dans les erreurs où les fausses démonstrations de la géométrie vous ont jeté" (339:111–12). For further comments on Pascal et *l'esprit de géométrie*, see Méré (78:XXIX [1922], 217; XXX [1923], 524–27; XXXII [1925], 73, 443, 452). On Méré's *esprit métaphysique*, see 78:XXIX [1922], 92, 223; XXX [1923], 79, 524; XXXI [1924], 492; XXXII [1925], 448, 452, 455.

33. "... tout d'un coup voir la chose d'un seul regard, et non pas par progrès de raisonnement." See also Pascal (393:576, #512–13); Méré (340:II, 27, 63, 71, 86, 127; 78:XXIX [1922], 86–87; XXX [1923], 522); La Bruyère (286:107, #2). "... il pense des choses délicates et voit les plus imperceptibles." In La Rochefoucauld, as in Pascal and Méré, *la délicatesse* is also associated with *l'esprit de finesse*; see Pascal (393:597, #751); Méré (340:I, 72; II, 51; III, 121; 78:XXXII [1925], 437); Bouhours (79:153–54). "J'ai ... beaucoup de sentiments intérieurs qui me conduisent plus sûrement que ma raison. Ce sont des conseils obscurs de mon instinct, ou d'un esprit familier qui me font sentir le bien et le mal." See also Méré (340:II, 39); Pascal (393:512–13, #110). "... qui sentent les plus fines délicatesses qui se peuvent remarquer dans la bienséance." "On ne saurait trop sentir les agréments et les bienséances ... pour atteindre la plus haute éloquence." "... on a besoin d'une grande justesse de goût et de sentiment." See also Méré (340:I, 73, 96; II, 107; III, 116; 339:21); Borgerhoff (77:183–84).

34. "... préférer son goût aux règles communes quand [il] est assuré de l'avoir bon."

Notes: 4. Process and Ethics of Production

See also Méré (340:I, 55–56; II, 127–29; 339:138–39); Bellegarde (58:9). "Ceux qui ne suivent que leur inclination pour guide ont d'ordinaire le goût mauvais, parce qu'ils ressemblent en quelque manière aux bêtes qui n'agissent que par instinct et par tempérament." "... est l'effet d'une raison droite et éclairée qui prend toujours le bon parti." "... une espèce d'instinct de la droite raison qui l'entraîne avec rapidité." Many other writers on honnêteté describe reason and intuition as syncretic partners, among them La Rochefoucauld in his comments on *le grand esprit*; "Ses lumières n'ont point de bornes.... Il discerne les objets éloignés, comme s'ils étaient présents; il comprend, il imagine les plus grandes choses; il voit et connaît les plus petites ... rien n'échappe à sa pénétration, et elle lui fait toujours découvrir la vérité, au travers des obscurités qui la cachent aux autres" (294:527). The very same synthesis recurs in the notion of *discernement*, a quality so essential that a person who has it "se peut rendre honnête homme sans voir la cour ou le monde" (340:II, 129). Méré traces it to "un esprit de grande étendue," on the one hand, and on the other, associates it with the "sentiment" of *l'esprit de finesse* (pp. 129–30). For an analysis of the complex question of reason/intuition in seventeenth-century esthetics, see Borgerhoff (77:passim). "La délicatesse du goût ... est absolument nécessaire pour connaître la juste valeur des choses, pour en choisir ce qu'on y peut voir de plus excellent, pour les exprimer de la manière qui leur vient le mieux, et pour les mettre dans leur jour, comme il faut qu'elles soient"; "je ne vois rien de si rare ni qu'on doive tant rechercher que d'avoir du goût et de l'avoir fin." "Il y en a qui, par une sorte d'instinct dont ils ignorent la cause ... prennent toujours le bon parti ... tout agit de concert en eux.... Cet accord les fait juger sainement des objets et leur en forme une idée véritable." "... se le peut rendre [le goût] bon à force de regarder les choses qui sont bien"; "s'y être formé le goût sur celui des personnes qui l'ont excellent"; "s'être exercé de bonne heure"; "beaucoup de soins et de réflexions." "... se faire du bon goût comme une science ou comme une habitude."

35. "... une législation aristotélique, un véritable code à la Boileau"; "... ne vit que d'originalité et de naïveté; l'imitation, l'assujettissement aux règles la décolorent, la glacent, la tuent ... c'est spontanément, c'est d'instinct, d'inspiration que se met la cravate. Une cravate bien mise, c'est un de ces traits de génie qui se sentent, s'admirent mais ne s'analysent ni ne s'enseignent pas ... la cravate est romantique dans son essence; du jour où elle subira des règles générales, des principes fixes, elle aura cessé d'exister." See also Barbey (38:IX, 250); Baudelaire (51:II, 578). "... (l'esprit de nos sens, peut-être!) qui nous porte toujours à choisir les choses vraiment belles ou bonnes.... C'est un tact exquis, dont le constant exercice peut seul faire découvrir soudain les rapports, prévoir les conséquences, deviner la place ou la portée des objets, des mots, des idées et des personnes." On *tact*, see also Raisson (415:65–66); Mortemart-Boisse (364:42); on *goût*, see Balzac (22:44; 19:IV, 611–12). "Toutes les inventions humaines découlent d'une observation analytique dans laquelle l'esprit procède avec une incroyable rapidité d'aperçus.... [Le grand homme de science], le grand peintre et le grand musicien sont tous des observateurs.... Mais ces sublimes oiseaux de proie qui, tout en s'élevant à de hautes régions, possèdent le don de voir clair dans les choses d'ici bas ... ont pour ainsi dire, une mission purement métaphysique... Ils sont emportés par le vol audacieux de leur génie, et par leur ardente recherche du vrai, vers les formules les plus simples. Ils observent, jugent et laissent des principes que les hommes minutieux prouvent, expliquent et commentent.... Il faut encore posséder ce coup d'oeil qui fait converger les phénomènes vers un centre, cette logique qui les dispose en

rayons, cette perspicacité qui voit et déduit, cette lenteur qui sert à ne jamais découvrir un des points du cercle sans observer les autres, et cette promptitude qui mène d'un seul bond du pied à la tête."

36. "... le sentiment de l'élégance ... le goût qui sert à donner à la vie une poétique empreinte ... l'éducation, l'habitude." "... l'étude peut conduire un homme riche à porter des bottes et un pantalon aussi bien que nous." "... l'espoir [d'y] parvenir par l'habitude." "... à la fois, une science, un art, une habitude, un sentiment."

37. "Je plains les poètes que guide le seul instinct." As with other Romantic catchwords, Baudelaire redefined inspiration: "L'énergie, l'enthousiasme intellectuel et le pouvoir de tenir ses facultés en éveil" (212:25). "... perçoit tout d'abord ... les rapports intimes et secrets des choses, les correspondances et les analogies." "Elle est l'analyse, elle est la synthèse. ... Elle décompose toute la création, et, avec les matériaux amassés et disposés suivant des règles dont on ne peut trouver l'origine que dans le plus profond de l'âme ... elle produit la sensation du neuf." "La sensibilité de l'imagination ... sait choisir, juger, comparer, fuir ceci, rechercher cela, rapidement, spontanément. C'est de cette sensibilité, qui s'appelle généralement le *Goût*, que nous tirons la puissance d'éviter *le mal* et de chercher *le bien* en matière poétique." "... infailliblement ... veulent raisonner leur art, découvrir les lois obscures en vertu desquelles ils ont produit, et tirer de cette étude une série de préceptes dont le but divin est l'infaillibilité dans la production poétique." "passion ... devenue doctrine." "... la précision et la logique rigoureuse d'un problème mathématique." "[Il] répétait volontiers ... que l'originalité est une chose d'apprentissage, ce qui ne veut pas dire une chose qui peut être transmise par l'enseignement. Le hasard et l'incompréhensible étaient ses deux grands ennemis ... son génie, si ardent et si agile qu'il fût, était passionnément épris d'analyse, de combinaisons et de calculs. ... Les amateurs du délire seront peut-être révoltés par [ses] cyniques maximes; ... Il sera toujours utile ... de faire voir aux gens du monde quel labeur exige cet objet de luxe qu'on nomme poésie."

38. "... consiste pour l'ordinaire en des choses si délicates, qu'encore qu'on les sente, à peine peut-on dire ce que c'est." "... est une de ces choses qui se sentent mieux qu'on ne les fait entendre." "... on le sent mieux qu'on ne le peut exprimer." "... encore quelque chose d'inexplicable qui se connaît mieux à le voir pratiquer qu'à le dire." See also Méré (340:I, 72, 74; II, 17); Courtin (140:3); Rapin (418:184); Fontenelle (195:III, 80).

39. "... ces impressions, ces penchants, ces instincts, ces sentiments, ces parentés"; "en disant tout cela et mille autres choses encore on ne dit rien. ... Ce ne serait plus un je ne sais quoi, si l'on savait ce que c'est; sa nature est d'être incompréhensible et inexplicable." On the relevance of the *je ne sais quoi* (< *nescio quid*) to seventeenth-century art, see Bouhours (79:148); Boileau (72:1); Borgerhoff (77:passim). Since the term is first used during the Renaissance by Italian (and Spanish) estheticians, seventeenth-century writers refer, as early as 1628, to "what the Italians call *le je ne sais quoi*" (77:190). For references to the Italian or Spanish term, see Bouhours (79:202–03); Jacoubet (269:*passim*); Monk (354:138–39). A speech on *le je ne sais quoi* was given at the Académie Française, but it has never been found (see Bouhours, 79:213; Borgerhoff, 77:187–88).

40. "... je ne sais quoi de gai et d'insinuant"; "... je ne sais quel charme secret qu'on ne peut décrire." "... je ne sais quoi de civil et de poli, je ne sais quoi de railleur et de flatteur tout ensemble." "... je ne sais quoi de doux et de tendre qui touche le coeur"; "je ne sais quelle aimable nonchalance"; "de pur et de noble"; "de fin"; "de naif"; "de subtil et relevé;" "de juste et d'insinuant." "... ce je ne sais quoi galant, qui est répandu en toute la

Notes: 4. Process and Ethics of Production

personne qui le possède, soit en son esprit, en ses paroles, en ses actions, ou même en ses habillements est ce qui achève les honnêtes gens et qui les rend aimables et ce qui les fait aimer." "Ainsi, ce qu'on en peut dire de plus raisonnable et de plus certain, c'est que le plus grand mérite ne peut rien sans lui et qu'il n'a besoin que de lui-même pour faire un fort grand effet. On a beau être bien fait, spirituel, enjoué, et tout ce qu'il vous plaira: si le je ne sais quoi manque, toutes ces belles qualités sont comme mortes, elles n'ont rien qui frappe, ni qui touche. Ce sont des hameçons sans amorce et sans appât, des flèches et des traits sans pointe. Mais aussi quelques défauts qu'on ait au corps et en l'esprit, avec ce seul avantage on plaît infailliblement, et on ne fait même rien qui ne plaise. Le je ne sais quoi raccommode tout." See also Méré (340:II, 32); Vaugelas (510:477); Bellegarde (58:12).

41. "... l'indéfinissable, le mystérieux secret de la séduction et des influences." "... [de nous entraîner] dans sa sphère par une puissance inexplicable." "... un air de grandeur, une contenance fière, enfin tout ce qu'on a nommé si justement le je ne sais quoi." "... il tient à l'air, à la démarche, au son de la voix, au lancer du regard, au geste, à une foule de petites choses que les femmes voient et auxquelles elles attachent un certain sens qui nous échappent." On the relation between the je ne sais quoi and nuances, see Bulatkin (44:266 ff.); see also Balzac (21:II, 34; 22:57); Barbey (38:IX, 229); Goncourt (225:171). "... était né pour régner par des facultés très positives, quoique Montesquieu un jour, dépité, les ait appelées le je ne sais quoi, au lieu de montrer ce qu'elles sont. Ce fut par là qu'il prima son époque. ... 'Il fut roi par la grâce de la Grâce.'" See Montesquieu (356:II, 1253–55). Barbey's attitude may reflect the trivialization of the je ne sais quoi from c.1850 onward. See Köhler (281:57–58). The term, for example, plays no part in Baudelaire's esthetics.

42. On this development, see Monk (354) and e.g., Plato's The Laws (#667); Cicero (131:III, 15, 91, 99; IV, 83). Quintilian used the word gratia, rather than venustas, when he referred to Pliny's account of Apelles, the text which was to become the Renaissance topos for the analysis of grace (413:IV, 453). Elsewhere, Quintilian insists that "the meaning of venustus is obvious; it means that which is said with grace and charm [cum gratia et venere]" (II, 447).

43. "La grâce elle-même, cette divine grâce ... qui fait des effets si admirables dans les âmes ... qui triomphe de la dureté du coeur sans blesser la liberté du franc arbitre, qui s'assujettit la nature en s'y accommodant, qui se rend maîtresse de la volonté en la laissant maîtresse d'elle-même, cette grâce, dis-je, qu'est-ce autre chose qu'un je ne sais quoi surnaturel qu'on ne peut ni expliquer ni comprendre. Les Pères de l'Eglise ont tâché de la définir, et ils l'ont appelé une vocation profonde et secrète, une impression de l'esprit de Dieu, une onction divine, une douceur toute puissante, un plaisir victorieux, une sainte concupiscence, une convoitise du vrai bien: c'est-à-dire c'est un je ne sais quoi qui se fait bien sentir, mais qui ne se peut exprimer et dont on ferait bien de se taire." See also Bouhours (79:202); Borgerhoff (77:198–99). Cf. Jansenist grace, that transcendent light (393:274), as incomprehensible as it is real (p. 521, #149), which gives us the sufficient and efficient pouvoir (p. 605, #829) to be born anew—"une seconde naissance" (p. 589, #662)—and achieve the highest spiritual ideal: "Pour faire d'un homme un saint, il faut bien que ce soit la grâce" (p. 613, #869). Leaving aside the question of source, the only notable difference between religious grace and le je ne sais quoi is that the former functions in terms of absence/presence, whereas the latter encompasses a negative and a positive component, as Bouhours explains: "Outre ce que je ne sais quoi qui répare ... tous les défauts naturels ... il y en a un autre qui fait un effet tout contraire, car il détruit, il gâte et il empoisonne, pour

parler ainsi, tout le mérite des personnes où il se rencontre. . . . On s'étonne quelquefois pourquoi un homme ne plaît point, on s'en demande une raison à soi-même, on en trouve mille qui font qu'il devrait plaire, et on n'en trouve pas une pourquoi il déplaît, sinon je ne sais quoi de choquant, qui fait dire, malgré qu'on en ait: Il est bien fait, il a bonne mine, il a de l'esprit, mais il a je ne sais quoi qui me déplaît. Il semble à quelques-uns que cela se dit par délicatesse ou par caprice, que ce n'est qu'un faux prétexte; cependant c'est une bonne et solide raison, mais cachée, mais inconnue à la philosophie" (70:205–06). For instances of the negative *je ne sais quoi*, see Balzac (24:II, 523); Méré (340:I, 23, 29, 109–10; II, 16, 53, 124; 339:9–10); La Rochefoucauld (294:388–89); Bellegarde (61:preface; 63:477).

44. ". . . la magie du je ne sais quoi, la toute puissance du je ne sais quoi." ". . . on voit parmi elles des nains, des bégués et des bossus; mais le nain du grand monde a bon air, le bégué énonce galamment, le bossu porte noblement sa bosse . . . l'ignorant lui-même décoche l'anachronisme en homme de bonne compagnie et l'imbécile se dandine avec grace, cherche ses mots et s'arrête court en parfait gentilhomme. Tel est le prestige du . . . je ne sais quoi masculin." ". . . ni gracieux ni déplaisant, vous ne citerez jamais de lui un mot inconvenant, et il ne lui échappe aucun geste de mauvais ton." "tout est gracieux, frais, recherché, poétique même . . . séduit sans plaire." ". . . Aussi l'aimerez-vous irrésistiblement. Vous [le] prenez pour type et lui vouez un culte."

45. ". . . en littérature comme en théologie les oeuvres ne sont rien sans la Grâce." ". . . le chef d'oeuvre d'un excellent naturel et d'un art consommé." See also Méré (340:I, 111; 339:502); Bellegarde (61:84–85). ". . . la souveraine perfection." See also J. de Caillières (106:313); F. de Caillières (103:252); Méré (340:I, 32; II, 65–66; III, 70; 339:405, 502); de Pure (410:I, 66). The same compound applies to art (see Borgerhoff, 77:183–84; Bray, 85:92). "Qu'il perfectionne sans cesse ses dons naturels, qu'il les aiguise avec soin, qu'il en tire des effets nouveaux, qu'il pousse lui-même sa nature à outrance, cela . . . est justement la marque principale du génie." ". . . une collection de règles réclamées par l'organisation même de l'être spirituel"; ". . . aiguiser sans cesse son génie de praticien." On the development from *génie* to *homme de génie*, see Smith (466:66–134). Although the term *homme de génie* is applied to innovative and creative beings in a wide variety of fields (e.g., Julien Sorel [487:I, 303, 308, 516]), the dandy generally assumes the characteristics of the poetic genius. For Saint-Rémy, in Sue's *Mystères de Paris*, there is no forsaking the ideal of dandyism to which he has sacrificed everything: "Autant dire au poète qui s'épuise, et dont le génie dévore sa santé: Arrêtez-vous au milieu de l'inspiration qui vous emporte" (492:562–63).

46. See Cicero (133:465); Quintilian (413:III, 185–187; IV, 495, 499).

47. "On ne se fait pas Brummell. On l'est ou on ne l'est pas. . . . Brummell a son droit divin et sa raison d'être comme les autres rois . . . [il] était une individualité des plus rares, qui s'était donné uniquement *la peine de naître*." "Une des premières impressions du futur Dandy fut donc de sentir le souffle de ces hommes forts et charmants sur sa tête. Ils furent comme les Fées qui le douèrent; mais ils ne lui donnèrent que la moitié de leurs forces, les plus éphémères de leurs facultés. Nul doute qu'en voyant, qu'en entendant ces esprits . . . le jeune Brummell n'ait développé les facultés qui étaient en lui." ". . . créatures d'élection"; "la faculté de Dandysme"; "dons célestes que le travail . . . ne peu[t] conférer." ". . . la grâce, le don gratuit." As Baudelaire also wrote of Alfred de Musset: "Je n'ai jamais pu souffrir *ce maître des gandins*, son impudence d'enfant gâté qui invoque le ciel et l'enfer pour des aventures de table d'hôte, son torrent bourbeux de fautes de grammaire et de

prosodie, enfin son impuissance totale à comprendre le travail par lequel une rêverie devient un objet d'art" (49:II, 38). "Etrange spiritualisme . . . pour ceux qui en sont à la fois les prêtres et les victimes." Baudelaire urged poets to pray to Poe as an intercessor, advice he himself apparently followed (51:I, 673; see also II, 287–88). On Baudelaire's identification with Poe's martyrdom, see 49:I, 195.

48. "L'art est la religion, le spiritualisme moderne." ". . . une lumière extraordinaire de l'âme par laquelle Dieu semble l'attirer à soi." ". . . quelque chose de divin, ou quelque génie particulier"; "[cette] espèce de génie [qui] a bien de la grâce." "Cette première disposition . . . nous vient quand nous venons au monde, c'est un présent du Ciel, c'est une lumière naturelle, qui ne se peut acquérir." ". . . la même voie." In the preface to the posthumous essays, Nadal contended that Méré became religious at the end of his life and withdrew from the world "en philosophe chrétien" (340:III, 68). It is difficult to accept Nadal's claims, although in one letter Méré does admit to no longer being "as unreligious as I used to be" (339:375). It is in the posthumous essays that Méré mentions the worship of God for the first and only time in his works (340:III, 101).

49. ". . . le meilleur moyen, et peut-être le seul pour se sauver c'est de lui plaire." "C'est un péché que de déplaire quand on s'en peut empêcher . . . et le scandale que le Sauveur défend sous des peines si rigoureuses, qu'a-t-il de mauvais que de déplaire ou d'apporter de l'ennui?" "Quand je pense que le Seigneur aime celui-ci et qu'il hait celui-là sans qu'on sache pourquoi, je n'en trouve point d'autre raison qu'un fonds d'agréments qu'il voit dans l'un et qu'il ne trouve pas dans l'autre." ". . . aimait tout ce qui se faisait de bonne grâce, commes ces excellents parfums qui furent répandus sur lui." "Il ne faut qu'un honnête homme pour inspirer les bonnes mœurs au plus méchant peuple de la terre, et pour donner envie à tous ceux d'une cour sauvage et grossière d'être honnêtes gens." ". . . nous peut rendre heureux en cette vie et dans l'autre."

50. Cf. Barbey's remark that Pascal was "un dandy comme on peut l'être en France" (38:IX, 218). Even after his purported conversion to Catholicism (XIV, 212, 284, 288–89, 300–01), which some contemporaries questioned (301:IV, 46–48), Barbey continued to depict priests as dandies in his novels, *L'Ensorcelé* (1855) and *Un Prêtre marié* (1860). Of course, the largest number of dandies in Barbey's work appears in the anti-Christian collection of tales he called *Les Diaboliques* (1874).

51. "Il avait fait préparer une haute salle destinée à la réception de ses fournisseurs; ils entraient, s'asseyaient les uns à côté des autres, dans des stalles d'église, et alors il montait dans une chaire magistrale et prêchait le sermon du dandysme, adjurant ses bottiers et ses tailleurs de se conformer, de la façon la plus absolue, à ses brefs en matière de coupe, les menaçant d'une excommunication pécuniaire s'ils ne suivaient pas, à la lettre, les instructions contenues dans ses monitoires et ses bulles." In the same vein, Baudelaire envisioned himself a warring Renaissance Pope (447:156). "En vérité, je n'avais pas tout à fait tort de considérer le dandysme comme une espèce de religion."

AFTERWORD

1. "Il n'existe que trois êtres respectables: le prêtre, le guerrier, le poète."

2. The seventeenth-century Lauzun should not be confused with his eighteenth-century descendant (1749–1793), the celebrated soldier and Don Juan whose memoirs were

Notes: Afterword

published in 1821. To avoid confusion, I have simply eliminated from consideration those nineteenth-century comments that do not specifically designate the seventeenth-century Lauzun. For examples of this ambiguity, see Raisson (415:191–92), Ancelot (8:584–85), Barbey (38:XI, 36–37).

3. "Je ne fais rien contre ma conscience ni contre ma gloire. C'est un parfaitement honnête homme." ". . . [je supplie] Votre Majesté . . . de me laisser marier avec le plus honnête homme de son royaume." Sévigné suggests the nobility's reaction to Montpensier's decision as she announces it to M. de Coulanges: "Je m'en vais vous mander la chose la plus étonnante, la plus surprenante, la plus merveilleuse, la plus miraculeuse, la plus triomphante, la plus étourdissante, la plus inouïe, la plus singulière, la plus extraordinaire, la plus incroyable, la plus imprévue . . . la plus brillante, la plus digne d'envie" (461:I, 181). "Je lui dis qu'il était tout comme le jardin d'Enghien, qu'il enchantait les gens toutes les fois qu'on le regardait, qu'on ne pouvait ni en imiter la beauté, ni la connaître." On Lauzun's attire and accoutrements, see 358:XLIII, 103, 160–61, 174; on his *air*, pp. 102–03, 125, 163. ". . . ce qui aurait paru une entreprise dans un autre devint pour lui une action naturelle." ". . . il y avait des moments que je trouvais que son mérite était au-dessus de tout ce que je voulais faire pour lui; que je pouvais me persuader cela avec plus de vérité que toute la France le croyait ainsi, tant il s'était acquis une réputation d'être singulier en tout." On Louis XIV's praise of Lauzun see 358:XLIII, 166, 290. Saint-Simon insists on the veracity of Montpensier's portrait of Lauzun (39:265).

4. "Il a dit de soi: *J'ai de l'esprit, j'ai du courage* et tous ont dit après lui: *Il a de l'esprit, il a du courage.*" "Le joli, l'aimable, le rare, le merveilleux, l'héroïque ont été employés à son éloge; et tout le contraire a servi depuis pour le ravaler: caractère équivoque, mêlé, enveloppé; une énigme, une question presque indécise." On Lauzun's negative characteristics, see Sévigné (461:I, 451); Bussy-Rabutin (99:II, 276–77); La Rochefoucauld (294:536); Choisy (128:II, 218, 222–23); Primi-Visconti (409:14); La Fare (288:LXV, 180); Saint-Simon (440:VII, 353). "Il veut, comme un autre César, forcer le destin, faisant même voir par-là, comme fit ce grand Empereur, que son grand coeur n'est pas moins disposé à résister hardiment à toutes les attaques de la mauvaise fortune, qu'à recevoir agréablement le fruit d'un heureux succès." On Lauzun's *hubris*, see Choisy (128:II, 220); La Fare (288:LXV, 181); La Rochefoucauld (294:537–38); Saint-Simon (440:VII, 367). "Rien ne lui échappait pour faire sa cour, avec un fond de bassesse et un extérieur de dignité."

5. On Lauzun as extraordinary, see Montpensier (358:XLII, 515; XLIII, 101–02, 104, 126, 147, 188, 274); Sévigné (461:III, 364); La Rochefoucauld (294:533); Saint-Simon (440:VII, 352, 367). "Polyecute a du nom, et sort du sang des rois." ". . . le juste sujet d'une tragédie dans toutes les règles du théâtre." ". . . le second tome de M. de Lauzun est fort beau et digne du premier." "Voilà un beau sujet de roman ou de tragédie, mais surtout un beau sujet de raisonner et de parler éternellement." On Lauzun's life as art, see also La Bruyère (286:245, #96); Saint-Simon (440:I, 230).

6. "Les gens qui ont assisté à ces singuliers évenements n'ont point compris ce que la conduite de Lauzun avait d'extraordinaire et de beau." ". . . le plus grand artiste en séduction qu'on ait jamais vu. . . . Il ne fallut rien moins que la volonté de Louis XIV pour renverser ce chef d'oeuvre." ". . . il savait également s'ouvrir les coeurs par ses manières aimables ou écraser un ennemi sous un monceau de ridicules." ". . . s'attachait . . . avec des clous ce coeur envoûté par lui." ". . . l'écaille de tortue en hypocrisie, dans laquelle il s'est enfermé."

Notes: Afterword

7. "Il avait . . . le plus terrible égoïsme qui ait existé depuis l'égoïsme romain. . . . Il eut la vanité impitoyable, la vanité tigre du Dandy." See also Beauvoir (57:II, 240). "Au lieu d'être un Caumont, je voudrais être né dans quelque grenier afin que les historiens à venir, parlant de ce règne, fissent un chapitre ainsi intitulé: Un homme sorti de la dernière classe du peuple et s'éleva par son habileté seule au point d'entrer dans la famille royale." ". . . qui ne porte point l'empreinte de [nos] semelles . . . la cime de cette montagne où nous cheminons est à peine visible." "N'avons-nous pas mis en usage . . . des calculs mille fois plus profonds que ceux par lesquels on gouverne un royaume?" On Lauzun's marriage as fact, see Musset (370:I, 168); Beauvoir (57:II, 8 ff.); Sue (491:97); Dumas (171:1011); Barbey (38:IX, 304). "Il faut absolument que je sois enfermé pour quelques semaines, puis j'en sortirai plus radieux que le Christ dans la nuit de Pâques." "Vingt fois la mort s'élança sur lui en allongeant les griffes jusque dans les plus beaux de ses vêtements; mais toujours elle se retira saisie de respect au moment d'entamer la chair de ses membres, comme Madeleine qui referma ses bras . . . quand le Seigneur lui dit: *Noli me tangere*. Il était écrit que cet homme épuiserait toutes les phases possibles d'une destinée humaine."

8. "Personne n'a tiré d'une destinée plus qu'il a fait . . . rien ne lui a échappé." "Il paraissait avoir une organisation semblable à celle de Lauzun. Sa jolie figure, son esprit railleur, son ambition, son habileté à manier les gens en les flattant, lui donnait avec le favori du roi plus d'un point de ressemblance, et cependant il lui manquait je ne sais quoi de grand qui éleva toujours Lauzun dans une région qu'il ne pouvait atteindre. . . . Il y avait entre eux la même différence qu'entre deux fruits du même arbre exactement pareils à l'oeil, dont l'un contient un suc délicieux tandis que l'autre n'a qu'une fade saveur." On Vardes as an honnête homme, see e.g., Choisy (128:II, 48–49); La Fare (288:LXV, 158–61); Saint-Evremond (438:III, 247).

9. ". . . une institution . . . très ancienne, puisque César, Cataline, Alcibiade nous en fournissent des types éclatants; très générale puisque Chateaubriand l'a trouvée dans les forêts et au bord des lacs du Nouveau Monde." On Baudelaire's dandyistic vision of Caesar, see Kempf (280:137–43); on Alcibiades (51:1059, 1260). Baudelaire planned to write a text on Chateaubriand, as the father and head of the nineteenth-century dandyistic clan (49:III, 212, 245, 274; V, 59). The numerous references to Alcibiades as a dandy in the nineteenth-century corpus include Balzac (21:II, 54); Chapus (121:112); Sue (491:25; 492:545); Gautier (213:299, 301); Barbey (38:I, 89; IX, 278; 142:88). In *Histoire d'Alcibiade et la république d'Athènes* (1873), Arsène Houssaye depicted Alcibiades as the Greek Don Juan, whose life was spent in orgies and debauchery (261:I, 110, 216, 218). ". . . [il] me paraît le plus grand homme du monde, et ce qui m'en plaît davantage, j'ai de la peine à imaginer un plus honnête homme." ". . . je ne sais quoi de brillant, qui le distinguait en quelque lieu qu'il fût." ". . . le faisait toujours souhaiter parmi les plus honnêtes gens et les plus belles femmes de ce temps." On Caesar, see *supra*, chapter 2, pp. 65–66. On Alcibiades, compare the ambivalent portrait in Plutarch's *Lives* (the Amyot translation, 1559 [402:I, 419–64]) and in Nepos' *De viris illustribus* (373:37–39) with the entirely favorable image of a model orator that appears in Cicero (131:III, 267) and Quintilian (413:III, 275), and of the exemplary aristocrat that can be found in Castiglione (113:38). Montaigne, who determined the *mondains*' view of Alcibiades, tried to counter the criticism usually directed at the controversial Athenian general (355:III.iv, 842; III.xiii, 1048, 1086). On Alcibiades as the incarnation of the *galant homme*, see Méré (340:III, 140) and Saint-Evremond (438:III, 276). On Alcibiades' protean suppleness, see Montaigne (355:I.xxvi, 166–67); and in the

seventeenth century, Refuge (421:127–28); Faret (188:70); Marmet (329:263). "... la parfaite honnêteté est toujours la même en tous les sujets où elle se trouve quoique la différence
du temps et de la fortune la fasse paraître bien différemment." "Les grâces d'un siècle sont
celles de tous les temps." "... ses manières sont de toutes les cours depuis un bout de la terre
jusqu'à l'autre, encore ne sont-elles pas plus des cours que des déserts. Le changement des
lieux, la révolution du temps, ni la différence des coutumes, ne leur ôtent presque rien."

10. "De dandy comme Brummell on n'en verra plus, mais des hommes comme lui ...
quelque livrée que le monde leur mette, on peut affirmer qu'il y en aura toujours." "Il n'est
pas une chose de société, mais de nature humaine." "... a sa racine dans la nature humaine
de tous les pays et de tous les temps, puisque la vanité est universelle." "... le gouffre lumi-
neux où il admire sa face de Narcisse." Aside from the basic Freudian text *On Narcissism*
(1914) (199:XIV, 73–102), see *Totem and Taboo*, where narcissism is interpreted as a
megalomanic belief in the "omnipotence of thought" and "the magic of art" (XIII, 90). See
also the study of Leonardo (XI, 63–137).

SELECTED
BIBLIOGRAPHY

1. Accetto, Torquato. *Della dissimulazione oneste*. Bari: G. Laterza e figli, 1928.
2. Alméras, Henri d'. *La Vie parisienne sous la Restauration*. Paris: Albin Michel, 1910.
3. —— *La Vie parisienne sous le Consulat et l'Empire*. Paris: Albin Michel, 1909.
4. —— *La Vie parisienne sous le règne de Louis-Philippe*. Paris: Albin Michel, 1911.
5. Alter, Jean V. *Les Origines de la satire anti-bourgeoise en France*. Geneva: Droz, 1966.
6. Amiguet, Philippe. *La Grande Mademoiselle et son siècle d'après ses mémoires*. Paris: Albin Michel, 1957.
7. Amossy, Ruth and Elisheva Rosen. "La Configuration du dandy dans 'Eugénie Grandet.'" *L'Année Balzacienne*. Paris: Garnier, 1975.
8. Ancelot, Jacques. "L'Homme du monde." *Oeuvres complètes*. Paris: Adolphe Delahays, 1855, pp. 579–672.
9. —— *Le Dandy*. Paris: Dondey-Dupré, 1832.
10. Ariste, Paul d'. *La Vie et le monde du boulevard; Un Dandy: Nestor Roqueplan*. Paris: Jules Tallandier, 1930.
11. Arnauld, A. V. "Les Dandys." *Revue de Paris* (March 1833): 262.
12. Ascoli, Georges. *La Grande Bretagne devant l'opinion française au XVIIe siècle*. 2 vols. Paris: Librairie Universitaire J. Gamber, 1930.
13. Atkinson, Nora. *Eugène Sue et le roman feuilleton*. New York: Meridian Books, 1956.
14. Aubignac, François Hédelin, Abbé d'. *Nouvelle histoire du temps ou la relation véritable du royaume de la coquetterie*. Paris: Marin le Ché, 1655.
15. —— *La Pratique du théâtre*. Munich: Wilhelm Fink, 1971.
16. Auerbach, Erich. *Mimesis*. New York: Anchor Books, 1957.
17. —— *Scenes from the Drama of European Literature*. New York: Meridian Books, 1959.

Selected Bibliography

18. Baird, A. W. S. "The 'Honnête Homme' and the Aesthetics in the *Pensées.*" *AUMLA* 28 (November 1967): 203–14.
19. Balzac, Honoré de. *La Comédie humaine.* 11 vols. Bibliothèque de la Pléiade. Paris: Gallimard, 1966.
20. —— *Lettres à l'étrangère.* 4 vols. Paris: Calmann-Levy, 1924–33.
21. —— *Oeuvres diverses.* 3 vols. Paris: Louis Conard, 1935.
22. —— *Traité de la vie élégante; La théorie de la démarche.* Paris: Bossard, 1922.
23. Balzac, Jean Louis Guez de. *Aristippe ou De la cour.* Paris: Augustin Courbé, 1658.
24. —— *Les Entretiens.* 2 vols. B. Beugnot, ed. Paris: Marcel Didier, 1972.
25. —— *Les Lettres diverses.* 2 vols. Paris: Louis Billaine, 1664.
26. —— *Lettres.* Paris: Imprimerie Nationale, 1873.
27. —— *Lettres choisies.* 2 vols. Paris: Augustin Courbé, 1647.
28. —— *Oeuvres.* 2 vols. Paris: T. Jolly, 1665.
29. Banville, Théodore de. *Mes Souvenirs.* Paris: G. Charpentier, 1882.
30. Barante, Amable Guillaume de. *Etudes littéraires et historiques.* Paris: Didier, 1857.
31. Barbey d'Aurevilly, Jules-Amédée. "Dandysme et critique." *La Sylphide.* 6th year, 2d ser., vol. 2 (1845): 119–22, 158–62, 167–70, 182–85, 198–200.
32. —— [Maximilienne de Syrène]. "De l'élégance." *Moniteur de la mode* 1 (April 20, 1843): 13–15; (April 30, 1843): 19–21.
33. —— *Disjecta membra.* 2 vols. Paris: La Connaissance, 1925.
34. —— *Le XIXe siècle.* Vol. 1. Paris: Mercure de France, 1964.
35. —— *L'Esprit de J. Barbey d'Aurevilly: Dictionnaire de pensées, portraits, jugements tirés de son oeuvre critique.* Paris: Société du Mercure de France, 1908.
36. —— "Les Lions d'autrefois," *La Mode* (July 4, 1840), p. 1.
37. —— [Maximilienne de Syrène]. "La Mode." *Le Constitutionnel* 244 (September 1, 1845): 3; 286 (October 15, 1845): 3; 314 (November 10, 1845): 3; 362 (December 28, 1845): 2; 21 (January 21, 1846): 2; 51 (February 25, 1846): 2.
38. —— *Les Oeuvres complètes.* 17 vols. Paris: François Bernouard, 1926–27.
39. Barine, Arvède. *Louis XIV et La Grande Mademoiselle.* Paris: Librairie Hachette, 1923.
40. Barthes, Roland. "Le Bleu est à la mode cette année." *Revue française de sociologie* 1 (1960): 147–62.
41. —— *Le Degré zéro de l'écriture; Eléments de sémiologie.* Paris: Seuil, 1964.
42. —— *Essais critiques.* Paris: Seuil, 1964.
43. —— "Langage et vêtement." *Critique* 142 (March 1959): 242–52.
44. —— "Pour une psycho-sociologie de l'alimentation contemporaine." *Annales* 5 (September–October 1961): 977–86.
45. —— "Rhétorique de l'image." *Communications* 4 (1964): 40–52.
46. —— *Système de la mode.* Paris: Seuil, 1967.

Selected Bibliography

47. Bary, René. *Journal de conversation, où les plus belles matières sont agitées de part et d'autre*. Paris: J. Couterot, 1673.
48. —— *L'Esprit de cour, ou les conversations galantes*. Paris: Charles de Sercy, 1662.
49. Baudelaire, Charles. *Correspondance générale*. Jacques Crépet, ed. 6 vols. Paris: Louis Conard, 1947–53.
50. —— *Oeuvres*. Bibliothèque de la Pléiade. Paris: Gallimard, 1958.
51. —— *Oeuvres complètes*. 2 vols. Bibliothèque de la Pléiade. Paris: Gallimard, 1975.
52. Bayard, Jean-François-Alfred, and Gustave de Wailly. *Anglais et français*. Paris: J.-N. Barba, 1827.
53. Beauvoir, Roger de. *Aventurières et courtisanes; Histoire de la mode; De la comédie de société; Contes de Saint-Germain; Les Caravanes d'Anarchasis le dandy*. Paris: Michel Lévy, 1857.
54. —— *Le Chevalier Saint-Georges*. Paris: Michel Lévy, 1857.
55. —— "David Dick." *Revue de Paris* 6 (June 1834): 273–92.
56. —— *Histoires cavalières*. Paris: Michel Lévy, 1857.
57. —— *Les Mystères de l'île Saint-Louis*. 2 vols. Paris: Librairie Nouvelle, 1859.
58. Bellegarde, Morvan de. *Lettres curieuses de littérature et de morale*. Amsterdam: Henri Schelte, 1707.
59. —— *Modèles de conversations pour les personnes polies*. Paris: Jean Guignard, 1697.
60. —— *Oeuvres diverses*. 2 vols. Paris: Claude Robustel, 1723.
61. —— *Réflexions sur ce qui peut plaire ou déplaire dans le commerce du monde*. Paris: Arnoul Seneuze, 1688.
62. —— *Réflexions sur l'élégance et la politesse du style*. Paris: A. Pralard, 1700.
63. —— *Réflexions sur le ridicule et sur les moyens de l'éviter*. Paris: Jean Guignard, 1699.
64. Benay, Jacques. "L'Honnête Homme devant la nature ou la philosophie du Chevalier de Méré." *PMLA* 79, no. 1 (March 1964): 22–23.
65. Bénichou, Paul, "Jeunes-France et Bousingots." *Revue d'histoire littéraire de la France* 71 (1971): 439–62.
66. —— *Morales du grand siècle*. Paris: Gallimard, 1948.
67. Benveniste, Emile. "Le jeu comme structure," *Deucalion* (1947): 161–67.
68. —— *Problèmes de linguistique générale*. 2 vols. Paris: Gallimard, 1966, 1974.
69. —— "La Sémiologie de la langue." *Semiotica* 1–2 (1969): 1–12, 127–35.
70. Béroul, Pierre. "Les Anglais de Balzac." *Revue des sciences humaines* 57 (January–July 1950): 70–93.
71. Boase, Alan M. *The Fortunes of Montaigne*. London: Methuen, 1935.
72. Boileau-Despréaux, Nicolas. *Oeuvres complètes*. Bibliothèque de la Pléiade. Paris: Gallimard, 1966.

Selected Bibliography

73. Bonnaffé, Edouard. *Dictionnaire des anglicismes.* Paris: Librairie Delagrave, 1920.
74. Boon, Jean-Pierre. "L'Idéal de 'l'honneste homme' est-il compatible avec la théorie évolutive des 'Essais' de Montaigne?" *PMLA* 83 (1968): 298–304.
75. —— *Montaigne gentilhomme et essayiste.* Paris: Editions Universitaires, 1974.
76. Borel, Petrus. *Oeuvres complètes.* Vol. 3: *Champavert, contes immoraux.* Paris: La Force Française, 1922.
77. Borgerhoff, E. B. O. *The Freedom of French Classicism.* Princeton, N.J.: Princeton University Press, 1950.
78. Boudhors, Charles H. "Divers propos du Chevalier de Méré en 1674–1675." *Revue d'histoire littéraire de la France* 29 (1922): 76–98, 214–24; 30 (1923): 79–89, 380–83, 520–29; 31 (1924): 490–96; 32 (1925): 68–78, 432–56, 596–601.
79. Bouhours, Dominique [le père Bouhours]. *Entretiens d'Ariste et d'Eugène.* Paris: Bossard, 1920.
80. —— *La Manière de bien penser.* Paris: Libraires associés, 1771.
81. —— *Pensées ingénieuses des anciens et des modernes.* Paris: Michel Brunet, 1707.
82. Boulenger, Jacques. *Sous Louis-Philippe, les dandys.* Paris: Calmann-Lévy, 1932.
83. Bouvier, René. *Le Courtisan, l'honnête homme, le héros, pour présenter "Le Héros" de Baltasar Gracian.* Zdislas Milner, trans. Paris: André Tournon, 1937.
84. Boyancé, Pierre. *Epicure.* Paris: Presses Universitaires de France, 1969.
85. Bray, René. *La Formation de la doctrine classique en France.* Paris: Université de Paris, 1927.
86. —— *La Préciosité et les précieux.* Paris: Albin Michel, 1948.
87. Brody, Jules. *Boileau and Longinus.* Geneva: Droz, 1958.
88. —— "Platonisme et classicisme." *Saggi e ricerche di letteratura francese.* Vol. 2. Milan: Feltrinelli, 1961.
89. —— "*La Princesse de Clèves* and the Myth of Courtly Love." *University of Toronto Quarterly* 38, no. 2 (January 1969), 105–35.
90. ——, ed. *From Humanism to Classicism: Essays by His Former Students in Memory of Nathan Edelman. L'Esprit créateur* 15, nos. 1–2 (Spring–Summer 1975).
91. Brooks, Peter. *The Novel of Worldliness: Crébillon, Marivaux, Laclos, Stendhal.* Princeton, N.J.: Princeton University Press, 1969.
92. Brunot, Ferdinand. *Histoire de la langue française des origines à nos jours.* Vols. 3, 4, 12, 13. Paris: Armand Colin, 1966–67.
93. Buffram, Imbrie. *Studies in the Baroque from Montaigne to Rotrou.* New Haven, Conn.: Yale University Press, 1957.
94. Bulatkin, Eleanor W. "The French Word *Nuance.*" *PMLA* 70 (1955): 244–73.
95. Bulwer-Lytton, Sir Edward. *Pelham or Adventures of a Gentleman.* Philadelphia: J. B. Lippincott, 1877.

Selected Bibliography

96. Burckhardt, Carl J. "Der honnête homme." *Deutsche Geist*. Vol. 2. Munich: Suhrkamp Verlag, pp. 938–56.

97. Burckhardt, Jacob. *The Civilization of the Renaissance in Italy*. London: P. Landon, 1951.

98. Bussy-Rabutin, Roger de Rabutin, Comte de Bussy. *Carte géographique de la cour et autres galanteries*. Cologne: Pierre Marteau, 1668.

99. —— *Histoire amoureuse des Gaules*. Paul Boiteau, ed. 4 vols. Paris: P. Jannet, 1857.

100. —— *Lettres*. 2 vols. Paris: Delaulne, 1697.

101. Byron, George Gordon, Lord. *Letters and Journal of Lord Byron, with Notes of his Life*. Thomas Moore, ed. 2 vols. New York: Harper, 1830.

102. —— *The Poetical Works of Lord Byron*. New York: Oxford University Press, 1946.

103. Caillières, François de. *De la science du monde et des connaissances utiles à la conduite de la vie*. Paris: Etienne Ganeau, 1717.

104. —— *Des mots à la mode et des nouvelles façons de parler*. Paris: Claude Barbin, 1692.

105. —— *Du bel esprit*. Paris: J. Anisson, 1695.

106. Caillières, Jacques de. *La Fortune des gens de qualité et des gentilshommes particuliers*. Paris: Estienne Loyson, 1661.

107. Caillois, Roger. *Les Jeux et les hommes*. Paris: Gallimard, 1958.

108. Camus, Albert. *L'Homme révolté*. Paris: Gallimard, 1951.

109. Carassus, Emilien. *Le Mythe du dandy*. Paris: Armand Colin, 1971.

110. *Le Snobisme et les lettres françaises de Paul Bourget à Marcel Proust*. Paris: Armand Colin, 1966.

111. Carter, Alfred E. *The Idea of Decadence in French Literature, 1830–1900*. Toronto: University of Toronto Press, 1958.

112. Cassagne, Albert. *La Théorie de l'art pour l'art en France*. Paris: Dorbon, 1959.

113. Castiglione, Baldesar. *The Book of the Courtier*. Charles S. Singleton, trans. New York: Anchor Books, 1959.

114. —— *Il Cortegiano*. Edited by Vittorio Cian. Florence: G. C. Sansoni, 1916.

115. Catel, Maurice. *Les Ecrivains de Port-Royal*. Paris: Mercure de France, 1962.

116. Chabrol, Claude, ed. *Sémiotique narrative et textuelle*. Paris: Larousse, 1973.

117. Chalesme, de. *L'Homme de qualité*. Amsterdam: Pierre Le Grand, 1671.

118. Chamaillard, Edmond. *Le Chevalier de Méré*. 2 vols. Paris: Niort G. Clouzot, 1921.

119. Chapelain, Jean. *De la lecture des vieux romans*. Paris: Auguste Aubry, 1870.

120. —— *Lettres*. Ph. Tamizey de Larroque, ed. 2 vols. Paris: Imprimerie Nationale, 1880.

121. Chapus, Eugène. *Manuel de l'homme et de la femme comme il faut*. Paris: George Decaux, 1862.

122. —— *Théorie de l'élégance*. Paris: Comptoir des Imprimeurs-Unis, 1844.

283

Selected Bibliography

123. Chasles, Philarète. "Mémoires de Lord Byron." *Journal des débats* (April 11, 1830): 3.
124. Chateaubriand, Vicomte François-René de. *Génie du christianisme.* 2 vols. Paris: Garnier-Flammarion, 1966.
125. —— *Mélanges politiques et littéraires.* Paris: Fermin Didot Frères, 1850.
126. —— *Mémoires d'outre-tombe.* 2 vols. Bibliothèque de la Pléiade. Paris: Gallimard, 1958.
127. Chinard, Gilbert. *En lisant Pascal.* Lille: Giard, 1948.
128. Choisy, François-Timoléon, Abbé de. *Mémoires.* 2 vols. Paris: Librairie de Bibliophiles, 1887.
129. Chomsky, Noam. *Cartesian Linguistics.* New York: Harper & Row, 1966.
130. Cicero, Marcus Tullius. *De officiis.* Walter Miller, trans. Loeb Classical Library. Cambridge, Mass.: Harvard University Press, 1951.
131. —— *De oratore.* Vols. 3–4. E. W. Sutton and H. Rackham, trans. Loeb Classical Library. Cambridge, Mass.: Harvard University Press, 1967–68.
132. —— *De finibus bonorum et malorum.* H. Rackham, trans. Loeb Classical Library. Cambridge, Mass.: Harvard University Press, 1961.
133. —— *Pro Caelio, De Provinciis Consularibus, Pro Balbo.* R. Gardner, trans. Loeb Classical Library. Cambridge, Mass.: Harvard University Press, 1958.
134. Clément, Catherine and Bernard Pingaud, eds. *Roland Barthes.* Special issue of *L'Arc* 56 (1st trim., 1974).
135. Cole, Hubert. *Beau Brummell.* New York: Mason/Charter, 1977.
136. Collas, Georges. *Les Sentiments de l'Académie Française sur la tragicomédie du Cid.* Geneva: Slatkine Reprints, 1968.
137. Collet, François. "Fait inédit de la vie de Pascal: l'auteur des Provinciales et le Chevalier de Méré." *La Liberté de penser.* Vol. 1. Paris: Joubert, 1848, pp. 246–62.
138. Conrart, Valentin. *La Journée des madrigaux; la Gazette de Tendre (avec la carte de Tendre) et du carnaval des précieuses.* Introductions and notes by Emile Colombey. Paris, 1896.
139. Corneille, Pierre. *Théâtre complet.* Maurice Rat, ed. 3 vols. Paris: Garnier Frères, n.d.
140. Courtin, A. de. *Nouveau traité de la civilité qui se pratique en France parmi les honnêtes gens.* Paris: Helie Josset, 1672.
141. Cousin, Victor. *La Société française au XVIIe siècle d'après "le Grand Cyrus" de Mlle de Scudéry.* 2 vols. Paris: Didier, 1858.
142. Creed, Elizabeth. *Le Dandysme de Jules Barbey d'Aurevilly.* Paris: Droz, 1938.
143. Croce, Benedetto. *Esthétique.* Henry Bigot, trans. Paris: V. Giard & E. Brière, 1904.
144. Dallas, Dorothy F. *Le Roman français de 1660 à 1680.* Paris: Librairie Universitaire J. Gamber, 1932.
145. Dash, la Comtesse Saint Mars [Gabrielle Anne Cisterne de Courtiras]. *Comment on fait son chemin dans le monde; code du savoir-vivre.* Paris: Calmann-Lévy, 1888.

Selected Bibliography

146. —— *Les Bals masqués.* 2 vols. Paris: Calmann-Lévy, 1857.
147. —— *Mémoires des autres.* Paris: A la Librairie Illustrée, n.d.
148. Debu-Bridel, Jacques. "La Préciosité, conception héroïque de la vie." *Revue de France* 5, no. 18 (September–October 1938): 195–216.
149. Dédéyan, Charles. "Deux aspects de Montaigne." *Bibliothèque d'humanisme et renaissance* 6 (1945): 313–27.
150. Delas, Daniel and Jacques Philliolet. *Linguistique et poétique.* Paris: Larousse, 1973.
151. Deleuze, Gilles. *Proust et les signes.* Paris: Presses Universitaires de France, 1971.
152. Delft, Louis van. *La Bruyère, moraliste: quatre études sur les "Caractères."* Geneva: Droz, 1971.
153. —— "Une Influence remise en question: La Bruyère et Gracián." *Revue d'histoire littéraire de la France* 71 (1971): 472–83.
154. Delvau, Alfred. *Dictionnaire de la langue verte.* New ed. with a supplement by Gustave Fustier. Paris: Flammarion, 1883.
155. —— *Les Dessous de Paris.* Paris: Poulet-Malassis et de Broise, 1860.
156. Demorest, J. J. "L'Honnête Homme et le croyant selon Pascal." *Modern Philology* 33, no. 4 (May 1956): 217–20.
157. —— "Une Notion théâtrale de l'existence." *L'Esprit créateur* 11, no. 2 (Summer 1971): 77–91.
158. Dériège, Felix. *Physiologie du lion.* Paris: J. Delahaye, 1842.
159. DeWitt, Norman Wentworth. *Epicurus and His Philosophy.* Minneapolis: University of Minnesota Press, 1954.
160. Descartes, René. *Oeuvres et Lettres.* Bibliothèque de la Pléiade. Paris: Gallimard, 1953.
161. Descotes, Maurice. *La Légende de Napoléon et les écrivains français du XIXᵉ siècle.* Paris: Minard, 1967.
162. *Dictionnaire de l'Académie Française.* 1st ed., 1694; 2d ed., 1718; 6th ed., 1835. Supplement to the 6th ed., 1859.
163. *Dictionnaire des dictionnaires, ou vocabulaire universel & complet de la langue française reproduisant le Dictionnaire de l'Académie Française.* 6th ed., augmented. Brussels, 1839.
164. *Dictionnaire des lettres françaises: Le Dix-septième siècle.* Paris: Arthème Fayard, 1954.
165. Diderot, Denis. *Oeuvres complètes.* J. Assezat and Maurice Tourneaux, eds. Vol. 16. Paris: Garnier, 1875–77.
166. Doolittle, James, "A Royal Diversion: Mademoiselle and Lauzun." *L'Esprit créateur* 11, no. 2 (Summer 1971): 123–90.
167. D'Ormesson, Jean. "Arrivisme, snobisme, dandysme." *Revue de métaphysique et de morale* 68, no. 4 (October–December 1963): 443–59.
168. Du Bled, Victor. *La Société française du XVIᵉ siècle au XXᵉ siècle.* Vol. 2, *Le XVIIᵉ siècle.* Paris: Perrin, 1908.
169. DuCamp, Maxime. *Souvenirs littéraires.* Paris: Hachette, 1962.

Selected Bibliography

170. Ducrot, Oswald and Tzvetan Todorov. *Dictionnaire encyclopédique des sciences du langage.* Paris: Seuil, 1972.

171. Dumas, Alexandre. *Les trois mousquetaires; Vingt ans après.* Bibliothèque de la Pléiade. Paris: Gallimard, 1962.

172. Du Puy de Clinchamps, Philippe. *La Noblesse.* Paris: Presses Universitaires de France, 1968.

173. Eco, Umberto. *La Structure absente.* Paris: Mercure de France, 1972.

174. —— *A Theory of Semiotics.* Bloomington: Indiana University Press, 1976.

175a. Edelman, Nathan. *The Eye of the Beholder.* Jules Brody, ed. Baltimore Md.: Johns Hopkins University Press, 1974.

175b. —— *Attitudes of Seventeenth-Century France toward the Middle Ages.* New York: King's Crown Press, 1946.

176. Ehrmann, Jacques. "Homo Ludens Revisited." *Yale French Studies* 41 (1968): 31–57.

177. —— *Un Paradis désespéré: l'amour et l'illusion dans "L'Astrée."* New Haven, Conn.: Yale University Press, 1963.

178. Eigeldinger, Marc. *Le Platonisme de Baudelaire.* Paris: A la Baconnière, 1951.

179. Ellington, Margery E. *Les Relations de société entre l'Angleterre et la France sous la Restauration, 1814–1830.* Paris: Champion, 1929.

180. *Encyclopaedia of Religion and Ethics.* 13 vols. New York: Scribner's 1908–27.

181. Engelson, Suzanne. "Napoléon vu par Stendhal." *Synthèses* 283–284 (January–February 1970): 78–83.

182. Erlich, Victor. *Russian Formalism: History, Doctrine.* The Hague: Mouton, 1969.

183. Escarpit, Robert. *Lord Byron, un tempérament littéraire.* Paris: Le Cercle du Livre, 1955.

184. Esprit, Jacques. *La Fausseté des vertus humaines.* 2 vols. Paris: Guillaume Desprez, 1678.

185. Estève, Edmond. *Byron et le romantisme français.* Paris: Hachette, 1907.

186. Estienne, Charles. *Dictionarium historicum ac poeticum.* . . . n.p., 1553.

187. Fales, Angela Bianchini. "Le Dévéloppement du mot 'ennui' de la Pléiade jusqu'à Pascal." *Cultura Neolatina* 12 (1952): 225–38.

188. Faret, Nicolas. *L'Honnête Homme ou l'art de plaire à la cour.* M. Magendie, ed. Paris: Presses Universitaires de France, 1925.

189. Fatta, Corrado. *Du snobisme: un chapitre d'anthropologie.* Paris: Buchet/Chastel, 1961.

190. Fernandez, Dominique. "Barbey d'Aurevilly." *La Nouvelle revue française* 155 (November 1, 1965): 873–87.

191. Féval, Paul. *Les Mystères de Londres.* Paris: Calmann-Lévy, 1849.

192. Fleuret, Colette. "Montaigne et la société civile." *Europe* 513–14, (January–February 1972): 107–23.

193. Flugel, J. C. *The Psychology of Clothes.* London: Hogarth Press and the Institute of Psychoanalysis, 1971.

Selected Bibliography

194. Fontaine, André. *Conférences inédites de l'Académie Royale de Peinture et de sculpture.* Paris: Albert Fontemoing, 1672.

195. Fontenelle, Bernard le Bovier de. *Oeuvres.* Vol. 3. Amsterdam: Francis Champion, 1764.

196. François, Simone. *Le Dandysme et Marcel Proust.* Brussels: Palais des Académies, 1956.

197. Franke, Max Walther. *Das "Artifizielle" in der französischen Literatur des XIX. Jahrhunderts.* Leipzig: Druck der Spamerschen Buckdruckerei in Leipzig. 1913.

198. Frémy, Arnould. "Le Roi de la mode." *Revue de Paris* (October 1836): 256–70.

199. Freud, Sigmund. *The Complete Psychological Works.* 24 vols. James Strachey, ed. London: The Hogarth Press, 1955.

200. Fromentin, Eugène. *Dominique.* Paris: Didier, 1966.

201. Fukui, Y. *Raffinement précieux dans la poésie française du XVIIᵉ siècle.* Paris: Nizet, 1964.

202. Furetière, Antoine. *Dictionnaire universel.* 1st ed., 1690.

203. Garrett, Helen Thompson. "Clothes and Character: The Function of Dress in Balzac." Ph.D. dissertation, University of Pennsylvania, 1941.

204. Gasté, Armand. *La Querelle du Cid.* Paris: H. Welter, 1898.

205. Gautier, Théophile. "Albertus." *Premières poésies.* Paris: Charpentier, 1871, pp. 1–54.

206. ——— *Critique artistique et littéraire.* Paris: Bibliothèque Larousse, 1929.

207. ——— *Histoire du romantisme.* Paris: Charpentier, 1877.

208. ——— *Le Capitaine Fracasse.* Paris: Classiques Garnier, 1967.

209. ——— *Les Grotesques.* Paris: Charpentier, 1913.

210. ——— *Les Jeunes-France.* Nouvelle bibliothèque romantique. Paris: Flammarion, 1974.

211. ——— *Mademoiselle de Maupin.* Paris: Classiques Garnier, 1966.

212. ——— "Notice" to Charles Baudelaire, *Fleurs du mal.* Paris: Calmann-Lévy, 1890, pp. 1–75.

213. ——— *Nouvelles.* Paris: Charpentier, 1898.

214. ——— *Portraits contemporains.* Paris: Charpentier, 1898.

215. ——— *Romans et contes.* Paris: Alphonse Lemerre, 1897.

216. ——— *Souvenirs de théâtre, d'art et de critique.* Paris: Charpentier, 1883.

217. Genette, Gérard. *Mimologiques.* Paris: Seuil, 1976.

218. Gilman, Margaret. *The Idea of Poetry in France.* Cambridge, Mass.: Harvard University Press, 1958.

219. Girard, René. *Mensonge romantique et vérité romanesque.* Paris: Bernard Grasset, 1961.

220. Giraud, Raymond. *The Unheroic Hero in the Novels of Stendhal, Balzac and Flaubert.* New York: Octagon Books, 1969.

221. Goethe, Johann Wolfgang von. *Faust et le Second Faust.* Gérard de Nerval, trans., M. Allemand, ed. Paris: Garnier Frères, 1964.

222. Goffman, Erving. *The Presentation of Self in Everyday Life.* New York: Doubleday, 1959.
223. Goncourt, Edmond de. *La Faustin.* Paris: Charpentier, 1892.
224. Goncourt, Edmond de and Jules de Goncourt. *Charles Demailly.* Paris: Librairie Internationale, 1968.
225. —— *Gavarni.* Paris: Plon, 1873.
226. —— *Journal.* 22 vols. Monaco: Imprimerie Nationale, 1956.
227. Gossman, Lionel. *Men and Masks: A Study of Molière.* Baltimore, Md.: Johns Hopkins University Press, 1963.
228. Goujon, Abel. *Manuel de l'homme de bon ton, ou Cérémonial de la bonne société.* n.p., 1821.
229. Gould, Charles. "Le Dandysme de Balzac et son influence sur sa création littéraire." *Cahiers de l'association des études françaises* 15 (March 1963): 379–93.
230. Gozlan, Léon. *Le Lion empaillé.* Paris: Dondey-Dupré, 1848.
231. Gracián y Morales, Baltazar. *L'Homme de cour.* Translated by Amelot de La Houssaie. Paris: Boudot, 1684.
232. Graña, César. *Bohemian versus Bourgeois: French Society and the French Man of Letters in the Nineteenth Century.* New York: Basic Books, 1964.
233. Greenblatt, Stephen J. *Sir Walter Raleigh: The Renaissance Man and His Roles.* New Haven, Conn.: Yale University Press, 1973.
234. Greimas, A. J. *Du sens: Essais sémiotiques.* Paris: Seuil, 1970.
235. —— *Maupassant: La Sémiotique du texte, exercises pratiques.* Paris: Seuil, 1976.
236. —— *Sémantique structurale.* Paris: Larousse, 1966.
237. —— *Sémiotique et sciences sociales.* Paris: Seuil, 1976.
238. Greimas, A. J., ed. *Essais de sémiotique poétique.* Paris: Larousse, 1972.
239. —— *Pratiques et langages gestuels. Langages* 10 (June 1968).
240. Grenailles, François de. *L'Honnête garçon.* 2 vols. Paris: Toussaint Quinet, 1642.
241. Grenville, Vicomte E. de. *Histoire du journal "La Mode."* Paris: La Mode nouvelle, 1861.
242. Groethuysen, Bernard. *Origines de l'esprit bourgeois en France.* Paris: Gallimard, 1927.
243. Gronow, Captain Rees Howell. *Reminiscences and Recollections.* 2 vols. London: John C. Nimmo, 1892.
244. Grubbs, Henry A. *Damien Mitton, bourgeois honnête homme.* Princeton, N.J.: Princeton University Press, 1932.
245. Grube, G. M. A. *The Greek and Roman Critics.* London: Methuen, 1975.
246. Guéret, Gabriel. *La Carte de la cour.* Paris: Pierre Trabouillet, 1663.
247. Guichardet, F. G. "Le Lion de contrebande." *Prisme* 1 (1840): 206–10.
248. Guiraud, Pierre. *La Sémantique. Que sais-je?* Paris: Presses Universitaires de France, 1966.
249. Guyot, Henri, ed. *Anthologie des lettres de femmes.* Vol. 1, 1500–1774. Paris: Librairie Delagrave, 1923.

Selected Bibliography

250. Hadas, Moses, ed. *The Stoic Philosophy of Seneca: Essays and Letters.* New York: Norton, 1958.

251. Hautel, d'. *Dictionnaire du bas-langage, ou des manières de parler usitées parmi le peuple.* 2 vols. 1808.

252. Hazlitt, William. *The Complete Works.* P. P. Howe, ed. Vol. 20. Toronto: Dent, 1934.

253. —— "The Dandy School." *The Examiner* (November 18, 1827): 152–53.

254. Hemmings, F. W. J. *Culture and Society in France, 1848–1898.* New York: Scribner's, 1972.

255. Hess, Gerard, "Wege des Humanismus im Frankreich des 17. Jahrhunderts." *Romanische Forschungen* 53 (1959): 262–99.

256. Hjelmslev, Louis. *Prolégomènes à une théorie du langage.* Paris: Minuit, 1968.

257. Holyoake, S. John. "Montaigne and the Concept of 'bien né.'" *Bibliothèque d'humanisme et de renaissance* 30 (1968): 483–98.

258. Hope, Quentin M. *Saint-Evremond, the "Honnête Homme" as Critic.* Bloomington: Indiana University Press, 1962.

259. Horatius Flaccus, Quintus. *Satires, Epistles and Ars Poetica.* H. Rushton Fairclough, trans. Loeb Classical Library. New York: Putnam, 1929.

260. Houssaye, Arsène. *Les Confessions.* Vols. 1, 2, 4. Paris: E. Dentu, 1885–91.

261. Houssaye, Henri. *Histoire d'Alcibiade et de la république athénienne.* 2 vols. Paris: Librairie Académique, 1873.

262. Hugo, Victor, *La Préface de Cromwell.* Maurice Souriau, ed. Paris: Oudin, n.d.

263. —— "William Shakespeare." *Oeuvres complètes.* Vol. 12. Jean Massin, ed. Paris: Club Français du livre, 1969, pp. 152–323.

264. Huizinga, Johan. *Homo Ludens.* Boston: Beacon Press, 1960.

265. —— *The Waning of the Middle Ages.* New York: Doubleday, 1924.

266. Huysmans, J. K. *A rebours.* Paris: Charpentier, 1905.

267. Ignatius of Loyola, Saint. *The Spiritual Exercises of St. Ignatius.* Louis J. Puhl, trans. Westminster, Md.: Newman Press, 1951.

268. Ivanoff, N. *La Marquise de Sablé et son salon.* Paris: Les Presses Modernes, 1927.

269. Jacoubet, Henri. "A propos du 'je-ne-sais-quoi.'" *Revue d'histoire littéraire de la France* 35 (1928): 73–77.

270. Jakobson, Roman. *Essais de linguistique générale.* Paris: Editions de Minuit, 1963.

271. —— *Questions de poétique.* Paris: Seuil, 1973.

272. Jakobson, Roman, and Morris Halle. *Fundamentals of Language.* The Hague: Mouton, 1956.

273. Jasinski, René. *Les Années romantiques de Théophile Gautier.* Paris: Libraire Vuibert, 1929.

274. Jesse, Captain William. *Beau Brummell.* 2 vols. London: Grolier Society, 1844.

Selected Bibliography

275. Jollivet, Gaston. *Souvenirs de la vie de plaisir sous le Second Empire*. Paris: Jules Tallandier, 1927.
276. Jouy, Etienne de. *L'Hermite de la Chaussée d'Antin, ou observations sur les moeurs et les usages au commencement du XIXe siècle*. 2 vols. Brussels: Aug. Wahlen, 1818.
277. —— *L'Hermite de Londres*. 2 vols. Paris: Pillet Ainé, 1821.
278. Jullian, Philippe, ed. *Dictionnaire du snobisme*. Paris: Plon, 1958.
279. Kaufmann,Walter. *Nietzsche*. Princeton, N.J.: Princeton University Press, 1968.
280. Kempf, Roger. *Dandies: Baudelaire et Cie*. Paris: Seuil, 1977.
281. Köhler, Erich. "Je ne sais quoi." *Romantisches Jahrbuch* 8–9 (1953–54): 21–59.
282. Koehler, Gustav. "Der Dandysmus im französischen Roman des XIX. Jahrhunderts." *Zeitschrift für romanische Philologie* 33 (1911).
283. Kristeva, Julia. *Recherches pour une sémanalyse*. Paris: Seuil, 1969.
284. Kuhn, Reinhardt. "Le roi dépossédé: Pascal et l'ennui." *French Review* 42, no. 5 (April 1969): 657–84.
285. La Bédollière, Emile de. *Histoire de la mode en France*. Leipzig: Alphonse Dürr, 1858.
286. La Bruyère, Jean de. *Oeuvres complètes*. Bibliothèque de la Pléiade. Paris: Gallimard, 1962.
287. La Calprenède, Gautier de Coste de. *Cassandre*. 10 vols. Paris: A. de Sommaville, A. Courbet, T. Quinet, N. de Sercy, 1644–67.
288. La Fare, Charles-Auguste, Marquis de. *Mémoires. Collection des mémoires relatifs à l'histoire de la France*. Vol. 65. A. Petitot and Monmerqué, eds. Paris: Foucault, 1828.
289. La Fayette, Marie-Madeleine, Comtesse de. *Mémoires de la cour de France pour les années 1688 et 1689. Collection des mémoires relatifs à l'histoire de la France*. Vol. 65. A. Petitot and Monmerqué, eds. Paris: Foucault, 1828.
290. —— *La Princesse de Clèves*. Emile Magne, ed. Geneva: Droz, 1950.
291. La Fontaine, Jean de. *Oeuvres complètes*. 2 vols. Bibliothèque de la Pléiade. Paris: Gallimard, 1958–59.
292. Lalande, André. *Vocabulaire technique et critique de la philosophie*. Paris: Presses Universitaires de France, 1968.
293. Lanson, Gustave, ed. *Choix de lettres du XVIIe siècle*. Paris: Hachette, 1909.
294. La Rochefoucauld, François, Duc de. *Oeuvres complètes*. Bibliothèque de la Pléiade. Paris: Gallimard, 1964.
295. Larousse, Pierre. *Grand dictionnaire universel du XIXe siècle*. 1st ed. Vols. 1–15, 1866–76; Vols. 16–17 (Supplément), 1877–90.
296. Lathuillère, Roger. *La Préciosité*. Vol. 1. Geneva: Droz, 1966.
297. Laubriet, Pierre. "La Légende et le mythe napoléoniens chez Balzac." *L'Année Balzacienne*. Paris: Garnier, 1968, pp. 285–301.
298. Laver, James. *The Concise History of Costume and Fashion*. New York: Harry N. Abrams, 1970.

Selected Bibliography

299. Leibnitz, Gottfried Wilhelm. *New Essays on Human Understanding.* Alfred G. Langley, ed. and trans. New York: Macmillan, 1896.
300. —— *Philosophical Papers and Letters.* Vol 1. Leroy E. Loemaker, ed. and trans. Chicago: University of Chicago Press, 1956.
301. Lemaître, Jules. *Les Contemporains.* Vol. 4. Paris: H. Lecène & H. Oudin, 1889.
302. Lembrick, Elaine. "La Conception de l'honnête homme chez Montaigne." *Revue de l'Université d'Ottawa* 41 (1971): 47–57.
303. Lemoinne, John. "Brummell." *Revue des deux mondes* 7 (August 1844): 467–84.
304. Lemoyne, Pierre. *Hymnes de la sagesse divine et de l'amour divin; Un discours de la poésie.* . . . Paris: Sebastien Cramoisy, 1641.
305. Léon, Pierre R., Henri Mittérand, Peter Nesselroth, and Pierre Robert. *Problèmes de l'analyse textuelle.* Ottawa: Marcel Didier, 1971.
306. Leroy, Claude. "L'Ecrivain en habit dandy." *Revue des sciences humaines* 38, no. 150 (April–June 1973): 261–76.
307. Lethève, Jacques. "Un Mot témoin de l'époque 'fin de siècle': esthète." *Revue d'histoire littéraire de la France* 64, no. 3 (July–September 1964): 436–46.
308. *Lettres de mademoiselle de Montpensier, des mesdames de Motteville et de Montmorenci, de mlle du Pré et de madame la marquise de Lambert.* Paris: Léopold Collin, 1806.
309. Lévêque, André. "L'Honnête Homme et l'homme de bien au XVIIᵉ siècle." *PMLA* 72 (1957): 620–32.
310. Lévi-Strauss, Claude. *Anthropologie structurale.* Paris: Plon, 1958.
311. —— *Le Cru et le cuit.* Paris: Plon, 1964.
312. —— *Entretiens.* Paris: Plon, 1961.
313. —— *Tristes tropiques.* Paris: Plon, 1955.
314. Lewis, Philip E. *La Rochefoucauld: The Art of Abstraction.* Ithaca, N.Y.: Cornell University Press, 1977.
315. Lotman, Juri. *Analysis of the Poetic Text.* D. Barton Johnson, ed. and trans. Ann Arbor, Mich.: Ardis Press, 1976.
316. —— *La Structure du texte artistique.* Paris: Gallimard, 1973.
317. Lough, John. *Introduction to Seventeenth-Century France.* New York: Longman, Green, 1954.
318. Lucid, David P., ed. *Soviet Semiotics: An Anthology.* Baltimore, Md.: Johns Hopkins University Press, 1977.
319. McGann, Jerome. "The Dandy." *Midway* 10, no. 1 (Summer 1969): 3–18.
320. —— *Fiery Dust: Byron's Poetic Development.* Chicago: University of Chicago Press, 1968.
321. McGowan, Margaret. *Montaigne's Deceits.* Philadelphia, Pa.: Temple University Press, 1974.
322. Mackenzie, Frazer. *Les Relations de l'Angleterre et la France d'après le vocabulaire.* Paris: Droz, 1939.

Selected Bibliography

323. Magendie, Maurice. *La Politesse mondaine et les théories de l'honnêteté en France de 1600 à 1660.* Geneva: Slatkine Reprints, 1970.

324. —— *Le Roman français au XVIIᵉ siècle, de "L'Astrée" au "Grand Cyrus."* Geneva: Slatkine Reprints, 1970.

325. Magne, Emile. *Voiture et l'hôtel de Rambouillet.* 2 vols. Paris: Emile-Paul Frères, 1930.

326. Maigron, Louis. *Le Romantisme et la mode.* Paris: Honoré Champion, 1911.

327. Maland, David. *Culture and Society in Seventeenth-Century France.* New York: Scribner's, 1970.

328. Marivaux, Pierre Carlet de Chamblain de. *Le Petit maître corrigé.* Frédéric Deloffre, ed. Geneva: Droz, 1955.

329. Marmet, Melchior de, Sieur de Valcroissant. *Maximes pour vivre heureusement dans le monde et pour former l'honnête homme.* Paris: Charles de Scery, 1662.

330. Marsan, Jules. *Bohème romantique.* Paris: Editions des Cahiers Libres, 1929.

331. Martinet, André, ed. *Le Langage.* Encyclopédie de la Pléiade. Paris: Gallimard, 1968.

332. —— "La double articulation linguistique." *Recherches structurales des Travaux du Cercle Linguistique de Copenhague* 5 (1949): 30–37.

333. Matejka, Ladislav and Irwin Titunik, eds. *Semiotics of Art: Prague School Contributions.* Cambridge, Mass.: MIT. Press, 1976.

334. Matoré, Georges. *La Méthode en lexicologie: Domaine français.* Paris: Marcel Didier, 1953.

335. —— *Le Vocabulaire de la prose littéraire de 1835 à 1845.* Geneva: Droz, 1951.

336. Matoré, Georges, and A. J. Greimas. "La Naissance du génie au XVIIIᵉ siècle." *Le Français moderne* 25 (October 1957): 256–72.

337. Medwin, Thomas. *Journal of the Conversations of Lord Byron Noted during a Residence of his Lordship at Pisa in the Years of 1821 and 1822.* London: Colburn, 1824.

338. Mercier, Louis Sebastien. *Tableau de Paris.* 6 vols. Amsterdam: n.p., 1783.

339. Méré, Antoine Gombaud, Chevalier de. *Lettres.* 2 vols. Paris: Au Palais, 1689.

340. —— *Oeuvres complètes.* Charles H. Boudhors, ed. 3 vols. Paris: Fernand Roches, 1930.

341. Mérimée, Prosper. "Littérature: Mémoires de Lord Byron, publiées par Mme Belloc." *Le National* (March 7, 1830): 7.

342. —— *Romans et nouvelles.* Bibliothèque de la Pléiade. Paris: Gallimard, 1962.

343. Merla, Louis, "Autour du Chevalier de Méré: Antoine Gombaud et sa famille." *Les Cahiers de l'ouest* 16 (1957): 29–43.

344. Mesnard, Jean. "Introduction à l'étude de Pascal mondain." *Annales Universitatis Saraviensis* 3 (1954): 75–94.

Selected Bibliography

345. Mickel, Emmanuel J. *The Artificial Paradise in French Literature.* University of North Carolina Studies in the Romance Languages and Literatures, no. 84. Chapel Hill: University of North Carolina Press, 1969.

346. Milner, J. M. "Théophile Gautier et le dandysme esthétique." *Studies in the French Language, Literature and History Presented to R. Graeme Ritchie.* Cambridge: Cambridge University Press, 1949, pp. 128–36.

347. Moers, Ellen. *The Dandy.* New York: Viking Press, 1960.

348. Moles, Abraham André. *Information Theory and Esthetic Perception.* Joel Cohen, trans. Urbana: University of Illinois Press, 1966.

349. Molière [Jean-Baptiste Poquelin]. *Théâtre complet.* 2 vols. Bibliothèque de la Pléiade. Paris: Gallimard, 1971.

350. Monet, Paul [le Père Philibert]. *Invantaire des deux langues françoise et latine, assorti des plus utiles curiositez de l'un et de l'autre idiome.* Lyon: C. Obert, 1636.

351. Mongrédien, Georges. *Les Précieux et les précieuses.* Paris: Mercure de France, 1963.

352. —— *La Vie de société au XVIIe et XVIIIe siècles.* Paris: Hachette, 1950.

353. —— *La Vie quotidienne sous Louis XIV.* Paris: Librairie Hachette, 1948.

354. Monk, Samuel Holt. "A Grace Beyond the Reach of Art." *Journal of the History of Ideas* 5, no. 2 (April 1944): 131–50.

355. Montaigne, Michel Eyquem de. *Oeuvres complètes.* A. Thibaudet and M. Rat, eds. Bibliothèque de la Pléiade. Paris: Gallimard, 1962.

356. Montesquieu, Charles Louis de Secondat. *Oeuvres complètes.* 2 vols. Bibliothèque de la Pléiade. Paris: Gallimard, 1958.

357. Montpensier, Louise d'Orléans, Duchesse de [Mlle de Montpensier]. *La Galerie des portraits de Mlle de Montpensier.* Edouard de Barthelemy, ed. Paris: Didier, 1860.

358. —— *Mémoires. Collection des mémoires relatifs à l'histoire de France.* Vols. 40–43. A. Petitot, ed. Paris: Foucault, 1824.

359. —— *Relation de l'isle imaginaire; Histoire de la princesse de Paphlagonie.* Paris: Ant. Aug. Renouard, 1805.

360. Moore, W. G. "Le Goût de la cour." *Cahiers de l'Association Internationale des Etudes Françaises* 9 (June 1957): 172–82.

361. —— *La Rochefoucauld: His Mind and Art.* Oxford: Oxford University Press, 1969.

362. Moreau, Pierre. *Le Classicisme des romantiques.* Paris: Plon, 1932.

363. Morgan, Lady Sydney. *La France en 1828 et 1830.* A. Sobry, trans. 2 vols. Paris: Fournier, 1830.

364. Mortemart-Boisse, Baron de. *La Vie élégante à Paris.* Paris: Hachette, 1857.

365. Mounin, Georges. *Introduction à la sémiologie.* Paris: Minuit, 1970.

366. Murray, James A. H. et al., eds. *A New English Dictionary on Historical Principles.* . . . 1888–1928.

367. Musset, Louis-Charles Alfred de. *Oeuvres complètes.* 3 vols. Bibliothèque de la Pléiade. Paris: Gallimard, 1957–60.

Selected Bibliography

368. Musset, Paul de. *Biographie d'Alfred de Musset*. Paris: Alphonse Lemerre, 1877.
369. —— *Extravagants et originaux du XVIIe siècle*. Paris: Charpentier, 1863.
370. —— *Lauzun*. 2 vols. Paris: Dumont, 1835.
371. —— *Originaux du 17e siècle: galerie des portraits*. Paris: Charpentier, 1848.
372. Nattiez, Jean-Jacques, ed. *Roman Jakobson*. Special issue of *L'Arc* 60 (1975).
373. Nepos, Cornelius. *Oeuvres*. Bilingual ed. Anne-Marie Guillemin, trans. Paris: Les Belles Lettres, 1923.
374. Nerval, Gérard de [Gérard Labrunie]. *Oeuvres*. Vol. 1. Bibliothèque de la Pléiade. Paris: Gallimard, 1960.
375. Nicole, Pierre. *Essais de morale*. 5 vols. The Hague: Adrian Moetjens, 1709.
376. —— *An Essay on True and Apparent Beauty*. J. V. Cunningham, trans. The Augustan Reprint Society, no. 24. Los Angeles: University of California Press, 1950.
377. —— *Recueil de poésies chrétiennes et diverses*. Vol. 1. Paris: Le Petit, 1671–78.
378. Nicolet, M. "Condition de l'homme de lettres au XVIIe siècle." *Revue d'histoire littéraire de la France* 63 (July-September 1963): 369–93.
379. Nicot, Jean. *Thrésor de la langue françoyse tant ancienne que moderne.* . . . n.p., 1606.
380. Nietzsche, Friedrich. *The Birth of Tragedy and the Genealogy of Morals*. Francis Golfling, trans. New York: Doubleday Anchor, 1956.
381. —— *Beyond Good and Evil*. Walter Kaufmann, trans. New York. Vintage Books, 1966.
382. —— *The Gay Science*. Walter Kaufmann, trans. New York: Vintage Books, 1974.
383. —— *Human, All Too Human: The Complete Works of Friedrich Nietzsche*. Vols. 7–8. Paul V. Cohn, trans. New York: Macmillan, 1911.
384. —— *On the Greeks (Early Greek Philosophy)*, vol. 2. *The Complete Works of Friedrich Nietzsche*. Oscar Levy, ed. London: Fowlis, 1911.
385. —— *The Will to Power*. Walter Kaufmann, ed. R. J. Hollingdale and Walter Kaufmann, trans. New York: Vintage Books, 1968.
386. —— *Thus Spoke Zarathustra*. Walter Kaufmann, trans. New York: Viking Press, 1968.
387. Nordon, Pierre. "Alfred de Musset et l'Angleterre: à la rencontre de l'Angleterre." *Les Lettres romanes* 20 (1966): 319–33; 21 (1967): 28–46, 123–40, 238–56, 354–68; 22 (1968): 3–19, 109–32.
388. *Les Objets. Communications* 13 (1969).
389. Oudin, Antoine. *Curiositez françoises pour servir de supplément aux dictionnaires*. N.p. 1640.
390. Papin, Claude. "Le Sens de l'idéal de 'L'Honnête Homme' au XVIIe siècle." *La Pensée* 104 (July-August 1962): 52–83.

Selected Bibliography

391. *Paris et les parisiens au XIXe siècle: Moeurs, arts et monuments.* (Anthology of articles by Gautier, Houssaye, P. de Musset, L. Enault, et al.) Paris: Morizot, 1856.
392. Partridge, Eric. *The French Romantics' Knowledge of English Literature (1829–1848).* Vol. 14. Bibliothèque de la littérature comparée. Paris: Librairie Ancienne Edouard Champion, 1924.
393. Pascal, Blaise. *Oeuvres complètes.* Louis Lafuma, ed. L'Intégrale. Paris: Seuil, 1963.
393a. —— *Pensées et opuscules.* Léon Brunschvicg, ed. Paris: Classique Hachette, 1961.
394. Perelman, Chaim, and L. Olbrechts-Tyteca. *La Nouvelle rhétorique: Traité de l'argumentation.* 2 vols. Paris: Presses Universitaires de France, 1958.
395. Perrault, Charles. *Parallèle des anciens et des modernes en ce qui regarde les arts et les sciences.* Munich: Eidos, 1964.
396. Peyre, Henri. *Qu'est-ce que le romantisme?* Paris: Presses Universitaires de France, 1971.
397. Pichot, Amédée. *Voyage historique et littéraire en Angleterre et en Ecosse.* Paris: Ladvocat et Gosselin, 1825.
398. Peirce, Charles S. *Selected Writings.* Philip P. Wiener, ed. New York: Dover, 1966.
399. Pizzorusso, Arnaldo. "Morvan de Bellegarde e une retorica delle 'bienséances.'" *Rivista di Letteratura Moderne e Comparate* 12 (December 1959): 261–78.
400. Planche, Gustave. "Bulwer." *Revue des deux mondes* (June 1832): 550–83.
401. Plato. *The Dialogues of Plato.* 4 vols. B. Jowett, ed. and trans. London: Oxford University Press, 1964.
402. Plutarque. *Les Vies des hommes illustres.* Vol. 1. Jacques Amyot, trans. Bibliothèque de la Pléiade. Paris: Gallimard, 1951.
403. Ponson du Terrail, Pierre-Alexis, Vicomte de. *Les Drames de Paris.* Vol. 4. Brussels: Alphonse Lebègue, 1858.
404. —— *Les Drames de Paris.* Vol. 5: *Le Comte Artoff.* Paris: E. Dentu, 1890.
405. —— *Les Drames de Paris: Rocambole.* 3 vols. Monaco: Rocher, 1963.
406. —— *Les Voleurs du grand monde.* Vol. 4. Paris: E. Dentu, 1890.
407. Praz, Mario. *The Romantic Agony.* Angus Davidson, trans. New York: Meridian, 1965.
408. Prevost, John C. *Le Dandysme en France.* Paris: E. Droz, 1957.
409. Primi-Visconti. *Mémoires sur la cour de Louis XIV.* Jean Lemoine, ed. and trans. Paris: Calmann-Lévy, 1908.
410. Pure, Michel, Abbé de. *La Précieuse ou le mystère des ruelles.* 2 vols. Paris: Droz, 1938.
411. *La Qualité de la vie au XVIIe siècle.* Actes du Colloque de Marseille, 109 (1977).
412. Quinet, Edgar. "De l'unité des lettres modernes." *Revue des deux mondes,* 4th ser., vol. 15 (1838): 318–35.

Selected Bibliography

413. Quintilianus, Marcus Fabius. *Institutio oratoria.* 4 vols. H. E. Butler, trans. Loeb Classical Library. New York: Putnam, 1921.
414. Raikes, Thomas. *A Portion of the Journal Kept by Thomas Raikes, Esq. from 1831 to 1847.* 2 vols. London: Longman, Brown, Green, Longmans, and Roberts, 1858.
415. Raisson, Horace M. *Code civil, manuel complet de la politesse.* Paris: J. P. Roret, 1828.
416. —— *Code de la conversation.* Paris: J. P. Roret, 1829.
417. —— *Six codes fashionables.* Paris: Charles Sedille, 1830.
418. Rapin, René. *Les Réflexions sur la poétique de ce temps et sur les ouvrages des poètes anciens et modernes.* E. T. Dubois, ed. Geneva: Droz, 1970.
419. Raynaud, Ernest. "Baudelaire et la religion du dandysme." *Mercure de France* 127 (August 16, 1917): 577–614.
420. Reboul, Pierre. *Le Mythe anglais dans la littérature française sous la Restauration.* Lille: Bibliothèque Universitaire de Lille, 1962.
421. Refuge, Eustache de. *Traicté de la cour, ou instruction des courtisans.* Leiden: Les Elseviers, 1649.
422. Regosin, Richard L. *The Matter of My Book: Montaigne's "Essais" as the Book of the Self.* Berkeley: University of California Press, 1977.
423. Rhodes, S. A. "Baudelaire's Philosophy of Dandyism." *Sewanee Review* 36 (1928): 387–404.
424. Richard, Jean-Pierre. *Etudes sur le romantisme.* Paris: Seuil, 1970.
425. —— *Littérature et sensation.* Paris: Seuil, 1954.
426. Richelet, César-Pierre. *Nouveau dictionnaire françois.* 2 vols. New ed., rev. and expanded. 1719.
427. Ridge, George Ross. *The Hero in French Decadent Literature.* Atlanta: University of Georgia Press, 1961.
428. —— *The Hero in French Romantic Literature.* Georgia: University of Georgia Press, 1959.
429. Riffaterre, Michel. *Essais de stylistique structurale.* Paris: Flammarion, 1971.
430. Robert, Paul. *Dictionnaire alphabétique et analogique de la langue française.* 6 vols. 1st ed., 1957–64.
431. Roederer, P. L. *Mémoire pour servir à l'histoire de la société polie.* Paris: Firmin Didot Frères, 1835.
432. Ronteix, Eugène. *Manuel du fashionable.* Paris: Audot, 1829.
433. Roqueplan, Nestor. *Regain; La Vie parisienne.* Paris: Librairie Nouvelle, 1857.
434. Rousseau, Jean-Jacques. *Lettre à d'Alembert sur les spectacles.* Paris: Garnier Frères, 1889.
435. Rousset, Jean. *La littérature de l'âge baroque en France.* Paris: José Corti, 1963.
436. Rubin, Barbara L. "'Anti-Husbandry' and Self-Creation: A Comparison of Restoration Rake and Baudelaire's Dandy." *Texas Studies in Literature and Language* 14 (1973): 583–92.

Selected Bibliography

437. Saineau, L. *Le Langage parisien au XIXe siècle.* Paris: E. de Boccard, 1920.
438. Saint-Evremond, Charles de Marguetal de Saint-Denis, sieur de. *Oeuvres en prose.* 4 vols. René Ternois, ed. Paris: Didier, 1962–69.
439. —— *Oeuvres mêlées.* Charles Giraud, ed. Vol 3. Paris: J. Léon Techener, 1861.
440. Saint-Simon, Louis de Rouvroy. *Mémoires.* Gonzague Truc, ed. Bibliothèque de la Pléiade. Paris: Gallimard, 1954–61.
441. Sainte-Beuve, Charles-Augustin. *Portraits littéraires.* Vol. 3. Paris: Garnier Frères, 1878.
442. Saisselin, Rémy G. "Dandyism and Honnêteté." *French Review* 29, no. 6 (May 1956): 457–60.
443. —— "L'Evolution du concept de l'honnêteté de 1660 à 1789." Ph.D. dissertation, University of Wisconsin, 1957.
444. Sallentre, Albert Henri de. "Les Entretiens de feu M. de Balzac." *Mémoires de littérature.* Vol. 1. The Hague: Henri du Sauret, 1715.
445. Sarasin, Jean François. *Les Oeuvres de Mr. Sarasin.* Paris: S. Marbre-Cramotis, 1694.
446. Sareil, Arsène. *Introduction à l'histoire de l'esthétique française.* Brussels: Palais des Académies, 1955.
447. Sartre, Jean Paul. *Baudelaire.* Paris: Gallimard, 1947.
448. Saussure, Ferdinand de. *Cours de linguistique générale.* Paris: Payot, 1973.
449. Sayce, R. A. *The Essays of Montaigne: A Critical Exploration.* London: Weidenfeld & Nicolson, 1972.
450. Schérer, Jacques, ed. *Théâtre du XVIIe siècle.* Vol I. Bibliothèque de la Pléiade. Paris: Gallimard, 1975.
451. Schneider, Marcel. *La Littérature fantastique en France.* Paris: Fayard, 1964.
452. Scott, Sir Walter. A Review of "Childe Harold's Pilgrimage, Canto III . . . and other poems by Lord Byron." *Quarterly Review* 16 (Oct. 1816): 172–208.
453. Scudéry, Madeleine de. *Artamène ou le Grand Cyrus.* 10 vols. Paris: Augustin Courbé, 1649–54.
454. —— *Clélie, histoire romaine.* . . . 5 vols. in 10. Paris: Thomas Iolly, 1658–66.
455. —— *Conversations sur divers sujets.* Paris: Claude Barbin, 1680.
456. —— *La Promenade de Versailles.* Paris: Devambez, 1920.
457. Sebeok, Thomas, ed. *Style in Language.* Proceedings of a Conference on Style, Indiana University, 1958. Cambridge, Mass.: Technology Press of MIT, 1960.
458. Séché, Léon. *La Jeunesse dorée sous Louis-Philippe.* Paris: Mercure de France, 1910.
459. Seneca, Lucius Annaeus. *Epistulae morales.* 3 vols. M. Gummere, ed. Loeb Classical Library. Cambridge, Mass.: Harvard University Press, 1953–62.
460. —— *Moral Essays.* 3 vols. John W. Basore, ed. Loeb Classical Library. Cambridge, Mass.: Harvard University Press, 1963.

Selected Bibliography

461. Sévigné, Marie de Rabutin-Chantal, Marquise de. *Lettres*. 3 vols. Bibliothèque de la Pléiade. Paris: Gallimard, 1953.
462. Showalter, English. *The Evolution of the French Novel, 1641–1782.* Princeton, N.J.: Princeton University Press, 1972.
463. Shroder, Maurice. *Icarus: The Image of the Artist in French Romanticism.* Cambridge, Mass.: Harvard University Press, 1961.
464. Simmel, Georg. "Fashion." *International Quarterly* 10 (1904): 130–55.
465. —— *The Sociology of Georg Simmel.* Kurt H. Wolff, ed. and trans. Glencoe, Ill.: Free Press, 1950.
466. Smith, Logan P. "Four Romantic Words." *Words and Idioms.* New York: Houghton-Mifflin, 1925, pp. 66–134.
467. Somaize, Antoine-Baudeau, Sieur de. *Dictionnaire des précieuses.* M. Ch.-L. Livet, ed. 2 vols. Paris: Hachette, 1861.
468. Soulié, Frédéric. *Le Lion amoureux.* Paris: La Tradition, 1937.
469. —— *Les Mémoires du diable.* Brussels: Société Générale d'Imprimerie et de Librairie, 1837.
470. Spanneut, Michel. *Permanence du stoïcisme.* Gembloux: J. Durulot, 1973.
471. Speier, Hans. *Social Order and the Risks of War.* New York: G. W. Stewart, 1952.
472. Spoelberch de Lovenjoul, Charles, Vicomte de. *Histoire des oeuvres d'H. de Balzac.* Paris: Calmann-Lévy, 1879.
473. Staël, Anne-Louise-Germaine Necker [Mme de Staël]. *De la littérature.* 2 vols. Paul van Tiegham, ed. Geneva: Droz, 1959.
474. —— *De l'Allemagne.* 5 vols. Paris: Hachette, 1958–60.
475. Starobinski, Jean. "La Rochefoucauld et les morales substitutives." *Nouvelle revue française* 163–164 (July–September 1966): 16–34, 211–29.
476. —— *Les Mots sous les mots: les anagrammes de Ferdinand de Saussure.* Paris: Gallimard, 1971.
477. —— *L'Oeil vivant.* Paris: Gallimard, 1961.
478. —— *Portrait de l'artiste en saltimbanque.* Geneva: Albert Skira, 1970.
479. —— "Sur la flatterie." *Nouvelle Revue de Psychanalyse* 4 (Autumn 1971): 131–51.
480. Stegmann, André. *Les Caractères de La Bruyère: bible de l'honnête homme.* Paris: Larousse, 1972.
481. Steiner, Herbert. *Der Chevalier de Méré.* Strasbourg: Heitz, 1930.
482. Stendhal [Henri Beyle]. *De l'amour.* Paris: Garnier Frères, 1959.
483. —— "Lord Byron en Italie." *Revue de Paris* (March 1830): 192.
484. —— *Oeuvres complètes.* Vol. 17, *Vie de Napoléon; Mémoires sur Napoléon.* Vol. 24, *Correspondance.* Paris: Pierre Larrive, 1953.
485. —— *Oeuvres intimes.* Bibliothèque de la Pléiade. Paris: Gallimard, 1955.
486. —— *Racine et Shakespeare.* Paris: Garnier Flammarion, 1970.
487. —— *Romans et nouvelles.* 2 vols. Bibliothèque de la Pléiade. Paris: Gallimard, 1963.
488. Streicher, Jeanne, ed. *Commentaires sur les remarques de Vaugelas par . . .*

Selected Bibliography

Bouhours, Conrart, Chapelain, Thomas Corneille, [*et al*]. New edition. 2 vols. Paris: Droz, 1936.

489. Sue, Eugène. *Arthur*. 4 vols. Paris: Plon, 1845.
490. —— *Latréaumont*. 2 vols. Paris: Charles Gosselin, 1838.
491. —— *Le Marquis de Létorière*. Paris: Charles Gosselin, 1840.
492. —— *Les Mystères de Paris*. Paris: Pauvert, 1963.
493. Sy, Pierrette. "L'Importance de la toilette chez le héros stendhalien." *Stendhal Club* 13, nos. 49–52 (1925): 127–37.
494. Taine, Hippolyte. *Essais de critique et d'histoire*. Paris: Hachette, 1858.
495. —— *L'Idéalisme anglais*. Paris: G. Baillière, 1864.
496. —— *Notes sur Paris: Vie et opinions de M. Frédéric-Thomas Graindorge*. Paris: Hachette, 1959.
497. Tallemant des Réaux, Gédéon. *Les Historiettes*. 2 vols. Bibliothèque de la Pléiade. Paris: Gallimard, 1960–61.
498. Thorslev, Peter Larsen. *The Byronic Hero: Types and Prototypes*. Minneapolis: University of Minnesota Press, 1962.
499. Thucydides. *The Peloponnesian War*. 2 vols. Thomas Hobbes, trans. David Grene, ed. Ann Arbor: University of Michigan Press, 1959.
500. Todorov, Tzvetan. *Introduction à la littérature fantastique*. Paris: Seuil, 1970.
501. —— "Introduction à la symbolique." *Poétique* 11 (1972): 308.
502. Todorov, Tzvetan, ed. *Le Discours de la poésie*. *Poétique* 28 (1976).
503. —— and trans. *Théorie de la littérature: Textes des formalistes russes*. Preface by Roman Jakobson. Paris: Seuil, 1966.
504. Toldo, Pietro. "Le Courtisan dans la littérature française et ses rapports avec l'oeuvre de Castiglione." *Archiv für das Studium der neueren Sprachen und Litteraturen* 103–104 (1899–1900): 75–121, 313–30; 105 (1900): 60–85.
505. Torche, Antoine, Abbé. *Les Démêlés de l'esprit et du coeur*. Paris: G. Quinet, 1667.
506. Toudouze, Georges G. *Le Costume français*. Paris: Larousse, 1745.
507. Tulard, Jean. *Le Mythe de Napoléon*. Paris: A. Colin, 1971.
508. Vannier, Bernard. *L'Inscription du corps: Pour une sémiotique du portrait balzacien*. Paris: Klincksieck, 1972.
509. Van Tieghem, Philippe. *Les Grandes doctrines littéraires en France*. Paris: Presses Universitaires de France, 1963.
510. Vaugelas, Claude Favre de. *Remarques sur la langue françoise*. Facsimile of the original edition. Société des textes français modernes. Introduction by Jeanne Streicher. Paris: Droz, 1934.
511. Vaumorières, Pierre d'Ortigue, Sieur de. *L'Art de plaire dans la conversation*. 2 vols. Bilingual edition. M. Ozell, ed. London: W. Feales, 1735.
512. Veblen, Thorstein. *The Theory of the Leisure Class*. Boston: Houghton-Mifflin, 1973.

Selected Bibliography

513. Vidocq, Eugène François. *Les Voleurs: physiologie de leurs moeurs et de leur langage.* 2 vols. Paris: Chez l'auteur, 1837.
514. Villey, Pierre. *Montaigne devant la postérité.* Paris: Ancienne Librairie Turne, 1935.
515. Vigny, Alfred de. *Oeuvres complètes.* 2 vols. Bibliothèque de la Pléiade. Paris: Gallimard, 1958.
516. Villiers de l'Isle-Adam, Philippe-Auguste, Comte de. *Contes cruels.* Paris: José Corti, 1952.
517. —— *L'Eve futur.* Paris: Jean Jacques Pauvert, 1960.
518. Voiture, Vincent. *Oeuvres.* 2 vols. M. A. Ubicini, ed. Paris: Charpentier, 1855.
519. Voivenel, P. *La Méconnaissance de soi.* Toulouse: R. Lion, 1954.
520. Voltaire, François-Marie Arouet. *Correspondence.* Vol. 1. Bibliothèque de la Pléiade. Paris: Gallimard, 1963.
521. —— *Dictionnaire philosophique.* Paris: Classiques Garnier, 1967.
522. —— *Mélanges.* Bibliothèque de la Pléiade. Paris: Gallimard, 1965.
523. White, John S. *Renaissance Cavalier.* New York: Philosophical Library, 1959.
524. Williet, Jean. "Baudelaire et deux autres mythes: le peuple et le bourgeois." *Revue des sciences humaines* 130 (April–June 1968): 217–38.
525. Wimsatt, William K., Jr. "Belinda ludens." *Poétique* 10 (1972): 137–52.
526. Wohlfarth, Irving. "*Perte d'Auréole*: The Emergence of the Dandy." *MLN* 85, nos. 4–6 (May–December 1970): 529–71.
527. Zévaco, D. "L'Honnête homme au XVIIe siècle," *Revue de Philologie Française,* 25 (1911–12), 1–8.
528. Zumthor, P[aul] and H. Sommer. "A propos du génie." *Zeitschrift für romanische Philologie* 66 (1950): 170–201.

INDEX

301

Index

Barbey d'Aurevilly, Jules, 234*n*; on Byronism, 38; on dandy as work of art, 43, 107, 244*n*; on Brummell, 43–44, 56–57, 104, 147, 149, 159, 163, 165, 166, 169, 170, 172, 209, 223; on *le fat*, 55, 258*n*; on *l'élégant*, 56; on *les beaux*, 56–57; on the *fashionable* and the dandy, 58; on *les lions*, 58, 59; on *le gentleman*, 59; on *gandin* vs. *petit crevé*, 59–60; on Napoleonism and dandyism, 66; on vanity of dandy, 68–69, 223; on Stendhal, 70; on dandy and the law, 73–74; conservatism of, 74; on dandy's search for exclusiveness, 85; on motto of dandyism, 86; on dandy's friendlessness, 86–87; on impossibility of fixed code, 89; patronym of, 92; on "natural" aristocrat, 93; on wealth and elegance, 94; on his own writing, 97–98; on ennui, 102–4; on dandy's heroism, 104; on *plaire en déplaisant*, 146; on dandy's esthetic, 148–49; masculine/feminine ambiguity in dandies of, 151; on dandy's *expression*, 152–53; on stiffness, 154; on dress, 159; on impertinence, 164; on love and women, 166–69; on irony, 172; on human needs, 180; on *être/paraître*, 189; on imposture, 190; on mask of dandy, 194; on dandyistic stoicism, 194–95; on *le je ne sais quoi*, 209, 273*n*; on "divine right," 213; on "Dandy-priest," 215; on Lauzun, 217, 220, 221; on universality of dandyism, 223; on vanity and *fatuité*, 236*n*; on cafés, 239*n*; on Faubourg St. Germain, 239*n*; on drugs, 243*n*; on *bizarrerie*, 254*n*; on elegance's position in esthetic paradigm, 255*n*; on dandy's dressing ritual, 256*n*; on dandy as *gant jaune*, 257*n*; on the *lorgnon*, 257*n*; on *le flegme*, 258*n*; on conversation, 259–60*n*; on monosyllabic speech, 260*n*; on Pascal as dandy, 275*n*; religious conversion of, 275*n*
—works mentioned: *Un Dandy avant les dandys*, 8–9, 217, 220–21; *Les Diaboliques*, 38, 55, 92, 148, 151, 275*n*; *Du Dandysme et de George Brummell*, 43–44, 55; *La Bague d'Annibal*, 55; *Un Amour impossible*, 55, 168; *Le Rideau cramoisi*, 57; *Les Lions d'autrefois*, 234*n*; *L'Ensorcelé*, 275*n*; *Un Prêtre marié*, 275*n*

Bardin, Pierre: *Le Lycée*, mentioned, 21, 227*n*, 232*n*

Barthes, Roland: semiological theories of, 5, 108–10; on "literature of worldliness," 11; on "connotative semiotics," 109; idiolect defined by, 114; on *écriture* and esthetic ideology, 118; Mounin's attack on, 244*n*; on the *champ de dispersion*, 245*n*; on problem of arthrology, 245*n*
—works mentioned: *Système de la mode*, 5; *Eléments de sémiologie*, 5, 110, 244*n*; *Le Degré zéro de l'écriture*, 118

Baudelaire, Charles; his theory of dandyism, 43–44; on *le roué*, 55; on *l'homme du monde*, 57; on Delacroix, 59; Gautier on, 59, 147; on passion for domination, 67; on dandy's pride, 69; on *déclassement* and aristocracy, 71; on conformity and revolt, 73; politics of, 74–76; on the bourgeois, 79–80; enclosure for, 84, 85; on Le Jockey Club, 85; on *le flâneur*, 86; on friendships, 87; on dandy's doctrine, 89; on dandy's natural aristocracy, 93; on money, 94; on utility, 95; on bourgeois professionalism, 95–96; on dandy's a-praxis, 96; on own writing, 98; on ennui, 103; drugs in, 104, 180, 199–200; on "productive" artists as dandies, 107; on dandy as poetic, 111; on *déplaire*, 147; on diversity, 147; on dandy esthetics of fear and astonishment, 148; on *bizarrerie*, 149–50; on dandy as system, 150; on dandy and modernity, 150, 182; on hands, 153; on physiognomy, 153; on fashion, 156; on black dress, 157; on sartorial perfection, 159; on iciness of manner, 165–66; on dandy and love, 166–67; on

Index

Index

Index

Don Juan, the (*Continued*)
as, 167–68; Lauzun as, 220; Alcibiades
as, 277*n*
Dress: as category of system, 5; in Cicero,
16; in Castiglione, 19; in Faret, 21; in
Montaigne, 22; of English dandies, 33; in
Pelham, 39; of Brummell, 41–42; as
recurrent element in semantic field of
dandyism, 54–61; as language, 110; art
of, in honnêteté, 127–30; as primary
category of elegance, 155; in dandy
system, 155–59; *see also* Adornment
Drugs: Baudelaire and, 104, 180, 199–200;
Barbey on, 243*n*
Du Bled, Victor, 248*n*; on hands and *race*,
255*n*; on Gautier's love of costumes, 256*n*
Duclos, Charles Pinot, Sieur, 9
Ducrot, Oswald: on linguistics and
semiotics, 244*n*
Dumas, Alexandre: on Lauzun, 220; works
mentioned, 225*n*

Eco, Umberto, 112, 245*n*
Ecriture, 113, 118; honnête homme's *parole*
as, 145
Egotism/altruism dichotomy, 67–68
Elegance: work vs., 96, 130; Méré on, 130,
154; as global category in dandy system;
154–63; training in, 205–6; grace and,
211; as religion, 215; *see also Homme
élégant, l'*
Eloquence: of rhetor, 16–17; as metonym of
self-as-art, 141; honnête homme's
conversation and, 141–46
Enchanter, 120
Enclosure, 78–90; secret society and, 78; as
spatial construct, 80–86; honnête
homme's modes of, 78–84, 87–88;
dandy's search for, 84–87; hostility
within, 86–88; *see also* Clubs; Salons
Ennui, 242*n*; as corollary of leisure, 99–105;
Pascal's notion of, 100–1; honnête
homme's repression of, 101–2, 104–5;
dandyism and, 102–4

Epictetus, 268*n*
Epicureanism: in *Pelham*, 39; in honnêteté,
192–93
Epicurus, 23: Seneca and, 193, 267*n*
Esprit, Jacques, 83; on *politesse*, 132; on
ennui, 242*n*
Esprit de finesse, l', 202–4, 206, 270*n*;
délicatesse and, 270*n*
Esprit de géométrie, l', 202, 204, 205, 270*n*
Esprit galant, l', 51
Esthète, l', 253*n*
"Esthetic function," 245*n*; *see also* Poetic
function
Esthetic of identity: esthetic of opposition
vs., 119
Etonnement, 148
Etre/paraître dichotomy: honnête homme
and, 184–89; dandy and, 189–91; *see also*
Actor; Dissimulation; Mask
Exclusivity: Seneca and, 15; Castiglione
and, 19; Montaigne and, 21–24; *la
chambre bleue* and, 25–26; *préciosité*
and, 28–29; Brummell and, 41; secret
society and, 77–78; bourgeois mentality
and, 78–80, 91, 93–98; loci of, 81–86;
anthroponyms and, 91–93
Eyes: as category in system, 109; of honnête
homme, 122; of dandy, 151–52

Face: of *cortegiano*, 19; of *précieuse*, 29; of
Byronic hero, 37; in system of honnête
homme, 122–23; of dandy, 152–54
Fainéant, le, 99
Faret, Nicolas, 44, 48, 249*n*; Méré
compared with, 11; Castiglione's
influence on, 20–21, 49, 227*n*; equation of
courtisan and *honnête* in, 20, 47; on
dress, 21; on conversation, 21; Montaigne
and, 21, 227*n*; on *homme de bien*, 49; on
strategy of conquest, 64; on the face, 122;
on *souplesse*, 133; on *complaisance*, 133,
250*n*; on "appealing coolness," 135; on
bons mots, 142; on self-mastery, 192; on
grace, 210; on genius, 214; on Alcibiades,
226*n*; work mentioned: *L'Honnête*

Index

Gournay, Marie de, 210
Gozlan, Léon: *Le Lion empaillé*,
    mentioned, 234*n*
Grace, Christian notion of: *le je ne sais quoi*
    and, 209–11; in honnêteté and dandyism,
    211–12, 214, 273–74*n*
Grâce, la: in system of honnête homme,
    118, 125, 126, 248*n*; Brummell and, 209
Gracián, Baltasar, 227*n*
Grand monde, le, 80–81, 141, 187
Grandiloquence: honnête contempt for,
    141–42
Greimas, A. J.: theory of actants, 175–76
Grenailles, François de: *L'Honnête garçon*,
    mentioned, 65, 232*n*
Guazzo: *Civil conversatione*, mentioned,
    227*n*
Guéret, Gabriel: on self and mask, 184–85
Guez de Balzac, *see* Balzac, Jean Louis
    Guez de
Guichardet, F. G.: *Le Lion de contrebande*,
    mentioned, 234*n*
Guirlande de Julie, la, 26–27
Guys, Constantin: Baudelaire on, 107, 156

Habile homme, l', 21–22, 50–52; as distinct
    from *l'homme habile*, 50–51
Hands: in dandy system, 153
Hazlitt, William, 42–43
Hedonism, dandyism and, 194
Helper (*Adjuvant*), 176, 178, 182, 189; *see
    also* Greimas, A. J.
Hjelmslev, Louis, 109; on types of relations
    between signs, 117
Holbach, Paul Henri Thiry, Baron d', 31
Homme comme il faut, l', 56, 61
Homme de bien, l', 46, 49–50, 52
Homme de génie, l', 274*n*
Homme de loisir, l', 241*n*
Homme de qualité, l', 46, 48, 52
Homme d'honneur, l', 46, 49, 50, 58, 233*n*
Homme du monde, l', 55–56, 61
Homme élégant, l', 56, 61
Homme galant, l', 51–52
Homme sensible, l', 10
Homosexuality, 259*n*

Honestus, 15, 45, 46
Honnêteté: as system, 6–7; introductory
    remarks on, 6–12; as literary typology,
    10; corpus of 11–12; Greek prototypes of,
    14–15; Roman pre-texts and prototypes
    of, 15–17; knightly tradition and, 17–18;
    Castiglione and, 18–21; Montaigne and,
    21–25; *la chambre bleue* and, 25–27;
    préciosité and, 27–30; semantic field of,
    45–53, 61–62; *le fat* contrasted with
    honnête homme, 54; conquest and,
    63–68; Caesar and Alexander and, 65–66;
    vanity and, 67–68; power of seventeenth-
    century nobility and, 69, 71 (*see also*
    Nobility); conformist/revolutionary
    dichotomy and, 71–73; secret society and,
    78; enclosure and, 78–84; bourgeoisie vs.,
    78–79; urbanity/provinciality dichotomy
    and, 80–81; ritual activities in, 82–83;
    attitude to peers in, 87–88; secret
    knowledge and, 88–90; aristocracy of
    merit and, 90–98; attitude to social rank
    of, 90–91; attitude to wealth of, 93–94;
    attitude to professional activity of, 94–96,
    99; writing and, 96–97; leisure and,
    98–100; repression of ennui and, 100–2,
    104–5, 242*n*; *divertissement* and, 100–2;
    honnête homme as work of art in, 107;
    poetic text and, 108–19 (*see also* Poetic
    function; Semiology; Signs); *l'art de
    plaire* as esthetic of, 119–46; Classical
    esthetics and, 120; magic and, 120–21;
    "femininity" and, 121–22, 139;
    captivation and, 119–22; body as
    signifying surface and, 122–27; language
    of adornment in, 127–31; meaning of
    manners in, 131–39; love and, 135–39; art
    of conversation and, 139–46; on
    superiority of *parole* to *écriture*, 145;
    semiological system of, compared to that
    of dandy, 172–74; process of production
    of, 175–216; actants in, 175–76; nature
    and *belle nature* in, 176–77; Platonism
    and, 177–78, 202, 203, 267*n*; artifice and,
    178; *être/paraître* and, 184–89, 193;
    acting and, 184–86, 189; self-mastery and,

Index

192–94, 197–98; stoic and epicurean strains in, 192–94; *askesis* and, 197–98, 212; *géométrie/finesse* and, 200–4; *bienséance* and, 200–3; rules and, 200–2; feeling and; 202–4; *le je ne sais quoi* and, 207–11; as substitute religion, 211–15; Lauzun and, 217–19; as universal phenomenon, 222–23, 277–78*n*

Hook, Theodore Edward: *Merton*, mentioned, 38, 40

Horace: *cura* in, 100; on *Natura* and *Ars*, 212; *Epistles*, mentioned, 100

Hôtel de Rambouillet, *see Chambre bleue, la*

Houssaye, Arsène, 74; on Alcibiades, 277*n*

Hugo, Victor, 146

Huizinga, Johan, 2–3, 6, 18, 22*n*

Humanism, Renaissance, 3

Huysmans, Jovis-Karl: *A rebours*, mentioned, 11–12, 43–44, 80, 237*n*; artificiality in, 44, 180–81; political opposition in, 75; attraction to criminality in, 76; friendship in, 86–87; ennui in, 104; on sartorial simplicity, 159; on Des Esseintes' food and home, 162; on nature, 179–81; *être/paraître* in, 189; Christianity and, 215–16; objectification of women in, 259*n*

Idiolect: artistocratic self as, 113–14; honnête homme's speech as, 140–42; dandy's speech as, 169–72

Idleness, *see Oisiveté, l'*

Ignatius of Loyola, Saint: *Spiritual Exercises*, mentioned, 196, 268*n*

Impertinence, 118; dandy and, 164

Incroyable, l', 55, 58, 60; diction of, 170

Ingenuus, 15

Insinuation, 120, 125; "feminine" strategy and, 121–22; *souplesse* as form of, 133; *le je ne sais quoi* and, 208; Pascal and, 247*n*

Insolence, 118

Irony, dandy's, 171–72

Jakobson, Roman, 225*n*; on poetic function, 111, 112, 245*n*, 246*n*; on synchrony/diachrony, 231*n*; metaphor/metonymy distinction of, 246*n*

Jansenists, 83: vanity of honnête homme for, 68; texts of, generated in salon milieu, 82; on ennui of honnête homme, 101; on stoicism, 267*n*; grace for, 273*n*; *see also* Nicole; Pascal

Je ne sais quoi, le, 207–11; positive and negative components of, 273–74*n*

Jesse, Captain William: on Brummell, 40–42

Jesus Christ: parables of, as model of eloquence, 142; dandy's asceticism and, 195; Poe as, 213; *l'art de plaire* and union with, 214; Musset on Lauzun and, 221–22

Jeunes-France, the: Byronism and, 37; attitude to bourgeoisie of, 79; dress of, 157–58; idiolect of, 170; mystification and, 253–54*n*; *see also* Borel, Pétrus; *Bouzingots*, the; Gautier, Théophile

Jockey Club, 85

Jouy, Etienne de, 44; on the English dandy, 55; on *l'élégant*, 56; on dandy as androgyn, 169; *L'Hermite de Londres*, mentioned, 32–34

καλός καγαθός, 14, 15

Kristeva, Julia, 244*n*

La Bruyère, Jean de, 226*n*; on Gothic order, 17; on *les courtisans*, 47, 231*n*; on *l'homme de bien*, 49; on *l'homme habile*, 50; on strategy of conquest, 64; on l'Hôtel de Rambouillet, 83; on ennui at Louis XIV's court, 100; on importance of dress, 127; on wigs, 128; on arbitrariness of sartorial styles, 129; on manners, 131; on eloquence, 143; on conversation, 145; on artifice, 178; on Lauzun, 218, 222; Gracián and, 227*n*; on *la mine*, 247*n*; on marriage, 251*n*; on self-mastery, 266*n*; *Les Caractères*, mentioned, 65, 226*n*

La Calprenède, Gautier de Coste de, 261*n*

Laclos, Pierre Ambroise François Choderlos de: *Les Liaisons dangereuses*,

311

Index

Index

Index

Romanticism: hero in, 10; Shakespeare and, 32; Byron and, 34–35, 53; narcissism and, 68; ennui in, 102–3; esthetics of, 146–49; view of women in, 166; dandy idiolect and, 170; nature and, 178; natural self and, 191; superior man as messianic for, 195; attitude to rules in, 204

Ronteix, Eugène: on *l'homme du monde*, 56; on *le fashionable*, 86, 97; on dress, 156; on *l'oisif*, 241*n*; on dandy's dressing ritual, 256*n*; on monosyllabic speech, 260*n*; *Manuel du fashionable*, mentioned, 57

Roqueplan, Nestor: on "Mascarilles," 92; dress of, 157; opposition to nature of, 179

Rotrou, Jean de: *Saint-Genest*, mentioned, 175

Roué, le, 55, 56, 61

Rousseau, Jean-Jacques, 9–10; influence on Byron of, 34–35; works mentioned: *Lettre à d'Alembert sur les spectacles*, 9–10; *Confessions*, 10; *Les Rêveries du promeneur solitaire*, 10

Ruelle, la, 81

Sablé, Madeleine de Souvré, Marquise de: côterie of, 82–83

Sadism, dandyism and, 103–4, 243*n*

Sainte-Beuve, Charles Augustin de, 267*n*; *Marion Délorme*, mentioned, 22*n*

Saint-Evremond, Charles de Marguetal de Saint-Denis, Sieur de, 15, 87–88; on *l'homme d'honneur*, 49; on *l'habile homme*, 50; own texts treated as *bagatelles* by, 97; on *divertissement*, 101, 242*n*; on power to *plaire*, 119–20; on love, 135–36; on self-mastery, 192–93; on Augustus, 226*n*; on Montaigne, 228*n*; on military *métier*, 235*n*; on court life, 238*n* —works mentioned: *Jugement sur César et sur Alexandre*, 65; *Le Cercle*, 229*n*

Saint-Simon, Louis de Rouvroy, Duc de, 8; on "vile bourgeoisie," 79; on professionalism and honnêteté, 97; on

Lauzun, 218, 276*n*; criticism of king by, 236*n*

Salons, 25; as locus of *le grand monde*, 81; honnête homme's search for exclusiveness through, 81–84; pastimes in, 81–83; nineteenth-century, 84; *see also Chambre bleue, la*

Sarasin, Jean-François, 193; on love, 136–37; *S'il faut qu'un jeune homme soit amoureux*, mentioned, 136–37, 227*n*

Sartorial speech, 110; *see also* Adornment

Sartre, Jean-Paul: on society of dandies, 86; on anti-Nature, 180; on Baudelaire's dandyism, 260*n*; on *askesis* and dandyism, 268*n*

Satanic component: in Byron, 35; in dandyism, 147–48

Saussure, Ferdinand de: on semiology, 4–5; art excluded from semiological enterprise by, 108; on syntax as one syntagmatic model among others, 117; on synchrony/diachrony, 231*n*; Todorov and Ducrot on, 244*n*; on linguistic unit of significance, 245*n*; *Anagrammes*, mentioned, 244*n*

Scarron, Paul: *L'Epître chagrin*, mentioned, 229*n*

Science du collège vs. *science du monde*, 89

Scott, Sir Walter, 36

Scudéry, Georges de, 120

Scudéry, Madeleine de, 26–28, 240*n*; as *précieuse*, 27; ideal of honnêteté for, 27–28; on *homme d'honneur*, 49; côterie of, 81–82; anthroponyms in circle of, 91; on writing as diversion, 97; on *l'oisiveté*, 99; on self-conquest, 104–5; on *complaisance*, 133–34; criticism of Chapelain by, 136; on love, 136–39; on *la galanterie*, 136–37; on *la Carte de Tendre*, 137; on *l'air galant*, 138–39; on conversation, 140; on *agrément* of speech, 145; on *le je ne sais quoi galant*, 208; on the provinces, 238*n*; on women in formation of honnête homme, 251*n*; on conversation as synchronization, 253*n*; on dissimulation, 264*n*

317

Index

Index

Index